THEORIES AND
THEORY GROUPS
IN CONTEMPORARY
AMERICAN SOCIOLOGY

THEORIES AND THEORY GROUPS IN CONTEMPORARY AMERICAN SOCIOLOGY

NICHOLAS C. MULLINS

Indiana University

with the assistance of
CAROLYN J. MULLINS

Harper & Row, Publishers
New York Evanston San Francisco London

To H.C.W.
N.W.S. and the
I.U.S.F., 1971–1972

Sponsoring Editor: Alvin A. Abbott
Project Editor: Holly Detgen
Designer: June Negrycz
Production Supervisor: Stefania J. Taflinska

**THEORIES AND
THEORY GROUPS
IN CONTEMPORARY
AMERICAN SOCIOLOGY**

Library of Congress Cataloging in Publication Data   73–6229

Mullins, Nicholas C
   Theories and theory groups in contemporary
American sociology.

   Includes bibliographies.
   1. Sociology.   2. Sociology—Methodology.
3. Knowledge, Sociology of.   I. Mullins, Carolyn J.,
joint author.   II. Title.
HM24.M83   301'.01   73–6229
ISBN 0–06–044649–8

CONTENTS

Don't be a fool! Close this book at once.
It is nothing but foma.
Foma, of course, are lies.

—Kurt Vonnegut, Jr.
Cat's Cradle

PREFACE

This book was both planned and serendipitous. I had planned a book that would offer original research on contemporary theory rather than the typically rehashed, predigested summaries too often found in textbooks. Also, contemporary theory should not be like the high school history courses that we all remember, which never managed to arrive at the present. My intent was simply to examine the social processes operative on social theory and to report on those, together with a summary of the intellectual aspects of the various theories. So much for the planned aspects of this venture.

Somehow an itch crept into my plans. As a sociologist of science, I had just finished (late 1970) the initial work on a model for theory development in the natural sciences, and I knew that there were a few relatively simply processes, characteristic of the social organization of science, that might well serve to explain many of the seeming problems and peculiarities of sociological theory development. At that point I realized that an adequate treatment of the social processes acting on sociology's intellectual processes required me to utilize a theory about theory development that would permit both explanation and prediction. The treatment also required very detailed research into both the theories and the theory groups so that the validity (or falsity) of the theory could be demonstrated. Perhaps more important, I was just plain curious to see whether the natural science model would explain sociological data. That curiosity produced the itch, and I started scratching in earnest—with the result that the book was completed roughly a year behind the original schedule for it.

For me this book has become a risky venture. First, it is always hazardous to write about intellectual history. As has frequently been argued, the view of history that any person holds is profoundly affected by where and by whom he was trained and by his present objective conditions. Second, the data are incomplete; space does not permit the inclusion of every possible person involved in every single theory group. Since the book's basic purpose is to examine contemporary theory groups in sociology, groups from the past are inevitably slighted in favor of contemporary groups. Third, my theory may not provide the best possible explanation for the development of social theory. Fourth, I've had the audacity to do this research on my own discipline; not even those few friends who have seen this book in draft form agree with me in every detail (others may disagree more strongly!). However, those who took the time to share their disagreements with me during the research and writing process have taught me much and have left their mark on the book. I thank them.

There will be both "insider" and "outsider" objections to this book. Insiders to the various groups may say, with quite a bit of justice, that I have not distilled the true essence of their ideas, that I do not have a true understanding of what is going on. They may also object that I have included people who were not really part of the group and excluded others who were. The reasons for this probable situation are explained in the Appendix. Outsiders will almost certainly object that I have not included their particular madness. I invite them, at least, to write research papers using my model on their groups. We need more data on theory development, and I would be delighted to be proved wrong by omission if the result were an increase in our knowledge of theory group development.

This book is intended for use as a text in courses in contemporary sociological theory and as a research monograph in the sociology of knowledge. The model for theory development presented is being tested for the first time on sociology groupings—a total of eight different developments. The data on all eight groups are original research data. Beyond actual discussion of theories and groups, the eight data sets have been summarized at two points in the book for comparison with the basic model and evaluation.

The dedication of this book reflects my debt to persons without whose help the project couldn't have been completed. Harrison C. White's teaching has shaped much of my understanding about theory building; indeed, this book was written from a structuralist perspective that originated in my study with him. His comments on both Chapter 10 and one full draft of this book slowed my progress but improved the book considerably. Norman W. Storer has been both a good friend and advisor; for ten years he has read and commented helpfully on virtually everything I have written, including a complete, earlier draft of this book (especially Chapters 5, 7, and 11). His influence on my writing style has been entirely beneficial. Finally, many of the Indiana University Sociology Faculty, 1971–1972, have given substantial help in terms of books lent and careful reviewing of drafts of one or more of these chapters.

In addition to White and Storer, the following persons deserve special thanks: Robert K. Merton (for reading initial drafts of Chapters 1, 2, and

3); Sheldon Stryker (both for his extensive comments on Chapter 4 and for his loan of numerous books on both symbolic interactionism and small group research); Aaron V. Cicourel, Lindsey Churchill, and Hugh Mehan (for the great amounts of time they gave to helping me with Chapter 8); O. D. Duncan, Elton Jackson, Patricia L. Krisch, Angela Lane, and Karl Schuessler (for their help with Chapter 9); David Sallach (for his help on Chapter 11); Robert W. Friedrichs, Norman Koller, Joel L. Levine, and Larry Newman (for their help and comments on various portions); Debby Foler (for painstakingly checking all my bibliographies); Donna Musgrove and Elsie Sniffin (at Dartmouth College), Sue Havelish, Betsy Hine, Mary Olguin, Janie Richardson, Lorie Simmons, and Marge Wright (Indiana University) for cheerful and competent typing; and the Indiana University Institute of Social Research and J. Michael Armer, its director during 1971–1972, for general help and support on this project. My wife Carolyn has provided assistance above and beyond her usual excellent editorial work.

Although I am extremely grateful to all these people for their help, in no way do I hold them responsible for any errors that may be included in this book. They are mine alone.

N. C. M.

PART ONE
THINKING ABOUT THEORY

CHAPTER 1
INTRODUCTION

DEFINING THEORY

This book discusses the intellectual content of contemporary American sociological theories as well as the people who developed them.

Defining the word "theory" is no easy task. For example, sociological literature contains a theory of relative deprivation—a single-topic theory developed in bits and pieces by many persons, but not completely written down anywhere—and Parsonian theory, which is a specific set of books and articles written largely by one man (Talcott Parsons) about many theoretical topics. If we examined a range of explicitly theoretical works, we would find that some treat single ideas; others, systems of ideas. Some are historical descriptions, for example, Smelser's (1959) discussion of the development of the British cotton textile industry. Others are based on propositions such as Homans' statement: "Persons who interact frequently with one another tend to like one another" (1950: 111). Still others are sets of formulas or the diagrams that are the equivalent of such sets. Figure 1.1 illustrates a hypothetical relationship among six variables: father's, mother's, and son's education, father's occupation, son's first job, and son's total lifetime income.

These theoretical works also differ in their underlying philosophies, assumptions, and implications; over the years, everything from descriptive studies (in which theory exists, at best, only in the implicit organization of the description) to highly abstract discussion (in which data are barely mentioned) has been categorized as theory. Usually, though, theory contains (1) abstract generalizations that move beyond simple descriptions of a particular incident or case and (2) an attempt to explain either why or how[1] something happened on the basis of acceptable general principles.

The establishment of these principles is done in many different ways, but common elements exist among all kinds of theories, and these can

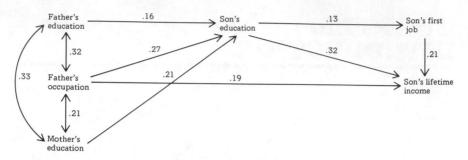

FIGURE 1.1 Example: diagrammatic presentation of variable relationships.

form the basis for defining theories and comparing theory types. When beginning an analysis, a theorist normally defines a set of standard terms that he will use in building his theory. Some of these are concepts; others, variables. A concept consists of (1) an idea (e.g., people being separated on the basis of race) and (2) a word associated with that idea (e.g., segregation). The idea comes from reading or thinking about a problem or situation. Concepts are part of a language or theory that results from, or is modeled after the results of, human communication. The theory is shaped by how terms are added to and used in it. Usually, the word part of a concept is defined using other terms already part of the theory or characterized through use in sentences. For example, we could define "segregation" in terms of "integration" if the second term were already included in the theory we were building. Alternately, we could define segregation with statements such as: "This is a segregated school," "Job openings here are held for Whites," and "This is a segregated restaurant; we don't serve Blacks."

A variable describes a situation and is often a compact summary in the form of a number selected from a set of numbers (e.g., one grade from all the grades for a course) or a word selected from a set of words (e.g., "cordial" from the set "cordial," "pleasant," "correct," "cool," and "hostile" to describe a diplomatic meeting).

Not every theory in sociology contains both concepts and variables. Some theories are simply sets of concepts for which relations have been stated; other theories are sets of variables that are statistically analyzed and then described. For still other theories, which include both elements, theorists differ about how concepts and variables are related. It is usually assumed, however, that a complete theory will include both concepts and variables and that they will be connected through a series of definitions associating specific variables with specific concepts. Theory structure can be analyzed into its parts, and there is disagreement about the way in which the parts of theory should be used (for one point of view, see Mullins, 1971).

It follows, then, that the concepts or variables used in any two or more theories can be compared. Many of the differences that usually appear result primarily from differences in subject matter; for instance, a theory about religious activity is not likely to use the same variables and concepts that go with a theory about behavior among small children. Other differences result from preferences for certain concepts and/or variables, and these preferences often signal different theory styles. Theories also differ in *how* concepts/variables are used; thus choice of form, like concept/variable choice, can also mark distinctive theory styles. For example, a theory including the concept "religiosity" might state that concept in an historical description, a proposition, an equation set, or a diagram (the styles noted on p. 3).

To summarize thus far, theories are productions (in any form, but usually written) that attempt to *analyze* and to *generalize* about the interaction of human beings, using a set of concepts and/or variables whose relations are governed by specific rules for theory building. One further element is needed in this basic definition: A theory is a statement that is an acceptable general principle to some group (Ziman, 1968). That important group is usually the scientists who can read and respond to what another scientist has written. For the purposes of this book, then, any block of material that meets the minimal criteria for a theory just noted and that is (or has been) held as such by a recognizable group in American sociology is defined as a sociological theory. Differences in theory content and form are noted, but no prescriptive criteria for either are applied. (Indeed, some of the more interesting points of difference among sociologists have centered on appropriate style or content.)

TYPES OF THEORETICAL WORK

Having determined what theory *is*, we can now consider types of theoretical work. Almost all characterizations of theory differentiate among works that *set* a new style for doing (or analyzing) theory and those that *follow* a style; work that *is* theory, and work that is *about* theory. We can cross-classify these distinctions as in Table 1.1. All four types are distin-

TABLE 1.1   Types of theory work

	Style Setter	Style Follower
Theory	Paradigmatic piece	Secondary material
About theory	Landmark in criticism	Secondary critical materials

guished only by content; materials typical of all four have appeared in many forms (articles, monographs, textbooks, lectures, etc.). For example, a series of lectures formed the initial material in symbolic interactionism; in other traditions, the first important piece has been a journal article.

With respect to content, a new and radical approach may not be recognized as such, even by its authors. This kind of work (or its author) may be seen as isolated, idiosyncratic, or wrong. Certainly C. Wright Mills (*The Power Elite*, 1956) received all these labels at one time or another, but he was crucial to the beginnings of the radical tradition (Domhoff and Ballard, 1968). Indeed, it is rare for a new tradition to be recognized immediately as a major challenge. Content issues between a new approach and the older, conventional wisdom are usually sharpened through debate (one form of debate reanalyzes important cases previously analyzed by the older tools). Sharpening and expanding, the tasks of secondary work, are usually done by a school's initiator and by his followers (normally his students). By collecting and publishing a series of articles in the ethnomethodological tradition, for example, Jack D. Douglas (1970) has been a major force in sharpening the ethnomethodological position.

Work about theory—critical materials—analyzes theory work. The conclusions of criticism may be positive, negative, or mixed. The analysis of a theory is done either by comparing that theory with a set of abstract criteria or by contrasting it to another theory. In such work, the critic usually develops his own theory about theories. The criterion for placing a piece of criticism in the "critical landmark" category is similar to that for placing theories in the paradigmatic category: Such work is a style setter. Its grounds for criticism are new. For example, Erik Erikson (*Young Man Luther*, 1958) used an extension of Freudian theory to analyze the life and work of an historical figure, Martin Luther, and, hence, to criticize previous analyses of Luther. Erikson's effort became a landmark, for it exceeded all similar, earlier writings in its depth of analysis.

Secondary critical material follows already established styles. For example, Coleman (1968) expressed highly negative views on ethnomethodology in his review of Garfinkel's (1967) *Studies in Ethnomethodology*. His review used a criterion for acceptable theory developed from his own work. No work as different from his as Garfinkel's could possibly pass the tests Coleman proposed; the two men theorized from totally different assumptions. Coleman's review was not a critical landmark because other reviews using similarly developed criteria had been published before (see Merton and Lazarsfeld, 1950).

PAST SCHEMES FOR
CATEGORIZING SOCIAL THEORIES

Other books have analyzed social theory, including contemporary social theory. In attempting this task, authors have asked: What concepts are being used? How? In what ways do theories change over time? To answer these and other questions, previous authors have needed a scheme for categorizing or grouping theories so that they could discuss similarities and differences.

Categorization is crucial because the volume of relevant material is immense. The social theory shelves in a college or university library stretch for hundreds of feet, holding works that have been written in many languages, over hundreds of years, by thousands of thinkers. Even if we limit our interest to sociological theory written in English, in the United States, between 1950 and 1970, there are still thousands of volumes of theory, about theory, or otherwise of interest to theoreticians. That number is expanding, with the addition of hundreds of books and thousands of articles each year. This rapid expansion forces us to search for a broad organizing principle, if only to catalog the books on our shelves.

There has been no lack of attempts to organize social theorists and their theories. Both the writers and their subject matter have been examined from many perspectives. For example, authors have taken large blocks of material, searched it for common sociological concepts (community, power, segregation, etc.), and catalogued various thinkers according to their treatment of those concepts (Nisbet, 1966). From a second perspective, it is possible to write biographies of particular thinkers (e.g., Max Weber) and to probe those for clues to the theorist's work; some writers have been studied by several people (Bendix, 1966, and Mitzman, 1970, both analyze Weber). A third perspective records the intellectual history of a group of similar theorists, either as a single tradition (e.g., structural functionalism; see Demerath and Peterson, 1967) or as part of a larger survey of several traditions (see Martindale, 1960). Still another perspective examines a total school of theorists (e.g., the Chicago school of the 1920s and 1930s; see Faris, 1967) for clues to the development and meaning of their theory.

These forms analyze either persons or ideas, by units or as systems. Table 1.2 cross-classifies these distinctions. Each of these forms has been

TABLE 1.2 Past attempts to organize social theory

	Ideas	Persons
Unit	Core concepts	Biographies
System	Intellectual history	Schools of social thought

utilized with some degree of success, but their real appeal is that each is *exhaustive* (i.e., permits the classification of each and every social theory) and open (i.e., can analyze any new theory that might occur).

My concern with theory is to understand (1) how different kinds of theory come to be written, (2) why some theories are similar to one another and others differ greatly, and (3) why any given social theory begins and, once started, eventually dies out. What answers to these questions are offered by the four types of explanation just outlined? Who finds which perspective valuable, and what are the strengths and weaknesses of each type of explanation?

CORE CONCEPTS

The perspective centering on core concepts adapts well to the traditional scientist's view of his own work. Indeed, every scientific paper begins by stating the concepts to be used, the origins and modifications of those concepts since their first use, and the special formulation of them being used in the research that is to be presented. In a larger context, the general sociological domain is supposedly established by the concepts being used. Within that domain, one way of explaining social realities signals one type of theory; another explanation, another type. For example, explanation of an objectively defined social fact (e.g., the growth pattern of a city) that assumes *imposition* of that reality on society by forces other than people (e.g., the physical location of transportation) signals a theory that can be termed social ecologism. A different kind of theory, technologism, produces an explanation of social realities in which the principal phenomena used in explanation are *generated* by the nonpersonal elements of the participants' environment (Wallace, 1969: 16).

The core-concepts approach is frequently used by those who are summarizing a field with the intent of adding to its findings. The emphasis is on what an idea means *now* rather than on what it has meant *historically*. Different kinds of theories are described as placing different emphases on the major concepts and using them slightly differently. Small differences within theory types are generally explained as modifications in concept usage. The rise and fall (starting and stopping) of specific theories is customarily seen as part of a process by which ideas are gradually modified in the direction of current usage.

This approach is strongest in its ability to compare the structure of many theories by highlighting the use of several concepts within each; the other elements of theory are eliminated, and the student is not confused in his understanding of similarities and differences. However, the core-concept approach does not deal with the way in which each concept is used within the structure of particular theories. For example, the concept of "status" is used by many theorists, including Marx and de Tocqueville, yet they employ this concept differently within their respective theories.

BIOGRAPHY

Biography is based on a wholly different philosophy of science. Central to this perspective is the individual who writes theory. Theory itself is perceived more as an individual task than as the gradual improvement of a schema over time. Emphasis is placed on interpreting the written words in light of the life and times of the individual who wrote them. Thus science is seen as the product of a series of individuals. The biographical approach is often used by (1) historians needing a focus for their histories of a period (e.g., Clark's, 1971, biography of Einstein), (2) psychologists testing a theory of psychological development or using it to illuminate a man (e.g., Coles's, 1970, biography of Erikson), and (3) scientists honoring another member of the profession (e.g., the festschrift celebrating Sorokin; Allen, 1963). Only the first two of these uses have an explanatory purpose. Biography serves frequently when a specific piece of written material needs interpretation; often a single work is best understood when it is considered simultaneously with earlier works. The battles that have occurred during the past forty years over the importance of Marx's *early* manuscripts illustrate the use of biography. (See Schaff, 1970, for an example of an analysis dependent on early manuscripts). The Marx case has been particularly interesting because the early manuscripts were not published until 1932 (see Marx, 1964); thus their influence on his 1850 and 1860 work in economics was not obvious until decades after its initial publication.

The biographical approach makes writing about theory quite easy. Each major theorist can be seen as explaining, in and of himself, the origin of his proposed way to do theory. The small differences that exist between a major theorist and lesser ones whose thought is similar are interpreted as natural differences between a leader and his followers. Those whose thoughts differ substantially are seen as competitors. The rise and fall of a viewpoint is either ignored (since the view is concentrated on the man) or interpreted as a response to the genius of the biography's subject (the rise) followed by his intellectual decline or death (the fall).

This explanation of rise and fall is clearly inadequate, since some theories live well beyond the lifetime of their originator, whereas others die long before their maker. Biographers try to use the simple fact of a theory type's rise and fall to define the theorist's success or failure: If a theory fails to survive its founder, it is because he has lost his powers; if it survives him, it is because he is a great theorist. If that theory is modified by subsequent workers (e.g., Marxism), the result is clearly not the true theory. This type of explanation can be used on all theories, but it is also tautological. More fundamentally, biographers tend to assume that a theorist is *always* consistent in his approach, always "developing" his approach from work to work, over a lifetime. The facts, however, show that even great theorists radically change perspectives. Between 1935 and 1950, for example, Talcott Parsons dropped the perspective of action theory for that of structural functionalism (see Parsons, 1937, 1951; Gouldner, 1970; also see Chapter 3).

The strength of the biographical perspective is that a theorist's work is examined as a whole; the effect of various events in the subject's life can be fully considered, and the result is an intensive interpretation. Biography's weaknesses issue from its strengths. Because it focuses on one person, it reduces the contributions of earlier thinkers to the development of a particular theory. Likewise, it reduces the contributions of the subject's followers. Furthermore, by emphasizing only major theorists, the factor of individual genius is overemphasized. Finally, as already noted, biography does not explain rise and fall, and it often fails to account for individual changes in perspective.

INTELLECTUAL HISTORY

Intellectual history, which analyzes interrelations among the works of several authors who are assumed to have influenced one another, is a very common way to attempt organizing the volume of material on social theory. This approach assumes a highly rationalistic philosophy of science. The student of a tradition discovers what sets of ideas occur together and discusses the meaning of those sets. Gouldner's *The Coming Crisis in Western Sociology* (1970) and Martindale's history of sociology (1960), which divides that history into the progression of several schools, are typical.

Intellectual historians do not tell us why particular theories exist. Small differences among theorists indicate that they belong in the same tradition; larger ones indicate peripheral or competitive figures. Traditions rise and fall; but as with biography, major and minor persons are seen as the major causative factors, and the resulting explanation is little better than biography's. Occasionally a dialectic argument (initial statement leads to counter-statement followed by a final synthesis) is used to explain rise and fall, with the final synthesis marking the end of the tradition.

The major strengths of this approach are (1) its emphasis on context, which clarifies the place of individuals in a group of authors and (2) its recognition of the rise and fall of theory (even though, as we know, the explanation has its weaknesses). Weaknesses include (1) the lack of adequate explanation for the rise and fall of theories and (2) the omission of what should be the most important aspect of this approach—the concept of influence. The process by which theories and theorists influence each other is not detailed.

SCHOOLS OF THEORY

A student of social theory (or theory in any field or intellectual system, for that matter) might observe that certain similar theories are written in roughly the same period of time by a limited group of authors. (Indeed, we can often use publication dates to pinpoint specific beginnings and endings for specific theories.) Attempts to make sense of these patterns of rising and falling have resulted in the study of social groups or schools of thought. Although the pure analysis of schools is rare, studies have been done on University of Chicago sociologists. Faris (1967) described the early Chicago school and emphasized the importance of institutionalization and professional training at the University of Chicago to the early development of sociology. School analysis is largely the product of a socially and psychologically informed philosophy of science which emphasizes the importance of early training and the acquisition of paradigms.

The school approach is widely used by genealogists of science who wish to discover a discipline's roots. Its strength is its emphasis on the social context of theory. Its weakness is that the actual product of science, the theories themselves, are not discussed. Moreover, this approach usually fails to try to explain how the same training (e.g., by Talcott Parsons at Harvard during the early 1950s) can produce such different persons as Harold Garfinkel (an ethnomethodologist) and Robert Bellah (a structural functionalist).

Each of these four approaches to analyzing social theory offers a means to order knowledge, but each has particular weaknesses. As we have noted, the exhaustive, open quality of these systems indicates that each is only a classification system rather than a theory itself. Being open, they can fit all possible future theories into their framework; being exhaustive, they include *all* theories and thus have no adequate explanation for (no way to predict) the rise and fall of different theoretical systems. Each provides some reasons for perceived changes in intellectual systems, but these reasons have not been systematized into a theory of sociological theory.

REORGANIZING THE ANALYSIS OF SOCIAL THEORY

Early in this chapter (p. 5) I stated a basic, operational definition of social theory. I then discussed the matter of grouping similar theories and accounting for similarities and differences among them. I pointed out that the weakness of past analysis has been its classificatory (exhaustive and open) rather than explanatory nature. Until now, however, the sociology of knowledge has not possessed the theoretical and empirical tools necessary to construct and test an adequate explanation for the development of theory—social or otherwise. These tools now exist, and Chapter 2 therefore presents a theoretical model for the development of theories. The model, which is based on recent findings in the sociology of knowledge, is used throughout the rest of this book to explain the development of sociological theories.

My organization of social theory is based on the model developed in Chapter 2. Briefly, two or more pieces of theory work are considered to be similar if their authors (1) cite similar sources, (2) are known to be colleagues or students, one of another, or all of yet another person; and (3) are considered to be similar by themselves and others. If these characteristics exist, it is assumed that the theoretical works involved are more like one another with respect to concepts, variables, styles, relations, and so on, than they are to other theories.[2] If major differences are found (and occasionally some are), they are considered unusual, and explanation is required.

There is obviously a scale of relative differences among theories, and determining relative similarity is important to understanding the present state of social theory. Distinctions can be made finely (so as to separate almost every theory) or grossly (so as to make only a few distinctions). For example, some sociologists lump together all theories that use numbers for any purpose other than page and footnote identification, whereas others find several distinct groups among those who use numbers in constructing their theories.[3] Fine distinctions are frequently made simply to indicate that a particular theory makes a unique contribution, even though that contribution may be marginal. The development of exchange theory within standard American sociology provides an example. By stating that the system-maintaining processes within stable social systems are exchanges between persons, exchange theorists have made a marginal contribution to sociology. Yet these sociologists (e.g., Homans) see their contribution as having produced a theory very different from other closely related functional theories (e.g., the work of Parsons and his followers).

This book analyzes theories that, according to the model discussed in Chapter 2, have been or presently are the major different kinds of American sociological theory. If you've read the Contents of this book, you already know that I have omitted exchange theory. Why? When we look at American sociology, we find that the different kinds of sociology developed at different times—some after 1960, others well before. Data on major theoretical shifts in other sciences, as discussed in Chapter 2, show that major changes occur when a small coherent group of theorists develops, works on a series of related problems of mutual interest, and gradually finds that (1) their theoretical formulations are becoming increasingly different from those of the rest of the discipline and (2) the members' formulations are becoming more alike. Exchange theory, and other systems of thought that meet the basic definition stated earlier, have been omitted because they have never generated sufficient enthusiasm to gather a coherent group; hence (for reasons elaborated in Chapter 2), their incipient formulations have never developed far enough to be differentiated distinctly and recognizably, by outsiders, as radical, theoretical breaks with the past. In short, one can still understand exchange theory if one first understands structural functionalism.

The model presented in Chapter 2, then, is not exhaustive; it includes only theories that have gained some acceptance within a communicating group. This model thus offers the possibility of predicting, for a given theory, its chance for progressing from incipient status to that of a theory position fully different from that which spawned it. Chapter 2's model is not open to all new theories for the same reason that it is not exhaustive; to those exhibiting the appropriate properties, though, this theory is quite open.

This book examines how, over time, groups of social theorists form, grow, and then cease to exist. One of our purposes is to examine the processes that bring persons together (through teacher–student relations, colleague relations, etc.) and create, sustain, and kill the groups that result. In addition to the social aspects, the model outlined in Chapter 2 considers the intellectual side of theory development: fundamental concerns, basic techniques, and how both aspects began and have changed over time.

The rest of the book follows a very simple outline. Chapter 2, which closes Part One, presents the theory on which the remainder of the book is based. Chapters 3 to 5 present and discuss data on three core perspectives in sociological theory: standard American sociology, symbolic interactionism, and small group theory. They are now part of sociology's history in that they no longer exist as groups and are no longer generating new intellectual insights; nevertheless, people trained in these perspectives are still teaching in many American universities, and the groups themselves have made essential social and intellectual contributions to the five perspectives that are now active, contemporary American sociological theories. Chapter 6 reviews the first three perspectives, compares their data for their fit with the theoretical model of Chapter 2, and summarizes Part Two. Part Three includes chapters on the forecasters, ethnomethodologists, new causal theorists, structuralists, and radical-critical theorists. Chapter 12 summarizes data on the last five groups, compares their fit with the model, and comments on the future of social theory groups. Finally, a technical appendix discusses such methodological matters as the data sources and the procedures used to determine group members and typical theory pieces.

NOTES

1. Obviously the "why" and "how" (i.e., what constitutes adequate explanation) are quite important in theory. This book is not the place for an extended discussion of their meaning. The interested reader should see Kaplan (1964), Ziman (1968), and Wilson (1970) for alternative approaches to explanation.
2. This assumption has not yet been proved by research. Many sociologists of science believe it to be true, however, and a more limited statement—that persons who are in communication with one another see their research in the same way—*has* been proved (Mullins, 1968).
3. There is a general tendency to group those theories that are perceived as quite different from one's own work into very few groups and to make many fine distinctions among theories that are similar to one's own work. My approach to grouping is analogous to the way in which Warner (1941) grouped his respondents by class. Warner began with respondents' perceptions of their own class. Fine discriminations were made nearest to the respondent's position, and Warner tried to objectify class perceptions by using the discriminations of many respondents. The dimensions of theory differences are at least as complex as those of perceived class.

BIBLIOGRAPHY

Allen, Philip J. (ed.).
    1963   *Pitirim A. Sorokin in Review.* Durham, N.C.: Duke University Press.
Bendix, Reinhard.
    1966   *Max Weber: An Intellectual Portrait.* London: Methuen.
Clark, Ronald W.
    1971   *Einstein: The Life and Times.* New York: World Publishing.
Coleman, James S.
    1968   "Review symposium." *American Sociological Review* 33 (February): 126–130.
Coles, Robert.
    1970   *Erik H. Erikson: The Growth of His Work.* Boston: Little, Brown.
Demerath, Nicholas J., III, and Richard A. Peterson (eds.).
    1967   *System, Change and Conflict: A Reader on Contemporary Sociological Theory and the Debate over Functionalism.* New York: Free Press.
Dohmoff, G. William, and Hoyt B. Ballard.
    1968   *C. Wright Mills and the Power Elite.* Boston: Beacon.
Douglas, Jack D. (ed.).
    1970   *Understanding Everyday Life: Toward the Reconstruction of Sociological Knowledge.* Chicago: Aldine.

Erikson, Erik H.
　　1958　*Young Man Luther: A Study in Psychoanalysis and History.* New
　　　　　York: Norton.
Faris, Robert E. L.
　　1967　*Chicago Sociology, 1920–1932.* San Francisco: Chandler.
Garfinkel, Harold.
　　1967　*Studies in Ethnomethodology.* Englewood Cliffs, N.J.: Prentice-Hall.
Gouldner, Alvin W.
　　1970　*The Coming Crisis of Western Sociology.* New York: Basic Books.
Homans, George C.
　　1950　*The Human Group.* New York: Harcourt Brace Jovanovich.
Kaplan, Abraham.
　　1964　*The Conduct of Inquiry: Methodology for Behavioral Science.* San
　　　　　Francisco: Chandler.
Martindale, Don A.
　　1960　*The Nature and Types of Sociological Theory.* Boston: Houghton
　　　　　Mifflin.
Marx, Karl.
　　1964　*Selected Writings in Sociology and Social Philosophy.* Translated by
　　　　　T. B. Bottomore. Edited by T. B. Bottomore and Maximilien Rubel.
　　　　　New York: McGraw-Hill.
Merton, Robert K., and Paul F. Lazarsfeld (eds.).
　　1950　*Studies in the Scope and Method of "The American Soldier."* (Also
　　　　　known as *Continuities in Social Research.*) New York: Free Press.
Mills, C. Wright.
　　1956　*The Power Elite.* New York: Oxford University Press.
Mitzman, Arthur.
　　1970　*The Iron Cage: An Historical Interpretation of Max Weber.* 1st ed.
　　　　　New York: Knopf.
Mullins, Nicholas C.
　　1968　"The distribution of social and cultural properties in informal com-
　　　　　munication networks among biological scientists." *American Socio-
　　　　　logical Review* 33 (October): 786–797.
　　1971　*The Art of Theory: Construction and Use.* New York: Harper & Row.
Nisbet, Robert A.
　　1966　*The Sociological Tradition.* New York: Basic Books.
Parsons, Talcott.
　　1937　*The Structure of Social Action: A Study in Social Theory with Spe-
　　　　　cial Reference to a Group of Recent European Writers.* New York:
　　　　　McGraw-Hill.
　　1951　*The Social System.* New York: Free Press.
Schaff, Adam.
　　1970　*Marxism and the Human Individual.* New York: McGraw-Hill.
Smelser, Neil J.
　　1959　*Social Change in the Industrial Revolution.* Chicago: University of
　　　　　Chicago Press.
Wallace, Walter L. (ed.).
　　1969　*Sociological Theory: An Introduction.* Chicago: Aldine.

Warner, W. Lloyd, and Paul S. Lund.
  1941   *The Status System of a Modern Community*. New Haven, Conn.:
         Yale University Press.
Wilson, Thomas P.
  1970   "Normative and interpretive paradigms in sociology." Pp. 57–79 in
         Jack D. Douglas (ed.), *Understanding Everyday Life: Toward the
         Reconstruction of Sociological Knowledge*. Chicago: Aldine.
Ziman, John M.
  1968   *Public Knowledge: An Essay Concerning the Social Dimension of
         Science*. London: Cambridge University Press.

CHAPTER 2
MODEL FOR THE
DEVELOPMENT OF
SOCIOLOGICAL THEORIES

T his chapter presents a general model for the development of sociological theories. The study of academic, scientific groups in general has
its roots in Kuhn's (1962) formulation regarding changes ("revolutions")
in scientific thinking and Price's (1963) presentation of a theoretical
social structure called the "invisible college," a group of roughly 100 consulting colleagues; these formulations have inspired considerable empirical investigation. In a characteristically nice turn of phrase, Price described those of us who study social structure in science as having set
a unicorn trap for the beautiful concept of the "invisible college" (in
Crawford, 1972: 2). Instead of unicorns, however, the trap first appeared
to have caught only sociological rabbits: very small, loosely organized
groups of scientists which behave much like ordinary groups and do
rather ordinary sorts of research.

Further research into both the broad communication structure encom-
passing all science and the specific groupings in diverse specialties[1] has
uncovered small coherent, activist theory groups whose work foreshadows,
and may eventuate in, major advances and changes in the direction of
a group's parent discipline. These groups seem to occur across a variety
of disciplines, periods of time, and types of research, and the findings
of research into these groups have suggested a model for theory group
development. An explicit theory of group formation and change in scientific thinking was first presented in Mullins (1968a, 1972). Griffith and
Miller (1970) delineated characteristics specific to scientific theory groups.
Griffith and Mullins (1972) then summarized empirical data on scientific groups as of early 1972 and emphasized the importance of such
groups to change in scientific thinking.

DEVELOPMENTAL STAGES

This theory is based on a four-stage model of group development, each stage being marked by empirically demonstrable social and intellectual characteristics. The four stages are: (1) normal, (2) network, (3) cluster, and (4) specialty or discipline.[2] The most important aspect of the development process is the communication structure, which is based on trusted assessors of work. As a distinguished scientist remarked: "The chief means of critical appraisal of any piece of work, the demonstration of its strong and weak points, its methodological inadequacies and its position among other investigations in the field is, even today, verbal, direct and immediate discussion in a circle of understanding colleagues" (Medvedev, 1971; 133–134).

Every active, productive scientist has a few trusted assessors, usually not in his own department and often not in the same specialty or even discipline (Mullins, 1968b; Crane, 1969, 1970; see also, pp. 20ff.) who act as friendly critics of his work. These scientists may or may not reciprocate the service. In fact, the people in one scientist's group of assessors do not necessarily share the same set of trusted assessors; often, there is not even one assessor in common. Storer (1967) conceptualized this situation, typical of the normal stage in science, as a personal invisible college for each scientist. Students of invisible colleges have noted that their structure and personnel shift as one moves from person to person within a set of scientists (Mullins, 1966).

The general scientific communication structure is depicted (in ideal–typical fashion) in Figure 2.1. The relationships among active scientists at any point within the general structure need not be, and usually are not, always the same. Hence Figure 2.1 also depicts (in similar ideal–typical fashion) the social relationships characteristic of the four stages noted previously. These stages are *always* imbedded within the general scientific communication structure. Furthermore, at any given point in time, several manifestations of each stage are probably happening simultaneously at different places within the network; the figure shows only one network and one cluster, but more are possible and, indeed, likely. There is no representation for either the normal or the specialty stage simply because, with respect to relationship patterns, the two are not differentiated within the general structure. From an historical standpoint, the specialty stage leaves a mark on formal structures (e.g., colleges) simply because its members and work become institutionalized as a department, a discipline, a specialty within a discipline, and so on. But we have no way to detect, in advance, people who will be showing up in, say, five years, as members of a network-stage group.

Connections between scientists in the general scientific communication structure are symbolized by four kinds of lines, each representing a social relationship that continually occurs in science. These relationships are: (1) communication (serious discussion about ongoing research; Mullins, 1968b), (2) coauthorship (a more intimate form of association in which two or more scientists jointly report their research results on some topic), (3) apprenticeship (a student is trained and sponsored by his teacher), and (4) colleagueship (two scientists work in the same laboratory). Most scientists who are at all active in research have some of these relationships. The purpose here is not simply to show that they occur but, rather, to describe the *pattern* in which they occur, since that pattern can roughly suggest the stage to which an intellectual group has developed itself.

An active scientist who continues to participate in the communication structure (many scientists *never* enter into it)[3] forms and breaks connec-

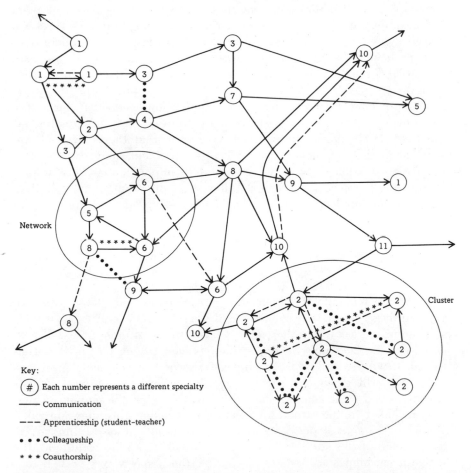

FIGURE 2.1   Ideal–typical communication structure in science.

tions throughout his research lifetime; during that lifetime, moreover, his research interests are likely to change several times. Network stages are created—some for short periods of time and others for longer—by the focusing of several scientists on a specific area of concern. Many scientists not engaged in network or cluster activity at one point in time may become involved later or may have been involved earlier. For example, in 1966, when standard American sociology and symbolic interaction were the dominant specialties in sociology, both ethnomethodology and new causal theory were making the transition from network to cluster stage. The majority of active sociologists took no part in either new group, nor were they aware of their developments. However, a few of these sociologists had been part of earlier group developments (e.g., symbolic interaction).

The making and breaking of the relations that constitute the general communication structure is a continuous process. Teacher–student pairs and coauthorships leave a permanent record, although such pairings are not always active. Colleague relations sometimes last a year; others span their participants' entire working career (e.g., Homans and Parsons were at Harvard together, except for brief periods, from 1932 until Parsons retired).

The foregoing discussion may have left the impression that, for a specific intellectual problem, the stages named are not only progressive but exclusive. It should be emphasized, therefore, that these divisions are artificial in that, for *any* given intellectual problem, they can overlap. Discussion of each stage is not intended to imply that aspects of preceding stages are no longer functioning; I simply want to suggest that, for a specific intellectual problem, at least a given additional amount of social structural progress has been made. Specific properties of the four stages of group growth are discussed in the following sections.

NORMAL STAGE

The general scientific communication structure is quite loose. We can say that the structure is loose because, if we select 50 scientists (a "wave") at random and ask whom they talk to about their research, they will generally provide the names of other scientists who *are not* part of the original 50. If we then ask *those* scientists (a second wave) the same question, they will generally, but not always, answer by citing scientists not yet named (who can become a third wave). Thus the number of persons included in the structure generated by using this question on a "snowball" sample of persons expands quite rapidly (see Mullins, 1966, for a sketch of this structure using a "snowball" sampling technique; the structure encompassed 2.6^N people per person per N waves or 17.6 in 3 waves). There is also evidence (Mullins, 1968b; Crane, 1969) that those chosen are not always in the same field of research. Not only does the number of persons expand rapidly; the number of fields represented also increases rapidly.

The normal stage is characterized by a low degree of organization both within the literature and within the social relationships. The literature in a normal-stage area (e.g., small group research before 1945) is produced by people at scattered institutions, one or two per institution. Few teacher–student relations are visible in the area, and—more important—no groups of students are being formed. The commitments of persons involved in normal areas are generally short in duration and constitute only one of several commitments, each to different areas (Mullins, 1966). Hence little *coordinated* effort is made to solve any particular problem.

If we take an area as defined by the literature (i.e., a research front; Price, 1965), we find that the degree of social organization varies from the normal-science condition of little organization to the high-organization characteristic of coherent clusters. Research literature may be produced either by a well-organized group or by single individuals acting largely alone. The evidence thus far suggests that the activity of science in the normal stage is "bit-and-piece" puzzle solving (Kuhn, 1970). There is little or no coauthorship.

In paradigm development, a group of scientists, either together or separately, undergo a "gestalt shift" (Kuhn, 1970) that changes their perception of the topic or topics they are analyzing. The development of a new perspective may be quite gradual, although *recognition* that a perspective is very different may be rather sudden. The group's subsequent research uses this new perception, and some of that research is published.

NETWORK STAGE

From time to time, in a few places, the normal-science pattern begins to undergo change. Figure 2.2 (p. 30) shows that the boundary between the normal and the network stages is frequently marked by the appearance of one or more exciting intellectual products around which several researchers gather. For structuralism (see Chapter 10), the important item was White's *Chains of Opportunity* (1970). A major discovery, a new idea, or an especially cogent criticism of the present state of affairs may begin to attract attention to one or several persons. Directly or indirectly, these persons come to focus on *each other* consistently as trusted assessors (in contrast with the normal stage, when one scientist's assessors most likely use *other* scientists as *their* assessors) and to recruit these like-minded scientists as colleagues.[4] A consensus gradually begins to develop among this group as its members focus on crucial intellectual issues. It is important that some success (e.g., a research breakthrough) or apparent success reward the group's effort during this early period, thus confirming and supporting the developing consensus.

The more frequent communication among a few persons, combined with the declining number of ties to scientists outside the circle of frequent communicators,[5] creates a "thickening" of the scientific communication network (Mullins, 1972; Griffith and Mullins, 1972). A second factor is the appearance of a few students and the creation of student–teacher links. The general science communication structure as a whole is not affected by such local thickenings; indeed, they are seldom noticed by most active scientists. It is only those directly involved who are likely to notice that the thickening has developed.

These changes in social relations are accompanied by specific changes in the intellectual content of the developing theory. During the network stage, successful groups generally make an explicit agreement regarding limits on the style and content of the research to be done by its members (Mullins, 1972). The directions for future research provided by this agreement generally appear in a program statement. For structural functionalism (the eventual outcome of standard American sociology; see Chapter 3), that implicit agreement was on the production of middle-range theories. The program statements were by Parsons (1949) and Merton (1948). Often the transition from network to cluster stage is marked by publication of research resulting from the consensus. For small group theory, note the large number of publications between 1949 and 1951. The literature shows somewhat greater organization, since it is being produced by fewer scientists, and they refer in footnotes to one another and to accepted common "forefathers" more frequently than they cite other scientists (e.g., Durkheim, Pareto, and Weber were forefathers of structural functionalism).

CLUSTER STAGE

The transition to cluster status is a major change. Communication becomes even more ingrown. Clusters of students and colleagues form around the key figures in a group in one or a few institutions. Students are important because only a few scientists in a field ever have any graduate students, and those who do usually perform most of the research and publish frequently, as well (see Price, 1963). The current American university situation is fairly open; nevertheless, junior faculty members do not usually have groups of students. Junior faculty cannot provide fellowship funds, and they seldom have the kind or number of research problems necessary to keep a group of students busy. A totally different factor, but also important, is the desire of students. Clusters in sociology usually form around the high producers mentioned earlier, at the universities which have traditionally had great sociology faculties (Berkeley, Chicago, Columbia, Harvard, Michigan, Wisconsin). Indeed, the students at these institutions have generally come to study with the top persons in their field of interest. These major universities have been the centers for both training and research.

A cluster generally includes three or more professionals (i.e., possessors of the Ph.D. degree), who reinforce one another's interests, and several graduate students. It constitutes a first institutionalization and is based on colleague and teacher–student relations rather than the less stable, informal communication relations of the network stage. The group members' outside contacts are largely with others in similar lines of work. The students, who have not developed the multiple interests of the professional, tend to be more focused on one interest. As Stinchcombe (1972) remarked: "Our students try to make sectarians of us."

As with the network stage, the cluster's social changes are accompanied by intellectual changes. Intellectually, such a group concentrates on the specific set of problems defined by the program statement. Usually large quantities of research results are generated, and some of these eventually prove to be critically important scientific work. The group's work gradually begins to reveal its divergence from the theoretical concepts of the parent discipline. The degree of divergence from standard work seems to be a function of the group's size, and that divergence affects the group's actual degree of isolation from the main discipline.

The literature in the group's area shows an even higher degree of organization than was true in the network stage, and for the same reasons. The theoretical connections among specific works are made even stronger by coauthorship, which becomes particularly important at this stage as the results of joint research projects are published.

It is worth repeating that the making and breaking of the relations that create networks and clusters is a continuous process. Even in a cluster, the relations are seldom long-lived, nor are cluster members likely to remain associated with other cluster members when the cluster stage is over. It is the *pattern* of associations and *not* the *characteristics* of those associations that make up a network or cluster. This finding may well explain why sociologists of science originally thought that they had caught only rabbits in their unicorn traps: They were looking for special kinds of relations, whereas, actually, the context and the pattern of relations give a group its character.

It is during the cluster stage that the parent discipline's reaction to the new work becomes known. This reaction establishes the group as either revolutionary or elitist (Griffith and Mullins, 1972). An elite group becomes the leading group in the parent discipline. Such a group's reformulation of theory is accepted by the rest of the discipline as different, but useful and important. The elite group is clearly not isolated from the parent discipline. The new causal theory group (see Chapter 9) exemplifies this type of group.

Sometimes, however, a group's work is seen as revolutionary and either dangerous or foolish by the main discipline, which rejects the proposed ideas. Then the cluster group becomes "encapsulated," isolated from and by the rest of the discipline, as the human body encapsulates an infection. With time, such a group may (1) die, (2) wait until the older discipline loses its ability to produce enough students to maintain itself, or (3) become the establishment point for a new specialty or discipline (which is what happened when phage workers became part of the foundation for molecular biology; see Mullins, 1972). The ethnomethodologists (see Chapter 8) exemplify the revolutionary type of group in sociology.

During the cluster period, secondary materials and critical work related to the group's emphasis begin to appear (for ethnomethodology, see Coleman, 1968; Douglas, 1970). Clearly this type of work could not have been done earlier; sufficient published work must exist to make the critical effort worthwhile. Being attacked is a measure of success for a group, and such academic assaults serve to buoy the morale of group members.

SPECIALTY STAGE

The transition from cluster to specialty stage begins as the students become successful themselves, and both they and others are hired away from their original locations. No location has yet been able to support a cluster indefinitely; it is expensive to retain successful people. Perhaps more important, most clusters form at teaching institutions that must offer a variety of courses; thus, of necessity, some of the persons in a cluster are replaced by other scientists with different interests. Ironically, then, the successful cluster pays for its success by ceasing to exist. During the breakup period, the old ties of personal contact are weakened by increased distance and responsibility (resulting from job promotions received by successful group members). When the original bonds fail to connect the group closely any more, the ultimately successful cluster's next effort is to institutionalize the work that has been done. This is usually accomplished through the establishment of journals, departments, and positions for the new specialty (discipline, program, etc.) The processes of institutionalization themselves are well reported in Ben-David (1960, 1971) and Ben-David and Collins (1966).

The crucial aspect of institutionalizing a new specialty is the establishment, either by creating new positions or reassigning old ones, of jobs for persons trained in that specialty. An elite specialty tends to grow more quickly, to attract more established investigators who have students, to stay clustered for a shorter time, to have less group feeling, and to take over established journals and positions rather than creating new ones—all because communication ties are made easily (see Chapter 9 on new causal theory). A rejected and, hence, revolutionary specialty attracts few established investigators, grows almost exclusively through the training of students, remains in the cluster stage longer, has a stronger group feeling, establishes new journals and positions, and may separate totally from the parent discipline—because communication ties are made less easily (see Chapter 8 on ethnomethodology).

In either case, a process of routinization, both of new social arrangements and of the new intellectual positions, occurs as (1) the students begin to develop divergent interests and (2) textbooks, critical material, and secondary works are written in order to maintain the purity of the group's theoretical reformation and to reduce the strangeness of the new position. The amount of research and publication may increase for a while, but it will be done by many more people. Either the core of early, very high producers is not producing as much, or it has already shifted to other lines of research. Gradually the dense network that had formed loosens again into the normal pattern of the general science communication structure. The remnants of the group hang together within scattered network thickenings for a while, but the making of other ties into other research areas inevitably begins, and many people fall out of the structure completely (Jahn, 1972). Soon, the only indication of the specialty is a name, sometimes a nostalgia for the good old days of clusterhood, and occasionally, a conscious history (e.g., Cairns, Stent, and Watson, 1966; Parsons, 1970).

From the flow of this discussion the reader may infer that transition from one stage to the next is necessary. As Figure 2.2 (p. 30) indicates, however, transition is not necessary. Groups can die off for many reasons at any point along the way (e.g., small group work died before reaching the specialty stage, and the forecasters may yet not develop a cluster). The characteristics required for success are discussed in the following section.

SOCIAL AND INTELLECTUAL PROPERTIES OF COHERENT GROUPS

In addition to documenting the stages of group growth, research has established that known theory groups exhibit empirical characteristics as follows.

1. A *theoretical orientation* (break) different from that of the parent discipline —developed and directed by an *intellectual leader*, verbalized in a *pro-*

gram statement, and supported by *intellectual successes*. These works usually include critiques of the parent discipline's current work.

2. A loss of disinterestedness—organized and directed by a *social organizational leader*; this aspect includes conscious group development ("social engineering"), seeking jobs for members, and acquiring students.
3. A *research center*—the site or sites of close interaction, often leading to aberrant work and recreation habits.[6]
4. *Training centers*—for teaching the students who are necessary to carry out the research program. The training center is usually a research center, but this situation is not mandatory.
5. Intellectual materials—a *textbook* in the orientation of the group, *critical material, and secondary material.*

These common aspects, as we have noted, presently exist in many ongoing natural and social science groups. Some of these groups will ultimately be judged as successes, others as failures. Similar groups have also existed in the past. Gouldner (1965), referring to the Socratic group of philosophers, noted many of the same aspects of social organization discussed previously, particularly the necessity for a theoretical break:

Both the difference and the continuity between Socrates and Plato are repeatedly paralleled throughout the history of social theory; they will be found in the paired relation between Marx and Engels, between Saint-Simon and Comte, and even among some contemporaries. In part, this is a relation between relatively speculative, sprawling, imaginative, and daring innovators on the one hand and their somewhat more disciplined disciples on the other who take the mentor's ideas, sometimes only verbally expressed, and with more or less brilliance, diligently codify, systematize, and elaborate their implications in selected directions.

It is notable that major breakthroughs in social theory are not the product of lonely genius but are often the product of a few men working closely together. Some kind of group support is helpful to those striving to elude conventional ways of looking at human behavior; the primary group, whether a *folie à deux* or a love affair, can be a sheltering enclave for theoretical innovations, for these are always precarious and especially need protection during their formative periods. Changes in social theory are always—in smaller, interpersonal influences as well as through larger institutional pressures—a social product. In particular, the master–disciple or teacher–student relation, when close and intense, constitutes a sheltering social system that functions to protect the novel and hence precarious creativity of the older man. The function of the student–disciple is not merely to do the routine, "dirty" work of his mentor, and it is not only in this way that the former obligates the master–teacher to him and wins his subsequent sponsorship. The more intellectually significant function of the admiring and friendly disciple is—through his favorable disposition to his mentor—to give consensual validation to the latter's innovations before they are given over to the public scrutiny of his peers. This enables the master–scholar to overcome his own work-blocking anxieties and provides him with socio-emotional support. This support is especially needed when the master's innovation is still precarious, when it is still only half-born, insufficiently documented, incompletely justified, and only dimly perceived, and when, in consequence, the creative innovation could be crushed by a full-scale critique inspired by the competitive animus of the older man's peers (Gouldner, 1965: 177–178).

We might hypothesize, then, that the foremost factor in determining whether a coherent group develops at some location in the general science structure is: Are the scientists involved proceeding only empirically (simply moving from one research problem to another, without benefit of broad, theoretical guidance) or, alternatively, are they carving out a new theoretical orientation and being guided by it? Certainly an overemphasis on the empirical was a factor in the failure of small group researchers to reach the specialty stage (see Chapter 5).

How do we distinguish successful groups from failures? One possibility is to define as a failure every potential group of scientists that does not develop the characteristics noted previously. If we take this approach, however, virtually every development in every time period is ultimately unsuccessful. This is a drastic but honest conclusion. Most scientists and most potential developments do *not* contribute to changing the course of science.

FITTING THE PROPERTIES WITH THE STAGES

To summarize briefly, theory groups develop in four stages; the beginning of each stage is signaled by changes in the group's social structure and intellectual output. Research has also produced a list of specific social (e.g., the development of a training center) and intellectual (e.g., a program statement) properties that characterize successful groups.[7] Table 2.1 lists these properties by stages, showing which properties are necessary at which points in time.

The normal stage of science shows no signs of a given future group that could be obvious to outsiders. At this point, the "founding father" of a new group has just started on his (new) career. By the specialty stage, he may have left that line of work to begin quite different research. In the normal stage, however, there is no way to predict which productive persons of all those in a discipline are likely to become future leaders of new specialties and which will continue working out older ideas.

An intellectual leader provides the original idea(s) around which a group can form; often, but not always, he (or they) also furnishes the program statement (during the network stage), which guides work in the cluster stage. A social organizational leader(s) becomes important

TABLE 2.1 Group properties by stages of group development

Properties	Normal Stage	Network Stage	Cluster Stage	Specialty Stage
1. Intellectual leader(s)	Founding father(s)	Probable integration of concept, etc.	Should have highly productive student groups	May leave
2. Social organizational leader(s)	—[a]	Organizes training center	Arranges jobs, publications, meetings	Continues activities
3. Research and training center(s)	—	Develops where people are starting to work together; usually at a university	Generally one or two more, at least one becomes a strong training center	No specific center; research is diffuse
4. Intellectual successes	First written success appears roughly at end of stage	Attracts other scientists, students	Many successes leading to divergencies	No longer important as the group institutionalizes
5. Program statement(s)	—	Stated during this stage	Becomes a "central dogma," particularly for revolutionary groups	Work becomes routine
6. Secondary material	—	—	Appears here	Limited to consolidation
7. Critical material by group	Can appear here (revolutionary)	Can appear here (revolutionary)	Possibly can appear here also (revolutionary)	—
8. Critical material about group	—	—	Appears here (revolutionary)	Becomes routine
9. Text	—	—	—	Appears here
Group size	Indeterminant	**(Informal relations)** Up to 40	**(More formal relations)** (7–25 in actual cluster)	20–100 +

[a] — = nonapplicable at this stage.

during the cluster stage. He is essential in establishing and then maintaining a cluster over its lifetime. The lack of such a leader was one important factor in the demise of small group work. A different kind of social organizational leader, one willing to become bureaucratized, may be needed in the specialty stage.

A research center ("center" implies more than one person) develops as soon as two people at a single place begin doing research in the new style. The necessity for more than one person is emphasized by the data on ethnomethodology. Research centers are distinct throughout the network and cluster stages and are diffuse during the specialty stage. A training center develops fully during the cluster stage. One of the more interesting (but still unexplained) findings of research into group development is that students do not join groups in even flows but in bunches. The ability to attract *several* groups of students seems to be crucial to a theory's survival and growth. Invariant theory in mathematics was killed by a lack of students (Fisher, 1967); in sociology, forecasting has been slowed in its development by a lack of students.

Intellectual successes of some sort signal continued development. Early successes attract attention to the group and its work, whereas later triumphs maintain continued interest. Successes need not be large, but they must seem like inevitabilities. Lack of success can kill a group; indeed, this lack was another important factor in killing small group work in sociology.

The other intellectual properties appear at quite predictable times. Material *by group members* that is *critical of the parent discipline* appears during the network and early cluster stages. During the late cluster stage and specialty stage (particularly for revolutionary-type groups), material that is *critical of the group* appears. Secondary materials—readers, review articles, collections of essays, and textbooks—appear during the specialty stage. An outline at the beginning of each data chapter (Chapter 11 excepted) details these properties for the theory group of concern in that chapter.

The properties in Table 2.1 enable us to determine how far a group has come in development (although, as I have noted before, development does not necessarily complete itself in every group). Figure 2.2 schematizes the process by which groups move from one stage to another and lists the necessary elements of each change.[8] The results of a lack of that development are also proposed. At any stage in a group's development, if a communicating group of scientists does not develop student or colleague relations that are more stable than communication relations, two forces will act to pull the group apart and return the area to the normal-stage pattern of communication again. The forces are: (1) changes in interest and (2) the attrition that eliminates some members of the group as active scientists. This return to the normal-stage pattern can

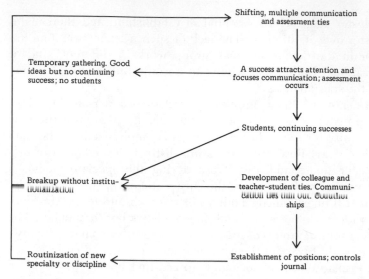

FIGURE 2.2 Process of group development and dissolution.

occur at any stage, and it is observed more frequently than the development of student or colleague relations. Stability is unlikely because ongoing transformations in pattern and personnel of the underlying communication structure make it impossible to maintain a permanent network pattern in a particular area. Long network stages such as that for symbolic interactionism (Chapter 4) occur when there are only a few students—enough to provide some stability, but not enough to cause a cluster to form.

This model assumes a largely academic environment because the characteristics of the model are developed from those of academe and academically trained scientists. It is assumed that most changes in science are made by academicians.

The communication structure of science is the model's basic element. That structure constitutes the basis for explanation of the development of other social structures in science. It is a *whole* composed of scientists (usually Ph.D. holders) and the relations among them (communication, trusted assessorship, colleagueship, coauthorship, and studentship). Because the model's concern is for the *patterns* of those relations among scientists rather than for individuals, it assumes that science has a wholeness as a relational system whose structure can be described and examined. Transformations in relations (e.g., colleagueship into coauthorship) are the fundamental process of interest. Transformations in a structure of relations determine whether a group will come into existence. The initial existence of groups and further transformations in relational structures result in the properties and stages already described.

The transformations are assumed to be self-regulating—that is, not requiring explanations based on individuals' personalities, general characteristics of American society, or the intellectual history of sociology. These three elements sometimes appear in the discussion of a specific group's structure, but they are neither necessary nor sufficient to explain that structure and its change over time. They simply clarify how one of the properties listed in Table 2.1 worked itself out in a given context.

This model would be seriously challenged if any of the following possibilities were true: (1) The communication structure for an area became stabilized over a period of time, with interest maintained by a set of scientists who were neither colleagues nor students of one another. (2) A stable set of colleagues successfully institutionalized an area without ever developing a training center or cluster stage. (3) Over time, one or two institutions both graduated large numbers of students trained in a certain style and maintained their clusters despite regular turnover among their faculty. Empirically, these possibilities have not happened, although logically they could. The failure rate of groups is emphasized because creating a new theoretical orientation is a relatively rare event; there have been nine in sociology since 1892, and only three were fully successful: the early Chicago school, symbolic interactionism, and standard American sociology.

With respect to time, the data on processes suggest that we can expect a network stage to last from four to fourteen years, and a cluster stage, from four to eight years. I can offer some tentative explanations for these time limits in terms of conditions for academic employment, necessity for institutions to teach a variety of courses, and the relative richness of the job market. Unless tenure is granted or special arrangements made, academic tenure rules in the United States forbid junior faculty to remain longer than seven years at one institution. If a cluster is formed largely of persons with short-term (e.g., research or postdoctoral) appointments, the transition to specialty may be a gradual occurrence. However, a cluster formed of persons on regular appointments may break up quite precipitously if all the members received their initial appointments simultaneously. We have already noted the need, at most establishments, to teach a range of courses. The third important factor in cluster breakup is the general condition of the job market. During a talent-hungry, job-rich time (for example, during the early 1960s for biology or sociology), the successful cluster is a prime candidate for raiders from other universities and laboratories, and the result is rapid special establishment.

The following chapters apply this model to original data on sociology groups. Part Two discusses groups from the recent past: standard American sociology (later, structural functionalism), symbolic interactionism, and small group work. Part Three discusses contemporary groups: the forecasters, ethnomethodologists, new causal theorists, structuralists, and radical-critical theorists.

NOTES

1. Rural sociologists (Crane, 1969), Skinnerian psychologists (Krantz, 1971), audition researchers (Griffith and Miller, 1970), phage workers in molecular biology (Mullins, 1972), and numerous other groups (see Griffith and Mullins, 1972) have been studied.

2. A specialty is part of a discipline (e.g., demography is a specialty within sociology).

3. Publication has been used as a measure of scientific activity. Derek deS. Price (1963: 40–45) estimated that 50 percent of all Ph.D.-holding scientists publish nothing beyond their dissertations. Publication is not communication, but it seems clear that those who do not publish, with very few exceptions, have little to communicate to active scientists and therefore are not sought as trusted assessors.

4. There are virtually no data publicly available on trusted assessors (gathering such data systematically would require the use of a questionnaire or interviews). The only public information available (aside from that in festschrifts or conscious retrospection; e.g., Parsons, 1970), is the "thanks to reviewers of previous drafts" which appear (irregularly) in a footnote at the beginning of a paper or as part of a book preface. Because sociology is virtually devoid of both festschrifts and retrospectives, my information has been drawn almost solely from published acknowledgments to reviewers; where possible, it has been confirmed by reports from in-group readers of the various chapters. Considerable public information is available on colleagueship, however, and that information has been presented in the basic data table for each chapter (e.g., Table 3.3).

5. Research suggests that each scientist communicates regularly with an average of three other scientists (Mullins, 1968). Obviously, if three is an accurate estimate for a scientist's number of regular communicators, the change of even one person for another may make quite a difference in a scientist's thinking. There is virtually no direct, public information on who talks to whom among sociologists. Hence the assertion that ties to non-group members are declining is an inference based on the increase of in-group ties. (Increased in-group ties are assumed to require decreased out-group ties, since there are only 18 hours at most in an average working day, and other duties—teaching, research, administration—do not change.) Increased in-group relationships can be inferred from public information on meetings, coauthorships, training, and colleagueships. When possible, I have confirmed my inferences from public data with information from in-group readers. Conversely, I have tried to avoid using informant data that could not also be inferred from public data.

6. See Mullins (1972) for a discussion of such habits (e.g., camping trips, which were part of the Phage Group's culture). The relative newness of sociology groups, particularly the contemporary ones, means that there is

very little retrospective data on groups and their behavior, such as Cairns, Stent, and Watson (1966) provided on the Phage Group. My conversations with members of the various groups, however, indicate that unusual characteristics do develop; for example, structuralists frequently terminate seminars and colloquia held in the Cambridge area with a mass descent on a specific Chinese restaurant not far from Harvard.

7. Although here divided into social and intellectual properties, these properties can also be viewed together in analogy to Lévi-Strauss's analysis of totemic systems (social properties have an obvious analogy to the social–structural kinship system whereas intellectual properties parallel marriage rules):

> To recognize that each tribe possesses two codes to express its social structure—kinship system and rules of marriage on the one hand, organization into sections or subsections on the other—does not at all entail, and even excludes, that the codes shall by nature be destined to transmit different messages. The message remains the same; only the circumstance and the recipients differ (1963: 50).

The message being delivered is about the similarities and differences of work among scientists, and how that work fits together. We can see the message of a new specialty unfold in both social and intellectual codes over its stages of development.

8. Clearly the next task for the sociology of knowledge is to develop estimates of the probabilities for moving from one stage to another; at present we lack sufficient data to make such estimates.

BIBLIOGRAPHY

Ben-David, Joseph.
  1960 "Scientific productivity and academic organization in nineteenth century medicine." *American Sociological Review* 25 (December): 828–843.
  1971 *The Scientist's Role in Society: A Comparative Study.* Englewood Cliffs, N.J.: Prentice-Hall.
Ben-David, Joseph, and Randall Collins.
  1966 "Social factors in the origins of a new science: the case of psychology." *American Sociological Review* 31 (August): 451–465.
Cairns, John, Gunther S. Stent, and James D. Watson (eds.).
  1966 *Phage and the Origins of Molecular Biology.* Cold Spring Harbor, N.Y.: Cold Spring Harbor Laboratory of Molecular Biology.
Coleman, James S.
  1968 "Review symposium." *American Sociological Review* 33 (February): 126–130.
Crane, Diana.
  1969 "Social structure in a group of scientists: a test of the 'invisible college' hypothesis." *American Sociological Review* 34 (June): 335–352.
  1972 *Invisible Colleges.* Chicago: University of Chicago Press.

Crawford, Susan (ed.).
   1972   *Informal Communication Among Scientists: Proceedings of a Conference on Current Research.* Chicago: American Medical Association.
Douglas, Jack D. (ed.)
   1970   *Understanding Everyday Life: Toward the Reconstruction of Sociological Knowledge.* Chicago: Aldine.
Faris, Robert E. L.
   1967   *Chicago Sociology, 1920–1932.* San Francisco: Chandler.
Fisher, Charles S.
   1967   "The last invariant theorists." *European Journal of Sociology* 8 (2): 216–244.
Gouldner, Alvin W.
   1965   *Enter Plato: Classical Greece and the Origins of Social Theory.* New York: Basic Books.
Griffith, Belver C., and A. J. Miller.
   1970   "Networks of informal communication among scientifically productive scientists." Pp. 125–140 in Carnot E. Nelson and Donald K. Pollock (eds.), *Communication Among Scientists and Engineers.* Lexington, Mass.: Heath-Lexington.
Griffith, Belver C., and Nicholas C. Mullins.
   1972   "Coherent groups in scientific change: 'Invisible Colleges' may be consistent throughout science." *Science* 177, 4053 (September 15): 959–964.
Jahn, Marilyn.
   1972   "Dispersion in Source Literature for Subject Areas in Biomedical Research." Philadelphia: Unpublished M.A. thesis, Drexel University.
Krantz, David L.
   1971   "The separate worlds of operant and non-operant psychology." *Journal of Applied Behavioral Analysis* 4 (61): 61–70.
Kuhn, Thomas S.
   1970   *The Structure of Scientific Revolutions.* 2nd ed. Chicago: University of Chicago Press. (1st ed. 1962.)
Lévi-Strauss, Claude.
   1963   *Totemism.* Translated by Rodney Needham. Boston: Beacon.
Medvedev, Zhores A.
   1971   *The Medvedev Papers.* Translated by Vera Rich. London: Macmillan.
Merton, Robert K.
   1948   "Discussion of Parsons." *American Sociological Review* 13 (April): 164–168.
Mullins, Nicholas C.
   1966   Social Communications Networks among Biological Scientists. Cambridge, Mass.: Unpublished Ph.D. thesis, Harvard University.
   1968a "The social origins of an invisible college: the Phage Group." Paper presented to the American Sociological Association meeting, Boston (August).
   1968b "The distribution of social and cultural properties in informal com-

munications networks among biological scientists." *American Sociological Review* 33 (October): 786–797.

1972   "A model for the development of a scientific specialty: the Phage Group and the origins of molecular biology." *Minerva* 10 (January): 51–82.

Parsons, Talcott.

1949   "The prospects of sociological theory." Pp. 348–369 in Talcott Parsons, *Essays in Sociological Theory*. 1st ed. New York: Free Press.

1970   "On building social system theory: a personal history." *Daedalus: The Making of Modern Science: Biographical Studies* 99 (Fall): 826–881.

Price, Derek J. deS.

1963   *Little Science, Big Science*. New York: Columbia University Press.

1965   "Networks of scientific papers; the pattern of bibliographic references indicates the nature of the scientific research front." *Science* 149 (3683, July 30): 510–515.

Stinchcombe, Arthur.

1972   Personal communication (February).

Storer, Norman W.

1967   "Remarks." To a Social Science Research Council Conference on the Social Study of Science. New York: Columbia University (February).

White, Harrison C.

1970   *Chains of Opportunity: System Models of Mobility in Organizations*. Cambridge, Mass.: Harvard University Press.

PART TWO
PAST THEORIES: THE BACKGROUND OF CONTEMPORARY AMERICAN SOCIOLOGY, 1892–1968

CHAPTER 3
STANDARD AMERICAN SOCIOLOGY

Faith of Our Fathers, Living Still . . .

**Social and intellectual properties
of standard American sociology**

Intellectual leaders	R. K. Merton
	T. Parsons
Social organization leader	T. Parsons
Research centers	Bureau of Applied Social Research (BASR), Columbia University
	National Opinion Research Center (NORC), University of Chicago[a]
Training centers for students	University of Chicago
	Columbia University
	Harvard University
Paradigm content	Social systems are closed; their parts may be studied empirically
Success	Parsons, **The Structure of Social Action** (1937)
	Merton, **Social Theory and Social Structure** (1949)
	Stouffer et al., **The American Soldier**, Volumes I and II (1949)
Program statements	Parsons, "The Position of Sociological Theory" (1949, Chapter 1; address delivered in 1947)
	Merton, "Discussion of Parsons" (1948)
Examples of secondary work	Merton et al. (eds.), **Sociology Today** (1959)
	Parsons, **American Sociology** (1968)
Examples of critical work	Black (ed.), **The Social Theories of Talcott Parsons** (1961)
	Demerath and Peterson (eds.), **System Change and Conflict** (1967)
	Gouldner, **The Coming Crisis of Western Sociology** (1970)
Text	Broom and Selznick, **Sociology** (various editions)

[a] NORC is not legally part of the University of Chicago, but the two institutions have long had many close ties (e.g., shared personnel).

riedrichs (1970) argues that a synthesis of theoretical traditions in sociology existed and dominated American sociology from 1951 through the middle of the 1960s. Friedrichs called this synthesis structural–functionalist theory and said that it included concepts of both "social system" and "function." The most important early works were Kingsley Davis' *Human Society* (1949); Robert K. Merton's collection of essays in *Social Theory and Social Structure* (1949); George C. Homans' *The Human Group* (1950); Talcott Parsons' *Essays in Sociological Theory* (1949) and *The Social System* (1951), and the collection of essays titled *Toward a General Theory of Action*, which he coedited with Edward A. Shils (1951); Robin M. Williams' *American Society* (1951); and Marion Levy's *The Structure of Society* (1953). This collection of books, together with those of this group's forefathers (e.g., Weber, Durkheim, Pareto) constituted the content of theory courses in sociology from 1951 through much of the 1960s.

These theories were loosely associated with empirical work such as Samuel A. Stouffer et al., *The American Soldier* (1949), Volumes I and II; the Columbia voting studies (Lazarsfeld, Berelson, and Gaudet, 1944; Berelson, Lazarsfeld, and McPhee, 1954). Close social ties of the sort described in Chapter 2 tie Davis, Homans, Levy, Merton, Parsons, Shils, and Williams into a social group. Looser ties—purely intellectual because of the length of time separating their lives from those of the seven so-

TABLE 3.1 Social and intellectual highlights in the development of standard American sociology

Stage	Social	Intellectual
Normal: to 1935	Chicago domination (1892–1935) Henderson's seminar on Pareto at Harvard	Some reexamination of the sources of social theory (1930–1935)
Network: 1935–1945	First generation of Harvard students (e.g., Merton, Williams)	Focus on action theory; Parsons' **The Structure of Social Action** (1937)
Cluster: 1945–1951	Second generation of Harvard students: Department of Social Relations brought into existence	Introduction of Freudian psychology Development of structural–functional theory (Merton, 1949) and survey research (Stouffer et al., 1949)
Specialty: 1951–	Third-generation Harvard students Columbia develops, followed by other centers	Development of empirical analysis

ciologists just named—connect Weber, Durkheim, and Pareto to this group.[1]

Structural functionalism is the specific term applied to the social theory that emerged toward the end of standard American sociology's cluster stage and took over the theory side of most sociology departments after 1951. Structural functionalism was standard American sociology's most coherent theoretical product. This chapter traces the development of standard American sociology from its beginnings through its eventual institutionalization in the sociology of this country. The major themes of this chapter's discussion are outlined in Table 3.1, which gives approximate dates marking the four stages of standard American sociology's development, plus an important event or characterization of the social and intellectual aspects of each period. In the sections that follow (and in each subsequent chapter on a theory group), my procedure is to discuss first the social and then the intellectual aspects of each period. Outlines of group characteristics and tables (e.g.,Table 3.1) describing group stages precede these discussions.

NORMAL STAGE:
TO 1935[2]

SOCIAL

In 1892 the University of Chicago established a Department of Sociology (the world's first). Its training of professional sociologists was the first offered in the United States, and the Chicago department thus began the processes being traced in this book.

Figure 3.1 maps relationships among some of the important figures in early sociology (largely to the left-hand side of the diagram) and some who were important to standard American sociology (right-hand side). The figure does not represent any particular stage of development; it is included for its value in showing how people connect with and affect each other intellectually. The map contains 26 names joined (with one exception) by three kinds of relations: (1) one person is a student of another; (2) one person is a colleague of another; (3) one person is known to have been influenced by another. These persons were selected by Wallace (1969) as authors of articles representative of American sociology.[3] In Figure 3.1, persons on the left-hand side of the diagram belonged to or were trained by those who belonged to the Chicago school of sociology.

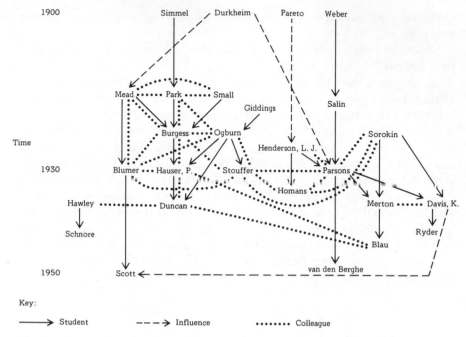

FIGURE 3.1 Linkages among some persons important to the development of standard American sociology.

The period 1892 to (roughly) 1935 was a normal science period for standard American sociology, and, with good reason, it has been termed the University of Chicago period (Faris, 1967). During the early years, the University of Chicago was virtually the only institution in the United States having a concentrated graduate curriculum. Later, as other departments emerged, Chicago retained its importance as a major force in the discipline for quite some time.

Of particular social importance to Chicago sociology was the organizational activity of the first chairman of the sociology department, Albion Small, who founded the *American Journal of Sociology*. Small had the advantage of being at a brand new institution which had no entrenched group of other disciplines to restrict the growth of his department. He had the further advantage of being dean of Chicago's graduate school from 1892 to 1925. He used those advantages to their fullest in making some brilliant appointments: in 1895, W. I. Thomas; in 1914, Robert E. Park. In 1908 a student named Ernest W. Burgess came to Chicago; he received his degree in 1913 and remained at Chicago for the rest of his life. After Small's time as dean, W. F. Ogburn (in 1927) and Louis Wirth (in 1931) were appointed.[4] Between 1894 and 1931, George Herbert Mead taught in the Department of Philosophy; he offered a course called Advanced Social Psychology, which was taken by most graduate students in sociology.

Small's importance becomes plainly evident when one notes that, beginning in 1894, his department had potential competition in the new Department of Sociology at Columbia University, initially chaired by Franklin Giddings. Although endowed with superior intellectual gifts, Giddings lacked Small's organizational ability, opportunism, and location at a new school. The result was that Columbia's department produced many fewer students than Chicago's (50 between 1894 and 1928, by contrast with Chicago's 113 between 1895 and 1935),[5] and the sociologists associated with it lacked the eminence of Chicago's personnel (Faris, 1967: 126–127). Columbia could not match, in quality or quantity, Chicago's production of books, papers, and students until the middle 1940s, after Merton and Lazarsfeld had joined the department. Perhaps most telling, it is Chicago and not Columbia that has drawn the attention of historians and sociologists of sociology.

Small and his staff had a profound effect on sociology. They published the *American Journal of Sociology*, the first professional journal in the field, and one of the most important. Two department members, Park and Burgess, wrote the most important early sociology text, *An Introduction to the Science of Society* (1921). This book was widely used and still sets the pattern for most contemporary sociology texts. Chicago's 113 Ph.D.'s were scattered in departments across the country, spreading their Chicago spirit and training, and teaching a fairly consistent style of sociology.

There were only a few sociology departments during the early period, and those were largely staffed with Chicago personnel. The American Sociological Society (founded in 1906 by an agreement among the men who became its first presidents—Albion Small, Franklin Giddings, Lester Ward, William Sumner, and Edward A. Ross; see Faris, 1967) had only a few hundred members even as late as the 1930s. American sociology was thus quite small, with personal contact the primary social factor joining its practitioners.

Faris points to the minor revolution in the American Sociological Society in 1935 as the end of the Chicago era. At that time Herbert Blumer, a Chicago faculty member with a doctorate from that university, was replaced as secretary–treasurer of the society, and a new society-sponsored journal, the *American Sociological Review*, which was *not* owned and edited by the University of Chicago, began publication.

If we look back at Figure 3.1, we can see the rough division between the already established (in 1935) Chicago group on the left (Blumer, Mead, Ogburn, Small, Stouffer, et al.) and the developing Harvard–Columbia group on the right (Henderson, Homans, Merton, Parsons, et al.). The two groups are linked by Blau and Stouffer; they show quite distinct aims and styles over the two periods, 1935–1946 and 1946–1951. Some in the former group (e.g., Blumer) later became members of the loyal opposition to standard American sociology (see Chapter 4): symbolic interactionism. In the latter group, the major figure was Talcott Parsons.

Figure 3.2 represents the outlines of American sociology in 1935. The dominant group was at the University of Chicago. Some sociologists were central to that group (e.g., Burgess and Wirth), whereas others (e.g., Blumer and Stouffer) were just beginning to modify their Chicago orientations. With hindsight, we see that the groups which became important in the late 1940s and 1950s—namely, standard American sociology, symbolic interactionism, and small group theory—could just be discerned.

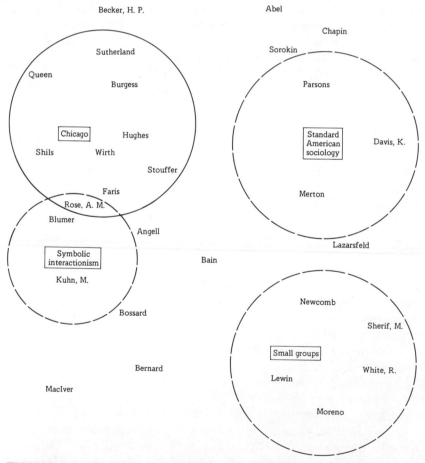

FIGURE 3.2 Outlines of theory groups in American sociology in 1935. (**Sources:** Data from this chapter and Chapters 4 and 5.)

The first two were beginning to form networks composed mainly of very junior sociologists. Parsons was still an instructor, although in the midst of a fight for promotion (see Parsons, 1970: 832); Blumer and Stouffer were assistant professors; Davis, Merton, and Arnold M. Rose were in the graduate student–new Ph.D. stage. Lewin was just beginning his small group research at Iowa. Other senior men were not part of any of the developments: Bossard at the University of Pennsylvania, MacIver at Columbia, and others. They continued as lone individuals and, lacking numbers of students, were not particularly important to growth and change in sociology.

INTELLECTUAL

The principal intellectual origins of American sociology are European. The French sociology of Tarde and Durkheim; the German sociology of Weber, Tonnies, and others; and the British social survey and social welfare traditions, as well as American pragmatism, all contributed to the intellectual beginnings of American sociology. Particularly important were four Europeans active at the turn of the century: Durkheim, Pareto, Simmel, and Weber.[6] All had ceased working by 1920, and at least some of their work was known to Americans before that date; but American sociologists needed the subsequent thirty years to digest the Europeans' thought, add a uniquely American flavor, and emerge with their own product—particularly, structural functionalism.

Standard American sociology's early intellectual center was the University of Chicago. Chicago's sociologists established a pattern that produced both students and research success, particularly between 1920 and 1930. The research was scattered across many topics: urban and mass behavior under Park; urban ecology under McKenzie and Wirth; and social psychology under Faris and Mead. The men directing this research were all leaders in their fields. Their research efforts continued well beyond the early 1930s, even though their success and productivity thereafter was not as high, nor was their morale as good (Faris, 1967: 119).

Characterizations of the original work at the University of Chicago as "dust bowl" empiricism—research undertaken without any theoretical understanding of the issues involved—are inaccurate. Some of the students did follow a research style without understanding why the research was important, but the main work itself was theoretically guided. The major theoretical perspectives were Park's interpretation of Simmel, Mead's analysis of social interaction, and "ecologism," the theory of community growth and development (soon to be identified with Wirth and Burgess) which was being distilled at Chicago during this period.[7]

The intellectual elements of standard American sociology were quite unclear during the normal stage. L. J. Henderson was leading a seminar on Pareto at Harvard, but the effects of his teaching were not felt until the network stage. In 1935 Parsons' work was small in quantity and largely unknown. Merton was still a graduate student. Stouffer was at Chicago, and the mathematically trained Lazarsfeld, new to the United States, had not yet begun his research into the effects of mass communication on public opinion (ASA, 1959). The potential existed, but there was no explicit pattern of ideas that clearly posed an alternative to the Chicago school.

NETWORK STAGE: 1935–1945

SOCIAL

The period from 1935 to 1945 was marked by World War II and, within sociology, the rising influence of the Harvard and Columbia Departments of Sociology and the founding of major research establishments (e.g., the National Opinion Research Center—NORC).

As I noted in Chapter 2, both social and intellectual strands can help to explain a movement's progress. One way to examine standard American sociology's growth is to analyze Parsons' role in the kind of sociology that was formally initiated by the publication of his books. By contrast with other possible leaders of the time—Robert M. MacIver, for example —Parsons could hardly have seemed a likely candidate to become the most important sociologist of his time. MacIver was a senior professor at a major sociology department (Columbia; he had switched from political science in 1929). He became president of the American Sociological Society in 1940 and published 15 books, over a range of topics. Yet he is now largely without influence (see Westie, 1972). Parsons was an instructor in economics at Harvard from 1927 to 1931. Also interdisciplinary, he became a sociology instructor in 1931 and remained one until 1936. (The only other sociologists at Harvard at that time were Pitirim A. Sorokin and Carle Zimmerman.) Parsons did not become president of the American Sociological Society until 1949.

Yet when writing a history of sociology between 1935 and 1970, one cannot ignore Parsons' towering presence (whatever value one may place on his work). By 1951 Parsons was a major figure in American sociology; by 1965 he was *the* major figure. He was central to the Harvard department, to the profession of sociology, and to the intellectual specialty of social theory. As Howard W. Odum (1951: 242–243) noted, Parsons effected a return (intellectually speaking) to an earlier tradition of grand systems in sociology. At Harvard he was a prime mover in converting a minor department into a major part of the university. The "ivory tower" of William James Hall at Harvard, while not built in Parsons' honor, is nevertheless an appropriate symbol of his achievement. Also a fitting monument is the number of his students who are now important sociologists (see Table 3.2, p. 51).

Besides Parsons, others in the early, Harvard-centered, standard American sociology network were Henderson, Sorokin, Merton, Homans, K. Davis, and Williams. Homans, Henderson, and Sorokin were colleagues; Merton, Homans, Davis, and Williams were students in the pre-World War II department. Henderson was a major figure even though he was not a sociologist but a physiologist. He had become interested in Pareto and, during the early 1930s, taught a seminar on Pareto that was attended by Homans, Parsons, and other social scientists (Parsons, 1970: 832–833). He also sponsored Parsons' promotion when Sorokin opposed it. Parsons (1970: 832) notes that he had

> . . . an extraordinary relationship with Henderson. I had known him through his Pareto seminar and in other respects before the manuscript of my book was referred to him for critical comment in connection with my appointment status. Instead of the usual limited response, he got in touch with me (stimulated I think mainly by my discussion of Pareto) and started a long series of personal sessions at his house, something like two hours, twice a week for nearly three months. In these sessions he went through the manuscript with me paragraph by paragraph. . . .
>
> This was an extraordinary experience, both personally and intellectually.

Sorokin was a noted scholar when, in 1930, he became the first chairman of Harvard's Department of Sociology. He had written *Social Mobility* (1927) and *Contemporary Sociological Theories* (1928) and was working on *Social and Cultural Dynamics* (1941), a complex and detailed study of the rise and fall of cultural traditions over time. As was just suggested, Sorokin was a consistent and bitter critic of Parsons. This enmity did not prevent Sorokin from influencing the intellectual development of standard American sociology, notably through his teaching of Merton and Davis and his numerous important publications, but he and Parsons were never close colleagues, striving to achieve a common intellectual goal. Merton's (1938) thesis work on seventeenth-century English science was clearly affected both by Sorokin's work and by Parsons' interest in Weber. Merton later became one of two major figures (the other was Lazarsfeld) dominating a revitalization of Columbia's Department of Sociology during the late 1940s and 1950s. He also led the introduction of empirical (particularly survey) research into the process of theory building.

Homans' first major work (written with Curtis, 1934) was an introduction to Pareto. Later, Harvard awarded Homans a Junior Fellowship, which permitted him to work on a topic without completing a degree. He chose English history and eventually wrote *English Villagers of the Thirteenth Century* (1941), a much neglected minor masterpiece. At least partly as a result of the fellowship, Homans was never Parsons' student but rather a junior colleague, through most of the 1930s. Homans returned to Harvard after wartime duty as a naval officer. His loud but not serious (although each thought so) debate with Parsons over petty tactics in theory building was a major fixture of theory discussion in the late 1950s and 1960s (e.g., see Homans, 1964).

Davis, a student at the same time as Merton, also graduated in 1936. His major career has been in demography, which is largely independent of sociology, but he has published several nondemographic works (e.g., Davis, 1949).

Williams was the youngest of the first student group. He received his Ph.D. degree in 1943. Between 1942 and 1946 he worked for the U.S. Army on the project that produced the two-volume work *The American Soldier* (1949), one of American sociology's major empirical products before 1950. (That project was headed by Samuel A. Stouffer, of whom more later.)

INTELLECTUAL

In 1937 Parsons published *The Structure of Social Action*. This book incorporated much that was important to Parsons' intellectual impact on the profession of sociology. Until that time, the intellectual tools of Chicago sociology had not included the works of Weber, Pareto, or any economists. Parsons, trained as an economist, had spent several years as both a student and a colleague (Parsons, 1970: 827–828) of Taussig, Schumpeter, and others in the Harvard economics department. These men were probing the role of technical economics in explaining social behavior (Parsons, 1970). By the mid-1930s he was ready to pull together work he had done in analyzing Weber (his German dissertation), Pareto (with Henderson), and Marshall (the foremost economic theorist of the time) into a general critical review of modern European writers; Durkheim, who was not an economist, was later included in the group. Parsons' recognition of a common orientation in all four, together with his expansion and comment on their themes, made the book an important piece.

Gouldner (1970: 175–178), certainly not a sympathetic witness, suggests that Parsons' theory of action was deeper than a simple focus on isolated parts or processes in society; rather, it was of a complexity commensurate with the profundity of current economic and political crises (the Depression, fascism, civil war in Spain, etc.). Gouldner also points out that the theory was open to new ideas, in need of work, and exciting to Parsons' original students. Action theory as Parsons developed it in 1937 was concerned with (1) the ordered pattern of values and norms which gave meaning to individual actions, providing motivation for behavior, as well as (2) interpretive structures through which others responded to this behavior. In seeking the primary subject for sociological inquiry, Parsons saw Durkheim, with his concept of "collective consciousness," Pareto, with his concept of "residues," and Weber, all moving to analyze not just the pattern of individual behavior but, rather, the pattern of values for some social unit.

This powerful and important work was central to the sense of high morale and closeness that marked the Harvard group from 1935 to 1940. Group members had a strong sense of participation in the shaping of the discipline's theory into a framework that subsumed all important earlier theories and completed their analysis (Gouldner, 1970: 176). This analysis was Parsons' basic statement until 1951, and it marked him as an intellectual leader.

This group might have achieved cluster status except for three factors. (1) Harvard had a very small sociology department—three regular faculty members (Parsons, Sorokin, and Zimmerman) plus an occasional visitor, such as Nicholas S. Timasheff. Henderson was a physiologist, and his only sociological interest was through Pareto. (2) The relationship between Parsons and Sorokin continued to be cool. This left the number of cooperating faculty too small to support a stable cluster. (3) The first students, Davis and Merton, left in 1936. They overlapped with some of the later students, but the student group was never very large at any point in time between 1936 and 1941 (Parsons lists only seven; see Table 3.2), and the only *group* of students to graduate in any year (Merton, Davis, John W. Riley, Jr.) graduated very early—1936. Clearly then, the minimum stable size for cluster status (between seven and 25 with three faculty members) was not achieved. Nevertheless, the members of this network group maintained their communication ties and became a core important to the later development of structural functionalism.

The training of students was virtually stopped during World War II. The postwar situation terminated the network stage: Parsons reorganized the social sciences at Harvard and established a cluster of faculty and students; he also began a massive reorganization of sociology's intellectual landscape.

CLUSTER STAGE:
1945–1951

SOCIAL

The Harvard academic year 1945–1946 was crucial. First, in 1945 Homans and Stouffer were appointed to newly created permanent positions in the department. Parsons played a major role in the prior negotiations—an indication of his importance as an organizational leader (see Parsons, 1970: 841). These additions broadened and strengthened Harvard sociology. Stouffer particularly added depth to the department's research experience. The addition of Stouffer and Homans to Parsons and Robert F. Bales (who had received his Ph.D. in 1945 and stayed on to teach at Harvard) brought the number of interested faculty above the critical level needed for a cluster to establish itself.

Second, the Department of Social Relations (a social expression of Parsons' desires to formulate an interdisciplinary theory of human activity) was formed; again, Parsons (1970: 841) was an important factor. The new department included social and clinical psychology (which had split from behaviorist psychology), social anthropology (which had split from physical anthropology and archaeology), and sociology. Parsons became chairman of this new department and remained chairman for ten years (Parsons, 1956). This creation of an interdisciplinary department—a research and training center able to serve his expanding concepts—changed student training at Harvard, producing a new, interdisciplinary group of students. At least during the department's early days, the faculty also made an effort to become more interdisciplinary in style: Parsons began psychoanalytic training, and Henry Murray participated in discussions on general social theory.[8]

Third, a second student group was born. The earliest and most important member (to structural functionalism) of this group was Bales, who was at Harvard as a graduate student during the war. The students who joined Bales at Harvard after World War II were a rather remarkable group. As Parsons notes (1970: 842):

> For my role as teacher, especially at the graduate level, the early years of the Department of Social Relations came to be a true golden age. Opening just a year after the end of the war, the department attracted, aided by the G.I. Bill, an unusually able sample of the backlog of young men whose training had been interrupted by the war. . . . Close association with advanced students of such caliber has been one of the most rewarding features of my academic career. Such young minds cannot fail, it seems to me, to have a most stimulating effect on their teachers.

Parsons' list of students (Table 3.2), although long, does not include all the well-known and important sociologists who were trained at Harvard during the period in question. (Parsons, 1956: 45–46, shows that 80 doctoral degrees in sociology were granted between 1946 and 1956 alone.) Yet it was the continuing wave of Harvard Ph.D.'s influenced by Parsons, Homans, Stouffer, Bales, and other students of Parsons, whose members dominated so much of sociology's intellectual content from 1950 through 1968 (Friedrichs, 1970).

Parsons' social organizational efforts were not only directed toward his

TABLE 3.2 Harvard Ph.D.'s taught by Parsons

	Year of Ph.D.
American	
Robert Merton	1936
Kingsley Davis	1936
John Riley	1936
Robin Williams	1943
Edward C. Devereux	1950
Logan Wilson	1939
Wilbert Moore	1940
Florence Kluckhohn	1941
Bernard Barber	1949
Albert Cohen	1951
Marion Levy	1947
Henry Riecken	1950
Francis Sutton	1950
Robert F. Bales	1945
David Schneider	(Anthropology)
Harold Garfinkel	1950[a]
David Aberle	(Anthropology)
Gardner Lindzey	(Psychology)
James Olds	(Psychology)
Morris Zelditch	1955
Joseph Berger	1958
Renée Fox	1954
Clifford Geertz	(Anthropology)
Robert Bellah	1955
Neil Smelser	1958
Jackson Toby	1950
Kaspar Naegele	No information
Theodore Mills	1952
Joseph Elder	1959
Ezra Vogel	1958
Winston White	No information
Leon Mayhew	1964
Jan Loubser	1964
Edward Laumann	1964
Charles Ackerman	1967
Victor Lidz	No information
Andrew Effrat	No information
Rainer Baum	1968
Mark Gould	No information
John Akula	No information
Gerald Platt	(Postdoctoral)
Foreign	
François Bourricaud	(From France)
Odd Ramsoy	(From Norway)
Bengt Rundblatt	(From Sweden)
C. Enno Schwanenberg	(From Germany)

Source: T. Parsons, "On Building Social Systems Theory," **Daedalus** 1970: 833–835. (The order is his.)
[a] Other sources (e.g., ASA, 1959) have Garfinkel's degree date as 1952.

local institution (as just noted), but also toward his students and the profession in general. Several of his students were enabled to work at Harvard during or after completion of their degrees (e.g., Naegele, Olds, and Sutton; see Parsons, 1956: 75–76). In 1949 Parsons became president of the American Sociological Society; that post was for a year only, but he returned later as secretary (for five years). During his tenure as president, the first full-time executive officer was hired (Parsons, 1970: 841).

By 1951 Parsons had succeeded at each of the tasks that must be completed to assure the survival of a new theory group. He was clearly the intellectual leader, a role that had been further established with his delivery of a program statement in 1947 (see next section). He had written a large number of books and articles (64 items by 1953; Parsons, 1954: 440–445), which had placed him in the intellectual forefront of his field. Second, he had trained outstanding groups of students (see Table 3.2). Third, he was the *organizational leader* of his profession.

The result of these efforts was a cluster group that produced structural functionalism. In addition to Parsons, Homans, Stouffer, and Bales on the faculty, the cluster included at minimum the nine students (see Table 3.2) who received Ph.D. degrees between 1947 and 1952. There were almost certainly others also (e.g., Naegele, Olds; see Parsons 1956: 75–76) who were at Harvard in various nonstudent capacities. The size of this minimum core of 13 to 15 active students, teachers, and researchers was more than adequate for the tasks a cluster must accomplish.

Not part of the Harvard cluster but still in close touch with Parsons were his very early students. Merton was at Columbia, but he as well as Parsons contributed a program statement to structural functionalism. K. Davis was also at Columbia (as of 1948) and Williams was at Cornell, but their books (Davis, 1949; Williams, 1951) show the continuing influence of Parsons. Parsons also had close ties with Shils of Chicago (Parsons, 1970: 877), who spent the 1949–1950 academic year at Harvard.

In addition to Davis, Merton had a methodological colleague at Columbia, Paul F. Lazarsfeld, who had been trained in applied mathematics at the University of Vienna. From 1929 to 1933 he taught at the University of Vienna as a psychology instructor. In 1933 he became a Traveling Fellow of the Rockefeller Foundation and came to the United States. Lazarsfeld first worked as Director of the Bureau of Radio Research at Princeton, and in 1939 he moved to Columbia as head of the Bureau of Applied Social Research (BASR). A full-fledged cluster never developed at Columbia (only six important students were graduated between 1946 and 1952; see Table 3.3). However, the effect of that developing faculty on structural functionalism became quite evident later (nine important students received Ph.D. degrees from Columbia between 1952 and 1959, whereas Harvard graduated only six; see Table 3.3).

The cluster, then, was Harvard-based, but its ties to Columbia and Chicago became quite evident in the specialty stage.

INTELLECTUAL

By the late 1940s Parsons' action theory, which had dominated the network period, had revealed a small but important shift from the individualistic and rational social theory underlying economics. Over the period 1945–1951 two important new ideas, one of "system" and the other of "function," began reorganizing that theory. A "system" is a collection of parts that may be concrete (e.g., the gears of a clock) or abstract (e.g., the roles in a social system), which interconnect in a definable way. Most analyses of systems emphasize the way in which a system's parts fit together and reduce the importance, for analysis, of factors external to that system. Such analyses also tend to emphasize orderliness: The way in which a system works now or will work is perceived as resulting from the operation of well-established processes rather than from radical change or unexpected events.

Functionalism is a subset of system analysis. A functional analysis is concerned with the *contribution* to a system by any part of it. Most functionalism does *not* try to explain the origins of specific system parts (e.g., religion, the economy). Hence most functional analysis is ahistorical.

The structural–functional synthesis was partly supported by an increase in empirical studies, such as surveys, including (1) those of Gallup and Roper; (2) those of several university-related organizations, such as Chicago's NORC; and (3) those of organizations such as hospitals (e.g., Merton et al. *The Student Physician*, 1957) and communities (e.g., Lynd and Lynd, 1937).

A pair of essays published in the late 1940s (Parsons, 1949; Merton, 1948) established a new focus in standard American sociology. Parsons initiated the change with a paper presented at the American Sociological Society meeting in 1947: "The Current State of Sociological Theory" (published in Parsons, 1949: Chapter 1). In this paper he called for a theoretical scheme developed along the lines of *The Structure of Social Action* (1937), but placing greater emphasis on creative theorizing and less on analyzing older theorists. Parsons was anxious to develop his action theory further, and in the fall of 1949 the Carnegie Corporation supported a seminar with Parsons, Edward Tolman of Berkeley (a noted behaviorist psychologist), and Shils (a senior member of the Chicago Department of Sociology). These social scientists, together with six members of the Harvard staff (Stouffer, Clyde Kluckhohn, and Murray were the major ones), consciously attempted a synthesis that would hold across the whole field of social relations (Parsons, 1951, pp. vii, viii). The seminar attempt can be seen either as an important theoretical gain

TABLE 3.3   Important standard American sociologists:[a] degree (date and place) and selected job locations

Name	Ph.D. Date	Ph.D. Place	1935	1946
Abel, Theodore	1929	COL	ni	ni
Alpert, Harry	1938	COL	CCNY	CCNY
Anderson, C. Arnold	1932	MINN	ni	KENT
Angell, Robert C.	1924	MICH	MICH	MICH
Bales, Robert F.	1945	HARV	*	HARV
Barber, Bernard	1949	HARV	*	HARV
Barton, Allen	1957	COL	*	*
Becker, Howard P.	1930	CHIC	SMIT	WISC
Bell, Wendell	1952	UCLA	*	*
Bellah, Robert	1955	HARV	*	*
Bendix, Reinhard	1947	CHIC	*	CHIC
Berelson, Bernard	1941	CHIC	CHIC	CHIC
Bernard, Jessie	1935	WSTL	USRR	LIND
Bierstedt, Robert	1946	COL	*	COL
Blau, Peter M.	1952	COL	*	*
Broom, Leonard	1937	DUKE	DUKE	UCLA
Caplow, Theodore	1946	MINN	*	MINN
Christensen, Harold	1941	WISC	*	BYU
Clausen, John A.	1949	CHIC	*	CORN
Clinard, Marshall	1941	CHIC	ni	ni
Cloward, Richard	1959	COL	*	*
Cohen, Albert K.	1951	HARV	*	HARV
Coser, Lewis A.	1954	COL	*	*
Davis, Kingsley	1936	HARV	HARV	PRIN
Devereux, Edward C.	1950	HARV	*	PRIN
Dodd, Stuart C.	1926	PRIN	AMBE	AMBE
Elder, Joseph	1959	HARV	*	*
Etzioni, Amitai	1958	BERK	*	*
Fox, Renée	1954	HARV	*	*
Glazer, Nathan	1962	COL	*	ni
Glock, Charles Y.	1952	COL	*	COL
Goode, William J.	1946	PNST	*	WAYS
Goodman, Leo A.	1950	PRIN	*	*
Gouldner, Alvin W.	1953	COL	*	ni
Gross, Neal	1946	IOST	*	IOST
Guttman, Louis	1942	MINN	*	CORN
Hauser, Philip M.	1938	CHIC	CHIC	CENS
Heberle, Rudolf	1923	KEIL	ni	LSU
Hollingshead, August	1935	NEBR	NEBR	INDU
Homans, George C.	none	none	HARV	HARV
Hyman, Herbert H.	1942	COL	ni	NORC
Inkeles, Alex	1948	COL	*	OSS
Janowitz, Morris	1948	CHIC	*	*
Katz, Elihu	1956	COL	*	*

Sources: American Journal of Sociology (various years); ASA (various years a, b, c).
[a] Criteria for selection are explained in the Appendix.

Job held in academic year ending in					
1950	1955	1959	1963	1967	1970
ni	ni	HUNT	HUNT	HUNT	UNME
BUD	NSF	ORE	ORE	ORE	ORE
KENT	KENT	CHIC	CHIC	CHIC	CHIC
MICH	MICH	MICH	MICH	MICH	MICH
HARV	HARV	HARV	HARV	HARV	HARV
SMIT	COL	COL	COL	COL	COL
*	COL	COL	COL	COL	COL
WISC	WISC	WISC	ni	d	
*	NWU	UCLA	YALE	YALE	YALE
*	HARV	HARV	HARV	BERK	BERK
BERK	BERK	BERK	BERK	BERK	BERK
CHIC	FORD	CHIC	POPC	POPC	POPC
PNST	PNST	PNST	PNST	ret	ret
ILL	CCNY	CCNY	NYU	NYU	NYU
COL	CHIC	CHIC	CHIC	CHIC	COL
UCLA	UCLA	TEX	TEX	TEX	TEX
MINN	MINN	MINN	COL	COL	COL
PURD	PURD	PURD	PURD	PURD	PURD
NIMH	NIMH	NIMH	BERK	BERK	BERK
ni	WISC	WISC	WISC	WISC	WISC
COL	COL	COL	COL	COL	COL
INDU	INDU	INDU	INDU	CONN	CONN
CHIC	BRAN	BRAN	BRAN	BRAN	STON
COL	COL	BERK	BERK	BERK	BERK
COL	CORN	CORN	CORN	CORN	CORN
WASH	WASH	WASH	WASH	WASH	WASH
*	HARV	OBER	WISC	WISC	WISC
*	BERK	COL	COL	COL	COL
*	ni	COL	COL	COL	PENN
ni	ni	BENN	HHFA	BERK	HARV
COL	COL	BERK	BERK	BERK	BERK
WAYS	COL	COL	COL	COL	COL
PRIN	CHIC	CHIC	CHIC	CHIC	CHIC
BUFF	ILL	WSTL	WSTL	WSTL	WSTL
MINN	HARV	HARV	HARV	HARV	PENN
HEBR	HEBR	HEBR	HEBR	HEBR	HEBR
CHIC	CHIC	CHIC	CHIC	CHIC	CHIC
LSU	LSU	LSU	LSU	LSU	LSU
YALE	YALE	YALE	YALE	YALE	YALE
HARV	HARV	HARV	HARV	HARV	HARV
NORC	COL	COL	COL	COL	WESL
HARV	HARV	HARV	HARV	HARV	HARV
ni	ni	MICH	CHIC	CHIC	CHIC
COL	CHIC	CHIC	HEBR	HEBR	HEBR

TABLE 3.3 (continued)

| | Ph.D. | | | |
Name	Date	Place	1935	1946
Kirkpatrick, Clifford	1925	PENN	MINN	MINN
Kormarovsky, Mirra	1940	COL	COL	COL
Lazarsfeld, Paul F.	1925	VIEN	ROTF	COL
Lee, Alfred McC.	1933	YALE	KANS	WAYS
Levy, Marion	1947	HARV	*	HARV
Lieberson, Stanley	1960	CHIC	*	*
Lipset, Seymour M.	1949	OOL		TORO
Loomis, Charles P.	1933	HARV	ni	MIST
Lundberg, George	ni	MINN	BENN	WASH
MacIver, Robert M.	1915	EDIN	COL	COL
Merton, Robert K.	1936	HARV	HARV	COL
Middleton, Russell	1956	TEX	*	*
Moore, Wilbert E.	1940	HARV	*	PRIN
Naegele, Kaspar	1952	HARV	*	*
Page, Charles	1940	COL	*	CCNY
Parsons, Talcott	1927	HEID	HARV	HARV
Petersen, William	1954	COL	*	*
Queen, Stuart	1919	CHIC	WSTL	WSTL
Riley, John W., Jr.	1936	HARV	HARV	RUTG
Riley, Matilda W.	none	none	*	ni
Rossi, Peter	1951	COL	*	COL
Schmidt, Calvin F.	1930	PITT	MINN	WASH
Schuessler, Karl	1947	INDU	*	INDU
Selznick, Philip	1947	COL	*	COL
Sewell, William H.	1939	MINN	MINN	WISC
Shils, Edward A.	none	none	CHIC	CHIC
Simpson, George E.	1934	PENN	TEMP	PNST
Smelser, Neil J.	1958	HARV	*	*
Sorokin, Pitirim A.	ni	STP	HARV	HARV
Stouffer, Samuel A.	1930	CHIC	ni	HARV
Toby, Jackson	1950	HARV	*	*
Trow, Martin A.	1957	COL	*	*
Tumin, Melvin	1942	NWU	WAYS	PRIN
Vogel, Ezra	1958	HARV	*	*
Williams, Robin M., Jr.	1943	HARV	*	res
Winch, Robert F.	1942	CHIC	*	VAND
Wrong, Dennis	1950	COL	*	*
Yinger, J. Milton	1942	WISC	*	OBER
Zelditch, Morris	1955	HARV	*	*

Key:

AMBE	American College, Beirut, Lebanon	BROO	Brooklyn College
		BROW	Brown University, Providence, R.I.
ASA	American Sociological Association	BUD	Bureau of the Budget
		BUFF	State University of New York, Buffalo
BENN	Bennington College	BYU	Brigham Young University
BERK	University of California, Berkeley	CCNY	City College of New York
BRAN	Brandeis University	CENS	U.S. Census

Job held in academic year ending in					
1950	1955	1959	1963	1967	1970
INDU	INDU	INDU	INDU	INDU	INDU
COL	COL	COL	COL	COL	COL
COL	COL	COL	COL	COL	COL
BROO	BROO	BROO	BROO	BROO	BROO
PRIN	PRIN	PRIN	PRIN	PRIN	PRIN
*	*	CHIC	WISC	WISC	WASH
BERK	COL	BERK	BERK	HARV	HARV
MIST	MIST	MIST	MIST	MIST	MIST
WASH	WASH	WASH	ret	ret	ret
COL	ret	ret	ret	ret	ret
COL	COL	COL	COL	COL	COL
*	TEX	FSU	WISC	WISC	WISC
PRIN	PRIN	PRIN	PRIN	RUSS	DENV
HARV	UBC	UBC	UBC	d	
SMIT	SMIT	SMIT	PRIN	UCSC	MASS
HARV	HARV	HARV	HARV	HARV	HARV
COL	BERK	COLO	BERK	BERK	OHST
WSTL	WSTL	ret	ret	ret	ret
RUTG	RUTG	RUTG	ind	ind	ind
ASA	ASA	ASA	RUTG	RUTG	RUTG
COL	CHIC	CHIC	CHIC	JHU	JHU
WASH	WASH	WASH	WASH	WASH	WASH
INDU	INDU	INDU	INDU	INDU	INDU
BERK	BERK	BERK	BERK	BERK	BERK
WISC	WISC	WISC	WISC	WISC	WISC
CHIC	CHIC	CHIC	CHIC	CHIC	CHIC
OBER	OBER	OBER	OBER	OBER	OBER
*	HARV	BERK	BERK	BERK	BERK
HARV	HARV	ret	ret	d	
HARV	HARV	HARV	d		
HARV	RUTG	RUTG	RUTG	RUTG	RUTG
*	COL	BERK	BERK	BERK	BERK
PRIN	PRIN	PRIN	PRIN	PRIN	PRIN
*	HARV	HARV	HARV	HARV	HARV
CORN	CORN	CORN	CORN	CORN	CORN
NWU	NWU	NWU	NWU	NWU	NWU
COL	BROW	BROW	NEWS	NYU	NYU
OBER	OBER	OBER	OBER	OBER	OBER
*	HARV	COL	STAN	STAN	STAN

CHIC	University of Chicago	EDIN	Edinburgh University, Scotland
COL	Columbia University	FORD	Ford Foundation, New York
COLO	University of Colorado	FSU	Florida State University
CONN	University of Connecticut, Storrs	HARV	Harvard University
CORN	Cornell University	HEBR	Hebrew University, Jerusalem
d	Deceased	HEID	Heidelberg University, Germany
DENV	Denver University	HHFA	Housing and Home Finance
DUKE	Duke University		Agency

Key (continued)

HUNT	Hunter College, New York	POPC	Population Council, New York
ILL	University of Illinois, Champaign–Urbana	PRIN	Princeton University
		PURD	Purdue University
ind	Industry	res	Miscellaneous research position
INDU	Indiana University, Bloomington	ret	Retired
IOST	Iowa State University	ROTF	Rockefeller Foundation Traveling Fellow
JHU	Johns Hopkins University		
KANS	University of Kansas	RUSS	Russell Sage Foundation
KEIL	Keil University, Germany	RUTG	Rutgers
KENT	University of Kentucky	SMIT	Smith College
LIND	Lindwood College, Missouri	STAN	Stanford University
LSU	Louisiana State University	STON	State University of New York, Stony Brook
MASS	University of Massachusetts		
MICH	University of Michigan	STP	St. Petersburg, Russia
MINN	University of Minnesota	TEMP	Temple University
MIST	Michigan State University	TEX	University of Texas
NEBR	University of Nebraska	TORO	University of Toronto
NEWS	New School for Social Research	UBC	University of British Columbia
ni	No information	UCLA	University of California, Los Angeles
NIMH	National Institute of Mental Health		
		UCSC	University of California, Santa Cruz
none	No degree earned	UNME	University of New Mexico
NORC	National Opinion Research Center	USRR	U.S. Railway Retirement Board
NSF	National Science Foundation	VAND	Vanderbilt University
NWU	Northwestern University	VIEN	University of Vienna, Austria
NYU	New York University	WASH	University of Washington, Seattle
OBER	Oberlin College		
OHST	Ohio State University	WAYS	Wayne State University
ORE	University of Oregon	WESL	Wesleyan University, Middleton, Conn.
OSS	Office of Strategic Services, U.S. government		
		WISC	University of Wisconsin
PENN	University of Pennsylvania	WSTL	Washington University, St. Louis
PITT	Pittsburgh University	YALE	Yale University
PNST	Pennsylvania State University	*	Not in system

or as intimidation (Friedrichs, 1970: 18–20). However, the resultant document, _Toward a General Theory of Action,_ along with the others mentioned at the beginning of this chapter, dominated the year 1951 and forced a theoretical break in sociology.

The break involved: (1) introduction of the term "social system" as a given and (2) discussion of society in terms of society's structure and functions. Park would not have recognized either concept. He had understood society as comprised of the activities of individuals; these activities occurred for many reasons, but they had no functions. Society might be thought of as an abstraction, but at bottom it was only groups of individuals. Parsons' group was no longer talking about individuals but, rather, about the articulations of social selves. Instead, systems of individual personality and of culture were conceived as articulated with the system of society. Parsons, who was simply not interested in the activities of individuals, chose to investigate the sets of rules and norms that ordered society. He assumed (1) the existence of a set of values that stretched across American society and (2) the operation of these values in a set of norms about how social life was lived.

Parsons' 1947 paper called forth a response that cemented standard American sociology's metamorphosis into structural functionalism. An article by Merton (1948) on sociological theories of the middle range was a direct response to Parsons. In 1949 Merton published *Social Theory and Social Structure*, a series of essays including a revised version of his response to Parsons, plus two other chapters that have had a major impact on the profession. Empirical research, sociological theory, and the bearing of sociological theory on empirical research were all affected.

Merton's emphasis was different from Parsons'; he proposed that the work of grand theorizing needed an empirical basis in the sort of studies then being done at Columbia by himself, Lazarsfeld, and others, and which had already been done on the Army by Stouffer. All this research was quite extensive for its time; the studies were not undertaken by one or two persons but rather by a research team, which could put together a number of systematic ideas and test them in a series of studies. Theory established the rationale for studies, and studies, in turn, provided either support for the theory or guidelines for its reconstruction.

Merton's particular theory was relatively small in scale, but it drew its fundamental support from the large-scale thinking (both in terms of society and number of variables) of Parsons et al. (published in 1951, but well known in advance). Merton's smaller-scale demands had the effect of shielding the larger theory from testing, since even the smaller-scale research required efforts that were close to current limits of research. Indeed, social scientists found it difficult to get support for research on a large scale until the 1960s. However, small-scale survey research—community studies and organizational analysis—proceeded throughout the 1950s on the theoretical base provided by Merton and Parsons. Along these research lines Lazarsfeld and, to a lesser but still real extent, Stouffer contributed a major theme to standard American sociology in their development of methods, especially those of statistical analysis.

The cluster stage ended, then, with the emergence of structural functionalism, a well-developed theoretical perspective buttressed by methodological competence. Most structural functionalists were clustered at Harvard, but several were at Columbia, and some were at other locations (e.g., Chicago had Shils; Cornell had Williams; see data in Table 3.3 on many of the important standard American sociologists).

SPECIALTY STAGE:
1951–

From 1951 on, structural functionalism was the most seriously regarded theory in the discipline. This status resulted from its apparent theoretical fruitfulness, the quantity of new theoretical development, the number of students and their central positions at major universities (see Table 3.3), and the lack of equally prominent alternatives. Furthermore, structural functionalism has continued to develop and change. The basic framework established by the concepts of system and function remain, but many newer developments have been built, using these ideas only as reference points.

SOCIAL

The second major social center (after Harvard) for structural functionalism was Columbia University. During the cluster period, the work of Merton and Lazarsfeld had been important in adding new elements to the developing theory. Also during this period, Columbia's Department of Sociology had begun training increased numbers of students. Table 3.3 reveals that Columbia granted 18 Ph.D.'s during 1946 or after; Columbia was particularly productive of Ph.D.'s during 1951–1955, which was a slow period for Harvard. (Again I should note that Table 3.3 is not an exhaustive list; it simply includes some major sociologists.)

Both institutions lost faculty to each other and to other schools. The latter occurrence resulted from a lack of positions at major universities after 1956 and the opening up of jobs in less prestigious locations. The effect was to spread the cluster group more thinly across more centers (again, see Table 3.3).

Referring now to Table 3.4, we can note the movement of important faculty members from one major department to another. The figures show that Columbia and Harvard interchange, that both send *to* Chicago (almost never receiving anyone in return), and that all three have contributed heavily to Berkeley but have received almost no returns. Each of the big three takes many of its own students for short periods, but few of these students remain to become permanent faculty. The figures for the

TABLE 3.4 Personnel interchanges among major departments, 1935–1970[a]

From	To Columbia	Harvard	Chicago	Berkeley	Total number of Ph.D.'s, 1954–1968
Columbia	8[b]	5	3	5	172
Harvard	5	9	2	3	120
Chicago	0	1	11	7	163
Berkeley	1	0	0	0	84

Source (of total Ph.D.'s, last column): ASA, **Guide to Graduate Departments** (1965, 1970).
[a] For persons listed in Table 3.3.
[b] Numbers indicate persons who remained for two or more years.

University of Chicago are somewhat distorted because Chicago was a major center for the training of symbolic interactionists (see the next chapter) as well as standard American sociologists; but neither Harvard nor Columbia hired any symbolic interactionists during this period. Columbia, Chicago, and Harvard remained the major graduate training centers throughout the 1950s and into the 1960s. Of the 85 people listed in Table 3.3, Columbia trained 23, Harvard 18, and Chicago 12. No other school trained as many as five. (Chapter 6 considers the entire system of Ph.D.-granting schools.)

A closer look at personnel exchanges shows that many people leave the top schools entirely, either to help found or to run departments in institutions that are not top rated. This turn of events was probably the inevitable effect of the process that earlier filled the top jobs with fairly young representatives of the dominant position, who subsequently squeezed out younger students simply by staying alive. An example is furnished by the Harvard department, whose permanent establishment was very small and not growing. Of the student cohorts from 1945 to 1970, only three of the almost 200 students (120 between 1954 and 1969) who graduated with Ph.D.'s were able to remain at Harvard. With the exception of Bales, Bellah, and Vogel, none of the students reported by Parsons as having worked closely with him could stay, and Bellah moved to Berkeley in 1967.

Consider the sociologists named by Parsons (1970) in Table 3.2 as his closest students—presumably, then, the very best of Harvard-trained standard American sociologists. Their employers by 1968 ranged over Stanford, University of Connecticut, the State University of New York at Buffalo, University of California at Los Angeles, Princeton, Pennsylvania, and so on; all these institutions could be considered as being in department-building situations. The building has been successful to very different degrees.

An important factor in the institutionalization of structural functionalism was a five-year series of conferences (1952–1957) on systems theory, held in Chicago and chaired by Dr. Roy Grinker. These conferences were interdisciplinary and provided both a forum and a testing place for system ideas (Parsons, 1970: 831).

Also important to structural functionalism's success in the specialty stage was Parsons' relationship with the Free Press. During the 1940s Parsons had experienced difficulty arranging for the continued publication of his work. *The Structure of Social Action* (1937) had been a small success outside of Harvard, but McGraw-Hill was not interested in publishing a second edition. At this juncture, Parsons learned that Shils, his friend and (later) coauthor, was consulting editor for a small house, the Free Press. Its editor, founder, and man of all work, Jeremiah Kaplan, became interested in collecting Parsons' essays up to 1949 and in reprinting *The Structure of Social Action*. After those publications, the Free Press became Parsons' publishing house, enabling those who were interested in his work to find it in a single place. Many of his students also began submitting most of their book-length material to the Free Press, with the result that this house became the major publisher of sociology for a time (Parsons, 1970: 877; Shils, 1970: 796).

The importance of Parsons' relationship with the Free Press during the late cluster stage and the specialty stage was the guarantee that his work would be published and made widely available. That availability was a continuing indicator of structural functionalism's success which, in turn, stimulated further intellectual development and publication.

The cumulative effect of departures in the late 1950s (including Stouffer's death) was to remove from Harvard all of those who had participated in the cluster-building effort, except Bales and Parsons. The establishment in Cambridge was simply too small to support the large number of people working on similar problems who would have been necessary to maintain morale and provide depth to the research effort.

Standard American sociology's growth as described previously is reflected in coauthorship data for the period between 1935 and 1965. Coauthorship is a particularly close form of association requiring that the people involved coordinate ideas, research, and writing. The 85 people named in Table 3.3 produced 925 publications (articles in the *American Sociological Review* or *American Journal of Sociology* and books) between 1935 and 1965. Some of those publications also involved a total of 316 persons not listed in Table 3.3; some are unknown, some are eminent sociologists (primarily involved in other developments), and some are prominent in other fields. The important point is that the networks formed by linking coauthors with each other indicate the total group's closeness. For standard American sociology, one group of 42 (49 percent of those in Table 3.3) are linked, in the coauthorship network of Figure 3.3, with 143 persons *not* listed in Table 3.3. The other persons in Table 3.3 are linked in other networks (not shown here), the largest of which includes only two members from the table and the smallest, just one.

The large coauthorship network includes the core of sociologists important to standard American sociology: Parsons, Merton, Lazarsfeld, Stouffer, Sorokin, Shils, Williams, and many others. The groups of coauthors of *The American Soldier* (1949), Volumes I and II, and *Toward a General Theory of Action* (1951) contribute much to the network's density (i.e., the same people are connected more than one time); but the same group of persons from Table 3.3 would be connected even if one book or the other (but not both) were dropped from consideration. The diagram shows some cluster-stage connections, but 111 of 141 connections (78.9 percent) were made during or after 1951. Clearly, then, as argued in

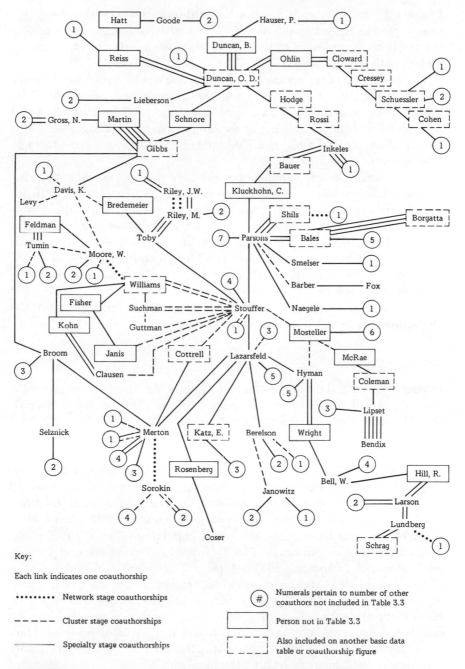

Key:

Each link indicates one coauthorship

•••••••• Network stage coauthorships

– – – – – Cluster stage coauthorships

——— Specialty stage coauthorships

(#) Numerals pertain to number of other coauthors not included in Table 3.3

☐ Person not in Table 3.3

⌐ ¬ Also included on another basic data table or coauthorship figure

FIGURE 3.3 Major coauthorship network among standard American sociologists, 1935–1965. (**Sources:** Books reviewed in ASR and AJS, and articles appearing in both journals.)

Chapter 2, coauthorship is a major factor during the specialty stage as a group spreads; it is a less significant factor earlier, although visible during the publication explosion of the cluster stage, and it is not important at all before the cluster stage.

The social side of the specialty stage was marked by two developments. First was the almost complete intellectual domination of sociology by structural functionalism (two exceptions are discussed in Chapters 4 and 5). Second was the remodeling of sociology from the undergraduate text level (Broom and Selznick, many editions, became the standard text) to more uniform graduate training.[9]

These changes exerted tremendous pressure for a more consistent discipline. The examinations for graduate students given at a series of major educational institutions in the United States (see Mack, ed., in the *American Sociologist*, 1969) indicate how similar the education of graduate students had become across the full range of departments that had any students at all. Finally, neither Parsons nor Merton shifted to new research. Furthermore, Parsons continued his social organizational efforts during the specialty stage by serving several years as the American Sociological Association's secretary and, at Harvard, by continuing to support the Department of Social Relations (see note 8).

INTELLECTUAL

Intellectually, standard American sociology in the specialty stage had a history of small successes but no major new insights. By the mid-1950s first Harvard, then Columbia, and then the Chicago department had working groups of standard American sociologists who developed high morale and produced research and books of high quality. During and after 1951, in addition to the works named at the beginning of this chapter, came such secondary work as Parsons, Bales, and Shils' *Working Papers* (1953), Stouffer's *Communism, Conformity, and Civil Liberties* (1955), Parsons and Smelser's *Economy and Society* (1956), from Harvard; Hauser and Duncan's ecology and population studies (1959) and Blau's studies of organizations (1963) from Chicago; Katz and Lazarsfeld's *Personal Influence* (1955), Lipset, Trow, and Coleman's *Union Democracy* (1956), Merton et al.'s *The Student Physician* (1957), and W. Goode's work on the family (1956, 1963) from Columbia. Each of these institutions had a major research branch that contracted for research and provided jobs and degree topics for graduate students. Harvard's Laboratory of Social Relations was the smallest. Columbia's BASR was larger, and Chicago's NORC, the largest of all.

By the mid-1960s techniques of survey research, the computer, and the intellectual materials that divided the field into sociology of occupations, sociology of science, social stratification, and so forth, had combined to produce hundreds of papers and many books. In terms of the original program (to develop middle-range theories), the work was virtually complete.

The high point of the specialty stage came with the publication of a piece of secondary work, *Sociology Today* (Merton et al., 1959, from papers written in 1957); in it Parsons wrote the theory chapter, Lazarsfeld, the methods chapter, and Merton, the introduction. Table 3.5 lists the participants along with their fields of interest, affiliations in 1957–1959, and Ph.D. location and date. This document, still being sold in the 1970s, shows the structural–functional synthesis as having (1) solved the range of problems reported in the chapters and (2) maintained an open-ended research program that could absorb the efforts of sociologists in the foreseeable future.

Parsons' perspective, which presupposed social order, had obvious implications for the examination of behavior. By the late 1950s structural functionalism was receiving substantial critical attention. Parsons' students and their students, in studying social order, had not always clarified the distinction between an *intellectual* focus on problems of order in a disorderly world and a *moral* commitment to order. Mills (1959), Gouldner (1970), and others, responding to this lack of clarity, have argued that too often the effect of this perspective is to label all nonconformist behavior as aberrant, no matter what the subject's intention. This labeling has political implications as well, since no mechanism for social change was built into structural functionalism. Change was not assumed, nor was it obvious how changes in a social system could occur or be accommodated. The emphasis on values rather than interests, on norms rather than behavior, very clearly underlined the orderly aspects of society. Nevertheless, Parsons was very clear in his explanation of why social order exists. His critics, by contrast, although claiming to be more radical, often assumed the existence of order; what needed explanation, they claimed, was change.

The work of Robin M. Williams, Jr., proves that structural–functional theory does not limit one to conclusions that society is changeless and without conflict. Williams has been analyzing American society since 1951, when he first stated that racism was a major American value (a quite unpopular assertion, then as now). Each edition of *American Society* since 1951 has reiterated, with additional support, that a set of common value orientations does not eliminate behavioral conflict, or even value conflict, across a total society.

During the 1960s, the budding ethnomethodologists began criticizing the positivistic basis of standard American sociology. There were also critics within (e.g., Demerath and Peterson, 1967; Gouldner, 1970). Homans, one of Parsons' original colleagues, had become more concerned with individual behavior (Homans, 1961). In addition, the philosophy of

TABLE 3.5 Participants in **Sociology Today**

Name	Field of Interest	Location, 1957–1959	Ph.D. Location and Date
Talcott Parsons	Theory	Harvard	Heidelberg, 1927
Robert K. Merton	Introduction	Columbia	Harvard, 1936
Paul F. Lazarsfeld	Methods	Columbia	Vienna, 1927
Seymour M. Lipset	Political	UC Berkeley	Columbia, 1949
Philip Selznick	Law	UC Berkeley	Columbia, 1947
Neal Gross	Education	Harvard	Iowa State, 1946
Charles Y. Glock	Religion	Columbia; UC Berkeley	Columbia, 1952
William J. Goode	Family	Columbia	Pennsylvania State, 1946
James H. Barnett	Art	Connecticut	University of Pennsylvania, 1930s
Bernard Barber	Science	Columbia	Harvard, 1949
George G. Reader, M.D.	Medicine	Cornell Medical School	Cornell, M.D., 1943
Mary Gross	Medicine	New York Hospital	Columbia, 1959
Alex Inkeles	Personality	Harvard	Columbia, 1948
Theodore M. Newcomb	Consensus	Michigan	Columbia, 1929
Robert F. Bales	Small groups	Harvard	Harvard, 1945
Kingsley Davis	Population	UC Berkeley	Harvard, 1936
Gideon Sjoberg	Urban	Texas	Washington State, 1949
C. Arnold Anderson	Rural	Kentucky–Chicago	Minnesota, 1932
George E. Simpson	Race and ethnic	Oberlin College	University of Pennsylvania, 1934
Milton J. Yinger	Race and ethnic	Oberlin College	Wisconsin, 1942
Alvin W. Gouldner	Organizational	Illinois–Washington (St. Louis)	Columbia, 1953
Leonard Broom	Stratification	UCLA	Duke, 1937
Everett C. Hughes	Occupations	Chicago	Chicago, 1928
Albert K. Cohen	Disorganization	Indiana	Harvard, 1951
John Clausen	Mental illness	NIMH	Chicago, 1949
Marshall Clinard	Criminology	Wisconsin	Chicago, 1941
John W. Riley, Jr.	Mass communication	Rutgers	Harvard, 1936
Matilda W. Riley	Mass communication	Rutgers	None
Charles Page	Teaching sociology	Smith	Columbia, 1940

Locations	No.	Ph.D.'s	No.
UC Berkeley	4	Columbia	8
Columbia	5	Harvard	6
Harvard	4	Chicago	3
Chicago	2	University of Pennsylvania	2
Oberlin	2	None	2
Rutgers	2		
One participant only	13	One Ph.D. only	8

science basis of standard American sociology as outlined by Hempel (1959) and other positivists was under attack from Popper (1959), Kuhn (1962), and linguistic philosophers (Black, ed., 1961).

In sum, the specialty stage saw standard American sociology—largely structural functionalism—spread itself throughout sociology, producing a noticeable standardization of training. The coauthorship network reflects this expansion in the increased number of persons involved in co-authorship during the specialty stage. The secondary and critical work expected during this period appeared, and some of the critical material (e.g., that by the ethnomethodologists) gradually gave impetus to new theory groups.

Although structural functionalism was the majority view in sociology from 1951 to 1968 (Friedrichs, 1970), it was not the only active school of thought. The next two chapters discuss two other active groups, symbolic interactionists and small group theorists. Still other sociologists were called demographers, a group that generated little excitement until some of its members began developing new causal theory (Chapter 9). There were also a few sociologists, belonging to none of these groups, who were nevertheless publishing actively in the field (see Chapter 6).

In addition, structural functionalism was not isolated from these other sociological thought systems. As I note in Chapter 4, the system concept linked this tradition with symbolic interactionism (see p. 96). The system–function combination bridged the gap to the small group tradition (pp. 119–120). These three thought systems together defined recognized sociology between 1951 and (roughly) 1968. What I have here termed contemporary theories were well underway by 1968, but they had not yet been noticed or deemed important, except by those actually doing the new work.[10]

NOTES

1. It should be noted that equally good connections can be made to many highly undistinguished scholars. However, in the same way that a family tree may show its connection to Charlemagne but not to an undistinguished relative who was kicked to death by a mule in his youth, theorists remember the Webers in their backgrounds but not the pedestrian teachers and researchers.

2. I noted in Chapter 2 that the normal stage at a given location in the general science communication structure ends when a network begins to form; the remainder of the general structure remains as it was, except for other locations marked by other groups that are developing. For each group, I have begun discussion with the events that had direct effects on the way in which a particular group and its tradition developed. The time

periods are from *the viewpoint of the group being analyzed only.* Other viewpoints and other groups are not considered in determining the stages for a specific group. For example, 1892–1918 marks, approximately, the network stage and 1918–1931 the cluster stage for Chicago sociology. However, these are not noted in discussion of standard American sociology.

3. Wallace's book, focused largely on the structural–functionalist school, marks a convenient endpoint to that school—not because people ceased to believe in it but because, since 1968, it has become clear that the target Wallace chose was too narrow to include all of American sociology. Other groups are also significant (see Part Three of this book). Wallace's book is important, however, because it describes the diversity of theoretical approaches contained within standard American sociology, even within the somewhat narrower range of structural functionalism which, after 1951, was the major theoretical product of standard American sociology.

The basic source of persons listed in Figure 3.1 was authors contributing to Wallace (1969): Peter M. Blau, Herbert Blumer, Fred Cottrell, Ralf Dahrendorf, O. D. Duncan, Philip M. Hauser, Amos Hawley, George C. Homans, George H. Mead, Robert K. Merton, William Ogburn, Talcott Parsons, Norman Ryder, Leo Schnore, John F. Scott, and Pierre van den Berghe. Of these, Fred Cottrell is a political scientist, and Ralf Dahrendorf is a German. Dahrendorf's relation to American sociology is obviously close—*Class and Class Conflict in Industrial Sociology* (1959) was written at the Center for Advanced Study in the Behavioral Sciences at Stanford, California. However, he is closer to the radical-critical part of contemporary American sociology than to standard American sociology.

This diagram connects the authors in Wallace with standard American sociology's origins in European and American thought. The connections represent one person's influence on another's work. Many persons who might have been on the diagram were not included if they did not directly connect parts of the diagram (e.g., Edgar Salin, a student of Weber's who taught Parsons). The major sources (see list below) for the linkages shown are Parsons (1970), Shils (1970), Faris (1967), personal communication from the parties themselves or others who were in a position to know, and inferences. The inferences should be defended here.

Sorokin was a likely teacher of Davis, since Davis was an early Harvard student, and Harvard then had only three sociologists, one of whom was Sorokin. We can say that Parsons trained van den Berghe because van den Berghe has a doctorate from Harvard, with some interests in theory, and he was trained when Parsons was the primary theoretician on the staff. The relation may be one of influence rather than teacher–student, but some relation almost certainly exists. The inference that Blumer trained Scott is probably the weakest. Scott has a 1966 Ph.D. degree from the University of California, Berkeley. From his discussion in Wallace, we discover that he is interested in Parsons' work and was probably introduced to his work by Smelser and Davis, both former students of Parsons who were at Berkeley—there is an introductory note thanking them. Yet Scott's discussion is critical of Parsons in a way that Blumer would approve; it emphasizes the early Parsons (*The Structure of Social Action*, 1937), whose action is closer to symbolic interactionism than is the later structural functionalism. The relationship is clearly one of influence and may be stronger than that. The Hawley–Schnore relation is inferred because Hawley was the University of Michigan's primary ecologist when Schnore received his degree there. The same sort of inference was made for the Burgess–Hauser and Davis–Ryder relations. Hauser and Duncan's colleague relation was inferred from Hauser and Duncan (1959). The student–teacher relation was inferred from Duncan's graduate study and faculty membership at Chicago while Hauser was there, and the subsequent publication of Hauser and Duncan (1959).

Sources for the remaining relations are:

Durkheim–Mead	Faris (1967: 8–9)
Durkheim–Cooley	Faris (1967: 8–9)
Cooley–Mead	Faris (1967: 92)
Simmel–Park	Faris (1967: 28)
Simmel–Small	Shils (1970: 783)
Pareto–Henderson	Parsons (1970: 830–831; Shils: 785)
Weber–Salin	Parsons (1970: 827)
Salin–Parsons	Parsons (1970: 827)
Sorokin–Merton	Merton (1968: xiii)
Henderson–Homans	Homans and Curtis (1934)
Henderson–Parsons	Shils (1970: 785); Parsons (1970: 832)
Giddings–Ogburn	Faris (1967: 113)
Park–Burgess	Faris (1967: 37–50)
Small–Burgess	Faris (1967: 26)
Mead–Blumer	Blumer (1969: 99)
Ogburn–Duncan	Duncan (1972)
Ogburn–Stouffer	Faris (1967: 114)
Ogburn–Hauser	Faris (1967: 115)
Durkheim–Parsons	Shils (1967: 785)
Davis–Scott	Wallace (1969: 262)

4. During the early period, Chicago also employed Ellsworth Faris, R. D. McKenzie, and Charles R. Henderson (see R. E. L. Faris, *Chicago Sociology 1920–1932*, 1967).

5. An appendix to Faris (1967) includes a complete list of those to whom Chicago granted Ph.D.'s from 1895 (the first two) to 1935; the Columbia data are in Odum (1951: 88).

6. See this chapter's bibliography for a selection of works by these men. The late translation of many of their works testifies to their importance to more recent sociology. In the original languages, the material was inaccessible to most American sociologists.

7. Following the fate of all good intellectual groups, the Chicago cluster's students were hired elsewhere, its best teachers and researchers aged and retired or died (Park retired in 1935 and Mead died in 1931), and Chicago sociology became routinized as a specialty (in this case as the majority of the discipline), both intellectually and socially. Clearly the data on the 1892–1935 period of Chicago sociology look very much like data on a group progressing through the four-stage model of Chapter 2. How-

ever, this period is sufficiently removed in time from contemporary sociology so that its contributions to today's sociology have been largely indirect, filtering through standard American sociology and symbolic interactionism. I have therefore chosen to treat early Chicago sociology not in and of itself but, rather, through its influence on later groups and persons. This group should be studied further to determine whether it fits the four-stage model.

8. Parsons' importance to this interdisciplinary operation became apparent after 1968, when illness forced his partial withdrawal from active participation in the department. Sociology then began withdrawing from Social Relations, and in 1970 a separate Department of Sociology was established. Clyde Kluckhohn (the anthropologist), Henry Murray (the clinician), and Gordon W. Allport (the social psychologist), who had been the other founding fathers of the department, were all dead by 1968 (Parsons, 1970: 841).

9. Uniformity in graduate training was encouraged in part by two sets of publications: the *Guide to Graduate Departments* of the American Sociological Association (ASA: various years, b) and the Sibley report (1963). The ASA was formerly the American Sociological Society; the name was changed in 1949.

10. The possible exception may be new causal theory (see Chapter 9).

BIBLIOGRAPHY

American Journal of Sociology.
　　various 　　*Cumulative Index to the American Journal of Sociology 1895–*
　　years 　　*1965.* Chicago: American Journal of Sociology.
American Sociological Association.
　　various 　　*Directory of Members 1959*; also for years 1963, 1967, 1970.
　　years a 　　New York and Washington, D.C.: American Sociological Association.
　　various 　　*Guide to Graduate Departments of Sociology 1965*; also for years
　　years b 　　1969, 1971. Washington, D.C.: American Sociological Association.
　　various 　　*Index to the American Sociological Review.* Vols. 1–25 (1936–
　　years c 　　1960) and Vols. 26–30 (1961–1965). New York and Washington, D.C.: American Sociological Association.
Barber, Bernard (ed.).
　　1970 　　*L. J. Henderson on the Social System.* Chicago: University of Chicago Press.
Berelson, Bernard, Paul F. Lazarsfeld, and William N. McPhee.
　　1954 　　*Voting: A Study of Opinion Formation in a Presidential Campaign.* Chicago: University of Chicago Press.
Black, Max.
　　1961 　　"Some questions about Parsons' theories." Pp. 268–288 in Max Black (ed.), *The Social Theories of Talcott Parsons.* Englewood Cliffs, N.J.: Prentice-Hall.
Black, Max (ed.).
　　1961 　　*The Social Theories of Talcott Parsons.* Englewood Cliffs, N.J.: Prentice-Hall.

Blau, Peter M.
   1963   *The Dynamics of Bureaucracy: A Study of Interpersonal Relations in Two Government Agencies.* Chicago: University of Chicago Press.
Blumer, Herbert.
   1969   *Symbolic Interactionism: Perspective and Method.* Englewood Cliffs, N.J.: Prentice-Hall.
Broom, Leonard, and Philip Selznick.
   1968   *Sociology: A Text with Adapted Readings.* 4th ed. New York: Harper & Row.
Dahrendorf, Ralf.
   1959   *Class and Class Conflict in Industrial Society.* Stanford, Calif.: Stanford University Press.
Davis, Kingsley.
   1949   *Human Society.* New York: Macmillan.
Demerath, Nicholas J., III, and Richard A. Peterson (eds.).
   1967   *System, Change and Conflict: A Reader on Contemporary Sociological Theory and the Debate over Functionalism.* New York: Free Press.
Duncan, O. D.
   1972   Personal communication (June).
Durkheim, Émile.
   1933   *The Division of Labor in Society.* Translated by George Simpson. New York: Free Press.
Faris, Robert E. L.
   1967   *Chicago Sociology 1920–1932.* San Francisco: Chandler.
Friedrichs, Robert W.
   1970   *A Sociology of Sociology.* New York: Free Press.
Goode, William J.
   1951   *Religion Among the Primitives.* New York: Free Press.
   1956   *After Divorce.* New York: Free Press.
   1963   *World Revolution and Family Pattern.* New York: Free Press.
Goode, William J., and Paul K. Hatt.
   1952   *Methods in Social Research.* New York: McGraw-Hill.
Goodman, Leo.
   1961   "Modifications of the Dorn–Stouffer–Tibbetts method for testing the significance of comparisons in sociological data." *American Journal of Sociology* 66 (January): 355–363.
Gouldner, Alvin W.
   1970   *The Coming Crisis of Western Sociology.* New York: Basic Books.
Gross, George R.
   1970   "The organization set: a study of sociology departments." *American Sociologist* 5 (February): 25–29.
Hauser, Philip M., and O. D. Duncan (eds.).
   1959   *The Study of Population.* Chicago: University of Chicago Press.
Hempel, Carl G.
   1959   "The logic of functional analysis." Pp. 271–307 in Llewellyn Gross (ed.), *Symposium on Sociological Theory.* Evanston, Ill.: Row, Peterson.

Henderson, L. J.
 1935   *Pareto's General Sociology: A Physiologist's Interpretation*. New York: Russell and Russell.
Homans, George C.
 1941   *English Villagers of the Thirteenth Century*. Cambridge, Mass.: Harvard University Press.
 1950   *The Human Group*. New York: Harcourt Brace Jovanovich.
 1961   *Social Behavior: Its Elementary Forms*. New York: Harcourt Brace Jovanovich.
 1962   *Sentiments and Activities: Essays in Social Science*. New York: Free Press,
 1964   "Bringing men back in." *American Sociological Review* 29 (December): 809–818.
Homans, George C., and Charles P. Curtis, Jr.
 1934   *An Introduction to Pareto, His Sociology*. New York: Knopf.
Katz, Elihu, and Paul F. Lazarsfeld.
 1955   *Personal Influence: The Part Played by People in the Flow of Mass Communication*. New York: Free Press.
Kuhn, Thomas S.
 1962   *The Structure of Scientific Revolutions*. 1st ed. Chicago: University of Chicago Press.
Lazarsfeld, Paul F., Bernard Berelson, and Hazel Gaudet.
 1944   *The People's Choice: How the Voter Makes Up His Mind in a Presidential Campaign*. New York: Duell, Sloan and Pearce. (2nd ed., 1948. New York: Columbia University Press.)
Lazarsfeld, Paul F., and Morris Rosenberg (eds.).
 1955   *The Language of Social Research: A Reader in the Methodology of Social Research*. New York: Free Press.
Levy, Marion.
 1953   *The Structure of Society*. Princeton, N.J.: Princeton University Press.
Lipset, Seymour M., Martin A. Trow, and James S. Coleman.
 1956   *Union Democracy: The Internal Politics of the International Typographical Union*. New York: Free Press.
Lynd, Robert S., and Helen M. Lynd.
 1937   *Middletown in Transition*. New York: Harcourt Brace Jovanovich.
Mack, Raymond W. (ed.).
 1969   "Written doctoral examinations in sociology at some leading universities." *American Sociologist* 4 (August): 189–226.
Merton, Robert K.
 1938   "Science, technology and society in seventeenth century England." *Osiris* 4 (Part II): 360–632.
 1948   "Discussion of Parsons." *American Sociological Review* 13 (April): 164–168.
 1949   *Social Theory and Social Structure*. New York: Free Press. (Rev. ed., 1968.)
Merton, Robert K., Leonard Broom, and Leonard S. Cottrell, Jr. (eds.).
 1959   *Sociology Today: Problems and Prospects*. New York: Basic Books.

Merton, Robert K., Marjorie Fiske, and Alberta Curtis.
    1946   *Mass Persuasion: The Social-Psychology of a War Bond Drive.* New York: Harper & Row.
Merton, Robert K., George G. Reader, and Patricia L. Kendall (eds.).
    1957   *The Student Physician: Introductory Studies in the Sociology of Medical Education.* Cambridge, Mass.: Harvard University Press.
Mills, C. Wright.
    1959   *The Sociological Imagination.* New York: Oxford University Press.
Odum, Howard W.
    1951   *American Sociology: The Story of Sociology in the United States Through 1950.* New York: Longmans, Green.
Pareto, Vilfredo.
    1935   *The Mind and Society.* 4 vols. Arthur Livingston (ed.). New York: Harcourt Brace Jovanovich.
Park, Robert E., and Ernest W. Burgess.
    1921   *Introduction to the Science of Sociology.* Chicago: University of Chicago Press.
Parsons, Talcott.
    1937   *The Structure of Social Action: A Study in Social Theory with Special Reference to a Group of Recent European Writers.* New York: McGraw-Hill.
    1949   *Essays in Sociological Theory.* New York: Free Press. (Revised in 1954.)
    1951   *The Social System.* New York: Free Press.
    1956   *Department and Laboratory of Social Relations, Harvard University; The First Decade, 1946–1956.* Cambridge, Mass.: Harvard University.
    1966   *Societies: Evolutionary and Comparative Perspectives.* Englewood Cliffs, N.J.: Prentice-Hall.
    1970   "On building social system theory: a personal history." *Daedalus: The Making of Modern Science: Biographical Studies* 99 (Fall): 826–881.
Parsons, Talcott (ed.).
    1968   *American Sociology.* New York: Basic Books.
Parsons, Talcott, Robert F. Bales, and Edward A. Shils.
    1953   *Working Papers in the Theory of Action.* New York: Free Press.
Parsons, Talcott, and Edward A. Shils (eds.).
    1951   *Toward a General Theory of Action.* Cambridge, Mass.: Harvard University Press.
Parsons, Talcott, and Neil J. Smelser.
    1956   *Economy and Society.* New York: Free Press.
Popper, Karl.
    1959   *The Logic of Scientific Discovery.* New York: Basic Books.
Selznick, Philip.
    1949   *TVA and the Grass Roots: A Study in the Sociology of Formal Organization.* Berkeley: University of California Press.
Shils, Edward A.
    1970   "Tradition, ecology and institution in the history of sociology."

Daedalus: The Making of Modern Science: Biographical Studies 99 (Fall): 760–825.

Sibley, Elbridge.
1963 *The Education of Sociologists in the United States.* New York: Russell Sage.

Simmel, Georg.
1950 *The Sociology of Georg Simmel.* Translated and edited by Kurt H. Wolff. New York: Free Press.

Sorokin, Pitirim A.
1927 *Social Mobility.* New York: Harper & Row.
1928 *Contemporary Sociological Theories.* New York: Harper & Row.
1941 *Social and Cultural Dynamics.* New York: American Book Company.

Stouffer, Samuel A.
1955 *Communism, Conformity and Civil Liberties: A Cross-Section of the Nation Speaks Its Mind.* Garden City, N.Y.: Doubleday.

Stouffer, Samuel A., E. A. Suchman, L. C. DeVinney, S. A. Star, and R. M. Williams, Jr.
1949 *The American Soldier.* Vol. 1: *Adjustment During Army Life.* Princeton, N.J.: Princeton University Press.

Stouffer, Samuel A., A. A. Lumsdaine, M. H. Lumsdaine, R. M. Williams, Jr., M. B. Smith, I. L. Janis, S. A. Star, and L. S. Cottrell, Jr.
1949 *The American Soldier.* Vol. II: *Combat and Its Aftermath.* Princeton, N.J.: Princeton University Press.

Wallace, Walter L. (ed.).
1969 *Sociological Theory: An Introduction.* Chicago: Aldine.

Weber, Max.
1947 *The Theory of Social and Economic Organization.* Translated by A. M. Henderson and Talcott Parsons. Edited by Talcott Parsons. New York: Oxford University Press.
1958 *From Max Weber.* Translated and edited by Hans H. Gerth and C. Wright Mills. New York: Oxford University Press.

Westie, Frank.
1972 "Academic expectations for professional immortality: a study of legitimation." *Sociological Focus* 5 (Summer): 1–25.

Williams, Robin M., Jr.
1951 *American Society: A Sociological Interpretation.* New York: Knopf.

CHAPTER 4
SYMBOLIC INTERACTIONISM
The Loyal Opposition

**Social and intellectual properties
of symbolic interactionism**

Intellectual leaders	H. Blumer
	G. H. Mead
Social organization leader	H. Blumer
Research centers	University of California, Berkeley
	University of Chicago
Training centers for students	University of California, Berkeley
	University of Chicago
Paradigm content	Behavior is the result of a self constructed in interaction
Success	Lindesmith, **Opiate Addiction** (1947)
Program statement	Blumer, "Social Psychology" (1938)
Examples of secondary work	Rose, **Human Behavior and Social Process** (1962)
	Manis and Meltzer, **Symbolic Interactionism: A Reader in Social Psychology** (1967)
	Shibutani, **Human Nature and Collective Behavior** (1970)
Examples of critical work	Glaser and Strauss, **The Discovery of Grounded Theory** (1967)
	Vaughan and Reynolds, "The Sociology of Symbolic Interactionism" (1970)
	Lofland, "Interactionist Imagery and Analytic Interruptus" (1970)
Text	Lindesmith and Strauss, **Social Psychology** (1956)

Any serious student of symbolic interactionism eventually becomes convinced that George Herbert Mead must have been a superb lecturer. Beginning in 1894, he taught for nearly forty years in the University of Chicago's philosophy department. One of his courses was in advanced social psychology, and it was taken by most sociology graduate students. He published no books during his career, yet his influence on American sociology through his Chicago graduate students alone has been enormous.

Mead's students were integral to the Chicago school's complex of persons and ideas. After Mead's death and the other events of the 1930s detailed early in Chapter 3, the Chicago school started to split up. Those who were primarily interested in the conceptions of mind, self, and society that were central to Mead's intellectual scheme rallied around Herbert Blumer. They developed a research style of their own and became a new, recognizable group. Others, influenced by the leadership of Edward A. Shils, NORC's survey research group, and the demographers at the University of Chicago began to integrate themselves with standard American sociology, particularly after 1951.

The opposition of symbolic interactionism and standard American sociology derives from their different intellectual positions. This opposition should be expected, since each group defined its position in terms of its own forefathers and in contrast to each other. Symbolic interactionists complained that Parsons and his students never understood Mead (Blumer, 1966); Parsons (1937) recognized Mead only in one footnote, simultaneously claiming to have discussed all major social theories. During the period before World War II, the opposition could be expressed as basically philosophical. The differences became striking after 1951, however, since standard American sociologists were willing to embrace the technology of survey research and data analysis, whereas most symbolic interactionists were not. Although some symbolic interactionists (e.g., Arnold M. Rose and Manford Kuhn) did surveys and tried to reconcile symbolic interactionism with the rest of sociology, others (e.g., Blumer and Erving Goffman) were working to keep the two separate, both theoretically and methodologically. Table 4.1 outlines highlights in the history of symbolic interactionism.

NORMAL STAGE: TO 1931

SOCIAL

Mead was the early intellectual leader of symbolic interactionism. At the turn of the century, he, Charles H. Cooley, W. I. Thomas, and William James were trying to formulate a theory of human interaction. They were

TABLE 4.1   Social and intellectual highlights in the
development of symbolic interactionism

Stages	Social	Intellectual
Normal: to 1931	Chicago base; Mead as leader	Thomas and Znaniecki, **Polish Peasant in Europe and America**; G. H. Mead lectures
Network: 1931–1945	Still Chicago base; Blumer becomes leader; more students	Mead's books: 1932, 1934, 1936, 1938 Program statement: Blumer, "Social Psychology" (1938)
Cluster: 1945–1952	Chicago cluster; other groups: Iowa and Minnesota	Lindesmith, **Opiate Addiction** (1947); Gerth and Mills, **Character and Social Structure** (1953)
Specialty: 1952–	Spread to Berkeley; many locations have one interactionist	Dalton, **Men Who Manage** (1959); Goffman, **Presentation of Self** (1959)

friends and corresponded frequently about their work.[1] Mead was a particularly forceful intellectual leader, strong enough to gain and hold students largely on the basis of his lectures (see Kuhn, 1964: 61). From 1920 on, he was helped by the impact of Thomas' *Source Book* and Thomas and Znaniecki's *The Polish Peasant in Europe and America* (5 volumes, publication beginning in 1918; see following discussion). The influence of these two works lasted long after Thomas' departure from the Chicago faculty in 1918.[2] Mead was also helped by two students of Thomas and himself, Ernest W. Burgess and Ellsworth Faris, who had both joined the faculty of Chicago's sociology department. Although Mead remained the recognized intellectual leader, all three were influential in training Herbert Blumer, Ruth Cavan, R. E. L. Faris, E. Franklin Frazier, Everett C. Hughes, Ernest T. Krueger, and Walter C. Reckless between 1920 and 1931.

Originally trained in the perspective of the old Chicago school, these students eventually became important symbolic interactionists (see Table 4.2, pp. 84–88). There were strong intellectual differences among them, but all felt that they were working together toward the common goal of a clearer understanding of sociology. Burgess' close relations with Park, the high esprit d'corps, and the small size of the entire department minimized potential conflicts between those who were influenced by Mead and those who were not. Of these students Blumer, Cavan (Ph.D., 1926) and Hughes (Ph.D., 1928; see Table 4.2) remained at Chicago and, with Burgess, formed the initial core of Chicago colleagues interested in what was to become symbolic interactionism. These were the Chicago sociologists who followed psychology and philosophy very carefully, early calling themselves "social psychologists." Indeed, Mead's course, previously mentioned, was called "Advanced Social Psychology," and Krueger and Reckless' textbook (1930) was entitled *Social Psychology*.

Comparision with standard American sociology on social properties at the end of the normal stage shows symbolic interactionism ahead in personnel—four faculty as opposed to one. The student situation was roughly comparable—Faris and Frazier were finishing degrees in 1931, as were K. Davis and Merton in 1936.

INTELLECTUAL

Until 1931 Chicago sociology contained within itself the entire range of sociology: social psychological, institutional, formal, and analytic studies and ideas were all present in the Chicago mix. People specialized in their own work; however, they also kept open communication lines to those with other interests, and they taught graduate courses taken by all students to provide common background. The technology of social research was still sufficiently limited that the whole range of techniques could be learned well enough to understand (if not actually practice).

Mead's influence focused attention on questions such as: How does the conception of self develop? How do interaction situations occur? Mead emphasized careful observation, participation, and introspection as proper techniques for answering these questions. The success that eventually converted Mead's (philosophical) and James's (psychological) thought into a major part of sociology was Thomas and Znaniecki's *The Polish Peasant*. By carefully analyzing the correspondence of Polish immigrants, the authors produced a successful research piece that explained a mass of empirical information. Their simple but powerful theoretical scheme was built around the ideas of (1) the "four wishes," (2) "the definition of the situation," and (3) the distinction between values (conceptions of what is valued) and attitudes (feelings toward external objects or persons).

The fundamental conceptions of symbolic interactionism were later stated by Manis and Meltzer (1967: 495):

1. Mind, self, and society are most usefully viewed as processes of human and interhuman conduct.
2. Language is the mechanism for the rise of mind and self.
3. Mind is an importation of the social process; that is, of interaction, within the individual.
4. Human beings construct their behavior in the course of its execution, rather than responding mechanically to either external stimuli or such internal "forces" as drives, needs, or motives.

5. Human conduct is carried on primarily by the defining of situations in which one acts.
6. The socialization of the human being both enmeshes him in society and frees him from society. The individual with a self is not passive but can employ his self in an interaction which may result in behavior divergent from group definitions.

In 1931 these elements were known only to many Chicago-trained sociologists. To outsiders, the intellectual outlines of symbolic interactionism were not visible.

NETWORK STAGE: 1931–1945

SOCIAL

In 1931 Mead died. Perhaps one would have expected Mead's influence to end with his death. Except for his extraordinary qualities as a lecturer, it might have. Instead, beginning in 1932 his lecture notes, which had been carefully preserved, were edited and published by his students.[3] Few professors have ever been able to claim such consistent clarity on behalf of their lectures or such devotion to the lecturer's content from their students!

Certainly student production was slowed. Of those who later became important symbolic interactionists, only Leonard Cottrell, Horace Dunham, Alfred R. Lindesmith, Francis Merrill, Anselm Strauss, Rose (who officially graduated in 1946), Paul Wallin, and S. K. Weinberg were trained at Chicago between 1931 and the end of World War II. Certainly these names represent more students than standard American sociology had during the same stage, but not enough over a 14-year period to establish a stable cluster. However, enough people had already been trained by 1931 to begin a slow network growth.

Communication is difficult to demonstrate in the specific. Vaughan and Reynolds (1970: 330–332) report for a later period that *formal* ties (e.g., teacher–student; colleagueship as either faculty or students, both of which existed during the normal stage) are very strong and will be followed by *informal* ties such as communication. Certainly the existence of a continuing core of activity at Chicago from 1931 to 1952 should have provided an impetus for communication and, hence, a network.

Crucial to the network's growth was the increasing influence of Herbert Blumer. A member of the Chicago sociology department from 1927 to 1952, he left an indelible mark on his students (see Shibutani, 1970). Perhaps more important, he succeeded Mead as intellectual leader and became the organizational chief for symbolic interactionism. His intellectual contributions are discussed later. Some of his more obvious social organizational activities were his secretary–treasurership (1930–1935) of the American Sociological Society (he was ousted in the revolt of 1935); his editorship (1935 to the present) of the Prentice-Hall sociology series; his editorship (1941–1952) of the *American Journal of Sociology (AJS)*; and his presidency (much later—1956) of the American Sociological Association (Shibutani, 1970, p. vii). Blumer's organizational leadership was important in establishing symbolic interactionism as a major kind of social psychology in contradistinction to experimental social psychology (another perspective beginning to develop within sociology as the study of small groups, see Chapter 5) and the analysis of survey research (which gained social psychological adherents interested in analyzing the relation between social groupings and attitudes; these researchers' interests fit more with those of standard American sociology).

As was true also of standard American sociology, symbolic interactionism's network stage was prolonged by World War II. By 1945, however, there existed a growing, communicating network of sociologists, linked by both current and past teacher–student and colleague relations, and largely based at Chicago. Chicago already had four faculty; hence a large student group could move the network into cluster status. Finally, Blumer had begun to establish himself as an intellectual and social organizational leader.

INTELLECTUAL

Probably the most important intellectual event during the network stage was the appearance of a program statement for symbolic interactionism, an article written by Blumer (1938). In that essay, Blumer established three major themes. First, he used the term "symbolic interactionism" with reference to a position developed largely from the work of Mead, Thomas, Cooley, and Wirth but also including a varied cast of others. Second, he focused on Mead's work as the essential part of the perspective. Third, he stated the fundamental three premises of symbolic interactionism. These premises were restated in a later work (Blumer, 1969: 2) as:

1. Human beings act toward things on the basis of the meanings that things have for them.
2. Meaning derives from social interaction.
3. Meanings are modified by their interpretations, used by persons in actual situations.

Blumer's statement also shaped interactionism by what it did *not* say. He offered no discussion of research methods; thus, by implication, he defined symbolic interactionism as largely a way of thinking.

More generally, Blumer's intellectual contribution to symbolic interactionism during the network stage was to state explicitly matters that, in former days, had been only implied by his mentors. For example, he worked out some of the implications of Thomas' contention that men's actions are generally governed by their definition of a situation (an extremely important concept).

Blumer insisted that the meaning of objects was primarily a property of behavior and depended only secondarily on the intrinsic character of the objects themselves. That idea is central to the fundamental theory of symbolic interaction. Furthermore, meanings were constructed, reconstructed, and reaffirmed in social interaction; they were not graven on stone tablets or determined totally by the behavior of parents or by some other factor in a person's background. Meanings were conceived as shaped mainly by the actual and anticipated responses of others. Human beings are thus neither creatures of impulse nor heedless victims of external stimulation. They are active organisms, guiding and constructing their lines of action *while* continuously coming to terms with the demands of an ever-changing world as they interpret it. This basic concept, as I demonstrate in later chapters, contrasts strongly on several levels with the perspectives of other social theories.

Symbolic interaction clearly takes an optimistic view of man because it affirms that man is a thinking animal, rational, and essentially in control of his own situation; he can make his own future. This view opposes those which perceived man as controlled by economic or political forces (e.g., Marxist analysis) or by internal drives and hormonal stimulation (e.g., Freudian psychology). Blumer's sociology thus required a rationalist psychology. Particularly important for Blumer was the object that each person formed of himself. If a person was unable to step back from himself and see his own behavior somewhat as other people saw it, he would have little or no opportunity to correct himself. He would also have little or no opportunity for planning, if he could not predict others' probable responses to certain behavior; thus he would be unprepared to deal with those responses.

From these basics, Blumer developed an analysis of concerted action: Each transaction is built up through communication as participants mesh their respective contributions. Repetition sometimes results in the formation of habitual modes of cooperation—social institutions. Blumer's forceful presentation of this viewpoint profoundly affected the thinking of several generations of graduate students. He was clearly juggling two concepts that had an uneasy relationship to each other. On the one hand, he took the social psychological view of man as a unitary self (Reynolds et al.: 422–438), a rational, thinking, symbol-using creature. On the other, he conceived social institutions simply as habitual modes of action, built up from people's willingness to behave in habitualized, ritualized fashion, over time. Man, the rational creature, willingly surrendered his self-control in crowd situations, and only thus were social institutions born.

The ambiguity in Blumer's formulations became clear later, during the specialty stage, as others calling themselves symbolic interactionists (see, e.g., Rose and Prell, 1955) began to recognize nonrational elements of behavior and external social controls separated from the self. In general, though, symbolic interactionism's strong emphasis remained with the rational and the individual. It should also be noted that Blumer was a pragmatist and that pragmatism is perhaps the one uniquely American philosophical school.

If we compare Blumer at this stage with Parsons, we see that Blumer was not the originator of symbolic interactionism as Parsons was of standard American sociology. Neither did he possess Parsons' towering stature in his field—Blumer's position was more that of first among equals (others being, e.g., Burgess, Hughes). Nevertheless, he led the school of thought that was Parsons' major competition for 20 years. Furthermore, he produced a program statement for symbolic interactionism during the midnetwork stage, whereas Parsons' was not made public until 1947—midcluster stage for standard American sociology. This comparison of the two men is simply to illustrate a point I made in Chapter 2—namely, that the *roles* the two men played in their developing specialties were the crucial factor. Their personalities may have set a style, but social theory building clearly did not require a person of Parsons' intellectual and organizational stature.

At the end of the network stage, the outlines of symbolic interactionism and its future program were apparent. That group was ready, as was standard American sociology, to take full advantage of the conclusion of World War II.

CLUSTER STAGE:
1945–1952

SOCIAL

With the return of graduate students to Chicago, symbolic interactionism experienced a flowering that paralleled, in time, the development of structural functionalism in the east. The network at Chicago thickened into a cluster. The information on degrees and jobs for 82 symbolic interactionists, presented in Table 4.2, is basic data for the remainder of this chapter. The group's growth during this stage is obvious. Twenty-six principal symbolic interactionists graduated from the University of

Chicago between 1945 and 1954, more than enough, with the faculty group, to form a stable cluster. Most were Blumer students, although some had worked also with other interactionists on the Chicago staff: Howard S. Becker, Everett C. Hughes, Ethel Shanas, T. Shibutani, and Strauss (Shanas, Shibutani, and Strauss, themselves had graduated early in this period). During the cluster period, Chicago was both the major research center and the training center. Of the 82 symbolic interactionists listed in Table 4.3, 45 (55 percent) are Chicago graduates. Wisconsin is next with six. Iowa and Berkeley (four) and Minnesota (three) follow.

These numbers confirm the notion that a group at a location can reproduce itself many times *if* it begins with a sufficient number of people. Table 4.2 shows that Chicago began 1945 with four symbolic interactionists on the faculty; by 1950 there were seven. Even on a very large staff such as Chicago's, particularly since there were several senior persons (e.g., Blumer, Hughes), these faculty constituted an important training unit. Such senior persons with a common orientation serve to protect a budding group from departmental infighting; they also attract students and money to support research. The combination of active and enthusiastic senior and junior faculty with good students is relatively rare. Chicago had it between 1948 and 1952, the result of a buildup that started in 1945. The cluster group experienced some departures, but the persons leaving were replaced. Although Rose (part of the network stage group) moved to Minnesota, and Haberstein and Stone (students between 1946 and 1949) moved to Missouri and Michigan State, respectively, Strauss returned to Chicago in 1950 and new students (e.g., Erving Goffman, Gladys E. Lang, and Kurt Lang) arrived to fill out the group.

Those who have studied the symbolic interactionist tradition (e.g., Manis and Meltzer, 1967; Vaughan and Reynolds, 1970) agree that, during the cluster period and after, a second (although minor) training center, headed by Manford Kuhn, existed at the University of Iowa (see Table 4.3). Intellectually, Kuhn's tradition was less differentiated from structural functionalism than was Blumer's. Kuhn was trained at Wisconsin when Kimball Young and Hans H. Gerth were on the staff. Young had a master's degree from the old Chicago school (1918) and a Ph.D. in psychology. Gerth, born and trained in Germany, taught a social psychology similar to Mead's. Kuhn graduated from Wisconsin in 1941 and settled at Iowa in 1946. From 1946 to 1963 he taught at Iowa, developing a series of pencil-and-paper tests for the concept of "self." This effort was his attempt to make operational the major concepts of symbolic interactionism (see Shibutani, 1970: 3–17). Kuhn trained only three students whom I can locate in the literature: C. J. Couch, T. S. McPartland, and H. A. Mulford. Couch succeeded Kuhn

TABLE 4.2 Important symbolic interactionists: degree (date and place) and selected job locations

Name	Ph.D. Date	Ph.D. Place	1925	1935
Bain, Read	1926	MICH	MICH	MIAO
Becker, Howard S.	1951	CHIC	*	*
Blumer, Herbert	1927	CHIC	CHIC	CHIC
Bolton, Charles	1959	CHIC	*	*
Bonner, Hubert	1949	CHIC	*	*
Bramson, Leon	1959	HARV	*	*
Burgess, Ernest W.	1914	CHIC	CHIC	CHIC
Cavan, Ruth	1926	CHIC	CHIC	CHIC
Coates, Charles H.	1955	LSU	*	*
Cottrell, Jr., Leonard S.	1933	CHIC	*	CHIC
Couch, C. J.	1955	IOWA	*	*
Coutu, Walter	1935	WISC	*	WISC
Cressey, Donald	1950	INDU	*	*
Dalton, Melville	1949	CHIC	*	*
Daniels, Arlene	1960	BERK	*	*
Davis, Fred	1958	CHIC	*	*
Denzin, Norman	1966	IOWA	*	*
Deutscher, Irwin	1959	MISO	*	*
Dubin, Robert	1947	CHIC	*	*
Emerson, Joan	1963	BERK	*	*
Farber, Bernard	1953	CHIC	*	*
Faris, R. E. L.	1931	CHIC	*	BROW
Foote, Nelson	1956	CORN	*	*
Frazier, E. Franklin	1931	CHIC	*	HOWD
Freidson, Elliott	1952	CHIC	*	*
Gans, Herbert	1957	PENN	*	*
Geer, Blanche (education)	1956	JHU	*	*
Gerth, Hans H.	1933	GOET	*	ni
Glaser, Barney G.	1961	COL	*	*
Glaser, Daniel	1954	CHIC	*	*
Goffman, Erving	1953	CHIC	*	*
Gross, Edward	1949	CHIC	*	*
Haberstein, Robert	1954	CHIC	*	*
Heiss, Jerold	1958	INDU	*	*
Horowitz, Irving L.	1957	BUEN	*	*
Hughes, Everett C.	1928	CHIC	CHIC	CHIC
Kerckhoff, Alan C.	1954	WISC	*	*
Keyfitz, Nathan	1952	CHIC	*	*
Killian, Louis M.	1949	CHIC	*	*
Kinch, John	1959	WASH	*	*
Klapp, Orrin E.	1948	CHIC	*	*
Kolb, William	1943	WISC	*	*
Kornhauser, William	1953	CHIC	*	*

Sources: AJS (various years); ASR (various years a, b, c). People were selected for Table 4.2 if they had authored either: (1) a selection in either Manis and Meltzer (1967) or Shibutani (1970), or (2) one of several widely used texts: Lindesmith and Strauss (1949), Bonner (1953), Gerth and Mills (1953), or Shibutani (1961).

Job held in academic year ending in						
1946	1950	1955	1959	1963	1967	1970
MIAO	MIAO	MIAO	MIAO	ret	ret	ret
*	CHIC	CHIC	CHIC	STAN	NWU	NWU
CHIC	CHIC	BERK	BERK	BERK	BERK	BERK
*	DENV	COLC	ILL	UCDA	POST	POST
*	ni	ni	OHWE	ni	ni	ni
*	*	*	HARV	HARV	SWAT	SWAT
CHIC	CHIC	ret	ret	ret	ret	ni
CHIC	ROCK	ROCK	ROCK	ret	ret	ret
*	*	LSU	MARL	MARL	MARL	MARL
CORN	CORN	RUSS	RUSS	RUSS	RUSS	UNC
*	*	IOWA	CMIU	MIST	IOWA	IOWA
PNST	PNST	PNST	PNST	ni	ni	ni
*	UCLA	UCLA	UCLA	UCSB	UCSB	UCSB
*	CHIC	UCLA	UCLA	UCLA	UCLA	UCLA
*	*	*	*	res	res	SFST
*	*	MARL	JFS	UCSF	UCSF	UCSF
*	*	*	*	*	ILL	BERK
*	*	KANC	KANC	res	res	CASE
*	ILL	ORE	ORE	ORE	ORE	UCIR
*	*	*	*	CARL	res	BUFF
*	*	ILL	ILL	ILL	ILL	ILL
SYRA	WASH	WASH	WASH	WASH	WASH	WASH
*	*	CORN	self	self	ind	ind
HOWD	HOWD	HOWD	HOWD	d		
*	*	res	CCNY	NYU	NYU	NYU
*	*	PENN	PENN	COL	res	MIT
mil	teac	res	res	res	SYRA	NEU
WISC	WISC	WISC	WISC	WISC	WISC	WISC
*	*	*	*	UCSF	UCSF	UCSF
*	res	ILL	ILL	ILL	ILL	USC
*	CHIC	BERK	BERK	BERK	BERK	PENN
CHIC	WAST	WAST	WAST	MINN	MINN	WASH
*	ni	ni	MISO	MISO	MISO	MISO
*	*	*	CONN	CONN	CONN	CONN
*	*	ni	ni	ni	WSTL	RUTG
CHIC	CHIC	CHIC	CHIC	BRAN	BRAN	BOSC
*	*	VAND	DUKE	DUKE	DUKE	DUKE
res	res	res	TORO	CHIC	CHIC	BERK
*	OKLA	FSU	FSU	FSU	UCLA	MASS
*	*	*	SFST	SFST	SFST	SFST
ni	ni	ni	SDST	SDST	SDST	SDST
OKST	TULA	TULA	TULA	CARL	BELO	BELO
*	ni	ni	BERK	BERK	BERK	BERK

TABLE 4.2 (continued)

Name	Ph.D. Date	Place	1925	1935
Krueger, Ernest T.	1925	CHIC	VAND	VAND
Kuhn, Manford H.	1941	WISC	*	*
Lang, Gladys E.	1954	CHIC	*	*
Lang, Kurt	1953	CHIC	*	*
Lee, Shu Ching	1950	CHIC	*	*
Lindesmith, Alfred R.	1936	CHIC	*	CHIC
Litman, Theodor J.	1961	MINN	*	*
Lofland, John	1964	BERK	*	*
Manis, Jerome G.	1952	COL	*	*
Martindale, Don A.	1948	WISC	*	*
McCall, George	1965	HARV	*	*
McPartland, T. P.	1953	IOWA	*	*
Meltzer, Bernard N.	1948	CHIC	*	*
Merrill, Francis	1937	CHIC	*	ROOS
Messinger, Sheldon	1969	UCLA	*	*
Mills, C. Wright	1940	WISC	*	*
Miyamoto, S. Frank	1950	CHIC	*	*
Mulford, Harold	1955	IOWA	*	*
Petras, John	1966	CONN	*	*
Quarantelli, Enrico	1959	CHIC	*	*
Reckless, Walter C.	1925	CHIC	CHIC	OHST
Rose, Arnold M.	1946	CHIC	*	*
Roth, Julius A.	1954	CHIC	*	*
Scheff, Thomas	1960	BERK	*	*
Schwartz, Michael	1962	ILL	*	*
Shanas, Ethel	1949	CHIC	*	*
Shibutani, Tamotsu	1948	CHIC	*	*
Solomon, David	1952	CHIC	*	*
Stone, Gregory P.	1959	CHIC	*	*
Strauss, Anselm L.	1945	CHIC	*	*
Stryker, Sheldon	1955	MINN	*	*
Swanson, Guy E.	1948	CHIC	*	*
Troyer, William	1942	CHIC	*	*
Turner, Ralph	1948	CHIC	*	*
Waller, William	1929	PENN	CHIC	PNST
Wallin, Paul	1942	CHIC	*	*
Warshay, Leon	1959	MINN	*	*
Weinberg, S. Kirson	1942	CHIC	*	*
Young, Kimball	1920	STAN	ORE	WISC

Key:			
		BROW	Brown University
ALBI	Albion College	BUEN	Buenos Aires University
BELO	Beloit College	BUFF	State University of New York, Buffalo
BENN	Bennington College		
BERK	University of California, Berkeley	CARL	Carleton College
BOSC	Boston College	CASE	Case-Western Reserve University
BRAN	Brandeis University	CCNY	City College of New York
BROO	Brooklyn College	CHIC	University of Chicago

Job held in academic year ending in						
1946	1950	1955	1959	1963	1967	1970
d						
MTHO	IOWA	IOWA	IOWA	IOWA	d	
OSS	CHIC	CHIC	BROO	QUEE	res	COL
*	CHIC	res	QUEE	QUEE	STON	STON
*	CHIC	WSTL	SEMO	SUSD	SUSD	OHIO
INDU	INDU	INDU	INDU	INDU	INDU	INDU
*	*	*	*	MINN	MINN	MINN
*	*	*	*	BERK	MICH	SOST
*	*	WMIU	WMIU	WMIU	WMIU	WMIU
*	MINN	MINN	MINN	MINN	MINN	MINN
*	*	*	*	*	ILL	ILCH
*	*	ni	ni	ni	res	ni
*	MCGI	CMIU	CMIU	CMIU	CMIU	CMIU
DART	DART	DART	DART	DART	DART	DART
*	*	UCLA	res	BERK	BERK	BERK
COL	COL	COL	COL	d		
WASH	WASH	WASH	WASH	WASH	WASH	WASH
*	*	NMST	IOWA	IOWA	IOWA	IOWA
*	*	*	*	*	CMIU	CMIU
*	*	SBIU	HARP	OHST	OHST	OHST
OHST	OHST	OHST	OHST	OHST	OHST	OHST
BENN	MINN	MINN	MINN	MINN	MINN	d
*	*	ni	res	COL	UCDA	UCDA
*	*	*	BERK	WISC	UCSB	UCSB
*	*	*	*	WAYS	INDU	FAU
*	CHIC	ni	NORC	CHIC	ILCH	ILCH
*	CHIC	BERK	self	UCSB	UCSB	UCSB
*	res	res	MCGI	res	MCGI	MCGI
*	MIST	MIST	MISO	MINN	MINN	MINN
LAWR	INDU	CHIC	res	UCSF	UCSF	UCSF
*	*	INDU	INDU	INDU	INDU	INDU
*	ni	ni	MICH	MICH	MICH	BERK
DRUR	ALBI	NCED	NCED	NCED	NCED	NCED
*	UCLA	UCLA	UCLA	UCLA	UCLA	UCLA
d						
mil	STAN	STAN	STAN	STAN	STAN	STAN
*	*	CHIC	KANC	KANC	OHST	WAYS
ni	ni	ROOS	ROOS	ROOS	ROOS	LOYO
QUEE	NWU	NWU	NWU	ret	ret	ret

CMIU	Central Michigan University	DRUR	Drury College
COL	Columbia University	DUKE	Duke University
COLC	Colorado College	FAU	Florida Atlantic University, Boca Raton
CONN	University of Connecticut		
CORN	Cornell University	FSU	Florida State University
d	Deceased	GOET	Goethe University, Germany
DART	Dartmouth College	HARP	Harpur College (State University of New York)
DENV	Denver University		

Key (continued)

HARV	Harvard University
HOWD	Howard University
ILCH	University of Illinois, Chicago
ILL	University of Illinois
ind	Industry
INDU	Indiana University, Bloomington
IOWA	University of Iowa
JFS	Jewish Family Service, New York
JHU	Johns Hopkins University
KANC	Kansas City University
LAWR	Lawrence College
LOYO	Loyola University, Chicago
LSU	Louisiana State University
MARL	University of Maryland
MASS	University of Massachusetts
MCGI	McGill University
MIAO	Miami University (of Ohio)
MICH	University of Michigan
mil	Military
MINN	University of Minnesota
MISO	University of Missouri
MIST	Michigan State University
MIT	Massachusetts Institute of Technology
MTHO	Mount Holyoke College
NCED	National College of Education, Chicago
NEU	Northeastern University
ni	No information
NMST	Northeast Missouri State College
NORC	National Opinion Research Center
NWU	Northwestern University
NYU	New York University
OHIO	Ohio University
OHST	Ohio State University
OHWE	Ohio Wesleyan University
OKLA	University of Oklahoma
OKST	Oklahoma State University
ORE	University of Oregon
OSS	Office of Strategic Services, U.S. government
PENN	University of Pennsylvania
PNST	Pennsylvania State University
POST	Portland State College, Oregon

QUEE	Queens College, New York
res	Miscellaneous research position
ret	Retired
ROCK	Rockford College
ROOS	Roosevelt University, Chicago
RUSS	Russell Sage Foundation
RUTG	Rutgers
SBIU	South Bend Center, Indiana University
SDST	San Diego State College
self	Self-employed
SEMO	Southeastern Missouri State College
SFST	San Francisco State College
SMIT	Smith College
SOST	Sonoma State College, California
STAN	Stanford University
STON	State University of New York, Stony Brook
SUSD	State University of South Dakota, Vermillion
SWAT	Swarthmore College
SYRA	Syracuse University
teac	Teaching (high school)
TEX	University of Texas
TORO	University of Toronto
TULA	Tulane University
UCDA	University of California, Davis
UCIR	University of California, Irvine
UCLA	University of California, Los Angeles
UCSB	University of California, Santa Barbara
UCSF	University of California, San Francisco
UNC	University of North Carolina
USC	University of Southern California
VAND	Vanderbilt University
WASH	University of Washington, Seattle
WAST	Washington State University
WAYS	Wayne State University
WISC	University of Wisconsin, Madison
WMIU	Western Michigan University
WSTL	Washington University at St. Louis
*	Not in system

at Iowa and has since trained only one promising graduate student: Norman Denzin. (George McCall, while an Iowa undergraduate, had gone quite deeply into symbolic interactionism.) Neither Mulford nor McPartland has held positions with access to any number of graduate students. This lack of students doomed the Kuhn tradition for future development.

Another variant position developed at Minnesota, where Rose, a Chicago Ph.D. trained largely before World War II, and Don Martindale, also a student of Gerth's from Wisconsin, taught the symbolic interactionist position after Rose's arrival in 1949. The variant taught at

Minnesota became intellectually important during this stage and the specialty stage.

Rose's background included an important training experience that varied from the usual. From 1940 to 1942 he was a research associate to Gunnar Myrdal, the Swedish economist and social scientist, in the latter's research on the position of the Negro in America. The result of that research, *An American Dilemma* (1944), was and is an important document in American social science. It is not, however, a symbolic interactionist work. As a result of his work with Myrdal, Rose began to modify his understanding of symbolic interactionism to include the results of survey research. This process of modification and accommodation to the techniques of standard American sociology reduced the distinctiveness of the symbolic interactionist perspective. In addition, the Minnesota faculty did not develop a new cluster situation. Although three interactionists were on the staff (Rose, Martindale, and, later, Stone), that number was not sufficient to attract the large group of distinctive students that has marked the development of other groups. There were, however, some good students over the several years of this period. Rose's apparent accommodation to standard American sociology's methods made his position less rather than more distinctive over time, and this factor probably contributed to the lack of cluster development at Minnesota.

In addition to the cluster at Chicago and the Iowa and Minnesota groups, Table 4.2 shows some symbolic interactionists (e.g., Cressey at UCLA; Dubin at Illinois and, later, Oregon) and their students in other locations. These persons probably maintained their communication ties with the Chicago group (see discussion of Vaughan and Reynolds p. 79). By 1950 at least 22 locations had at least one interactionist. Indiana had two, Lindesmith and Strauss, who made good use of their colleagueship to write *Social Psychology* (first published in 1949), the textbook for symbolic interactionism. No location was as strong a second to Chicago as Columbia was to Harvard for standard American sociology, but interactionists were quite widely spread, and they became even more widely dispersed during the specialty stage.

A final note to the social side of this stage is that Blumer continued his editorship of the *AJS* and of the Prentice-Hall sociology series; both were important social organizational activities for the group.

INTELLECTUAL

The Chicago cluster's strong social bonds were paralleled by equally close intellectual bonds. Vaughan and Reynolds (1970) demonstrated this with a questionnaire study in which they asked leading symbolic interactionists to judge, among other things, whether symbolic interactionism was able to incorporate "the topic of change."

Among the 15 respondents who said that symbolic interactionism could handle change, a multibonded network of relations emerges. Twelve received their degrees from the University of Chicago.

> Although each one had no direct relationship with *all* others, all were linked in a chain of relationships. And this chain was heavily intertwined: nine of the twelve received the degree during the period 1948–1952. . . . The other three Chicago products received the degrees prior to 1948. Inasmuch as two of these earlier graduates were on the faculty during the period 1948 to 1952, the entire group of Chicago products, with but one exception, was concentrated at Chicago during this one period. While some of the group were on the faculty *after* 1952, it is noteworthy that no member of this group received a degree there after that date (1970: 330).[4]

Two of the three non-Chicago respondents who said symbolic interactionism *could* handle change received their degrees from the same institution in the same year and did their work under the supervision of the same interactionist. Among all 15 (1948–1952) there was heavy interaction. Not only were they exposed to the same intellectual tradition, they were also bound by a solid chain of intermediaries. For example, there were tendencies for two men to exchange postdoctoral students; or, one man would grant the M.A. and his colleague, at a different school, would grant the Ph.D. Various faculty would spend visiting years away from their home campuses, at the locations of their fellow interactionists.

This kind of agreement on major issues, however, did not prevent squabbles on lesser ones. As Gouldner (1965) has pointed out, social theories do not develop simply through the cooperative efforts of friendly groups who want to protect and extend their mentor's work. Indeed, theory develops as much from hostility and competition as from friendly cooperation. Once an idea is established, a group of disciples gathers who work *against* one another competitively, *within* the group, to gain position within it. They stand together only against the outside world, which does not perceive things as they do. This kind of infighting certainly occurred at Chicago, over such relatively minor matters as tenure decisions. However, the internal struggles did not destroy the group's theoretical solidarity, which had its roots in Blumer's (1938) program statement and his subsequent essays.

Vaughan and Reynolds assert that their data indicate the existence of a tightly related school of thought. They characterize the Chicago group as *strong* symbolic interactionists, strongly bonded and confident of their theory. The remainder of Vaughan and Reynolds' respondents are characterized as *weak* symbolic interactionists, who asserted that symbolic interactionism could adequately explain some social problems, but not change. These social scientists reported degrees from many different places, and their social connections differed from those characterizing the strongly bonded group. Members of the so-called weak group never gathered in groups larger than two, although they sometimes met in different pair combinations. It is unlikely that their judgment on symbolic interaction theory results solely from their lack of personal interaction; rather, it is probably related to their failure to gather to work out issues in full detail, under the criticism of like-minded others. Chicago, by contrast, had long been a hotbed of interactionist thought, criticism, and development.

It is important to note that, unlike standard American sociology and contrary to the model in Chapter 2, symbolic interactionism did *not* experience a publication explosion during either the cluster or the specialty period (Kuhn, 1964: 62ff). Relative to standard American sociology, there is a lack of articles and monographs written from the symbolic interactionist position. The explanation for this difference is fairly simple. The expectation (in the model) of a publication explosion is based on a rapidly increasing number of persons in the area who, upon completing their degrees, will begin adding to the literature. The symbolic interactionists, however, have taken longer than the average amount of time to complete degrees (Lofland, 1970). A second factor, important mainly to the production of books, is that symbolic interaction has been a social psychological specialty and, as such, has produced studies of the interpersonal rather than the institutional. Monographic work based on interpersonal research is more difficult to produce since it does not utilize the unique aspects of each social institution to "pad out" a presentation.

Perhaps most significant has been the effect on publication of symbolic interactionist research methods. Denzin (1970: 456–465) discusses five methods long available to interactionists: experiment, social survey, participant observation, life history, and records originally collected for other purposes (often called unobtrusive measures). Of these, the survey and the experiment have been generally distrusted (Kuhn's use of pencil-and-paper tests, however, constituted an important exception). The unobtrusive measures have not been much utilized, although they were later picked up by structuralists (see Chapter 10). As a result, participant observation and life history have been the basic interactionist methods. Both methods require considerable time to complete and are very difficult to treat adequately when reporting results. Life history, although highly praised, is less used, notwithstanding the early example of Thomas and Znaniecki (reprinted in 1956). Participant observation, then, has become the chief research method. It is very difficult to participate in many situations, and hence interactionists, like anthropologists, have tended to do and report one field study, usually as a dissertation, and to write essays about it from then on. This description is an over-simplification, but it helps to explain the relative rarity of interactionist publications.[5]

Among the few publications, Lindesmith's *Opiate Addiction* (1947) constitutes a notable research success of the cluster period. By careful use of observation, interviews, and inductive thinking about what he was finding, Lindesmith developed a picture of opiate addiction based on the meanings that individual persons have and develop in interaction with their situation and with other persons.

SPECIALTY STAGE: 1952–

SOCIAL

In 1952 Herbert Blumer left Chicago for the Berkeley campus of the University of California. This move marked the end of symbolic interactionism's cluster stage and the dissemination of Blumer's thought and students to other institutions. His importance to symbolic interactionism at Chicago, however, is underscored by the failure of any significant new symbolic interactionists to begin studying at Chicago after 1953 (Quarantelli and Stone, e.g., have 1959 degrees, but both had been students before Blumer left), whereas several were subsequently graduated at Berkeley. Evidently, Blumer was the kind of prestigious older man who both had students and could attract more. Table 4.2 clearly reveals the disintegration of Chicago symbolic interactionism. In 1950 eleven interactionists were at Chicago. By 1955 there were only five, students and faculty combined. Some of those who left did not complete degrees until much later (e.g., Stone, who joined the Michigan State faculty in 1950, and did not receive his degree until 1959).

Shortly after Blumer moved to Berkeley, he was joined by Erving Goffman, a former student of his. In time, important symbolic interactionists began graduating from Berkeley. Although there are no data to indicate that these individuals were students only of Blumer, it is likely that he exerted major influence on Arlene Daniels (Ph.D., 1960), Thomas Scheff (Ph.D., 1960), Joan Emerson (Ph.D., 1963), and John Lofland (Ph.D., 1964), because all produced articles for Shibutani's (1970) festschrift. Blumer was probably instrumental in recruiting them to Berkeley.

Despite the appearance of strengthening symbolic interactionism that Blumer's move to Berkeley must have given, that move actually marked the beginning of the end. Blumer failed to continue as a strong organizational leader. For example, he resigned as editor of the *AJS*; Everett C. Hughes took over that job (*AJS*, 1966: 1), but he was not a strong enough social organization leader to stop the disintegration that is so apparent in Table 4.2. Here the specialty stage of symbolic interactionism differs markedly from that of standard American sociology, possibly because Parsons remained at Harvard and continued to be a strong social organizational leader. The Harvard cluster also disintegrated, but much more gradually, and over a period of eight years.

Indeed, Parsons' ties to Chicago may have been part of symbolic interactionism's problem. The interactionists left at Chicago were not strong enough to counter the infusion of standard American sociology that was due to the influence of Shils and the hiring of Fred Strodtbeck, Peter M. Blau, and other Harvard and Columbia students. Even though Berkeley had both Blumer and Goffman, that Department of Sociology was not then a unified or well-known center for the production of sociologists or sociological theory. It remained a fragmented department (Shils, 1970: 796–797) and Blumer's position, although strong, has never been dominant.

Finally, as I noted earlier, the Iowa and Minnesota groups, while still in existence, failed to grow. Elsewhere, symbolic interactionists became widely scattered, and no large groups existed anywhere. Some interactionists became competitors for the social psychological positions that were available on many faculties; others moved into pure research (e.g., Becker for a time, Geer, B. Glaser, and Strauss; see Table 4.2).

Both symbolic interactionism's lack of organization and the danger it faced of being engulfed by standard American sociology are reflected in Figure 4.1, the coauthorship network for symbolic interactionism. Unlike Figure 3.3, which contained a large, well-connected central network, Figure 4.1 shows five separate ones. The largest network includes two loosely connected groups of seven symbolic interactionists each from Table 4.3—a total of 14 members. This network is not only smaller, it is not as well connected as the large standard American sociology group. It is also not much larger than the next group in size. Furthermore, Figure 4.1 shows that three of the five groups are connected to standard American sociology groups: Cloward, Cohen, L. S. Cottrell, Schrag, Schuessler, Shils, Star, and Williams are in Table 3.3 and/or Figure 3.3. Unlike Parsons and Merton, Blumer, who is the intellectual leader of symbolic interactionism, does not appear in the figure. He simply does not coauthor.

Figure 4.1 reveals that symbolic interactionism is less well organized than standard American sociology. The number of coauthorships is smaller, the coauthorship networks are smaller, and parts of the large

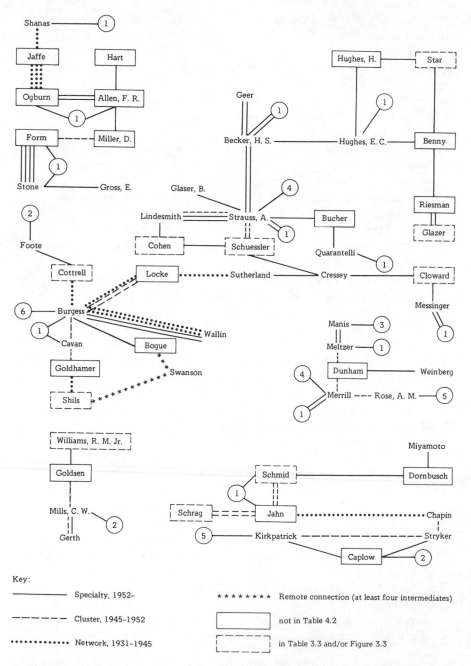

Key:

————————— Specialty, 1952–	★ ★ ★ ★ ★ ★ ★ Remote connection (at least four intermediates)
— — — — — Cluster, 1945–1952	▭ not in Table 4.2
•••••••••••••• Network, 1931–1945	⌐ ¬ in Table 3.3 and/or Figure 3.3

FIGURE 4.1 Coauthorship networks among symbolic interactionists, 1935–1965.(**Sources: American Journal of Sociology** [1966]; ASA [1961, 1966].)

network are connected only through the standard American network (the large network is linked through Karl Schuessler, a criminologist and statistician who has spent his entire career at Indiana University; see Table 3.3). Second, it is truly a loyal opposition to standard American sociology; while disagreeing with the fundamental theoretical position, many interactionists continue to publish jointly with standard American sociologists. In trying hard to cooperate with the opposition, the symbolic interactionists seem to have weakened both their social and their intellectual positions.

Symbolic interactionism was also hurt by some of the problems of social psychology in general (see Chapter 5 for more detail), and the lack of further training centers led to a general aging of the group: Table 4.2 lists 34 interactionists with degree dates in the 1950s, 11 with degree dates in the 1960s, and none in the 1970s. Goffman has had very few students.[6] He is a good participant observer, but his research has not lent itself to graduate student participation. In 1970 Strauss and B. Glaser were at medical schools. Klapp was in a department that lacks a graduate program. Miyamoto has not trained many students. Blumer's Berkeley students—with the exception of Scheff—have had little access to graduate students (see their locations on Table 4.2). There have been occasional students from one of the small interactionist groups at Indiana, Minnesota, or UCLA, for example; but in the specialty stage, symbolic interactionism has lacked a major training and research center to produce the lively core of research and new students that keep a perspective alive.

Still another social factor has been the frequently delayed degree dates for many interactionists, leaving them with significantly shortened careers. Also important was the early death (in 1969) of Arnold Rose, at fifty-one years of age. He was a major figure in symbolic interactionism, even though his use of survey and other data had made him controversial within the group. He was thus not available to take over Blumer's social and intellectual functions in the group as Blumer grew older.

By contrast with standard American sociology then (see pp. 60–64), symbolic interactionism in the specialty stage was not as successful socially.

INTELLECTUAL

The agreement between the Minnesota and Iowa groups and the structural functionalists on (1) the scientific method and (2) the determined character of behavior had brought this branch of symbolic interactionism and standard American sociology very close together. The conceptual differences between Kuhn and Blumer gradually resulted in substantial methodological differences, quite obvious by the beginning of the specialty stage; those following Kuhn used his pencil-and-paper tests, whereas Blumer's students favored interviews and participant observation (Manis and Meltzer, 1967: iv, 3, 215–216). Further methodological differences from Blumer's conceptions, which became expressed in a weak symbolic interactionism (Vaughan and Reynolds, 1970), were developed by those who were beginning to interpret survey materials and experimental data from the interactionist perspective. Rose, influenced by his experience with Myrdal, was a leader in this exploration.

The rest of symbolic interactionism moved into a form of coexistence with structural functionalism. During the late 1930s and 1940s, both groups had agreed on the subject matter of sociology (it must include study of both institutional systems and collective behavior); they had disagreed, however, on the methods of study. In that disagreement lay the grounds for potential confrontation between the two schools. Standard American sociologists' preferred methods were survey research and institutional analysis of major societal parts rather than case studies and participant observation, which were popular with interactionists.

Between 1937 and 1951, however, Parsons had gradually reshaped his viewpoint into structural functionalism, which was much more concerned with total institutions than with the behavior of the individual. By doing so, he left individual and collective behavior as subjects for the concern of symbolic interactionists and thus walked away from a potential confrontation on the subjects of precisely how people relate to institutions and whether institutions control individuals. At a result, during the specialty stage the two views coexisted as a combination—a synthesis—which became *the* view of what society was all about. Each school could discuss its area independent on the other; there was no issue to bring them into conflict.

Also important during the specialty stage was the group of content problems shared, in general, by Chicago symbolic interactionists. The National Science Foundation (NSF) had divided sociology by content matter (political sociology, economic sociology, etc.). Within the NSF's categories, Chicago symbolic interactionists were social scientists who claimed social psychology and collective behavior (see, e.g., Kornhauser, 1959) as their specialties. The institutional areas of family (e.g., Stryker, 1956), medical sociology (e.g., Emerson, 1963; Freidson, 1970a), and occupations (e.g., Hughes, 1958; Dalton, 1959) were also strong areas for symbolic interactionists. These areas are reflected in the secondary work produced during the specialty stage (see Rose, 1962; Manis and Meltzer, 1967).

During the 1950s and early 1960s, the criticism characteristic of the specialty stage gradually developed. Manis and Meltzer (1967: 495) summarize:

Among the major adverse criticisms leveled at symbolic-interaction theory have been (1) the indeterminism of many of its exponents, (2) its presumed inapplicability to broad, societal phenomena, (3) its neglect of the emotional dimension in human conduct, (4) its failure to come to grips with the unconscious, and (5) the limited researchability of some of its concepts. . . .

Put differently, interactionists encountered a crisis of analysis and method. As Lofland, a young interactionist (1970: 35) pointed out, interactionists have engaged in "analytic interruptus"; they have left unanswered questions about the usefulness of their approach. Lofland confined his remarks to those (including himself) whom he described as doing strategic analysis in the symbolic interaction tradition, but his comments are more generally applicable. He noted the need for developing a better connection between research and theory (Glaser and Strauss, 1967, exemplifies an effort to bridge this gap). Symbolic interactionists and structural functionalists were condemning one another (Bales, 1966) for failure to produce empirical research. Both parties were certainly right at that time. The research had not been done. Symbolic interaction for its part had not researched the possible means by which individuals might control either situations or one another.

This weakness of analysis gradually resulted in attacks by some who were not structural functionalists. Symbolic interactionism has been particularly criticized by the new group of everyday life sociologists. Particularly relevant here is Zimmerman and Wieder's (1970) response to Norman Denzin's (1970) attempt to show how interactionism and ethnomethodology—the major variety of everyday-life sociology—are related. Glaser and Strauss' (1967) call for the discovery of grounded theory has gone unanswered, even by the authors. Symbolic interactionism's analytic difficulties have only become more visible as radicals and ethnomethodologists have attacked both it and structural functionalism. The earlier, comfortable synthesis of symbolic interactionism with structural functionalism clearly proved inadequate once other options were available.

Intellectually, the symbolic interactionists are now caught between ethnomethodology, which is based on phenomenological philosophy rather than pragmatism (see Chapter 8), and standard American sociology. It has affinities with both, but both (see Zimmerman and Wieder, 1970) have rejected attempts to draw them into the interactionist perspective. Ethnomethodology has been as important a factor as the lack of students (noted above) in the decline of symbolic interactionism. Indeed, ethnomethodology appears to be drawing many students who might otherwise become symbolic interactionists (see Chapter 8). Garfinkel and Cicourel are now more discussed than Mead.

It is clear that the original ideas that developed within symbolic inter-actionism, like those of standard American sociology, have run their course intellectually and socially. Some symbolic interactionists are still actively publishing and, as a theory in social psychology, symbolic inter-actionism still has respectability (Stryker, 1964). As a change-maker and general orientation for sociology and as the loyal opposition to structural functionalism, however, it has come to an end. Some research-oriented analysis with a symbolic interactionist flavor will continue to be done, but the area has become socially and intellectually diffuse, and its problems are being divided up among new areas (e.g., ethnomethod-ology). An eventual redefinition for the boundaries of sociological social psychology appears to be the most likely outcome of symbolic interac-tionism's demise and the stillbirth of that part of experimental social psychology which was based on small group work.

NOTES

1. Certainly these three had the potential for developing a network from their original relationship. Cooley, however, was at Michigan with very few students. James was a psychologist, and before his death in 1910, he had become an intellectual leader in that field. Only Mead continued to teach and influence large numbers of sociologists with his particular world view, and that from a base in a philosophy department.
2. Thomas retired for several years and later taught at the New School for Social Research in New York City.
3. *The Philosophy of the Present*, edited by Arthur E. Murphy (1932); *Mind, Self and Society*, edited by Charles W. Morris (1934); *Movements of Thought in the Nineteenth Century*, edited by Merritt H. Moore (1936); and *The Philosophy of the Act*, edited by Morris (1938).
4. It should be noted, however, that Goffman received a degree in 1953 (although he was out of the country for part of that year) as did Kurt Lang, who was also important to symbolic interactionism.
5. Support for this point can be found in the figures for total publications, publications alone, publications coauthored, and number of coauthors, which I compiled in the process of researching the coauthorship networks. Symbolic interactionists average 6.8 papers for the period 1935–1965, distinctly less than the 11.2 authored by standard American sociologists. They also coauthor less: 72 percent of their papers between 1935 and 1965 are published alone, by contrast with 66 percent of those written by standard American sociologists. As I have suggested, this may be the result of different research styles. Finally, interactionists average 1.97 coauthors over 1935–1965, to the standard American sociologist's 3.81. This large discrepancy in average numbers of coauthors is a direct cause of the weakly connected coauthorship network among interactionists.
6. Goffman's books (now all in paperback editions) are very popular with

undergraduate students. His thinking is also popular with some ethnomethodologists (see Chapter 8). However, his lack of symbolic interactionist students continues.

BIBLIOGRAPHY

American Journal of Sociology.
  various   *Cumulative Index to the American Journal of Sociology 1966*;
  years   also for year 1971. Chicago: American Journal of Sociology.
  various   *Directory of Members 1959*; also for years 1963, 1967, 1970.
  years a   New York and Washington, D.C.: American Sociological Association.
  various   *Guide to Graduate Departments of Sociology 1965*; also for
  years b   years 1969, 1971. Washington, D.C.: American Sociological Association.
  various   *Index to the American Sociological Review*. Vols. 1–25 (1936–
  years c   1960) and Vols. 26–30 (1961–1965). New York and Washington, D.C.: American Sociological Association.
Bales, Robert F.
  1966   "Comment on Herbert Blumer's paper." *American Journal of Sociology* 71 (March): 545–547.
Becker, Howard S.
  1963   *Outsiders: Studies in the Sociology of Deviance*. New York: Free Press.
  1970   *Sociological Work: Method and Substance*. Chicago: Aldine.
Becker, Howard S., Everett C. Hughes, and Blanche Geer.
  1968   *Making the Grade: The Academic Side of College Life*. New York: Wiley.
Becker, Howard S., Everett C. Hughes, Blanche Geer, and Anselm L. Strauss.
  1961   *Boys in White: Student Culture in Medical School*. Chicago: University of Chicago Press.
Blumer, Herbert.
  1938   "Social psychology." Pp. 144–198 in Emerson P. Schmidt (ed.), *Man and Society: A Substantive Introduction to the Social Sciences*. Englewood Cliffs, N.J.: Prentice-Hall.
  1966   "The sociological implications of the thought of George Herbert Mead." *American Journal of Sociology* 71 (March): 535–544.
  1969   *Symbolic Interactionism: Perspective and Method*. Englewood Cliffs, N.J.: Prentice-Hall.
Blumer, Herbert, and Philip M. Hauser.
  1933   *Movies, Delinquency, and Crime*. New York: Macmillan.
Bonner, Hubert.
  1953   *Social Psychology: An Interdisciplinary Approach*. New York: Harcourt Brace Jovanovich.
Cooley, Charles H.
  1902   *Human Nature and the Social Order*. New York: Scribner.
  1909   *Social Organization: A Study of the Larger Mind*. New York: Scribner.

Coutu, Walter.
  1949 *Emergent Human Nature, A Symbolic Field Interpretation.* New York: Knopf.
Dalton, Melville.
  1959 *Men Who Manage: Fusions of Feeling and Theory in Administration.* New York: Wiley.
Daniels, Arlene.
  1970 *Academics on the Line.* San Francisco: Jossey-Bass.
Davis, Fred.
  1959 "The cab driver and his fare: facets of a fleeting relationship." *American Journal of Sociology* 65 (September): 158–165.
Denzin, Norman.
  1969 "Symbolic interactionism and ethnomethodology: a proposed synthesis." *American Sociological Review* 34 (December): 922–934.
  1970 "The methodologies of symbolic interaction: a critical review of research techniques." Pp. 447–465 in Gregory P. Stone and Harvey A. Farberman (eds.), *Social Psychology Through Symbolic Interaction.* Waltham, Mass.: Ginn-Blaisdell.
Dubin, Robert.
  1965 *Leadership and Productivity: Some Facts of Industrial Life.* San Francisco: Chandler.
Emerson, Joan.
  1963 Social Functions of Humor in a Hospital Setting. Unpublished Ph.D. dissertation. Berkeley: University of California at Berkeley.
Faris, R. E. L.
  1952 *Social Psychology.* New York: Ronald.
Frazier, E. Franklin.
  1957 *Black Bourgeoisie.* New York: Free Press.
Freidson, Eliot.
  1970a *Professional Dominance: The Social Structure of Medical Care.* New York: Atherton.
  1970b *Profession of Medicine: A Study of the Sociology of Applied Knowledge.* New York: Dodd, Mead.
Gerth, Hans H., and C. Wright Mills.
  1953 *Character and Social Structure: The Psychology of Social Institutions.* New York: Harcourt Brace Jovanovich.
Glaser, Barney G., and Anselm L. Strauss.
  1965 *Awareness of Dying.* Chicago: Aldine.
  1967 *The Discovery of Grounded Theory: Strategies for Qualitative Research.* Chicago: Aldine.
Goffman, Erving.
  1959 *The Presentation of Self in Everyday Life.* Garden City, N.Y.: Doubleday.
  1961a *Asylums.* Garden City, N.Y.: Doubleday.
  1961b *Encounters.* Indianapolis: Bobbs-Merrill.
  1967 *Interaction Ritual: Essays on Face-to-Face Behavior.* Garden City, N.Y.: Doubleday.

Gouldner, Alvin W.
   1965   *Enter Plato: Classical Greece and the Origins of Social Theory.* New
          York: Basic Books.
   1970   *The Coming Crisis of Western Sociology.* New York: Basic Books.
Gross, Edward, and Gregory P. Stone.
   1964   "Embarrassment and the analysis of role requirements." *American
          Journal of Sociology* 70 (July): 1–15.
Heiss, Jerold.
   1968   *Family Roles and Interaction: An Anthology.* Chicago: Rand Mc-
          Nally.
House, Floyd N.
   1936   *The Development of Sociology.* New York: McGraw-Hill.
Hughes, Everett C.
   1958   *Men and Their Work.* New York: Free Press.
James, William.
   1890   *The Principles of Psychology.* New York: Holt.
Killian, Lewis M., and Charles Grigg.
   1964   *Racial Crisis in America: Leadership in Conflict.* Englewood Cliffs,
          N.J.: Prentice-Hall.
Klapp, Orrin E.
   1962   *Heroes, Villains and Fools: The Changing American Character.* Engle-
          wood Cliffs, N.J.: Prentice-Hall.
Kornhauser, William.
   1959   *The Politics of Mass Society.* New York: Free Press.
Krueger, Ernest T., and Walter C. Reckless.
   1930   *Social Psychology.* New York: Longmans, Green.
Kuhn, Manford H.
   1964   "Major trends in symbolic interaction theory in the past twenty-five
          years." *The Sociological Quarterly* 5 (Winter): 61–84.
Lang, Kurt, and Gladys E. Lang.
   1961   *Collective Dynamics.* New York: Crowell.
Lee, Grace Chin.
   1945   *George Herbert Mead.* New York: King's Crown.
Lindesmith, Alfred R.
   1947   *Opiate Addiction.* Bloomington, Ind.: Principia.
Lindesmith, Alfred R., and Anselm L. Strauss.
   1956   *Social Psychology.* New York: Dryden. (1st ed., 1949.)
Lofland, John.
   1970   "Interactionist imagery and analytic interruptus." Pp. 35–45 in T.
          Shibutani (ed.), *Human Nature and Collective Behavior.* Englewood
          Cliffs, N.J.: Prentice-Hall.
Manis, Jerome G., and Bernard N. Meltzer (eds.).
   1967   *Symbolic Interaction: A Reader in Social Psychology.* Boston: Allyn
          & Bacon.
Martindale, Don A.
   1960   *The Nature and Types of Sociological Theory.* Boston: Houghton
          Mifflin.

102 SYMBOLIC INTERACTIONISM

Mead, George Herbert.
1932 *The Philosophy of the Present.* Arthur E. Murphy (ed.). Chicago: Open Court.
1934 *Mind, Self, and Society from the Standpoint of a Social Behaviorist.* Charles W. Morris (ed.). Chicago: University of Chicago Press.
1936 *Movements of Thought in the Nineteenth Century.* Merritt H. Moore (ed.). Chicago: University of Chicago Press.
1938 *The Philosophy of the Act.* Charles W. Morris (ed.). Chicago: University of Chicago Press.
Miyamoto, S. Frank.
1939 *Social Solidarity Among the Japanese in Seattle.* Seattle, Wash.: The University of Washington.
Myrdal, Gunnar.
1944 *An American Dilemma: The Negro Problem and Modern Democracy.* New York: Harper & Row.
Parsons, Talcott.
1937 *The Structure of Social Action: A Study in Social Theory with-Special Reference to a Group of Recent European Writers.* New York: McGraw-Hill.
Pfuetze, Paul E.
1954 *The Social Self.* New York: Bookman.
Reck, Andrew J. (ed.).
1964 *Selected Writings: George Herbert Mead.* Indianapolis: Bobbs-Merrill.
Reckless, Walter C.
1940 *Criminal Behavior.* New York: McGraw-Hill.
Reynolds, Larry T., Ted R. Vaughan, Janice M. Reynolds, and Leon Warshay.
1970 "The self in symbolic interaction theory: an examination of the social sources of the conceptual diversity." Pp. 422–438 in Larry T. Reynolds and Janice M. Reynolds (eds.), *The Sociology of Sociology.* New York: McKay.
Rose, Arnold M.
1962 *Human Behavior and Social Processes: An Interactionist Approach.* Boston: Houghton Mifflin.
Rose, Arnold M., and Arthur E. Prell.
1955 "Does the punishment fit the crime? A study in social valuation." *American Journal of Sociology* 61 (November): 247–259.
Roth, Julius A.
1963 *Timetables: Structuring the Passage of Time in Hospital Treatment and Other Careers.* Indianapolis: Bobbs-Merrill.
Schwartz, Michael, and Sheldon Stryker.
1971 *Deviance, Selves and Others.* Washington, D.C.: American Sociological Association (Rose Series).
Shibutani, Tamotsu.
1961 *Society and Personality: An Interactionist Approach to Social Psychology.* Englewood Cliffs, N.J.: Prentice-Hall.

1970   *Human Nature and Collective Behavior: Papers in Honor of Herbert Blumer*. Englewood Cliffs, N.J.: Prentice-Hall.
Shils, Edward A.
1970   "The history of sociology." *Daedalus: The Making of Modern Science: Biographical Studies* 99 (Fall): 760–825.
Solomon, David.
1969   "The soldierly self and the peace keeping role: Canadian officers in peace-keeping forces." Pp. 52–69 in Jacques A. A. van Doorn (ed.), *Military Profession and Military Regimes: Commitments and Conflicts*. The Hague: Mouton.
Stone, Gregory P., and Harvey A. Farberman (ed.).
1970   *Social Psychology Through Symbolic Interaction*. Waltham, Mass.: Ginn-Blaisdell.
Strauss, Anselm L. (ed.).
1956   *The Social Psychology of George Herbert Mead*. Chicago: University of Chicago Press.
Stryker, Sheldon.
1956   "Relationships of married offspring to their parents: a test of Mead's theory." *American Journal of Sociology* 62 (November): 308–319.
1964   "The interactional and situational approaches." Pp. 125–170 in Harold T. Christensen (ed.), *Handbook of Marriage and the Family*. Chicago: Rand McNally.
Swanson, Guy E.
1960   *The Birth of the Gods*. Ann Arbor: University of Michigan Press.
Swanson, Guy E., Theodore M. Newcomb, and Eugene L. Hartley.
1952   *Readings in Social Psychology*. Prepared for the Committee on the Teaching of Social Psychology of the Society for the Psychological Study of Social Issues. New York: Holt.
Thomas, W. I. (ed.).
1909   *Source Book for Social Origins, Ethnological Materials, Psychological Standpoint: Classified and Annotated Bibliographies for the Interpretation of Savage Society*. Chicago: The University of Chicago Press.
Thomas, W. I., and Florian Znaniecki.
1956   *The Polish Peasant in Europe and America*. 2 vols., rev. ed. New York: Dover.
Turner, Ralph.
1956   "Role taking, role standpoint and reference group behavior." *American Journal of Sociology* 61 (January): 316–328.
Turner, Ralph, and Lewis M. Killian.
1957   *Collective Behavior*. Englewood Cliffs, N.J.: Prentice-Hall.
Vaughan, Ted R., and Larry T. Reynolds.
1970   "The sociology of symbolic interactionism." Reprinted from *The American Sociologist* 3 (August, 1968): 208–214, as pp. 324–339 in Larry T. Reynolds and Janice M. Reynolds (eds.), *The Sociology of Sociology*. New York: McKay.

Zimmerman, Don H., and D. Lawrence Wieder.
   1970   "Ethnomethodology and the problem of order: comment on Denzin."
          Pp. 285–298 in Jack D. Douglas (ed.), *Understanding Everyday
          Life: Toward the Reconstruction of Sociological Knowledge*. Chicago:
          Aldine.

CHAPTER 5
SMALL GROUP THEORY
The Light That Failed

Social and intellectual properties
of small group theory

Intellectual leader	Kurt Lewin (until 1947)
Social organization leader	None
Research centers	Harvard
	Iowa
	MIT
	Michigan
Training centers for students	Harvard
	MIT (1945–1947)
Paradigm content	Explanation of the effects of social context on the psychological makeup of participants; dynamics of group development
Successes	Lewin, Lippitt, and R. K. White, "Patterns of Aggressive Behavior in Experimentally Created 'Social Climates'" (1939)
	Bales, **Interaction Process Analysis** (1950)
	Homans, **The Human Group** (1950)
Program statement	None
Examples of secondary work	Cartwright and Zander, **Group Dynamics** (1953)
	Hare, **Handbook of Small Group Research** (1962)
	Hare, Borgatta, and Bales, **Small Groups** (1955)
Example of critical work	McGrath and Altman, **Small Group Research: A Synthesis and Critique of the Field** (1966)
Text	None

Not every theory group that becomes a definable social and intellectual entity and transforms itself from one stage to another survives long enough to become a specialty. Small group theory exemplifies an area that failed. The model of group development presented in Chapter 2 suggests that failure rather than success is the likely ultimate outcome of group development. It is also true, however, that most research which actively affects a field is done within ultimately successful groups. The small group theorists are unusual in that, although failing as a theory group, they nevertheless left an important mark on the sociology literature. Indeed, one bibliography (Hare, 1962) listed 1,382 items published by these social scientists. This theoretical literature was produced by a group which had an incomplete social and intellectual structure and whose members have now diffused into a number of applied areas. Numerous well-known, empirical generalizations have developed from these group applications, but no general theory of group processes and effects has evolved.

The outline on p. 105 indicates that the small group theorists were blessed with most of the characteristics necessary for a successful group. This chapter's task, then, is to explain (1) the ways in which this group was not a success and (2) why the failure occurred. Why did a theory that adequately explained all the material of interest to this group fail to develop? Despite what are, in retrospect, obvious weaknesses in structural–functional and symbolic interaction theory, there is no question that both areas developed comprehensive, analytic theoretical perspectives. Furthermore, the social growth of both groups paralleled their intellectual growth. The small group theorists, by contrast, developed no single, analytic theory.

The small group theorists focused on social groups including two or more persons but less than a whole society, usually less than 15. Table 5.1 summarizes the highlights of this group's development. The normal and network stages proceeded in customary fashion; the cluster stage was incomplete, and a specialty stage within sociology never occurred. Following discussion of these stages, I examine the reasons for this group's failure and the future of its intellectual concerns.

NORMAL STAGE:
TO 1945

The normal stage shows four developments, two social and two intellectual, that eventuated in small group study. First, a series of professions grew up which either used the results of small group research or contributed to it. Second, several institutions provided a favorable climate for this research. The development of empirical social science, particu-

TABLE 5.1   Social and intellectual highlights in the
development of small group theory

Stage	Social	Intellectual
Normal: to 1945	Independent developments of both professions and institutions	Development of empirical social science; specific development of sociograms
Network: 1945–1950	MIT and Harvard become major research and teaching centers	Lewin, **Field Theory** (1951); ideas were influential before that date No agreement on an intellectual focus
Cluster: 1950–1958	Harvard is the major center; cluster gradually dissipates	Multiple theory starts, but no theory completed Increased emphasis on empirical findings

larly within psychology, was intellectually important, as was the specific set of techniques (e.g., sociograms) that became incorporated into small group work.

SOCIAL

During the 1930s a series of professional areas developed which had particular use for the results of small group work. These included social work and group psychotherapy, as well as the burgeoning management concerns of education and administration. Social work awaited the development of social welfare on a large scale during the Depression, but the appearance of great numbers of social workers, who needed to understand family and peer-group effects (see discussion of Whyte below), provided one important impetus for small group research. Group psychotherapy was developed quite accidentally by Pratt in Boston. For troubled individuals, the substitution (for professional guidance) of discussion with others similarly troubled had proved extremely useful when the professionals at a particular facility were overloaded, ineffective, or both (Mills, 1968: 47). Classroom situations were characterized by dynamics of which expert teachers had long been aware. However, with the impact of decreasingly authoritarian teaching systems and increasingly large numbers of professionally trained educators, the ways in which classroom situations developed became a major concern (Gronlund, 1959). Indeed, a much later survey of sociograms (Davis, 1970) determined that the majority had been done on classrooms. Finally, the development of business schools and the concomitant growth of human relations and industrial psychology were also important. One of the first intensive group studies was done by Elton Mayo and associates at the Hawthorne, N.J., plant of Western Electric (Roethlisberger and Dickson, 1939).

Supportive institutions that gave small group work a base for experimentation developed within both educational and industrial institutions. At Lewin's Child Welfare Research Station at Iowa, the primary interest was in education and social work, whereas the Group Dynamics Center at Massachusetts Institute of Technology (MIT) was supported by MIT's general concern with industrial management.

INTELLECTUAL

The intellectual foundation for later work had been well laid. The Hawthorne studies had recognized the effects on productivity of primary ties within a work group. This finding, plus the later discovery of group norms which limit productivity, represented a major shift in the way that management was studied. Jose L. Moreno had written *Sociometry* (1934), in which he presented new techniques and made powerful claims for the psychological effects of groups. Muzafer Sherif (1936) had developed a theory of norms supported by experimental manipulation, in natural and laboratory settings, of norm formation within groups. At the same time, Theodore M. Newcomb was developing methods for analyzing small groups in "natural settings" by examining the formation and changes of norms among girls at Bennington College (Newcomb, 1942). In 1937 William F. Whyte began his three and one-half year study, based on Harvard, of natural groups within an Italian community in Somerville, Mass. (Whyte, 1943). Whyte's study dramatically revealed the existence of group effects on performance.

Although each of these pieces of research was important in establishing the area, the most influential work was done by Kurt Lewin. Lewin, R. Lippett, and R. K. White (1939) combined a theoretical sweep with careful laboratory study of the effects of different group compositions on behavior. Their study showed that it was possible to use social conditions in a laboratory setting to change the psychological states of persons participating in a group situation.

These persons, research efforts, and institutions were much more independent of each other than were the parallel components of the normal stages for standard American sociology and symbolic interactionism. The war broke up the Iowa group and stopped other small group studies (except for some being done by the Army) until 1945.

NETWORK STAGE:
1945–1950

The network stage of development began in 1945, when Lewin founded the Research Center for Group Dynamics at MIT. During the same year Robert F. Bales joined Harvard's staff.

SOCIAL

The core of small group theorists is listed in Table 5.2. All are high producers (five or more entries) as shown by Hare's (1962) bibliography. Twenty-nine are part of a coauthoring network composed of two strongly intraconnected groups joined only weakly (see Figure 5.1, p. 117). One of the two groups includes largely sociological social psychologists (grouped around Bales) and the second, psychological social psychologists (grouped around Lewin and his students). Both groups focused on small group research but from different perspectives. The two groups are marked separately in Table 5.2. Also included in the table are six high producers who coauthored no papers, and 11 others whose coauthors are not further listed in Hare (1962). Hence these 17 do not link up with the network.

Kurt Lewin's death in 1947 deprived the group of its intellectual leader. On the surface it appears that his absence bolstered the spread of small group work. In 1949 Dorwin Cartwright and Alvin Zander moved the Center from MIT to the University of Michigan, where it became one part of the Institute for Social Research. Not all members of the MIT group transferred to Michigan; for example, Table 5.2 shows that Alex A. Bavelas, a theoretically inclined member of the original group with Lewin at Iowa, chose to remain at MIT. In any case, the Michigan group became active, and the MIT group gradually disintegrated.

In addition to the MIT and Michigan centers, there was a group at Harvard (see locations, Table 5.2). In 1946 MIT had the largest number of persons—eight. Harvard and Michigan had three each. At that point we would have expected a cluster to develop at MIT, if one was going to develop. By 1950, however, the picture had changed radically. Michigan had ten persons, Harvard eight, and MIT one. Although, as I have already noted, communication is difficult to demonstrate in the specific, it is highly likely that the formal colleague ties of the 1946 MIT group were maintained through informal communication after some members of that group moved to other locations (mainly Michigan). Nevertheless, the outstanding feature of this group's network stage is not informal communication but the unusual number of formal ties (networks are usually characterized by the dominance of informal communication ties).

TABLE 5.2   Important small group theorists: degree (date and place) and selected job locations

Name	Ph.D. Date	Ph.D. Place	1939
[a] Asch, S.	ni	ni	ni
[b] Back, Kurt W.	1949	MIT	*
[c] Bales, Robert F.	1945	HARV	*
Bass, B.	1949	OHST	*
[a] Bavelas, Alex A.	1948	MIT	*
Berkowitz, L.	1951	MICH	*
[a] Bion, W. R. (British)	*	*	*
[b] Blake, R. R.	1947	TEX	*
[c] Borgatta, Edgar F.	1952	NYU	*
[a] Bovard, E.	1949	MICH	*
[a] Caplow, Theodore	1946	MINN	*
[c] Carter, Lewis F.	1941	PRIN	WASH
[b] Cartwright, Dorwin	1940	HARV	HARV
Chapple, E.	1933	HARV	HARV
[c] Cottrell, Jr., Leonard S.	1933	CHIC	CORN
Deutsch, Morton	1948	MIT	*
[b] Festinger, Leon	1942	IOWA	*
[b] French, J. R. P.	1940	HARV	HARV
Guetzkow, Harold	1948	MICH	*
[b] Harary, Frank (mathematician)	1948	BERK	*
[c] Hare, A. Paul	1951	CHIC	*
[b] Homans, George C.	none	none	HARV
[d] Jennings, Helen H.	1942	COL	*
[b] Kelley, Harold H.	1948	MIT	*
[c] Kogan, N.	ni	ni	ni
[c] Lanzetta, John T.	1952	ROCH	*
[b] Lewin, Kurt	ni	ni	IOWA
[b] Lindzey, Gardner	1949	HARV	*
[b] Lippitt, R.	1940	IOWA	IOWA
Luchins, A. S.	1940	NYU	NEWS
[c] Mills, Theodore M.	1952	HARV	*
[d] Moreno, José L.	1917	VIEN	ni
[b] Newcomb, Theodore M.	1929	COL	BENN
[b] Riecken, Jr., Henry W.	1950	HARV	*
[b] Schachter, Stanley	1950	MICH	*
Shaw, M.	1953	WISC	*
[b] Sherif, Muzafer	1935	COL	ANKA
[c] Slater, Philip	1955	HARV	*
[c] Strodtbeck, Fred L.	1950	HARV	*

Sources: AJS (various years); **American Men of Science** (1968); ASR (various years a, b, c). Table 5.2 lists all the high producers (five or more entries) from Hare's (1962) bibliography of the small groups area; this bibliography includes 1382 items covering the period 1900–1960.

[a] Works alone.
[b] Psychological social psychologist.
[c] Sociological social psychologist.
[d] Another group of social psychologists.

Job held in academic year ending in					
1946	1950	1953	1955	1959	1970
ni	ni	ni	ni	ni	ni
MIT	CENS	COL	PURI	DUKE	DUKE
HARV	HARV	HARV	HARV	HARV	HARV
OHST	LSU	LSU	LSU	LSU	ROCH
MIT	MIT	MIT	MIT	res	ni
NYU	MICH	res	WISC	WISC	WISC
*	*	*	*	*	*
TEX	TEX	TEX	TEX	TEX	TEX
*	HARV	HARV	RUSS	CORN	WISC
MICH	TORO	TORO	TORO	res	QUCC
MINN	MINN	MINN	MINN	MINN	COL
ROCH	ROCH	res	res	res	res
MIT	MICH	MICH	MICH	MICH	MICH
res	res	res	res	res	res
CORN	CORN	RUSS	RUSS	RUSS	UNC
MIT	NYU	NYU	NYU	res	ni
MIT	MICH	MINN	STAN	STAN	NEWS
res	MICH	MICH	MICH	MICH	MICH
MICH	MICH	CIT	CIT	NWU	NWU
BERK	MICH	MICH	MICH	res	MICH
*	CHIC	HARV	HARV	HARV	HAVE
HARV	HARV	HARV	HARV	HARV	HARV
STAN	STAN	BROO	BROO	BROO	ni
MIT	MICH	YALE	YALE	MINN	USC
ni	ni	ni	ni	ni	ni
*	*	res	res	DELA	DART
MIT	d				
HARV	HARV	HARV	HARV	MINN	TEX
MIT	MICH	MICH	MICH	MICH	MICH
YESH	MCGI	MCGI	ORE	FLA	ALBA
*	HARV	HARV	HARV	HARV	BUFF
ni	ni	ni	ni	self	self
MICH	MICH	MICH	MICH	MICH	MICH
*	HARV	HARV	MINN	NSF	SSRC
*	MINN	MINN	MINN	MINN	COL
*	*	JHU	JHU	MIT	FLA
PRIN	OKLA	OKLA	OKLA	OKLA	PNST
*	*	HARV	HARV	HARV	BRAN
UCLA	HARV	YALE	CHIC	CHIC	CHIC

TABLE 5.2 (continued)

| Name | Ph.D. | | 1939 |
	Date	Place	
[b] Tagiuri, Renato	1951	HARV	*
Talland, G. A.	1953	LOND	*
Thelen, H.	ni	ni	ni
[b] Thibaut, John W.	1949	MIT	*
Torrence, E. Paul	1951	MICH	*
[b] White, R. K.	ni	ni	IOWA
[a] Whyte, William F.	1942	CHIC	*
[b] Zander, Alvin	1942	MICH	MICH

Key:

		DART	Dartmouth College
		DELA	University of Delaware
ALBA	State University of New York,	DUKE	Duke University
	Albany	FLA	University of Florida
ANKA	Ankara University, Turkey	HARB	Harvard Business School
BENN	Bennington College	HARV	Harvard University
BERK	University of California, Berkeley	HAVE	Haverford College
BOSU	Boston University	IOWA	University of Iowa
BRAN	Brandeis University	JHU	Johns Hopkins University
BROO	Brooklyn College	KAST	Kansas State University
BUFF	State University of New York,	LOND	University of London
	Buffalo	LSU	Louisiana State University
CENS	Bureau of the Census	MCGI	McGill University
CIT	Carnegie Institute of Technology	MICH	University of Michigan
COL	Columbia University	MINN	University of Minnesota
CORN	Cornell University	MIT	Massachusetts Institute of
d	Deceased		Technology

Also unusual—perhaps just another way of looking at the many formal ties—is the large number of faculty at both Harvard and Michigan. By 1950 the Harvard faculty included Bales, Borgatta, Homans, Lindzey, and Riecken. In addition, these five faculty had three students who show up in Table 5.2: Mills, Strodtbeck, and Tagiuri. Michigan was even more top-heavy: Cartwright, Festinger, French, Guetzkow, Harary, Kelley, Lippitt, Newcomb, and Zander were all on the staff, but only one of their students (Berkowitz) appears in Table 5.2. Neither standard American sociology nor symbolic interactionism was able to gather this many faculty until each was well into the cluster stage. Purely on the basis of social properties, therefore, the numerous faculty at both Harvard and Michigan would lead us to expect the rapid development of successful clusters. The relative lack of students at this stage might well be overcome during the cluster stage.

As Table 5.2 and Figure 5.1 reveal, the groups at Harvard and Michigan were internally coordinated but following separate research lines. The fundamental reason for this situation is obvious in Table 5.2: The Harvard and Michigan groups were composed of sociological social psychologists and psychological social psychologists, respectively. In retro-

Job held in academic year ending in					
1946	1950	1953	1955	1959	1970
*	HARV	HARV	HARV	HARB	HARB
*	*	res	res	res	ni
ni	ni	ni	ni	ni	ni
*	BOSU	HARV	UNC	UNC	UNC
*	KAST	res	res	MINN	ni
ni	ni	ni	ni	ni	ni
CHIC	CORN	CORN	CORN	CORN	CORN
SPRC	MICH	MICH	MICH	MICH	MICH

NEWS	New School for Social Research		RUSS	Russell Sage Foundation
ni	No information		self	Self-employed
NSF	National Science Foundation		SPRC	Springfield College
NWU	Northwestern University		SSRC	Social Science Research Council
NYU	New York University		STAN	Stanford University
OHST	Ohio State University		TEX	University of Texas
OKLA	University of Oklahoma		TORO	University of Toronto
ORE	University of Oregon		UCLA	University of California,
PNST	Pennsylvania State University			Los Angeles
PRIN	Princeton University		UNC	University of North Carolina
PURI	University of Puerto Rico		VIEN	University of Vienna
QUCC	Queensborough Community		WISC	University of Wisconsin
	College		YALE	Yale University
res	Miscellaneous research position		YESH	Yeshiva University
ROCH	University of Rochester		*	Not in system

spect, we can see that the lack of coordination was permitting research to drift without a central focus.

The multiple applications possible from small group research linked researchers quite naturally with the group dynamics movement (see Back, 1972), which acted as a force pulling the group apart both socially and intellectually before it was properly started. The group dynamics work was centralized in the National Training Laboratory (NTL) in Bethel, Maine. There were exchanges of personnel and expertise between NTL and the MIT Group Dynamics Center, and the MIT people who went to Michigan retained their ties with NTL. In addition, the practical experience of the NTL group was always available to solve problems. This emphasis on the practical drained off support and people from the attempt to develop a systematic understanding of small group behavior.

INTELLECTUAL

Usually during the network stage, an area's previously independent lines of development become knit together by a mutual awareness; in addition, the circumstances of mutual citation and use of one another as trusted assessors are factors that begin to cut off members from the rest of the discipline (or in this case, disciplines). This process usually begins moving the group toward development of an independent theoretical position. For small group study, though, this degree of integration was not achieved. The only numerous linkages other than colleague and student–teacher relations were coauthorship relations (see Figure 5.1). Lewin had started teaching a group of students (e.g., Kurt W. Back, Morton Deutsch, Harold Kelley; see Table 5.2) who later graduated possessing the basics of his perspective. There were also many small intellectual successes (e.g., Bales, 1950; Homans, 1950[1]), but the research groups were largely unconnected. Hence no theoretical sweep was developing. Lewin's ideas were collected posthumously into one book (Lewin, 1951) and published, but although it shows a systematic intent, this work never influenced small group research as Mead's posthumously published lectures did symbolic interactionism.

Overall, a pattern had begun to develop in which researchers were producing small-scale studies with limited goals. Bales had developed the *Interaction Process Analysis* (IPA) system (1950), which emphasized observational techniques. First, data had to be collected on several groups, over several time periods. The data were recorded on tape, by notes, or with the IPA recorder, and data reduction and analysis were begun. Much effort was spent on data display techniques (e.g., graphs of interactions). Often the lengthy efforts required made data analysis and theory building prohibitively time-consuming. Regardless of whether time pressure is the reason, though, the emphasis of much small group work has been on the small research team (one or two persons) observing a specific number of groups and writing them up in a paper that employs a small number of variables and rigid statistical tests, and contains a discussion section in which the results are stretched and prodded into some shape (McGrath and Altman, 1966: 53–54).

Certainly this choice of research style partly reflects the ways of psychologists, who were accustomed to it. Sociologists acquired it as they became familiar with psychological literature. Even Lewin's work was not fully systematic, although a systematic intent can be seen in *Field Theory* (1951).

Other models for work (e.g., extended studies, summary books, and analytical models) were relatively rare, although Festinger, Schachter, and Back (1950) did provide one. Festinger, a clever observer and experimentalist, based his theoretical analysis on startling observational results of extended studies (e.g., of a housing project, Festinger et al., 1950).

By 1950 there had still been no effort to develop a central analytical model. Nevertheless, at the end of the network stage in 1950, the group looked quite exciting. Several scientists (e.g., Bales, Festinger, and Homans) were competing for intellectual leadership. The group's work was being directly applied in both group therapy (e.g., Bion, 1948, 1952) and management (e.g., Guetzkow, 1951). The group had two centers, Michigan and Harvard. In retrospect, however, we note the absence of a program statement, an intellectual leader (after Lewin's death), and a social organization leader. The centers were internally coherent, but they did not mesh either socially or intellectually. Lacking these necessities, no coherent research pattern was developing across the whole of small group research.

CLUSTER STAGE:
1950–1958

By 1950 and the beginning of what should have been the cluster stage, small group research appeared to be progressing well. The MIT center was gone, but Harvard and Michigan had reached the minimum personnel level necessary for a cluster. Numerous researchers were working in the area, and there was a sense of excitement. By 1958, however, this atmosphere had vanished. There were few students, and the Harvard center had disintegrated. Intellectually, the area had not progressed much since the early 1950s, and much of the work was becoming routine. Examination of events after 1950 reveals an explanation for this occurrence; these events clearly show the effects of small group theory's earlier social and intellectual deficiencies.

SOCIAL

The Harvard group, strong in 1950, had increased its numbers to ten by 1953. Indeed, to an outsider this group would have looked—in numbers at least—very much like Harvard's cluster of structural functionalists in 1949. The 1950 cluster (minus Strodtbeck) was still intact and had been joined by Slater (a student) and Hare and Thibaut (faculty; see Table 5.2). Significantly, though, Slater was the only student of later note. By 1953 the Michigan group's membership had dropped to six: Berkowitz was no longer a student; Festinger had moved to Minnesota (to join Caplow and Schachter); Guetzkow had gone to the Carnegie Institute of Technology; and Kelley had shifted to Yale. Clearly the Michigan group had not retained its strength long enough to be termed a cluster. As of 1953, then, Harvard's was the only strong group. Furthermore, the data show that no other location (save Minnesota, with three) had more than one small group theorist.

Nevertheless, by 1955 the lack of students had begun to weaken the

Harvard cluster. The faculty was down to six (Bales, Hare, Homans, Lindzey, Mills, and Tagiuri), and Slater, the one graduate student, was finishing degree work. Michigan was still the same size and still had the same people. Minnesota had also remained the same size (although Riecken had replaced Festinger, who by 1955 had moved to Stanford).

In 1959 Harvard was down to five small group researchers—Bales, Hare, Homans, Mills, and Slater—all faculty. Michigan, minus Harary, was down to five. Minnesota had increased to five: Caplow, Kelley, Lindzey, Schachter, and Torrence—all faculty. The process that increased Minnesota's size, however, was an increase in colleague relations, not the addition of students and the creation of student–teacher relations. Indeed, the relationship underlying all these shifts in visible structure is colleagueship; previously trained people are simply moving from one location to another. Without students, one location's gain is another's loss. The largest loser in the whole process was not individual locations but the potential that lay in small group theory.

Certainly these locations may have been turning out students who are not listed in Table 5.2. However, many students, particularly from Michigan, may have gone completely into psychology, thus removing themselves from any importance to group development in sociology. More to the point, however, whatever students were graduated did not subsequently produce enough small group research to be important to the profession. That is, none is listed as a producer of five or more articles or books in Hare's (1962) very comprehensive bibliography.

The social reasons for this disintegration—as well as the collapse of the area in general—are (1) the fractionated, noncooperative nature of research; (2) social psychology's interdisciplinary status, with both sociology and psychology gradually providing fewer positions for social psychologists over time; and (3) the lack of students and both intellectual and social leaders in this period (plus the cumulative effects of this lack prior to 1950).

The fractionation of the field is reflected in Figure 5.1, which sets forth coauthorship links among small group workers. These links produce five weakly connected groups within the general network. The first includes Kogan, Tagiuri, Blake, and colleagues, who were primarily concerned with cognitive processes. The second (Festinger, Schachter, Back, Thibaut, Kelley, Brehm, and others) represents the core of Lewin's MIT students. The third is Carter and Lanzetta's group; their interest has been primarily in equity problems (whose focus is determining the rates of return for certain activities under specific conditions). The fourth group, the old Iowa group which moved to MIT, includes Lewin, Lippitt, Zander, Cartwright, and others. The fifth group is basically Harvard's sociological social psychologists: Bales, Borgatta, Hare, Mills, Slater, Strodtbeck. These five groups are more tightly connected internally than they

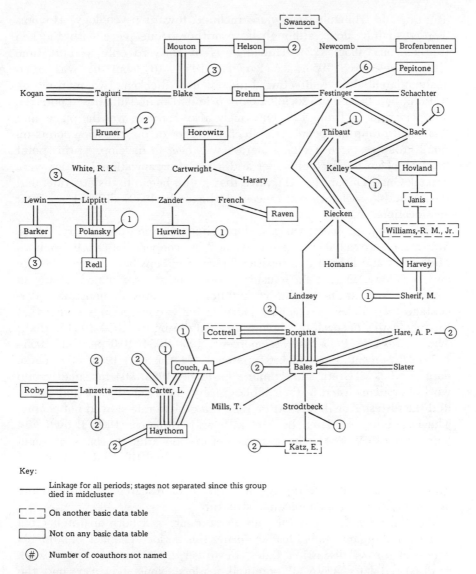

FIGURE 5.1 Coauthorship network among small group researchers, c. 1935–1960. (**Source:** Hare [1962].)

are to one another, but they are all interconnected. Of those in the table, 64 percent (29/45) appear in the figure.

The focus at Harvard, which had had the cluster's stage's most promising group, was similarly fractionated. Bales, Borgatta, Hare, Mills, and Strodtbeck, whose principal orientation was sociological, worked together, coauthoring several papers and bibliographies. Lindzey, Riecken,

Taguiri, and Thibault were more inclined toward psychology. Homans worked mainly alone, although he coauthored one piece with Riecken (see Parsons, 1956: 122). Thibaut was at Harvard only a short time (July 1951–March 1953; see Parsons, 1956: 76), but he was obviously influential in redirecting Lindzey and Riecken, two men whose training had been more sociologically oriented than Thibaut's[2] (note the *b* superscripts in Table 5.2). Obviously also, Harvard was the place, and this small group the people, to effect a merger of the two viewpoints on small group research if such a merger was ever to develop. At this point the lack of an intellectual leader and a social organizational leader were crucial. Once Thibaut left Harvard, that group began to disintegrate, and the favorable social circumstances of the early 1950s did not recur at any location.

The second problem was social psychology's interdisciplinary status. Many social psychologists were trained in cooperative efforts such as Michigan's and Harvard's interdisciplinary programs between psychology and sociology. During the cluster period, social psychology's status in sociology was at its height, as publication figures demonstrate. Percentages of articles in sociology journals for various periods reveal that the whole area of social psychology peaked during the 1950–1954 period.[3] The figures are: 1945–1949, 3.3 percent; 1950–1954, 10.0 percent; 1955–1959, 9.6 percent; 1960–1964, 6.2 percent (McCartney, 1970: 33). These data parallel McGrath and Altman's findings (1966: 50) for small group work. For items listed in their bibliography, the 1950–1955 period exhibited the fastest growth rate. After 1958 the growth rate slowed noticeably. The last date considered by McGrath and Altman is 1960. Brown and Gilmartin (1969: 284), citing years before and after the peak of small group research, report that only three articles in 1940–1941 and two of 202 articles in two sociological journals for 1965–1966 dealt with small groups.[4] These data are typical of a group of researchers participating only in the normal communication structure.

The third problem was the lack of students and both an intellectual and a social organizational leader during this period. The lack of students needs no further discussion. Bales, Festinger, and Homans, whose work is discussed later, were all potential leaders. None, however, had the record of continuing research success or the concentrated set of intellectual concerns that creates an intellectual leader. The loss of Lewin, the early intellectual leader, meant that serious intellectual problems did not receive the focused attention they merited.

Given the lack of direction from a social organizational leader, the existence of multiple centers and several journals contributed to a diffusion of effort rather than to the strength that can result from control of several power bases. It might be argued that the small group researchers "jumped the gun," moving from network status into a sort of specialty stage (semi-institutionalized at Harvard and Michigan in interdisciplinary departments) without going through a real cluster stage. If so, it would also have to be argued (contrary to Ben-David, 1960) that institutionalization is not a vitalizing force.

INTELLECTUAL

During the cluster stage the same intellectual pattern of early success and later fractionation shows in the narrow, empirical style of small group work, the emphasis on bibliographies made necessary by the scattered literature, and the continuing, fundamental division between sociologically and psychologically oriented researchers.

The data suggest clearly that a successful cluster does not inevitably develop if a group of persons who are interested in the same subject at the same time are at the same location. The group must also agree on its research goals (this group did not), and it must have leaders to state and enforce research directions. Many of the important small group researchers were at Harvard from 1951 to about 1956. There was also a sense of excitement at Harvard. Bales was using his interaction process analysis, and Homans had just written *The Human Group* (1950). The fractionation was not necessarily bad; the problem was that no one synthesized the two approaches.

From the perspective of small group work, Bales had been somewhat sidetracked. He was working on two books with Parsons: the extremely difficult *Working Papers in the Theory of Action* (1953) and *Family Socialization and Interaction Process* (1955). Both were more along structural–functional lines, and neither proved theoretically fruitful for small group work. Thus Bales could not act as an independent intellectual leader for small group research.

For a time it seemed that Homans would produce the necessary synthesis. His range of interest had been responsible for much of sociology's early excitement about this area. Although he has never run an experimental group on which he has published, he had done some observation. *The Human Group* brought together five studies performed by sociologists and anthropologists, including some of Mayo's work, a study of an island community, and data on a small rural community. The data combination alone suggested exciting possibilities, but his theory was also partly responsible for the excitement. Using a limited number of concepts, Homans deduced propositions that have been the basis for much further work (see Simon, 1952; H. White, 1970). The set of propositions was simple and understandable. Their logical form seemed consistent and yet powerful, although Maris (1970) has made some less favorable comments on the logical consistency of Homans' propositions.

Homans divided group activities from the conditions under which a group operated; he thus conceptualized an "internal system" and an "external system." These two operated in relation to each other, but they could be conceived in isolation. This simple distinction permitted researchers to posit that small groups in laboratory situations, where the external system was under experimental control, were essentially similar to small groups in field situations, where the external system was the rest of the world. Hence small communities, laboratory groups, and parts of organizations could all be analyzed within the same framework, and the possibility existed that social psychology was about to provide a neat synthesis of sociology, psychology, and anthropology.

However, Homans' *Social Behavior: Its Elementary Forms* (1961) was a great disappointment to those who had anticipated a synthesis. The author retreated to a psychological reductionist position in which he tried, unsuccessfully, to demonstrate that all sociological phenomena necessarily follow from psychological laws (in particular, those of behaviorist psychologist B. F. Skinner). The psychological position was unacceptable to most social psychologists, and the deduction itself, dubious. In short, the connection between field observation and experimental observation, applied work in group dynamics and therapy, and theoretical work in group processes, was just not made.[5]

Alternative research models continued to exist; of these, the small study model seemed the most successful. Festinger repeated the style of his 1950 housing research with analysis of an unsuccessful prophetic group (Festinger et al., 1956). He also published an apparent theoretical synthesis, *A Theory of Cognitive Dissonance* (1957), which caused considerable excitement initially. However, the theory later proved to be quite limited in scope; it was not the needed synthesis after all. Other, much later theoretical efforts, were also failures as syntheses (e.g., Thibaut and Kelley, 1959; McGrath and Altman, 1966). There were also research failures, including the simulation of small group behavior that originally had seemed so promising (see Bales, 1959); simulation, however, usually fails in the absence of a clear understanding of the processes involved.

An event that occurred early in connection with *A Theory of Cognitive Dissonance* (1957) illustrates the importance of an intellectual leader and a program statement. In 1951 Festinger was faced with a choice. Bernard Berelson, then Director of the Behavioral Sciences Division of the Ford Foundation, asked whether Festinger "would be interested in undertaking a 'propositional inventory' of the substantive area of 'communication and social influence,'" an area of social psychology that "had never been integrated at a theoretical level" (Festinger, 1957: v). Festinger admits that the question posed a theoretical challenge, and he took it.

With Ford money he was able to gather a research group including

May Brodbeck (philosopher), Dan Martindale (symbolic interactionist), and fellow experimentalists Jack Brehm and Alvin Boderman. This group finally decided to study the spread of rumor (Festinger, 1957: vi), a topic quite removed from the normal focus of experimentalists. Since Festinger had been originally interested in both experimentation and field work— e.g., his housing research (1950) was a field study—this decision effectively moved him away from the center of activity in small group research.

This story demonstrates that if prior decisions about research style and problems (i.e., a program statement) have not been made and encouraged by prestigious intellectual and social leadership, then the very best of a group's members will, when faced with other alternatives, begin moving away from the group's general concerns. As this process continues, an area becomes pulled apart into many pieces. The very success of the rumor project (published as *A Theory of Cognitive Dissonance*, 1957) accelerated the process. Given group leadership, Festinger might have declined Berelson's initial request on the ground that he already had his next research project planned. Or, had the request fitted his plans, he would have guided the final selection of topic in the directions required by the program statement.

The area's lack of intellectual focus is reflected in the early importance of bibliographies: Strodtbeck and Hare (1954) is a bibliography; Hare (1962) is primarily a bibliography. These materials are simply not needed in focused areas whose researchers are well connected to one another socially. The lack of focus also appears in Hare's (1962) need to survey 19 journals (nine in sociology, eight in psychology, and two miscellaneous) in order to locate all the writings important to small group research.

As we have noted, there was a fundamental difference between sociologically and psychologically oriented researchers. The fundamental failure, therefore, was the lack of an intellectual leader or leaders with the abilities to perceive theory and research choices, to select among them, to present those choices as a program statement, and (in concert with a social organizational leader) to encourage the following out of that program statement in all the group members' research. From this perspective, it is tremendously important to observe that, during the early 1950s, Bales chose primarily to follow out Parsons' strong program statement for structural–functional theory development, rather than any of the diffuse strands of small group research.

The result was the field's noncohesiveness. Research conditions always pose multiple contingencies and a high number of choices; and, initially at least, all look equally good. Without guidance, different research directions were chosen by different centers and small group theory never gained a strong focus; furthermore, the results of experiments seldom could be compared.

I noted earlier that the style of small group research also contributed to the lack of comprehensive theory development. That style involved small, nonreplicating, empirical studies, reported without reference to any broad theoretical framework. McGrath and Altman (1966: 79–85) offer several reasons for this style. One was the high cost, in resources and time, of doing any data analysis. This high cost led in the direction of producing more data for computer analysis. The lack of theory, however, made most computer analysis into elegant, number-crunching exercises with little point. Other causes were as follows:

1. The historical roots of small group study in a revolt against nonempirical, armchair theory.
2. "Publish or perish," which caused authors to cut extensive research reports into pieces in order to produce more publications.
3. The search for funds and the administration of those funds becoming central in the field.
4. The low value placed on replication.

On balance, the effect of these pressures was to destroy those conditions which emphasize the creative aspects of science. It is worth noting that although McGrath and Altman's book is subtitled *A Review and Synthesis of the Field*, the authors produced not a theoretical synthesis but, rather, a report of the types of research results; their book thus typifies the field's theoretical poverty. Steiner (1964) referred to this condition as a "theoretical staleness."

Eventually the problems that had belonged exclusively to small group workers were picked up by other areas. Psychologically oriented researchers have appropriated equity problems, a major research area. Social perception, once a major theme of small group work, has disappeared into a psychological group that is itself in trouble (Griffith and Miller, 1970). The most prominent social psychologist of this era, Leon Festinger, has become heavily involved in problems of perception (Festinger, 1971), thus continuing his drift away from small group research.

By 1968 the situation had deteriorated to the point that Theodore Mills' (1968) summary of small group study made no effort to cite new findings, to synthesize, or to summarize ongoing research. He only produced the rationale for small group research and suggested a few examples of use. This lack of currency, excitement, and depth of work strongly suggests that the area was by then quite dead. Perhaps more crucial yet was the continued lack of a textbook, even though more than 20 years had passed since the network had begun spreading.

In general, those still interested in small groups per se were concentrating on personal psychological adjustment goals: T-groups, the "self-awareness" movement, and groups such as Esalen. This activity had always existed simultaneously with other small group work, but the decline of the original research tasks combined with the mass popularity of personal adjustment work to emphasize that area to those professionals still interested in small group work (see Back, 1972, for a more complete discussion).

IS THERE ANOTHER EXPLANATION?

I have provided an explanation, in terms of the model presented in Chapter 2, for the failure of small group research to develop a single theory incorporating all the research elements. Now I want to consider other possible explanations and my reasons for rejecting them.

One possible explanation for the lack of theory is that small group work simply does not lend itself to generalizable research. A second is that the people involved in research were either unlucky or insufficiently. bright. Either hypothesis could explain the lack of theory; however, I find the results unsatisfactory because ungeneralizable. The first contention does not specify why this particular area of interest is ultimately intractable. Unless one argues that all social science is impossible, there is no reason to believe that small group study is inherently any harder to theorize about than, for example, demography, the family, or voting behavior.

The individual explanation is similarly opaque. At bottom, one is in the position of echoing the biographers of the past: If the theory worked, its developers were the right people; if it didn't, they weren't. And as I remarked in Chapter 1, that statement explains nothing. Lewin *was* important, but his death left the role of intellectual leader vacant and that role, as we know, was potentially open to many persons. Furthermore had Lewin lived and produced a program statement to give direction to research, the lack of a social organizational leader might still have hindered development. In short, my argument against this explanation is based on the importance of specific roles rather than persons.

Use of the model presented in Chapter 2, however, provides a nontautological, generalizable explanation for the failure of small group work. To summarize, the causes underlying the failure are both social and intellectual: (1) the lack of graduate students; (2) social psychology's interdisciplinary status between sociology and psychology; (3) the early loss of (and failure to replace) the intellectual leader, and the total lack of a social organizational leader; (4) the lack of either a program statement or any kind of research direction from a senior, important figure (by 1950 small group research was largely a young man's game); and (5) the basic research style.

These difficulties were both social and intellectual. Their ultimate effect, however, has been intellectual: Social theory has thus far been deprived of the theoretical synthesis promised by small group research as late as the early 1950s. The anthropological materials, field studies, and small group laboratory data that Homans had attempted to synthesize are still unincorporated in a theory of small groups. The large bank of collected and reasonably accurate data which exists, plus the need for a synthetic theory (believed attainable by me and many other social scientists), make this area of research ripe for the birth of a new theory group. Chapter 10 suggests that mathematical modeling of some small group work combined with a concern to synthesize the above-mentioned materials has been incorporated into the program of a new theory group, the structuralists.

This negative case of development, then, illustrates my hypothesis that good ideas alone do not necessarily issue in a theory. Specific social conditions are also needed.

NOTES

1. Structural functionalists considered Homans' book a successful piece of structural functionalism. Small group workers considered it a success in their area.
2. Tagiuri had been trained principally by Jerome Bruner, a psychologist; this student–teacher link is reflected in later coauthorship links (see Hare, 1962: 428, 454–455).
3. Study of three journals, *American Journal of Sociology, American Sociological Review*, and *Social Forces*, reported for category "social psychology, collective behavior, and small groups."
4. The journals were the *American Journal of Sociology* and the *American Sociological Review*.
5. There are some who doubt that small group research ever held the potential to develop into a complete theory. I believe that the potential did exist but that developing it lay in making the connections just noted. The same small group researchers and ideas crisscrossed time and time again, yet the connections remained uncompleted.

BIBLIOGRAPHY

Allport, Gordon W.
  1937   *Personality: A Psychological Interpretation*. New York: Holt.
American Journal of Sociology.
  various   *Cumulative Index to the American Journal of Sociology 1895–*
  years   *1965*. Chicago: American Journal of Sociology.
————.
  various   *American Men of Science*. 10th ed. The Jacques Cattell Press
  years   (ed.). Tempe, Ariz.: Cattell. 11th ed. The Jacques Cattell Press
          (ed.). New York: Bowker.

American Sociological Association.
  various   *Directory of Members 1959*; also for years 1963, 1967, 1970.
    years a   New York and Washington, D.C.: American Sociological Asso-
      ciation.
  various   *Guide to Graduate Departments of Sociology 1965*; also for
    years b   years 1969, 1971. Washington, D.C.: American Sociological As-
      sociation.
  various   *Index to the American Sociological Review*. Vols. 1–25 (1936–
    years c   1960) and Vols. 26–30 (1961–1965). New York and Washing-
      ton, D.C.: American Sociological Association.
Bach, George R.
  1954   *Intensive Group Psychotherapy*. New York: Ronald.
Back, Kurt W.
  1972   *Beyond Words: The Story of Sensitivity Training and the Encounter
    Moment*. New York: Russell Sage.
Bales, Robert F.
  1950   *Interaction Process Analysis: A Method for the Study of Small Groups*.
    Reading, Mass.: Addison-Wesley.
  1959   "Small group theory and research." Pp. 293–305 in Robert K. Merton,
    Leonard Broom, and Leonard S. Cottrell, Jr. (eds.), *Sociology Today*.
    New York: Basic Books.
Barnard, Charles I.
  1938   *The Functions of the Executive*. Cambridge, Mass.: Harvard Uni-
    versity Press.
Bavelas, Alex A.
  1942   "Morale and the training of leaders." Pp. 143–165 in G. Watson
    (ed.), *Civilian Morale*. New York: Reynal and Hitchcock.
  1948   "A mathematical model for group structures." *Applied Anthropology*
    7(3): 16–30.
Ben-David, Joseph.
  1960   "Scientific productivity and academic organisation in nineteenth cen-
    tury medicine." *American Sociological Review* 25 (December): 828–
    843.
Bion, W. R.
  1948   "Experiences in groups: I." *Human Relations* 1(3): 314–320.
  1952   "Group dynamics: a review." *International Journal of Psychoanalysis*
    33: 235–247.
Borgatta, Edgar F., L. S. Cottrell, Jr., and H. J. Meyer.
  1956   "On the dimensions of group behavior." *Sociometry* 19 (December):
    223–240.
Brown, Julia S., and Brian G. Gilmartin.
  1969   "Sociology today: lacunae, emphases and surfeits." *American Sociolo-
    gist* 4 (November): 283–290.
Busch, H. M.
  1934   *Leadership in Group Work*. New York: Association Press.
Cartwright, Dorwin, and Alvin Zander.
  1962   *Group Dynamics: Research and Theory*, 2nd ed. Evanston, Ill.: Row,
    Peterson. (1st ed., 1953.)

Coyle, Grace L.
  1930   *Social Process in Organized Groups.* New York: R. R. Smith.
Davis, James A.
  1970   "Clustering and hierarchy in interpersonal relations: testing two graph
          theoretical models on 742 sociomatrices." *American Sociological Re-
          view* 35 (October): 843–851.
Deutsch, Morton.
  1949   "An experimental study of the effects of cooperation and competition
          upon group processes." *Human Relations* 2(3): 199–231.
Festinger, Leon.
  1957   *A Theory of Cognitive Dissonance.* New York: Harper & Row.
  1971   Personal interview.
Festinger, Leon, Henry W. Riecken, Jr., and Stanley Schachter.
  1956   *When Prophecy Fails.* Minneapolis: University of Minnesota Press.
Festinger, Leon, Stanley Schachter, and Kurt W. Back.
  1950   *Social Pressures in Informal Groups: A Study of Human Factors in
          Housing.* Cambridge, Mass.: MIT Press.
Griffith, Belver C., and A. J. Miller.
  1970   "Networks of informal communication among scientifically productive
          scientists." Pp. 125–140 in D. K. Pollock and Carnot E. Nelson (eds.),
          Communication Among Scientists and Engineers. Lexington, Mass.:
          Heath.
Gronlund, Norman E.
  1959   *Sociometry in the Classroom.* New York: Harper & Row.
Guetzkow, Harold (ed.).
  1951   *Groups, Leadership and Men: Research in Human Relations.* Pitts-
          burgh: Carnegie.
Hare, A. Paul.
  1962   *Handbook of Small Group Research.* New York: Free Press.
Hare, A. Paul, Edgar F. Borgatta, and Robert F. Bales.
  1955   *Small Groups: Studies in Social Interaction.* New York: Knopf.
Homans, George C.
  1950   *The Human Group.* New York: Harcourt Brace Jovanovich.
  1961   *Social Behavior: Its Elementary Forms.* New York: Harcourt Brace
          Jovanovich.
  1964   "Bringing men back in." *American Sociological Review* 29 (Decem-
          ber): 809–818.
Hovland, Carl I., Irving L. Janis, and Harold H. Kelley.
  1953   *Communication and Persuasion: Psychological Studies of Opinion
          Change.* New Haven, Conn.: Yale University Press.
Lanzetta, John T.
  1971   Personal Interview.
Lewin, Kurt.
  1951   *Field Theory in Social Science.* New York: Harper & Row.
Lewin, Kurt, Robert Lippitt, and R. K. White.
  1939   "Patterns of aggressive behavior in experimentally created 'social
          climates.'" *Journal of Social Psychology* 10: 271–299.

Lindzey, Gardner.
1954   *The Handbook of Social Psychology.* Reading, Mass.: Addison-Wesley.
Maris, Ronald.
1970   "The logical adequacy of Homans' social theory." *American Sociological Review* 35 (December): 1069–1080.
Martindale, Don A.
1960   *The Nature and Types of Sociological Theory.* (Particularly Chapter 19, "Micro-Functionalism: Group Dynamics," pp. 501–522.) Boston: Houghton Mifflin.
Mayo, Elton.
1933   *The Human Problems of an Industrial Civilization.* New York: Macmillan.
McCartney, James L.
1970   "On being scientific: changing styles of presentation of sociological research." *American Sociologist* 5 (February): 30–35.
McGrath, Joseph E., and Irwin Altman.
1966   *Small Group Research: A Synthesis and Critique of the Field.* New York: Holt.
Mills, Theodore M.
1968   "On the sociology of small groups." Pp. 45–53 in Talcott Parsons (ed.), *American Sociology.* New York: Basic Books.
Mitchell, G. Duncan.
1965   *A Hundred Years of Sociology.* (Particularly Chapter 17, "Microsociology," pp. 280–297.) London: Duckworth.
Moreno, José L.
1934   *Who Shall Survive?* Washington, D.C.: Nervous and Mental Diseases Publishing Co. (Revised in 1953; Beacon, N.Y.: Beacon House.)
Newcomb, Theodore M.
1942   "Community roles in attitude formation." *American Sociological Review* 7 (October): 621–630.
1950   *Social Psychology.* New York: Dryden.
Parsons, Talcott.
1956   *Department and Laboratory of Social Relations, Harvard University, The First Decade, 1946–1956.* Cambridge, Mass.: Harvard University.
Parsons, Talcott, and Robert F. Bales in collaboration with James Olds, Morris Zelditch, Jr., and Philip Slater.
1955   *Family Socialization and Interaction Process.* New York: Free Press.
Parsons, Talcott, Robert F. Bales, and Edward A. Shils.
1953   *Working Papers in the Theory of Action.* New York: Free Press.
Roethlisberger, Fritz J., and W. J. Dickson.
1939   *Management and the Worker.* Cambridge, Mass.: Harvard University Press.
Schachter, Stanley.
1959   *The Psychology of Affiliation: Experimental Studies of the Sources of Gregariousness.* Stanford, Calif.: Stanford University Press.

Sherif, Muzafer.
   1936   *The Psychology of Social Norms.* New York: Harper & Row.
Sherif, Muzafer, O. V. Harvey, B. V. White, W. R. Hood, and C. W. Sherif.
   1961   *Intergroup Conflict and Cooperation: The Robbers' Cave Experiment.*
          Norman, Okla.: University of Oklahoma Press.
Simon, Herbert A.
   1952   "A formal theory of interaction of social groups." *American Socio-
          logical Review* 17 (April): 202–211.
Steiner, I. D.
   1964   "Group dynamics." Pp. 421–446 in P. Farnsworth (ed.), Vol. 15,
          Annual Review of Psychology. Palo Alto, Calif.: Annual Review.
Strodtbeck, Fred L., and A. Paul Hare.
   1954   "Bibliography of small group research: from 1900 through 1953."
          Sociometry 17 (May): 107–178.
Strodtbeck, Fred L., Rita M. James, and Charles Hawkins.
   1958   "Social status in jury deliberations." Pp. 379–388 in E. E. Maccoby,
          T. M. Newcomb, and E. L. Hartley (eds.), *Readings in Social Psy-
          chology.* 3rd ed. New York: Holt.
Thibaut, John W., and Harold H. Kelley.
   1959   *The Social Psychology of Groups.* New York: Wiley.
White, Harrison C.
   1970   "Simon out of Homans by Coleman." *American Journal of Sociology*
          75 (March): 852–862.
Whyte, William F.
   1943   *Street Corner Society: The Social Structure of an Italian Slum.* Chi-
          cago: University of Chicago Press.
Wilson, Gertrude, and Gladys Ryland.
   1949   *Social Group Work Practice: The Creative Use of the Social Process.*
          Boston: Houghton Mifflin.

CHAPTER 6
EVALUATION AND CONTEXT

We have examined three theory groups in sociology. Now we should consider how well the data on these groups fit the model proposed in Chapter 2. That model, which grew out of data on natural science groups, may well need modification for coherent groups in sociology. If clear differences exist, can they be explained? We must also consider whether there have been any changes in sociology's intellectual patterns that did not originate in small, coherent groups.

The profession of sociology in general goes on largely outside these coherent groups. There were roughly 1700 professional[1] sociologists in 1959 (ASA, 1959) and about 5000 in 1970 (ASA, 1970). Even though we have included peripherally related sociologists as well as the core coherent groups on the basic data tables, only 85 sociologists show up as central to standard American sociology, 82 to symbolic interactionism, and 47 to small group work. The coherent groups trained during the cluster stage have been small in each case: 12 at Harvard for standard American sociology, 29 at Chicago for symbolic interactionism, and 5 for small groups at Harvard.

Socially, these core persons constitute only a small fraction of the total profession. Intellectually, however, they were central to the development of sociology's major intellectual viewpoints during the 1950s and 1960s. The point of these chapters has been, quite simply, that a small, coherent group can produce massive changes in the theoretical orientation of a field.

Outside the groups themselves, changes that occurred between 1950 and 1970 in the number and location of sociology training centers have affected the growth of the newer theory groups in sociology. Outside the profession, the rise of other important intellectual traditions and methodologies has had noticeable effects, as have certain events in the society at large.

EVALUATION OF THE MODEL

No theory is ever completely developed in all its ramifications, nor is it ever the work of one person alone. Theory is the content of a shared understanding, held by a group of scientists, of how some part of the world operates. Books, articles, and lectures are all attempts to specify in more detail or with greater clarity how this theory works. The model presented in Chapter 2 holds that these understandings are initially the property of a coherent group; the theory is transmitted and modified by those who share its essential features, although particular details and style of presentation may vary somewhat from one adherent of a theory to another. I assume that the active adherents—and hence carriers or transmitters—of social theory are those who:

1. Have had some professional training.
2. Are active in teaching, research, or both.
3. Are publishing or contributing members of the coherent carrier group.

Obviously passive carriers of theories also exist. These either: (1) learn a theory at some point in time—usually during graduate training—and thereafter teach it to others virtually unchanged; or (2) follow the problems, successes, and changes in the theory, even though they contribute nothing to research efforts. Given the data cited earlier, it is clear that passive carriers constitute a large majority of the profession at any time. Members of coherent groups are active carriers.

Theories are not static; they change continually as carriers try to apply or improve them. Verbal and written reports, detailing a particular theory's successes and failures at specific tasks, are constantly circulated in coherent theory groups. The strength of a coherent group derives from its ability to concentrate on a theoretical scheme for an extended period of time.

Table 6.1 (based on Table 2.1) summarizes the first three chapters. Each column is dated for each group. The rows (characteristics) are also divided by groups. Thus for standard American sociology the intellectual leader is Parsons in the normal stage; and Parsons and Merton share this designation in the cluster stage. The parenthetical material at the top of each cell summarizes what the general model proposes for that stage. I now want to discuss several general matters raised by the data as well as concerns specific to one or another of the four stages.

GENERAL CONSIDERATIONS

Comparison of the data with the model reveals sloppiness in the transition from stage to stage. The transformation from stage to stage occurs as it should, but the boundary between stages is less clearly

TABLE 6.1 Outline of model, including data from Chapters 3–5

Feature	Stage			
	Normal	Network	Cluster	Specialty
Group[a]				
SAS	to 1935	1935–1945	1945–1951	1951–1968
SI	to 1931	1931–1945	1945–1952	1952–
SG	to 1945	1945–1950	1950–1958	None
Intellectual leaders	(Founding fathers)	(Integration)	(Many students)	(May leave)
SAS	Parsons	Parsons	Parsons, Merton	No
SI	Mead	Blumer	Blumer	No
SG	Lewin	Lewin (to 1947)	None	—[b]
Social organizational leaders	—	(Training center organized)	(Arranges jobs, publications)	(Continues activity)
SAS	—	Parsons	Parsons	Parsons
SI	—	Blumer	Blumer	No strong leadership
SG	—	None	None	None
Research and training centers	—	—	(2 or 3)	(Many)
SAS	—	Harvard	Harvard, Columbia (late)	Many
SI	—	Chicago	Chicago	Berkeley, Chicago (sometimes), Iowa, Minnesota
SG	—	MIT	Harvard, Michigan	—
Intellectual success	(First here)	(Attracts others)	(Many successes)	(No longer important)
SAS	Parsons (1937)[c]	Lazarsfeld et al. (1944)	Stouffer et al. (1949)	Many
SI	Thomas and Znaniecki (1918; rev. 1956)	Mead (1932–1938)	Lindesmith (1947)	Dalton (1959); Goffman (1959)
SG	Lewin, Lippitt, and White (1939)	Bales (1950)	Homans (1950)	—
Program statement	—	(Stated)	(Carried out in research)	(Becomes routine)
SAS	—	None	Parsons (1949); Merton (1948)	Yes

TABLE 6.1 (continued)

Feature	Normal	Network	Cluster	Specialty
		Stage		
Group[a]				
SI	—	Blumer (1938)	Yes	Yes
SG	—	None	None	—
Secondary work	—	—	(Appears)	(Limited)
SAS	—	—	Merton (1949)	Merton et al. (1959); Parsons (1968)
SI	—	—	Lee (1945)	Rose (1962); Manis and Meltzer (1967)
SG	—	—	Cartwright and Zander (1953); Hare, Borgatta, and Bales (1955); Hare (1962)	—
Critical work by group	(Can appear in normal or network stage and be an impetus for development)			(Routine)
SAS	—	Parsons (1937)	—	Demerath and Peterson (1967); Gouldner (1970)
SI	—	—	—	Glaser and Strauss (1967)
SG	—		—	—
Critical work of group			(Appears here for revolutionary group)	(Routine)
SAS	—	—	—	Mills (1959),
SI	—	—	—	Bales (1966); Vaughan and Reynolds (1968)
SG	—	—	McGrath and Altman (1966)	—

TABLE 6.1 (continued)

Feature	Stage			
	Normal	Network	Cluster	Specialty
Textbook				(Appears here)
SAS	—	—	—	Broom and Selznick (1954)
SI	—	—	Lindesmith and Strauss (1949)	Same
SG	—	—	—	—
Group size[d] (roughly)	(Interdeter-minant)	(Up to 40; many in-formal re-lations)	(Up to 40; more formal relations)	(20–100+)
SAS	26 (1935)	9 (1946)	20 (1946–1951)	81 (1970)
SI	16 (1932)	14 (1946)	42 (1946–1952)	65 (1970)
SG	31 (1945)	19 (1950)	21 (1950–1955)	—

Key:
[a] SAS = standard American sociology; SI = symbolic interactionism; SG = small group theory.
[b] — = Not applicable in this stage.
[c] See Chapter 3–5 bibliographies for full references on all works.
[d] Counts:
Normal: All persons listed in Tables 3.3, 4.2, and 5.2 for appropriate dates.
Network: SAS: Persons listed at Harvard in 1946 in Table 3.3 plus all Parsons' earlier students.
  SI: All persons listed at Chicago in 1946 in Table 4.2 plus all Blumer's earlier students.
  SG: All persons listed at Harvard, MIT, and Michigan in 1950 in Table 5.2.
Cluster: SAS: Same as for network, but for period 1946–1951; includes people who received Ph.D.'s through 1955. Shils included; other data have shown his importance. Also Garfinkel and Riecken (see Table 3.2).
  SI: Same as for network, but for period 1946–1952. Includes people who received doctorates as late as 1959 but studied during the cluster period.
  SG: Persons listed at Harvard and Michigan during 1950, plus additional people at those locations in 1953 and 1955.
Specialty: SAS and SI: All persons listed on Tables 3.3 and 4.2 as active in 1959; these numbers are intended only as indicative, not absolute, size of specialty, since the tables selected **important** rather than **all** persons in an area.
  SG: Not applicable.

marked than that between stages in natural science groups (e.g., see Mullins, 1972). Although this situation is due partly to the difficulty of discerning boundaries for stages, it is also attributable to a fundamental difference between social science and natural science literature. Griffith (1972), summarizing the work of others on social science groups, notes that social science literature is not as closely linked across time and people as natural science literature. Figure 3.3, for example, showed coauthorships over a 30-year period, yet most of the authors, young and old, are linked in some way. Such a graph has not occurred for the natural science groups studied. The reason is that social science citations and coauthorships have a lower currency rate and, hence, they exhibit less precise groupings than do the natural sciences. Griffith reports one study that showed that between 70 and 80 percent of all citations in natural science literature were to material published within the five years immediately prior to the publication dates of the papers studied, whereas only 50 to 60 percent of social science citations were that recent.[2]

Sociology is also marked by its lack of a single, dominant journal. There are at least three major journals: *American Sociological Review, American Journal of Sociology,* and *Social Forces.* Additional factors contributing to the murkiness of the literature are (1) the length of time (up to a year or more after a manuscript has been submitted) taken by journals to make publication decisions and (2) the rejection rate (about 65 percent) and the varying selection criteria for material received. Garvey (1972) has referred to the "recycling" of social science manuscripts through the journals with, for example, 95 percent of all papers presented at one ASA meeting having been published by a date four years later, but in many scattered journals and after several papers had received many refusals. Such factors do not deny publication, they only delay it; the effect of this delay, however, is to make it extremely difficult for either a profesional sociologist or a student of science to discover what research is really current.

With reference to the network thickenings mentioned in Chapter 2, I have noted my lack of direct data on informal communication. In light of the coauthorship networks, though, we can infer that communication. Not all informal communication eventuates in coauthored publication, but we can certainly presume that some communication preceded each coauthorship. Furthermore, as predicted, the coauthorship networks indicate little coauthorship in the normal and network stages, more in the cluster stage, and even more in the specialty stage. Hence some thickening in the network is gradually occurring over time, and that thickening involves most of the persons who are important to a given development.

Comparison of the persons included in a given coauthorship network with those linked at some time by colleague or student–teacher ties shows that the social links indicated by the latter match closely with the intellectual links implied by the former: If two people think very differently, they are not likely to coauthor with each other (at least not frequently). The small group researchers provide a particularly good example of this implication. Their social links divide them largely by training and job location (some Harvard researchers excepted); the coauthorship links fall into the same groupings as the social links. Only rarely does coauthorship transcend the subgroup boundaries. Obviously, then, some data suggest that the social and intellectual groupings are identical.

This inference cannot be considered to be proved, however. We would need more accurate data on research similarities and real communication data (e.g., that gathered on biologists; see Mullins, 1968) to provide a real test.

I should also note that, unlike natural scientists, sociologists have few jobs open to them at which they can do research exclusively. Thus the distinction between teaching and research centers is probably not particularly meaningful for sociology. Research is usually performed at locations that have both research facilities and students.

STAGE-SPECIFIC EVALUATION

The *normal stages* conform quite nicely to the natural science model with one small exception: In terms of the theoretical end product, symbolic interactionism (thanks largely to Mead's lectures) achieved relatively greater intellectual development than either standard American sociology or small group work. The latter two groups were in an intellectual state roughly comparable to that of the Phage Group in 1945 (Mullins, 1972: 55–56).

During the *network stage*, we normally expect a program statement, and symbolic interactionism fulfilled this requirement at the proper time. However, Parsons' statement for standard American sociology was not given until 1947 and not published until 1949—near the end of the cluster stage. Merton's was published in 1948. Yet it was obvious that Parsons' statement had circulated widely before publication and had influenced research that began appearing in 1949. The late appearance of this program statement seems to be clearly related to the disorganized nature of the literature that I discussed earlier. The 1947 program statement was included in that first book of Parsons' essays, put out by the Free Press after Parsons had resolved his publishing difficulties. The small group theorists never produced a program statement, but they were ultimately an unsuccessful group.

With respect to revolutionary and elite characteristics, which normally become apparent during the cluster stage, it seems clear that at least two of the three were elite types. Parsons was heartily disliked by Sorokin, and there were some who felt that Parsons' 1949 seminar on structural functionalism was an act of intimidation (Friedrichs, 1970: 20–21); nevertheless, there was no hint of the virulent hostility that characterized the reactions of some biochemists to phage work in general (Mullins, 1972) and of some sociologists to ethnomethodology (see Chapter 8). Chicago could have rejected Blumer, but instead it obviously approved—hiring others like him and eventually making him editor of the *AJS*. Small group work never developed fully or successfully enough to generate such a response.

The only departures from the model during the *cluster stage* are symbolic interactionism's production of a textbook and failure to produce a publication explosion. The textbook probably resulted because, relatively speaking, the group's theory was more nearly complete during the normal and network stages. The reasons for the publication failure seem to be quite understandable and quite specific to the group. Neither difference appears to suggest a necessity to alter the general model.

During the *specialty stage*, the data show continued work along earlier lines by both Blumer and Parsons, rather than a change to other kinds of sociology. The phenomenon of change, therefore, may be peculiar to Max Delbrück (Mullins, 1972). For many of the nonleaders, however, commitments to a specific line of research are of short duration; for example, many coauthors appear only once in the data for a group, and many (e.g., Bales, as the coauthorship networks also show) have multiple commitments.

In sum, the data fit the model quite closely. The only consistent difference for the two ultimately successful groups is in clarity of transformation from stage to stage, and that difference seems to be related to sociology's relatively looser social and intellectual organization (by contrast, say, with molecular biology). As a result of that relaxed organization, connections among the elements of the group development model are not as well defined as in the areas from which the model was originally drawn.

One further point should be made. The group sizes vary wildly from stage to stage (see bottom of Table 6.1). It is particularly interesting to note that standard American sociology had a much smaller network group than either of the other two groups, and the smallest cluster. Yet it was ultimately the most successful in the specialty stage. Symbolic interactionism had a fantastically successful cluster stage but only a moderately successful specialty stage. The two Harvard clusters— standard American sociology and small groups—look very much alike at points, if we simply count populations of faculty and populations of students. Yet the two had very different endings. Clearly size—within limits—is not terribly important. It does seem clear that a cluster will not develop without a "guaranteed" annual base population of seven to ten at the institution involved. (Symbolic interactionism's Chicago group in the 1930s was very close to that size, but a cluster did not result until the war's end had brought an influx of new students.) The important point suggested by these situations is simply that we cannot look only at one or two characteristics—or even, as we noted in the case of small groups, five. Without all the required characteristics, the largest group in sociology will not succeed. With them, a small group can and may totally reorganize the intellectual landscape when everyone else's back is turned.

Thus far, the data indicate that small coherent groups are agents for altering theory. At the core of each development that shaped American sociology throughout the 1950s and 1960s, similar groups developed in parallel ways, within looser constraints but still well within the outlines of Chapter 2's model. Part Three, therefore, continues to use the existence of small coherent groups as a good indicator that a lasting theoretical change is occurring.

It has been important to the intellectual quality of sociology that these groups are not closed at the top. If we compare the three coauthorship networks (Figures 3.3, 4.1, and 5.1), we find several sociologists linked to two of them, and some that are linked with all three (this phenomenon becomes even more pronounced when we examine the networks for contemporary groups).[3] Swanson is linked to both symbolic interactionism and small groups. Katz is linked to both standard American sociology and small groups. Cloward, Cohen, Schrag, Schuessler, Shils, and Star are all linked to both standard American sociology and symbolic interactionism. L. S. Cottrell and Williams are linked to all three groups. Although he appears only in the small groups network, I have already noted George C. Homans' contributions to both standard American sociology and small group work. The better professionals shift positions from one intellectual group to another as their research interests change; for example, Homans shifted from an early functionalism in his *English Villagers of the Thirteenth Century* (1941), to a combination of structural functionalism and small group work (1950), to a kind of psychologism (1961). The more outstanding men in the field also read and cite one another's research; for example, Goffman (1961) cited two scientists who were developing ethnomethodology—Harold Garfinkel and Harvey Sacks.

This limited flow of persons and information back and forth between groups fosters some degree of unity within the profession at large. This function of important group members helps hold the discipline together and supports Merton's (1957) finding that it is the students and followers of those engaged in priority disputes, rather than the principals themselves, who carry on such battles. In contemporary sociology groups, we observe both this kind of exchange and the growth of hostility toward some of the groups as they develop. Both reactions are quite possible, since a new group's early formulations may show only small differences between its fundamental theory and that of the parent discipline; these differences grow and intensify, however, as the group develops.

OTHER SOURCES?

The small size of the groups examined versus the size of the entire profession (measured by ASA membership) prompts us to ask whether, perhaps, other theoretical developments of note occurred outside these groups. What were those several thousand other professionals doing? Two developments exemplify the kind of theoretical work being done outside of coherent groups: exchange theory (associated with Blau and Homans, among others) and conflict theory (associated with Dahrendorf, Coser, and others).[4] Both are variants of structural functionalism (see Wallace, 1969; Friedrichs, 1970). Neither has yet been able to establish a truly separate theoretical scheme, probably because neither has generated sufficient excitement to attract a coherent group to its particular research concerns. The model in Chapter 2 does not assert that developments cannot occur without a coherent group, only that there can be *no radical theoretical break* in the absence of a group to work out those differences. As of 1972, exchange theory and conflict theory were important, potentially seminal ideas for radically different theories; however, they lacked the necessary support of productivity, as measured by both students and publications, to become coherent groups.

Even good ideas that are not supported by a group will not develop enough difference to become distinctive. Variants arise, but not radically different theories. The obverse of that assertion is that, had more sociologists become interested in, for example, conflict theory, and had a group of students developed in this area, there could have been (and may yet be) a theory that separates itself radically from the structural functionalism out of which it has grown.

SOCIOLOGY'S CONTEXT:
THE PROFESSION AND
THE OUTSIDE WORLD

This section examines the profession of sociology, commenting in particular on the spread of training centers within the profession and on some developments outside sociology which have especially influenced the development of sociological theory.

THE PROFESSION

Professionalization in sociology generally restricts positions to persons holding Ph.D.'s in the discipline from accredited institutions. Several of the major figures still active in the 1950s, 1960s, and 1970s never received doctoral degrees in sociology (Parsons has a doctorate in economics;

Homans and Shils have earned only B.A. degrees); but they are now the exceptions among important figures. A major effect of professionalization has been the standardization of professional training and the establishment of a specific context within which research questions, methods, and criteria for sound research are determined. For most people, most of the time, that context defines their work world; they do not deviate from it.

From 1892 to the 1930s, Columbia and Chicago were the principal training grounds for professional sociologists, Chicago being much the larger and better organized. The boundaries of sociology were sufficiently ill defined that nonprofessionals (e.g., Park and Mead) moved in and out of the area with little difficulty.

The period of Chicago's numerical dominance extended into the 1950s (see Table 6.2). During that decade Chicago's was still one-third larger than any other program. By the 1966–1970 period, though, (1) the absolute sizes of the Chicago program and of several other programs had declined and (2) there were six major locations producing eleven or more Ph.D. graduates per year. Four large state universities, Wisconsin, Michigan State, Minnesota, and Berkeley, had surpassed the

TABLE 6.2 Average number of Ph.D.'s granted per year for selected graduate training programs

Program	Average Number of Ph.D.'s Per Year		
	1950–1960	1960–1966	1966–1970
Chicago	18.0	14.3	11.6
Columbia	12.5	10.9	14.0
Harvard	9.4	7.7	6.4
Cornell	7.6	7.1	4.8
University of North Carolina	6.6	5.1	5.2
University of Wisconsin	6.5	4.7	13.8
Ohio State University	6.5	8.0	7.4
University of Minnesota	5.4	6.4	11.6
New York University	5.1	6.7	ni
Yale	4.9	4.7	5.8
University of Southern California	4.8	4.9	5.6
University of Pennsylvania	4.7	3.6	2.0
Michigan State	4.5	7.4	11.0
University of Washington	4.5	4.7	7.0
University of California, Berkeley	3.8	10.6	12.4
University of Michigan	3.6	6.3	7.0
Catholic University	3.2	4.1	3.4
University of Iowa	3.2	3.3	4.0
Pittsburgh	3.2	1.6	5.6
University of Illinois	2.7	4.0	3.6

Sources: Sibley (1963); ASA (1969, 1971).

large private universities (Chicago and Columbia) within which sociology had begun. Harvard, interestingly enough, had become one of the smaller centers. A third massive change during this period was the spread of graduate training to many more centers (most producing considerably fewer than eleven Ph.D.'s per year, however).

According to Sibley (1963), the total number of Ph.D's per year remained stable throughout the 1950s at 156 per year. Of these, three institutions (Chicago, Columbia, and Harvard) granted roughly 25 percent, nine institutions almost 50 percent, and 23 institutions, four-fifths of all the degrees in the field. By 1969 this situation had changed. Total production was up to 362 (ASA, 1971), and more centers (ASA, 1971: iii) were granting more of the degrees. This "democratization" of Ph.D. production for the discipline weakened any central control of the discipline that the Big Three could have had.

If we review the data in Chapters 3 through 5, we see that only two universities fostered cluster development: Chicago housed its own cluster in the 1920s and that of symbolic interactionism in the late 1940s. Standard American sociologists and small group researchers developed clusters at Harvard. Clearly the relationship between major centers and cluster development is more than casual. We might infer, then, that a minimum size (for faculty, available funds to support students, and research facilities) is necessary for cluster development. Obviously, the small number of major centers limited both potential students' choices of location to pursue a degree and professors' choices of places to send good students to do research (Shichor, 1970).[5]

Over the ten-year period preceding 1970, however, many more institutions opened graduate programs and the number of potential centers for cluster development became greater. The number of centers with sociology Ph.D. candidates increased from 68 in 1960 (Sibley, 1963) to 125 in 1970 (Roose and Andersen, 1970). Expansion is important because alternative views can exist in a professional system only if some people are free to deviate and experiment without correction (most graduate students are not). Furthermore, if they are to survive, new ideas need institutional support in the establishment of a research center and a training center. (Without the expansion of training centers, ethnomethodology might not have developed.) In the 1970s, as a result of expansion during the previous decade, more centers have become capable of supporting a cluster. Hence several clusters could (potentially) develop simultaneously.

The older centers will not necessarily grind out students in the old pattern only, but such is their overwhelming tendency. People came to Harvard to study with Parsons and Homans. Very few actually studied closely with them, but Parsons' students in particular hold important positions in many departments. Most students leaving Harvard in the 1960s were either Parsons' students or students of his students. No theory is ever complete and consistent, and those transmitting it are too intelligent and competitive merely to parrot a position; but a strong similarity in style and problem selection is usually apparent.

I mentioned earlier the large number of passive carriers of a tradition. Their effect is to perpetuate theories, often without change, long after substantial modifications have been made. Hence coherent groups *are* tremendously important to the history of ideas, but at the time of their actual existence they affect their parent profession only indirectly. Most professionals, who tend to be passive carriers, teach students a subject different from that being reported in the professional journals—specifically, they teach the theories they learned in graduate school (see Oromaner, 1969). Moreover, passive carriers do research that is shaped by concepts long established (Kuhn, 1970); in the meantime, coherent groups, either quietly or with fanfare, are changing the rules of the intellectual game.

Outside the American sociological profession itself, the support for sociology as a profession in terms of (1) research money and positions, (2) technical and conceptual discoveries in other disciplines, and (3) basic social changes have provided a context for coherent groups. Although research and job support are not completely separable, some separate, over-time data for each exist. First, the number of jobs for sociologists has increased during the last 20 years, and increasing numbers of sociologists have found jobs.[6] For the short-term future, it is likely that the earlier expansion in numbers of positions in sociology, brought on by increasing college enrollments and a shift to sociology from other possible majors, is probably at an end. Hence academic employment, which has been the largest part of sociological employment, will remain nearly static for a time. In 1970 about three-quarters of all sociologists were academically employed: 5674 out of 7658 (NSF, 1972: 60).

Federal support for sociological research is relatively new (Dupree, 1957). Support for research has increased across the last ten years from roughly $2 million in 1959 to $53.5 million in 1969 (Smelser and Davis, 1969: 147). From 1969 to 1972 the research and development budget for areas supporting sociology has changed very little; thus $53.5 million is probably quite accurate for 1972 also (NSF, 1971). Most of this research has been applied research in the area of President Lyndon B. Johnson's Great Society programs and their successors (see Smelser and Davis, 1969: 148). The increase in research funds has had an effect on sociology, particularly with respect to the concern with forecasting and social indicators (see Chapter 7).

TECHNICAL
AND CONCEPTUAL
INNOVATION
OUTSIDE SOCIOLOGY

Technical innovations enable investigators to explore different approaches to analysis. The computer is a classic example. By making possible the examination of large quantities of data, as well as comparison among, additions to, and storage of those data, the computer opened many possibilities for new forms of analysis. Most people use the computer only as a very fast adding machine or counter-sorter and thus do not benefit from its unique features; but even traditional analyses (e.g., table production, computation of statistics) can be done much more rapidly. Deutsch, Platt, and Senghaas (1971) found 62 such developments between 1900 and 1968, and all had effects in one or another of the social sciences (see Table 6.3). They also found that ten to fifteen years elapse before a technological innovation has visible effects on social science. In general, they attribute the early (1950 and before) developments in sociology to innovations in sociology and anthropology and the later developments (1960–1970) to innovations from psychology, political science, politics, anthropology, psychology, and mathematics.

American sociology benefited early (see Chapter 3) from European social thought; and European sociology, in turn, imported standard American sociology during the 1940s and 1950s. However, beginning in the 1930s, American thought became isolated from European currents. Much of European sociology was destroyed by the fifteen years of turmoil surrounding World War II. Subsequently the insularity of the 1950s and early 1960s prevented American sociology from reestablishing contact with European thinking. During that interim there had been two generations of European intellectuals: the World War I–World War II generation (including George Gurwitch, Georg Lukács, Karl Mannheim, Alfred Schutz, and Werner Stark) and the post-World War II generation (including Basil Bernstein, Elizabeth Bott, Raymond Boudon, Jürgen Habermas, Émile Jantsch, and Claude Lévi-Strauss). Translation and reading of the first generation's work began roughly in 1959; study of the second generation's work began having an influence after 1966. As the subsequent chapters reveal, many of these thinkers have been very important to contemporary sociology. Not all, of course, have had an equal influence. Any given development tends to be less important than the uses of it by those who introduced it. The overall effect of innovations and conceptions has been to make the development of contemporary theory groups the result of both international and interdisciplinary influences.

SOCIAL CHANGE

In the interests of brevity I have selected only two occurrences that had major, well-defined impacts: the student radical movement and the Great Society programs. The student radical movement (linked, at least rhetorically, to the Black movement, the antiwar movement, and third-world development since World War II) has reintroduced a series of concerns for radical change that had been removed from sociology. Early sociology had a radical aspect (e.g., Veblen, 1921), but the professionalization of the 1940s and 1950s had removed that element. As Chapter 11 shows, moral outrage, backed by the analysis of specific situations, has been reintroduced into the sociological literature.

Lyndon Johnson used the term the Great Society to designate a series of domestic reform programs that had the effect of introducing sociologists into the policy-making aspect of society. Until the early 1960s sociology had been quite isolated; no one in government cared what sociologists thought or did. As these programs developed, though, government officials called on sociologists to design new programs, evaluate old ones, and forecast the potential effects of proposed programs. Sociology thus acquired the position that economics had held in 1945. I now sense a humbleness in sociology about this experience. We sociologists found that we were technically unable to make accurate predictions. We were caught between good intentions (a sense that the programs we thought were right ought to be both advocated and instituted) and the need to make decisions (based on the realities of situations we did not fully understand; see Moynihan, 1969). A reassessment of sociologists' ability to make predictions has become central to the forecasters' group (see Chapter 7).

Other significant events are examined with respect to the groups they affected.

IN CONCLUSION

The theories that dominated sociology from 1951 to 1968 were based on a combination of pre-1920 European and American social theory, survey research, and cross-tabulation methodology. Part Three examines the groups in sociology that have surfaced since 1968 and are now shaping the sociology of the next decade or so. Standard American sociology and its alternatives are still alive but no longer dominant. New groups are developing in the elbow room of the much larger discipline. This is a period of recognized revolutions in sociological theory.

As the old groups lost their hold, people began looking for something new. Much to their surprise (or shock), alternatives did, indeed,

TABLE 6.3 Selected "basic innovations in social science"

Innovation	Innovator(s)	Date	Place	Chapter in this book to which it is important
Functionalist anthropology and sociology (anthropology)	A. R. Radcliffe-Brown	1925	Capetown	3
	B. Malinowski	1925–1945	London	
	T. Parsons	1932–1950	Cambridge, Mass.	
Ecosystem theory (sociology)	R. Park	1926–1938	Chicago	3 (early Chicago school)
	E. Burgess			
Community studies (sociology)	R. Lynd	1929–1962	New York	3
	H. Lynd			
	L. Warner	1941	Chicago	
	C. Kluckhohn			
Sociology of bureaucracy, culture, and values (sociology)	M. Weber	1900–1921	Germany	3
Multivariate analysis linked to social theory (sociology)	S. Stouffer	1944–1954	Washington, D.C.	3
	T. W. Anderson		Cambridge, Mass.	
	P. F. Lazarsfeld		New York	
Attitude survey and opinion polling (psychology)	G. Gallup	1936	Princeton	3
	H. Cantril	1937–1952		
	P. F. Lazarsfeld	1940	New York	
	A. Campbell	1942	Ann Arbor, Mich.	
Pragmatic and behavioral psychology (psychology)	J. Dewey	1905–1925	Ann Arbor, Mich.	4
	G. H. Mead	1900–1934	Chicago	
	C. Cooley	1900–1930	Ann Arbor, Mich.	
	W. I. Thomas	1900–1940	Chicago New York	
Laboratory study of small groups (psychology)	K. Lewin			5
	R. Lippitt	1932–1936	Cambridge, Mass.	
	R. Likert			
	D. Cartwright			
Sociometry and sociograms (sociology)	J. Moreno	1915 1934–1943	Innsbruck, Austria	5
Computers (mathematics)	V. Bush	1943–1958	Cambridge, Mass.	7–10

Source (Columns 1–4): Karl W. Deutsch, John Platt, and Dieter Senghaas, "Conditions Favoring Major Advances in Social Sciences," **Science** 171, 5 February, 1971. Copyright 1971 by the American Association for the Advancement of Science. Used by permission.

TABLE 6.3 (continued)

Innovation	Innovator(s)	Date	Place	Chapter in this book to which it is important
	S. Caldwell			
	D. P. Eckert		Philadelphia	
	J. W. Mauchy			
Computer simulation of economic systems (economics)	L. Klein G. Orcutt	1947–1960	Philadelphia Madison, Wisc.	7
Computer simulation of social and political systems (political science)	W. McPhee H. Simon A. Newell	1956–1966	Pittsburgh	7
	I. Pool	1958–1964	Cambridge, Mass.	
	R. Abelson		New Haven, Conn.	
Structural linguistics (mathematics)	R. Jakobson	1927–1967	Brno, Czecho-slovakia and Cambridge, Mass.	8, 10
Correlation analysis and social theory (mathematics)	K. Pearson F. Edgeworth R. A. Fisher	1900–1948	England	9
Large-scale sampling in social research (mathematics)	M. Hansen	1930–1953	Washington, D.C.	3, 9
Structuralism in anthropology and social science (anthropology)	C. Lévi-Strauss	1948–1966	Paris	10
Peasant and guerrilla organization and government (political science)	Mao Tse-tung	1929–1949	China	11
Theory of one-party organization and revolution (political science)	V. I. Lenin	1900–1917	Siberia, London, Munich	11
Large-scale nonviolent political action (political science)	M. K. Gandhi	1939–1944	Ahmedabad, India	11
Authoritarian personality and family structure (psychology)	M. Horkheimer H. Marcuse E. Fromm	1930–1932	Frankfurt	3, 11
	T. Adorno, et al.	1950	Stanford	
	A. Mitscherlich	1962	Heidelberg	

exist. Those who had been central to the development of the new sociologies were quite unsurprised by their own developments. The field as a whole, however, was shocked suddenly to find so many different kinds of sociology when only two major kinds had existed before. Furthermore, none of the new alternatives was a simple variant of one of the older types. All the new groups represented combinations with other disciplinary areas—combinations that differed from the mixture of social structural studies, anthropology, psychiatry, economics, and social psychology that had constituted the sociology of the past 20 years.

The serious consideration of politics has been combined with engineering and systems analysis thinking by the social forecasters. Ethnomethodologists have been reexamining the philosophical basis of the discipline with an emphasis on linguistic problems. New causal theory has accepted standard American sociology's mix of psychology and social structure, but it has also introduced formalizations from genetics, economics, and psychology. The new causal theory group is more concerned with the *form* of theory than with its content. Structuralism, like ethnomethodology, has also rejected the philosophical basis of standard American sociology and has reconstructed the discipline without a social psychology. The introduction of serious social and political considerations, together with Marxist theory, has been central to radical-critical thinking.

Each of these groups, then, has its own differences with earlier sociology, and these differences are not identical. The new groups' one element in common, as Deutsch, Platt, and Senghaas (1971) noted of sociology as a whole, is that they have been absorbing and adopting, rather than totally creating, their new theories. Hence we do not appear to be on the brink of any major synthesis of these theory groups.

Nevertheless, since the job market is presently static, and the flow of research money is not increasing, the new groups will not find it easy to continue growing during the next few years; and it is even more unlikely that other new groups will start. I do not expect all these groups to survive separately. One or some combination will almost inevitably push into a dominant position. Chapter 12 includes some suggestions regarding the eventual outcome.

NOTES

1. Professional is defined as a "fellow" or "active" member of the American Sociological Association.
2. It is largely for this reason that I have not used citation data in these chapters. I question the significance of citation data when the degree of recency is so much lower than for natural science groups. For the latter, recency virtually guarantees that the relationship or lack of it between social groups

and groups defined by citation data will be significant. There is no such assurance for sociology data.

3. This interchange has also been true of natural science groups. Development of some of the groups reported in Griffith and Mullins (1972) was not completely independent. For example, Harold Bohr, Niels's brother, was a mathematician trained at Göttingen under Hilbert (Reid, 1970). Max Delbrück, one of the founders of molecular biology, was resident at Bohr's institute for several years during the 1930s (Mullins, 1972: 55). Such exchanges suggest a "social epidemiology" in which the pattern of successful development is recognized, either consciously or unconsciously, and subsequently repeated elsewhere. The same "contagion" seems to exist for sociology. For example, Parsons helped train Harold Garfinkel (a later founder of ethnomethodology); Ogburn trained O. D. Duncan (a later leader in new causal theory work).

   Comparison of a list of these more central scientists in social science's coherent groups with various prestige rankings, citation and high publication lists, and so on, reveals that a majority of the top persons on those lists are also those who have been active at some time in one or another coherent group. Others occur on these lists also, but they are not a majority. (See Broadus, 1952, 1967; Crane, 1965; Glenn and Villemez, 1970; Lightfield, 1971; Oromaner, 1968, 1969, 1972; Shamblin, 1970; Straus and Radel, 1969; Westie, 1972; and Yoels, 1971, among other discussions of these subjects.)

4. For examples of exchange theory and conflict theory, see Blau (1969) and Dahrendorff (1969), respectively.

5. For further discussion of graduate schools and departments, see Blalock (1969); Borgatta (1969); Cartter (1966); Gross (1970); Knudsen and Vaughan (1969); Lewis (1968); and Shichor (1970).

6. We can infer that the number of jobs has increased during the last two decades, since unemployment has not been a serious problem for the profession; according to the NSF (1972: 60), only 612 out of 7658 were unemployed in 1970. We noted earlier the increase in ASA membership over the decade.

BIBLIOGRAPHY

American Journal of Sociology.
   1966   *Cumulative Index to the American Journal of Sociology.* Vol. 1–70, 1895–1965. Chicago: University of Chicago Press.
American Sociological Association.
   1959, 1970   *Directory of Members 1959*; also for year 1970. New York and Washington, D.C.: American Sociological Association.
   1969, 1971   *Guide to Graduate Departments*; also for year 1971. Washington, D.C.: American Sociological Association.
Blalock, H. M., Jr.
   1969   "On graduate methodology training." *American Sociologist* 4 (February): 5–6.

Blau, Peter M.
   1969   "The structure of social associations." Pp. 186–200 in Walter L.
          Wallace (ed.), *Sociological Theory: An Introduction*. Chicago: Al-
          dine.
Borgatta, Edgar F.
   1969   "Some notes on graduate education, with special reference to sociol-
          ogy." *American Sociologist* 4 (February): 6–12.
Broadus, Robert N.
   1952   "An analysis of literature cited in the *American Sociological Review*."
          American Sociological Review 17 (June): 355–357.
   1967   "A citation study for sociology." *American Sociologist* 2 (February):
          19–20.
Brown, Julia S., and Brian C. Gilmartin.
   1969   "Sociology today: lucunae, emphases and surfeits." *American Sociolo-
          gist* 4 (November): 283–290.
Caplow, Theodore, and Reece J. McGee.
   1965   *The Academic Marketplace*. New York: Anchor-Doubleday.
Cartter, Allan M.
   1966   *An Assessment of Quality in Graduate Education*. Washington, D.C.:
          American Council on Education.
Cole, Jonathan, and Stephen Cole.
   1971   "Measuring the quality of sociological research: problems in the use
          of the Science Citation Index." *American Sociologist* 6 (February):
          23–29.
Crane, Diana.
   1965   "Scientists at major and minor universities: a study of productivity
          and recognition." *American Sociological Review* 30 (October): 699–
          714.
Dahrendorf, Ralf.
   1969   "Toward a theory of social conflict." Pp. 213–226 in Walter L. Wal-
          lace (ed.), *Sociological Theory: An Introduction*. Chicago: Aldine.
Deutsch, Karl W., John Platt, and Dieter Senghaas.
   1971   "Conditions favoring major advances in social sciences." *Science* 171
          (February 5): 450–459.
Dupree, A. Hunter.
   1957   *Science in the Federal Government: A History of Policies and Ac-
          tivities to 1940*. Cambridge, Mass.: Belknap Press of Harvard Uni-
          versity Press.
Friedrichs, Robert W.
   1970   *A Sociology of Sociology*. New York: Free Press.
Garvey, W. D.
   1972   Presentation to the COSATI (Committee on Scientific and Technical
          Information) Review Group, Elkton, Md. (January 6, 1972).
Glenn, Norval D., and Wayne Villemez.
   1970   "The productivity of sociologists at 45 American universities." *Ameri-
          can Sociologist* 5 (August): 244–252.

Glenn, Norval D., and David Weiner.
  1969   "Some trends in the social origins of American sociologists." *American Sociologist* 4 (November): 291–302.
Goffman, Erving.
  1961   *Encounters*. Indianapolis: Bobbs-Merrill.
Gold, David.
  1957   "A note on statistical analysis in the *American Sociological Review*." *American Sociological Review* 22 (June): 332–333.
Griffith, Belver C.
  1972   "On the nature of social science and its literature." Philadelphia: Drexel University, Graduate School of Library Science. (mimeo)
Griffith, Belver C., and Nicholas C. Mullins.
  1972   "Coherent social groups in scientific change: 'invisible colleges' may be consistent throughout science." *Science* 177 (4053, September 15): 959–964.
Gross, George R.
  1970   "The organization set: a study of sociology departments." *American Sociologist* 5 (February): 25–29.
Homans, George C.
  1941   *English Villagers of the Thirteenth Century*. Cambridge, Mass.: Harvard University Press.
  1950   *The Human Group*. New York: Harcourt Brace Jovanovich.
  1961   *Social Behavior: Its Elementary Forms*. New York: Harcourt Brace Jovanovich.
Knudsen, Dean D., and Ted R. Vaughan.
  1969   "Quality in graduate education: a re-evaluation of the rankings of sociology departments in the Cartter report." *American Sociologist* 4 (February): 12–19.
Kuhn, Thomas S.
  1970   *The Structure of Scientific Revolutions*. 2nd ed. Chicago: University of Chicago Press.
Lewis, Lionel S.
  1968   "On subjective and objective rankings of sociology departments." *American Sociologist* 3 (May): 129–131.
Lightfield, E. Timothy.
  1971   "Output and recognition of sociologists." *American Sociologist* 6 (May): 128–133.
Lin, Nan, and Carnot E. Nelson.
  1969   "Bibliographic reference patterns in core sociological journals, 1965–66." *American Sociologist* 4 (February): 47–50.
McCartney, James L.
  1970   "On being scientific: changing styles of presentation of sociological research." *American Sociologist* 5 (February): 30–35.
Merton, Robert K.
  1957   "Priorities in scientific discovery: a chapter in the sociology of science." *American Sociological Review* 22 (December): 635–659.

Meyers, C. Roger.
    1970   "Journal citations and scientific eminence in contemporary psychology." *American Psychologist* 25 (November): 1041–1048.
Moynihan, Daniel P.
    1969   *Maximum Feasible Misunderstanding: Community Action in the War on Poverty.* New York: Free Press.
Mullins, Nicholas C.
    1968   "The distribution of social and cultural properties in informal communication networks among biological scientists." *American Sociological Review* 33 (October): 786–797.
    1972   "The development of a scientific specialty: the Phage Group and the origins of molecular biology." *Minerva* 10 (January): 51–82.
National Science Foundation.
    1971   *An Analysis of Federal R & D Funding by Budget Function.* Washington, D.C.: National Science Foundation.
    1972   *American Science Manpower 1970.* Washington, D.C.: National Science Foundation.
Oromaner, Mark J.
    1968   "The most cited sociologists: an analysis of introductory text citations." *American Sociologist* 3 (May): 124–126.
    1969   "The audience as a determinant of the most important sociologists." *American Sociologist* 4 (November): 332–335.
    1972   "The structure of influence in contemporary academic sociology." *American Sociologist* 7 (May): 11–13.
Reid, Constance.
    1970   *Hilbert.* New York: Springer Verlag.
Roose, Kenneth D., and Charles J. Andersen.
    1970   *A Rating of Graduate Programs.* Washington, D.C.: American Council on Education.
Schichor, David.
    1970   "Prestige of sociology departments and the placing of new Ph.D.'s." *American Sociologist* 5 (May): 157–160.
Shamblin, Don H.
    1970   "Prestige and the sociology establishment." *American Sociologist* 5 (May): 154–156.
Shanas, Ethel.
    1945   *"The American Journal of Sociology* through fifty years." *American Journal of Sociology* 50 (May): 522–533.
Sibley, Elbridge.
    1963   *The Education of Sociologists in the United States.* New York: Russell Sage.
Simpson, Richard L.
    1961   "Expanding and declining fields in American sociology." *American Sociological Review* 26 (June): 458–466.
Smelser, Neil J., and James A. Davis (eds.).
    1969   *Sociology.* Englewood Cliffs, N.J.: Prentice-Hall.

Solomon, Warren E.
  1972 "Correlates of prestige ranking of graduate programs in sociology."
      American Sociologist 7 (May): 13–14.
Sorokin, Pitirim A.
  1956 *Fads and Foibles in Modern Sociology and Related Sciences*. Chi-
      cago: Regnery.
Straus, Murray A., and David J. Radel.
  1969 "Eminence, productivity and power of sociologists in various regions."
      American Sociologist 4 (February): 1–4.
Useem, Michael.
  1972 "Federal government influence on social research." Paper prepared
      for a seminar session at the annual meeting of the American Socio-
      logical Association, New Orleans (August).
Veblen, Thorstein.
  1965 *The Engineers and the Price System*. New York: Augustus M. Kelly.
      (Reprinted from 1921 ed.)
Wallace, Walter L. (ed.).
  1969 *Sociological Theory: An Introduction*. Chicago: Aldine.
Westie, Frank R.
  1972 "Academic expectations for professional immortality: a study of
      legitimation." *Sociological Focus* 5 (Summer): 1–25.
Williams, Melvin J.
  1968 "Some observations of recruitment in sociology." *American Sociolo-
      gist* 3 (May): 127–129.
Yoels, William C.
  1971 "Destiny or dynasty: doctoral origins and appointment patterns of
      editors of the *American Sociological Review* 1948–1968." *American
      Sociologist* 6 (May): 134–139.
Ziman, John M.
  1968 *Public Knowledge: An Essay Concerning the Social Dimension of
      Science*. London: Cambridge University Press.

PART THREE
CONTEMPORARY THEORIES
AND THEORY GROUPS:
THE CHANGING SCENE

CHAPTER 7
THE SOCIAL FORECASTERS
Waiting for Godot

**Social and intellectual properties
of social forecasting**

Intellectual leader(s)	None
Social organization leader(s)	None
Research centers	Hudson Institute
	Institute for the Future
	Russell Sage Foundation
Training center for students	—
Paradigm content	Predictions for the future, given certain programs or policies; measurement of society.
Successes[a]	Kahn and Wiener, **The Year 2000** (1967); Forrester, **Urban Dynamics** (1969)
Program statement	**Toward a Social Report** (1969)
Examples of secondary work	Bell, **Toward the Year 2000** (1968)
	Rainwater and Yancey, **The Moynihan Report and the Politics of Controversy** (1968)
Examples of critical work	Horowitz, **The Rise and Fall of Project Camelot** (1967)
	Duncan, "Social Forecasting: The State of the Art" (1969a)
Text	None

[a] For this group, the successes listed are only potential; they have not yet been recognized as such.

The social forecasters are a group presently in the network stage. As such, they have some research to their credit and have attracted the interest of several scientists. They are full of possibilities—including that of collapse. The area may prove to have been a fad, or it may organize further into a cluster, do more research, produce a distinct theory, and then institutionalize. The present group probably includes some persons who will not participate in further development, and the content of the intellectual model that may eventually constitute the group's theory is not yet very clear. Numerous possibilities will undoubtedly be proposed and discussed by group members.

The term "social forecasters" here refers to social scientists who are actively involved, on both the theoretical and practical planes, with forecasting societal activity; the term "social planners" refers to persons doing city (especially architectural), business, or government planning. Planning is a necessary partner to forecasting; the latter's concern, however, is theoretical and practical, whereas planning stresses application and practicability. Social forecasters lack a common theoretical orientation but share a desire to predict the future, either for policy-making purposes or to validate a theory. Forecasters' work is composed primarily of discussions of the rationale and means for predicting the future. The means proposed for making predictions are a series of technical devices whose purpose is to produce believable estimates of the future.

Analysis of the outline on p. 155 points up the group's lack of social development. There are no recognized intellectual and social leaders; yet a program statement and both secondary and critical work have been produced. The table also reveals one of the forecasters' major problems: the three major research centers have no students, since they are research institutes rather than universities. The group's potential successes are similar—each attempts to predict the future, using techniques that are more systematic than simply thinking about a problem; nevertheless, the systematization of a well-developed theory is lacking. Table 7.1 summarizes highlights in the development of this infant group.

TABLE 7.1 Social and intellectual highlights in the development of social forecasting

Stage	Social	Intellectual
Normal: to 1965	Commission on the year 2000 Johnson administration social programs	**Recent Social Trends** (1934): population forecasts
Network: 1965–	Several joint projects	Bauer (ed.), **Social Indicators** (1966) Program statement: **Toward A Social Report** (1969)

NORMAL STAGE:
TO 1965

SOCIAL

During the normal stage, nine people who later became important to forecasting during the network stage were at work, independent of each other for the most part. These nine were Raymond A. Bauer, Daniel Bell, Albert Biderman, O. D. Duncan, Amitai Etzioni, Bertram Gross, Wilbert E. Moore, Daniel P. Moynihan, and Eleanor Sheldon. All except Gross are at least nominally sociologists.

Ray Bauer received his Ph.D. degree in social psychology from Harvard in 1950. After a short time as a lecturer in Harvard's social relations department, he spent a year at Stanford's Center for Advanced Study in the Behavioral Sciences and then returned to the Harvard Business School. His specialty has been the administration of large-scale activity, and he has maintained continuing interest in the Soviet Union. His effect on the group has been more to push the use of social indicators than to produce great amounts of new research.

Daniel Bell was managing editor of *The New Leader* (1941–1944; ASA, 1959) and labor editor of *Fortune* (1948–1958; ASA, 1959). In 1958 he was appointed as associate professor at Columbia, even though he had still not completed his doctorate. (He finally received this degree in 1960, from Columbia.) The author of several books, he has provided some intellectual leadership for the group.

Albert Biderman has been a research associate with the Bureau of Social Science Research since 1958. He has done contract research on many topics for various federal agencies. He has been a consistent group member but has provided no special leadership.

O. D. Duncan was trained by William Ogburn, who was responsible for *Recent Social Trends* (see below). Based at the University of Michigan since 1962, Duncan has become a leading demographer and sociologist (see Chapter 9 for another aspect of Duncan's work). His interest in prediction dates from at least 1949 (Ohlin and Duncan, 1949). The most technically competent of the group members, he has been a consistent data analyst and contributor to the literature.

Bertram Gross, a political scientist, was the executive secretary of the first Council of Economic Advisors. He has made consistent efforts to improve the data available for political decision making.

Like Duncan, Wilbert E. Moore and Eleanor Sheldon have done demographic research; both were staff members of the Russell Sage Foundation, which is a principal research center for the forecasters (the Institute for the Future and the Hudson Institute, also a futurist research center, are the others). Sheldon and Moore have been important as organizers of the group (e.g., they have organized conferences); but they have not been sufficiently active to be considered social organization leaders. They are also coauthors (Sheldon and Moore, eds., 1968).

Amitai Etzioni, the most nearly traditional sociologist who is important to the group, received his Ph.D. degree from Berkeley in 1958. He has been at Columbia University since that time. His interests were originally in complex organization, and he has written several good books in this area, including a frequently used reader (Etzioni, 1961).

Daniel P. Moynihan is perhaps the most interesting member of the group. One of America's foremost practitioners (during the 1960s) of the art of moving between academe and government without becoming fully identified with either, he wrote the "Moynihan Report" on Negro family disintegration in 1964 (published in Rainwater and Yancey, 1968); soon afterward, he left government service to become director of the joint MIT–Harvard Urban Center.

In 1965 all these people were established professionals whose interests were quite separate.

INTELLECTUAL

Social planning is not a new idea. Indeed, the census reported in Numbers 1:1–49 was probably not the first attempt by a governing body to learn what conditions existed in the territory it ruled. The United States Census (mandated by the Constitution) was first taken in 1790. As the social sciences have developed over the last half-century, so also has a strong relationship sprung up between the Census Bureau and some social scientists, particularly demographers. Demography, which is now almost an independent discipline, developed rapidly during the 1950s and has been an important root for the social planning tradition. It has also produced some of the more successful work in future prediction (however, see Duncan, 1969a). Demography's population growth model has an obvious need for and usefulness to census data. The accomplishment of a worldwide census in the 1950s and early 1960s has had enormous effects on our conceptions of the world.[1]

A second social science model important for social forecasting derives from the collecting of economic statistics and the 1930s work of Simon Kuznets which, combined with the economic theories of Keynes and others, provided a prediction model for national economic growth levels. This predictive ability has been institutionalized, in the President's Council of Economic Advisors, since 1946. The 25 years of experience in prediction and policy change since then have helped economic theory as well as (presumably) the country (Taeuber, 1970). Bertram Gross, an important student of social indicators, was the first executive secretary of the

Council of Economic Advisors. His work has been heavily influenced by the economic model.

The work of University of Chicago sociologist William Ogburn has also been important to social forecasting. In 1928 Ogburn was engaged as research director for the President's Research Committee on Social Trends. Their report, *Recent Social Trends* (1934), constituted a pioneering effort which, although largely disregarded by sociologists for a long period, has been pointed out recently as a major effort. Indeed, many contemporary commentators have suggested that, for its sheer effort as well as for its blend of the theoretical and the practical, this work has not been surpassed by any of the more contemporary research efforts.

Forecasting became increasingly possible as the technology of social data handling improved. Computers have enabled the simultaneous consideration of hundreds of variables in hundreds of equations, or the statistical analysis of thousands of items. Deutsch, Platt, and Senghaas (1971) note that simulations of economic systems have developed separately from social and political simulations. Simulations have the advantage of being able to work in the absence of a well-developed theory (the relation between simulation and theory is discussed below). The increasing speed and size of computer operations in the 1960s and 1970s have only made it increasingly natural to think about responsible planning for a country whose population exceeds 200 million persons and whose economy passes the billion dollar mark.

NETWORK STAGE: 1965–

SOCIAL

During the network stage, as a rule, independent investigators in a research area are gradually drawn together. The forecasters, however, were *called* together. First, a series of projects developed during the mid-1960s (some funded by the federal government and others by private sources) needed social science forecasting techniques and data that were sufficiently accurate to permit the formal setting of policy by reference to scientific information. This interest developed under President John F. Kennedy and carried over into the Johnson administration. The concern is attributable to the need of several operating federal programs for information pertinent to the issues raised by governmental (local, state, and federal) involvement in programs relating to housing, schools, welfare and family assistance, urban development, and other issues. Government actions clearly had produced effects that had not been foreseen by the policy makers who designed those actions. Foreknowledge of these effects (e.g., the breakup of neighborhoods under urban renewal; see Anderson, 1964) might have resulted in alternate plans.

Second, these plans and their consequences had paralleled in time, and sharply contrasted with, the seemingly rational planning and management of business firms (e.g., Robert MacNamara's work at Ford) and of countries such as Sweden, France, and the Soviet Union. Indeed, MacNamara himself became Secretary of Defense under the Kennedy administration. Such management calls for the ability to predict the outcomes of certain actions; management of social programs, hence, requires enough information on the society affected to permit the assessment of activities. William the Conqueror's "Domesday Book" (see Bean, 1968), a list of the property and supplies in his country, is a very early example of management information. Today census data provide our government with certain types of management information, as do tax records, Social Security records, veterans records, and so on.

There were many people potentially able to serve these two social needs; but the nine persons mentioned previously became exceptionally active in several consulting activities. The normal stage was brought to an end by the beginning establishment of advisory committees (e.g., the Commission on the Year 2000, convoked in 1965 by the American Academy of Arts and Sciences), which created social links among numerous people. In addition, several persons have participated even more actively in government activity. In 1968 Moynihan joined President Richard M. Nixon's staff, and he was influential in establishing the White House National Goals staff. He left that administration in 1970 to return to Harvard. Bauer served on the National Goals staff during part of Nixon's first term. For a selection of people who have participated in forecasting work, see Table 7.2.

Table 7.2 contains the basic data for the rest of this chapter. It lists those who have participated in developments up to 1972. The table names many more persons than are central to forecasting. Many will never contribute to this work again. Even so, this list has been pared down from the total of all persons who have ever been involved in any way with this work. The job locations are noteworthy because most of the institutions named have no graduate training program and, consequently, no current students (see table).

This group thus far has been as fractionated in its research focuses as were small group researchers. Therefore, many names in the table have been marked to indicate the individual's primary research interest. Social indicators (S), futurism (F), and simulations (M) are all strong and somewhat separate focuses. Forecasting's social and intellectual center, though, is provided by the social scientists whose chief interest is social indicators. Their concern is to diagnose contemporary society (i.e., to determine what indicators provide good indexes of the near future). The futurists, by contrast, concentrate not on the near future but on prediction over a longer range (25–100 years). Their work has provided both a logical and a methodological extension of that done with social indicators. The simulators, who can be seen as providing a methodology for both concerns, have worked to build computer models that show (1) interdependence among the parts of social systems and (2) how changes ramify throughout the systems. All three intellectual concerns are discussed later; for the present, I will concentrate on the social aspects of these focuses.

Social Indicators   Scientists explicitly interested in social indicators have produced five major documents. These are: three issues of the *Annals* (two volumes in 1967, and one in 1970); *Toward a Social Report* (U.S. Department of Health, Education, and Welfare, 1969); *Indicators of Social Change* (Sheldon and Moore, 1968); *Social Indicators* (Bauer, 1968); and *Toward the Year 2000* (Bell, 1968). Bauer, Bell, Biderman, Duncan, Etzioni, Gross, Moore, Moynihan, and Sheldon have been involved in more than one of these projects. All are well known and their work has been solid if not exciting. Of them, however, only Duncan has had regular students, and these have not been concentrated in one area. Thus far, this group has maintained itself solely by attracting a few new professionals over time. Real growth must wait until (1) one or more of these persons relocates where he can train students or (2) a major social scientist *and* his group of students are recruited to the group (an unlikely occurrence without some exciting intellectual breakthrough). The present pattern of recruiting established professionals is important, however, because it enables those interested in social indicators to act as a "glue," holding the futurists and the simulators with them into a somewhat coherent forecasting group.

The impetus of government support does not affect the other theory groups discussed in this book; however, it strongly favors the maintenance of social forecasting research. The government is now heavily involved in both forecasting and social planning activity. Robert MacNamara's attempt to rationalize the Defense Department's organization and the introduction of Programming and Planning Budgeting Systems (PPBS) into many government agencies has widened the knowledge of systems work. Federal agencies have even officially participated in the activities of the Commission on the Year 2000.

This Commission, established to probe the shape of the future, included the persons listed in Table 7.3. Daniel Bell was selected as chairman. The Commission considered what the world, and in particular the United States, would be like in A.D. 2000. The involvement of federal agencies in this program was twofold. First, Housing and Urban Development,

TABLE 7.2 Important social forecasters: degree (date and place) and selected job locations

| Name[a] | Ph.D. | | 1950 |
	Date	Place	
F Abt, Clark	1965	MIT	*
S Bauer, Raymond A.	1950	HARV	*
F Bell, Daniel	1960	COL	*
S Biderman, Albert	1964	CHIC	IIT
F Cetron, Michael	*	*	*
F Dror, Yehezkel	ni	ni	*
S Duncan, O. D.	1949	CHIC	WISC
Etzioni, Amitai	1958	BERK	*
S Fisher, Joseph	1949	HARV	ni
M Forrester, Jay W.	ni	ni	MIT
S Glaser, Daniel	1954	CHIC	*
S Gordon, Kermit	ni	ni	ni
F Gordon, Theodore J.	ni	ni	*
S Gross, Bertram M.	ni	ni	PCEA
F Helmer, Olaf	ni	*	*
F Ikle, Fred C.	1950	CHIC	COL
M Inbar, Michael	ni	JHU	*
F Jantsch, Erich (French)	*	*	*
F Kahn, Herman	none	none	res
S Keyserling, Leon	1931	HARV	PCEA
S Lebergott, Stanley	1958	HARV	BURB
Lehman, Edward	1964	MSST	*
F Lenz, Ralph	*	*	*
F Linstone, Harold	*	*	*
S Long, Norton	1937	HARV	WERE
F Martino, Joseph	*	*	*
Mitchell, Joyce M.	1964	BERK	*
Mitchell, William C.	ni	BERK	*
S Moore, Wilbert E.	1940	HARV	PRIN
S Moriyama, Iwo M.	1937	YALE	PHS
Moynihan, Daniel P.	1961	PENN	*
S Russett, Bruce M.	1961	YALE	*
S Sheldon, Eleanor	1949	CHIC	COL
M Stoll, Clarice	1967	RUTG	*
S Taeuber, Conrad	1929	MINN	UN
S Verba, Sidney	1959	PRIN	*
Wilensky, Harold	1955	CHIC	*

Sources: American Men of Science (1968); ASA (various years a,b,c); **The Annals** (various years); **Directory of American Scholars** (1969); **Technological Forecasting and Social Change** (various years).

[a] Abbreviations are as follows: S = primary interest in social indicators; F = primary interest in future; M = primary interest in simulation.

Job held in academic year ending in			
1960	1965	1968	1970
res	ABT	ABT	ABT
HARB	HARB	HARB	HARB
COL	COL	COL	HARV
BSSR	BSSR	BSSR	BSSR
*	*	res	res
ni	ni	ni	RAND
CHIC	MICH	MICH	MICH
COL	COL	COL	COL
RFI	RFI	RFI	RFI
MIT	MIT	MIT	MIT
ILL	ILL	RUTG	NYNA
ni	ni	ni	BROI
*	ni	IFF	IFF
SYRA	SYRA	SYRA	WAYS
*	RAND	IFF	IFT
RAND	MIT	RAND	RAND
*	*	*	JHU
*	*	*	*
res	HUDI	HUDI	HUDI
pri	pri	pri	pri
BURB	WESL	WESL	WESL
*	NCST	MSTL	MSTL
*	res	res	res
*	ni	res	res
NWU	BRAN	ILL	BRAN
*	res	res	res
ORE	ORE	ORE	ORE
ORE	ORE	ORE	ORE
PRIN	RUSS	RUSS	DENV
PHS	HEW	HEW	HEW
SYRA	HARV	HARV	WHS
YALE	YALE	YALE	YALE
UCLA	RUSS	RUSS	RUSS
*	RUTG	JHU	JHU
CENS	CENS	CENS	CENS
PRIN	STAN	STAN	CHIC
MICH	BERK	BERK	BERK

Key:

ABT	Abt Associates
BERK	University of California, Berkeley
BRAN	Brandeis University
BROI	Brookings Institution, Washington, D.C.
BSSR	Bureau of Social Science Research, Inc.
BURB	Bureau of the Budget
CENS	U.S. Census Bureau
CHIC	University of Chicago
COL	Columbia University
DENV	Denver University
HARB	Harvard Business School
HARV	Harvard University
HEW	U.S. Department of Health, Education, and Welfare
HUDI	Hudson Institute
IFF	Institute for the Future, Middletown, Conn.
IIT	Illinois Institute of Technology
ILL	University of Illinois
JHU	Johns Hopkins University
MICH	University of Michigan
MINN	University of Minnesota
MIT	Massachusetts Institute of Technology
MSST	Mississippi State University
MSTL	University of Missouri, St. Louis
NCST	North Carolina State University
ni	No information
NWU	Northwestern University
NYNA	New York Narcotic Addiction Control Commission
ORE	University of Oregon
PCEA	President's Council of Economic Advisors
PHS	U.S. Public Health Service
pri	Private practice, consultant
PRIN	Princeton University
RAND	RAND Corporation, Santa Monica, Calif.
res	Miscellaneous research position
RFI	Resources for the Future, Inc.
RUSS	Russell Sage Foundation
RUTG	Rutgers
STAN	Stanford University
SYRA	Syracuse University
UCLA	University of California, Los Angeles
UN	United Nations
WAYS	Wayne State University
WERE	Western Reserve University
WESL	Wesleyan College
WHS	White House Staff
WISC	University of Wisconsin
YALE	Yale University
*	Not in system

State, and Health, Education, and Welfare were involved for the purpose of shaping present programs for the cities, the international order, and the health and education of the population, since these programs would have effects in the coming years. Second, the agencies wanted to plan ahead for future changes. It is interesting to note that representatives of federal agencies spent little work time with social scientists before the introduction of systems work to the federal government.

Futurism   The futurists have been important to the social forecasters primarily as a source of techniques (to be discussed below). Courses in futurism, most of them undergraduate, are taught at many locations (Eldridge, 1970); but the futurists' lack of both graduate students and an academic basis hampers growth of their work, just as it blocks progress on social indicators.

Social connections between the futurists and the students of social indicators have been tentative at best (a further indication of the forecasters' early network status). Indeed, in his Presidential Address to the American Sociological Association (Moore, 1966) Wilbert Moore asked why sociology had not considered the future in more depth in its professional work. However, Bell and Moore provide some social links between the study of social indicators and futurism through their efforts on the Commission on the Year 2000, where they worked with Herman Kahn and Anthony Weiner of the Hudson Institute.

TABLE 7.3 Commission on the Year 2000

Member	Identification as of 1967[a]
Bell, Daniel, Chairman	Professor of sociology
Bowie, Robert	U.S. Department of State
Brzezinski, Zbigniew	U.S. Department of State
Deutsch, Karl W.	Professor of political science
Dobzhansky, Theodosius	Professor of zoology
Donovan, Hedley	Editor-in-chief, **Time** magazine
Duhl, Leonard	Psychiatrist, special assistant, HUD
Erikson, Erik H.	Psychiatrist, professor of human development
Frank, Lawrence K.	Social psychologist and retired foundation officer
Gorham, William	Assistant Secretary, HEW (RAND, 1953–1962)
Graubard, Stephen R.	Professor of history; editor of **Daedalus**
Haar, Charles M.	Assistant Secretary, HUD, on leave from Harvard Law Sch.
Huntington, Samuel P.	Professor of Government
Ikle, Fred C.	Professor of political science
Kahn, Herman	Director, Hudson Institute (RAND, 1948–1961)
Kalven, Harry	Professor of law
Leontief, Wassily	Professor of economics
Mayr, Ernst	Professor of zoology
Mead, Margaret	Curator, ethnology, American Museum of Natural History
Meselson, Matthew	Professor of biology
Miller, George A.	Professor of psychology
Moore, Wilbert E.	Sociologist, Russell Sage Foundation
Moynihan, Daniel P.	Director, Joint Center for Urban Studies
Orlans, Harold	Senior staff, Brookings Institute
Perloff, Harvey S.	Resources for the Future, Inc.
Pierce, John R.	Executive Director of the Research and Communications Sciences Division of Bell Telephone Laboratories
Pifer, Alan	President, Carnegie Corporation (consultant, USAID)
Piore, Emanuel R.	Vice President and Chief Scientist at IBM
Pool, Ithiel de Sola	Chairman, politcal science department
Postan, Michael	Professor emeritus of economic history
Quarton, Gardner C.	Program Director, Neurosciences Research Program of MIT, psychiatrist
Revelle, Roger	Professor of population
Riesman, David	Professor of social sciences
Rostow, Eugene V.	Undersecretary of State
Schon, Donald A.	President, Organization for Social and Technical Innovation
Shubik, Michael	Professor of economics
Stendahl, Krister	Professor of biblical studies
Wiener, Anthony	Hudson Institute
Wilson, James Q.	Professor of government
Wood, Robert C.	Undersecretary, HUD, (professor of political science)
Wright, Christopher	Professor of political science
Ylvisaker, Paul N.	New Jersey Commissioner of Public Affairs until 1967; director of public affairs programs at Ford Foundation.

Source: Bell (1968).
[a] Abbreviations as follows: HUD = U.S. Department of Housing and Urban Development; HEW = U.S. Department of Health, Education, and Welfare; RAND = RAND Corporation; USAID = U.S. Agency for International Development.

Futurism has had the following very pragmatic concern: to predict *any* part of the future using *any* technique that can produce reliable or even interesting information. Most futurists, however, have concentrated on technological forecasting. The improvement of such work (from its beginnings in simple imagination and "brainstorming" sessions) began in earnest in the 1960s (Jantsch, 1967a).

Some of the most interesting techniques have been developed by Olaf Helmer and Ted Gordon. Helmer has been a productive theoretician of the future, examining the foundations of prediction in the inexact sciences. He has also been an active methodologist, developing predictive techniques such as Delphi (see pp. 171–172). In 1968 Helmer and Gordon founded the Institute for the Future, in Middlebury, Conn. The intent of this organization was to act as a "lookout" organization for the whole society. Helmer and Gordon are also involved in the World Future Society and in its publication, *The Futurist*.

The futurist researchers work in 15 institutions, more or less, ranging from the RAND Corporation through the Institute for the Future and the government of Sweden. Most, as noted, lack an academic base. They are not well connected with other forecasters, although they have some connections with one another (sharing employment in the same institution, etc.). Their institutions have few, if any, sociologists. Futurists are usually employed either in government staff positions or for research in a non-profit organization that does studies for governmental agencies.

The futurists are sufficiently self-conscious as a subgroup to have organized an International Futures Conference in Kyoto, Japan (April 10–16, 1970). Several sociologists spoke at this meeting (Dror, 1970: 3).

Simulation   The scientists doing simulation are even less well organized than the futurists, despite a recent, substantial increase in the number and size of simulation centers engaged in many different kinds of simulation (brain models, urban land use, language acquisition, ecological systems, marketing, etc.), involving persons from many academic disciplines. One center of such activity is the Massachusetts Institute of Technology, where groups (although not sociologists) under Jay W. Forrester and Ithiel de Sola Pool are working on social systems simulation. Other simulations centers are at the University of Colorado, the University of California (Davis), and the Yorktown, N.Y., facilities of IBM.

Three types of simulations are being done: pure computer simulation, game simulation, and hybrid simulation. Those who do pure simulation and those who develop game simulations are distinct from one another. The hybrid (of gaming and pure simulation) was initiated by the game simulation people.

Forrester and Pool are the most prominent pure simulators. Allan

G. Feldt, formerly of Cornell, Richard D. Duke of Michigan State, James S. Coleman at Johns Hopkins, and Clark Abt[2] have been particularly active in developing "games" that attempt to describe parts of real social systems. Of these, Coleman has had several students, particularly Clarice Stoll and Michael Inbar, who have been actively involved in gaming research. Efforts made to collect this group have included the founding of a journal, *Games and Simulation*, and the processing of numerous bibliographies (see Nagelberg and Little, 1970; this point is another similarity that the forecasters bear to the small group theorists).

Socially speaking, then, the forecasters are a disparate group. There has been little cooperation except on a few projects, generally directed by one of the social indicators people (Daniel Bell has been particularly active). The lack of a common project involving people from all three subgroups, a cooperative location in which the parallel kinds of work could be learned together, a successful synthesis of the three emphases, or even a simple ordering of the various techniques, leaves the present social situation confused. The current group at Harvard and MIT (including Bell, Bauer, Moynihan, Forrester, and Pool; see Figure 7.1) offers some hope for a future synthesis or cooperative project.

It should be reemphasized that the forecasters differ from any other group discussed in this book. Its members are linked not by colleagueship but rather by membership on various commissions. No more than two have been together at any job location during the network stage (see Table 7.2). Of locations with two forecasters, only MIT and Oregon have graduate programs. MIT has no graduate program in sociology, however, and Oregon's two faculty members are political scientists. No subgroup of these professionals even shares a common prior training under the same person and might, therefore, serve as a core for the group. This collection of scientists, then, very much resembles the social perception group in psychology, which was brought together by government money, served for a while, and broke apart when government support was withdrawn (Griffith and Miller, 1970).

Two factors presently favor the group's survival: relatively easy access to government funding and to publication. Daniel Bell has been the editor of *The Public Interest* since its founding in 1968, and Gross, who has been a special editor of three issues of *The Annals*, is in an advantageous position with respect to that publication. In addition, Forrester operates his own press, the Wright Allen Press, in Cambridge, Mass. (Forrester, 1968).

At the present, though, discrete groups are still doing their own research. Communication links developed through various projects exist, but the network they form has not been developed. Further development must await (1) recognition of an intellectual success (two possible candidates are Kahn and Wiener's *The Year 2000*, 1967, and Forrester's *Urban*

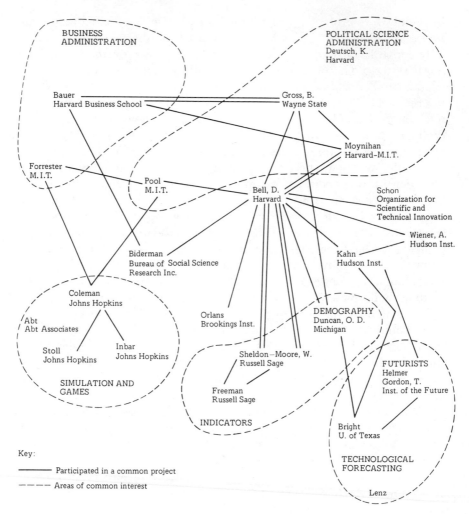

FIGURE 7.1   The forecasters group. No coauthorship network
is shown for this group because none exists;
the group is too underdeveloped. (**Sources: The
Annals** [various years]; Bauer [1966]; Bell [1968];
Duncan [1969a].)

Dynamics, 1969) and (2) students. Forecasting needs both the cohesive-
ness that a success would bring and the sheer increase in numbers that
would result from an influx of students. Without these ingredients, forecasting will continue as a low-level area, attracting interest because of
its obvious social importance and the availability of funds but never
becoming organized and developed.

INTELLECTUAL

Social planning is not unique to sociologists nor to any particular combination of sociologists and others. It goes on all the time, involving hundreds of people in and out of official positions. Most of this planning activity is done without the explicit consideration of theory or impact on the theory process (indeed, this was the criterion we noted for distinguishing forecasters from planners). The planning of laws by the staffs of government bureaus provides a good example of the usual planning process. The process involved is political and economic but not theoretical. Such planning attempts to balance the interests of those who recognize their (usually short-term) interests. However, the short-term interests of those who can *articulate* their interests and the long-term interests of all (including those who can define their short-term interests) may be quite different. Assessing long-term impact is the kind of theoretical problem that most social planning thus far has not faced.

Social Indicators The content of work on social indicators has been systems analysis of social systems. This work is basically present-oriented: What information that we are now receiving can we use to predict the immediate future? Or, How can this information help us with respect to the present? The emphasis is on the careful collection of time-series data for items that, in the past, have seemed to be reliable indicators of future changes; this pattern is that of the demographers and economists who have supplied models for this group. Bauer has given some intellectual leadership on the basis of his research into social indicators (1966). His work has not been particularly technical, although his study of second-order effects does approach many technical questions (Bauer, 1969).[3]

Should it seem unnecessary to try to "predict the present," consider the following situation. The 1970 census was still incomplete in late 1971. At that point, then, many facts about the American population in 1970 were still unknown. Many social conditions are similar in the sheer size of their data and data analysis problems. Sound techniques *"predictive"* of the present are thus necessary if we are to know the present population's mobility and growth rates. The development of such techniques is a theoretical process, since the estimates produced can be checked against the actual data when these finally become available, and the theory can be improved for future use. The *indicators* chosen must be both theoretically sound and practicable (comprehensible and useful as guides to policy makers). The analysts' specific model thus far has been the Economic Report and its indicators (unemployment, the price index, etc.).

Forecasters have also done *program evaluation* (Moynihan, 1969) on both the immediate and the long-range effects of particular programs, although most evaluation research has been done by others (see Clark and Hopkins, 1970). The ultimate goal of evaluation research has been to develop schemes to analyze program costs and benefits, both financial and social, which will facilitate the making of better future decisions about social programs. Both efforts have a central theoretical concern: the need for a useful, elegant theory of social systems which will permit future prediction *and* assessment of past effects. Development of such a theory—which does not presently exist—would probably affect forecasting much as Parsons' 1937 work affected standard American sociology.

It has been since 1965 that Etzioni's interest in this area has flourished. Relatively recently he gave a paper at the American Academy of Management (Etzioni, 1967) in which he proposed a major reorganization of sociological thinking about macrosociological systems to include both structural–functional and cybernetic ideas. His *Active Society* (1968) continued this line of thought. Etzioni can still be considered a scholar within a traditional area (standard American sociology), but he is moving away from standard formulations. The model suggests that he will not move very far unless his deviations receive support from a group that actively uses them. Although the forecasters might use his ideas as a basis for theory building, they have not yet done so.

Interestingly enough, this area has had a program statement, even though it has no recognized intellectual leader. *Toward a Social Report* (U.S. Department of Health, Education, and Welfare, 1969) contains a series of reports broken down by areas (e.g., health, education, and housing in the United States). When appropriate statistics were available, they were reported; otherwise, the estimates offered were based on whatever was available. This work constitutes a program statement in that it indicates the kind of research needed by the government from the social indicators group. However, the document's origin, in the U.S. Department of Health, Education, and Welfare, was not with a person but a committee, and no individual has yet achieved sufficient success in the social indicators area to become a recognized intellectual leader. Rather than testifying to a stage of intellectual development, therefore, the program statement simply indicates the federal government's past interest in forecasting. This evidence reinforces my suspicion that forecasting as an entity would disappear from sociology without government support.

The group's special character comes from its having been force-fed by the federal government, in part as a result of pressure from social scientists. When President Johnson announced, in a State of the Union address, that he had asked the Secretary of Health, Education, and Welfare to establish measures of the health and happiness of society which would parallels economic indicators (Springer, 1970: 2), he was responding to the impact of the social sciences on policy making in his administration. His response was to try to systematize the collection of indicators for how the society (and by extension, his programs) was doing.

The pressures had been generated quite deliberately by persons such as Gross and Bell, who believed that society would be better run if accurate information were available for decision-making in such areas as national health and education (Olson, 1969; Springer, 1970). These pressures built slowly, and the responses to them were not without problems. For example, the so-called Moynihan Report (1968) on the Negro family was originally a document prepared for internal planning use by Daniel P. Moynihan, then a junior official in the Department of Labor. Its intent was to discover what sorts of measures the federal government should propose in order to stabilize the Negro ghetto family. Before such proposals could be made, however, a profile of the Negro ghetto family was needed. The response to Moynihan (Rainwater and Yancey, 1968) and to Project Camelot (see pp. 174–175; also Horowitz, 1967) produced secondary and critical material even though this theory group is only in the network stage.

My explanation for this divergence from the model is that the federal government's interest in, and willingness to take advice from, researchers in social indicators made the group much more visible than groups developing by themselves (i.e., without strong nonacademic support) can become until late in the cluster stage. Partly because social indicators work was being taken quite seriously (and was thus able to affect our lives directly) and partly because of forecasters' high visibility, they drew numerous attacks in the form of secondary and critical material. Government's attempts to interest more sociologists in social indicators have also provoked some of the secondary and critical work. In 1968 Wilbur Cohen, Secretary of the Department of Health, Education, and Welfare, spoke at the Annual Meeting of the ASA. That address provoked a spirited response from radical-critical sociologists (see Chapter 11).

Futurism Table 7.4 lists some of the major techniques that have been contributed to forecasting by futurists. *Delphi,* developed by Olaf Helmer, attempts to force expert opinion into agreement. It permits use of a committee's advantages (e.g., having several persons' information and ideas expressed) without the disadvantage of having a single, strong personality dominate the proceedings. A full description of this technique is available in Bright (1968) and in Helmer (1966). The other techniques are described in Jantsch (1967a).

Because the futurists' interests are in the long range, their techniques try to move beyond strict, trend-line extrapolation. Lacking explicit theory to guide them, they use morphological techniques, scenario writing, historical analogy, probabilistic networks, and other techniques. Much of

TABLE 7.4 Futurist techniques

Type	Content
Delphi	Pooling of expert opinions
Morphological techniques	Exploration of possible and feasible alternative uses of present components of systems
Scenario	Systematic statement of one alternative (usually the most likely)
Historical analogy	Description of historical case that has common features (e.g., the railroad is an analogy for the space program)
Gaming	Operational—takes present situations and plays out alternatives
	Normative—takes desirable future situations and plays toward them
Simulation models	Given a theory, assesses alternative outcomes from different inputs to system over time
Imagination	Use of mind without technique (science fiction)

Sources: Bright (1968); Helmer (1966); Jantsch (1967a).

their work has been technological rather than strictly social forecasting. The technological element, like the population element, is clearly important in trying to estimate the future; for the futurists, the purely social changes that have occurred and their effects are generally of less interest.

In the main, the futurists' techniques have been unexplored by sociologists. They have been used by technologists and managers interested in technological development. However, occasional use of these techniques in social areas (e.g., the RAND Corporation's attempts to improve public services in the City of New York) suggests that their application has broader promise. If the future as a topic were carefully introduced through the social indicators group, it might well become a more respectable area for sociological study. At present, however, as Moore (1966) pointed out in his discussion of sociologists and the future, sociologists have *not* tried to predict much beyond the immediate future. Such prediction has generally been seen as projection of a utopia and, as Boguslaw (1965) has observed, the new utopians share many problems with the old: Utopia-making is like social philosophy—a not-quite-professional activity.

Simulation A simulation is a proposed order (or theory) for the variables included in the simulation. Forrester's *Urban Dynamics* (1969) constitutes his theory about cities. Not all theories lend themselves to simulation. Only those proposing relations between variables which can be described logically or mathematically can be simulated. Good simulations are those which either (1) promote interest in an area, although the simulations may be quite wrong (e.g., *Urban Dynamics*) or (2) are faithful to a theory and the available data on the variables of interest (e.g., *Industrial Dynamics*, Forrester, 1961). If theory development is to benefit from simulation, researchers should always be moving from type 1 to type 2.

We have already listed the three kinds of simulation techniques. Pure simulation developed in several areas characterized by basic phenomena that were either natural or a series of small, independent transactions. The simulation of the electorate for the 1960 election exemplifies the latter (Pool et al., 1964); weather system simulations, the former, A simulation is built on the asumption that the system being simulated responds to a limited series of external forces which can be defined. More recent simulations have become so complicated internally that the results of external changes are not at all obvious; they may, in fact, be systematically counterintuitive (see Forrester, 1971a).

The result of a pure simulation is a description of a series of system states produced by changes in external parameters as they are worked out in the simulation itself. These system states constitute predictions about the results of the changes introduced. In Forrester's *Urban Dynamics* (1969), for example, we find that the building of housing will attract so many new people that the housing situation deteriorates into a condition even worse than that with which the model began.

The game simulation is used when there are a few scarce resources in the system to be studied and the information desired covers the behavior of individual decision makers in such competitive situations (Meier and Duke, 1966). One example of such gaming models is Democracy (Coleman, 1966), in which legislative votes are the scarce good.

Hybrid models use the computer simulation of small segments of a system to provide feedback to decision makers on the results of their decisions. The intention is to increase the reality of the gaming situation by subjecting decision makers to both the pressures of other players and the "reality" of the effects of their decisions. Hybrid modeling had advanced quite far in urban planning, even as early as the mid-1960s; Duke's (1966) METRO and Feldt's (1965) CLUG exemplify two of several computer-assisted models.

IN CONCLUSION

Each of the forecasting techniques discussed attempts to say something about situations in which real decisions are being made about real problems. The intellectual picture follows the earlier description of social conditions: The forecasters' intellectual bag is filled with techniques and ideas that have been neither synthesized nor discarded. Thus we see a collection of possible parts rather than of a finished product. Considering the group's newness, however, this picture is not surprising.

In the recent past, sociology has deliberately chosen *not* to approach problems of high economic or political concern. We should ask, however, what kind of intellectual potential social scientists have in such areas of concern. The forecasters now include a mix of people who have enough experience in both conventional social science research and social planning to be able to talk to professional planners and sociologists, alike; they thus have the potential for taking the best from each for their own work. The absolute number of professional sociologists who hold degrees from major universities and who are involved in applied social research is still very small, however. Indeed, the distinction that has long separated pure social researchers and applied (client-oriented) workers is still quite strong and still very much to the detriment of both forecasters and planners, despite today's cry from students for relevance.

The forecasters have benefited, in recent years, from a substantial influx of money and a modest influx of people. Nevertheless, it has been some of the best planning reports rather than forecasters' works that have become social science classics in their own right. As Karl E. Taeuber (1970) has pointed out, work such as the Kerner Commission Report and the Eisenhower Commission Report, the Nader documents (e.g., Fellmeth, 1970), and other strong social statements will have considerably more effect on the world than will the work that the forecasters have produced to date. In order to be effective in the future, the forecasters will have to do more than collect federal money; they will also have to produce theoretically sound social forecasting that is also practicable.

The forecasters' other major problem will be ethical. Take one familiar example. Project Camelot, a piece of research based on social indicators and funded by the Department of Defense, was begun in 1965, in an attempt to understand the relationship between social organization and political stability in several countries. There were political repercussions from this presumed interference by Americans in the internal affairs of other countries. Irving L. Horowitz' *The Rise and Fall of Project Camelot* (1967) describes the situation. The closing of the international scene to this type of research has been paralleled by another familiar concern within the United States—the dismay over the development of the "dossier society." In such a society everything known about every single individual from every government source would be pooled, and the files would be made available to authorized persons. This system has the disadvantage, however, of being a massive invasion of privacy. The growing reluctance of foreign governments to permit research, coupled with present Congressional disinclination to permit dossier building and other developments of the National Data Center, make future development of the social indicators group through the use of such natural new data sources unlikely.

The option now open to forecasters is the improvement of data presently available for use. The quantity of information that is being collected is probably excessive for any reasonable need; however, its lack of organization often forces researchers to try several different locations when searching for specific data. Second, forecasters can use the futurist's techniques to improve currently available, practical, decision-making methodologies; if the consequences of present decisions are better understood, perhaps better decisions will be made in the future. Finally, with improved understanding of the consequences—which can be developed only through experience in the actual policy process—forecasters will be able to develop more sophisticated (but not necessarily more complicated) simulations. In turn, these simulations will provide even more information on the possible outcomes of decisions, and particularly on the interactions of decisions.

The forecaster group faces an uncertain future. It is small; few members have students. Social planning is still quite separate from forecasting, but forecasters have the potential to bridge the gap between the academic world and social planning. Interest in both social planning and forecasting will continue to be nourished to some extent by the federal government's interest in forecasting technology and planning.

The forecasters' difficulties as a group are its lack of (1) an intellectual leader, (2) a social organizational leader, (3) a strong training center, and (4) an intellectual success (although two possible candidates for this role exist). With respect to the model, the forecasters are in the early network stage; Figure 7.1 shows connections (largely through advisory positions) among a few persons. If development continues, we should expect (1) emergence of intellectual and organizational leaders, (2) the development of a training center, and (3) in the near future, a clear intellectual breakthrough—a piece of research that achieves something beyond the ordinary. If these factors do not appear, the group will survive only as long as government support continues.

Indeed, this group may already have failed (which is only to say that the network has dissipated). As of 1972, Eleanor Sheldon had become President of the Social Science Research Council; Wilbert E. Moore was at Denver University; the group of Forrester's students (who were not sociologists) who had worked on the world dynamics model (Forrester, 1971) had moved to Dartmouth College, which has no graduate program. On the positive side, social indicators have attracted the attention of new causal theorists (see Chapter 9) as they begin to examine the over-time implications of their basic models. Indeed, the sheer number of new causalists interested in time-series data (both Wisconsin and Michigan have been graduating several each year) may produce a situation in which the forecasters will lose their independent existence and become simply an adjunct of the new causal theory group. Second, even though removed from research herself, Sheldon is in a position to organize the area and to encourage SSRC funding of research on social indicators. Third, the National Science Foundation has decided to become involved in major funding of social indicators projects.

Positive aspects notwithstanding, however, the group itself has produced neither a clear success nor an intellectual breakthrough. Its members are still trying to become as good at what they do as Ogburn was. For that task, a new foundation and a new start may eventually be necessary.

NOTES

1. The "population crisis" and all that the phrase implies can be attributed to our realization of (1) the absolute size of the world's population and (2) the prevailing birth rates (crucial because they offer a means to predict later population size, given population facts about the present and assumptions about future birth rates).
2. Abt is the president of a nonprofit research group, Abt Associates. His organization has done both futurist and game work under contract but thus far has not combined the two.
3. Second-order effects—the delayed effects of programs—tend to crop up, usually unanticipated, to plague program administrators.

BIBLIOGRAPHY

Ackoff, Russell L.
  1970   *A Concept of Corporate Planning.* New York: Wiley.
Alamo Area Council of Governments.
  1969   *Social Indicators and a Social Accounting System for the AACOG Region: A Preliminary Statement.* San Antonio, Texas: Alamo Area Council of Governments.
American Journal of Sociology.
  1966   *Cumulative Index to the American Journal of Sociology 1895–1965.* Chicago: American Journal of Sociology.
————.
  1968   *American Men of Science.* 11th ed. The Jacques Cattell Press (ed.). New York: Bowker.
American Sociological Association.
  various   *Directory of Members 1959;* also for years 1963, 1967, 1970.
  years a   New York and Washington, D.C.: American Sociological Association.
  various   *Guide to Graduate Departments of Sociology 1965;* also for

years b   years 1969, 1971. Washington, D.C.: American Sociological As-
           sociation.
various   *Index to the American Sociological Review.* Vols. 1–25 (1936–
years c   1960) and Vols. 26–30 (1961–1965). New York and Washing-
           ton, D.C.: American Sociological Association.
Anderson, Martin.
    1964   *The Federal Bulldozer: A Critical Analysis of Urban Renewal, 1949–
            1962.* Cambridge, Mass.: MIT Press.
————.

various   *The Annals of the American Academy of Political and Social Sci-
years   ence.* 1967a, 1967b, 1970. Philadelphia: The American Academy
           of Political and Social Science.
Aron, Raymond.
    1968   "Remarques sur l'evolution de la pensée strategique (1945–1968)."
            Archives Européenes de Sociologie 9 (2): 151–179.
Bauer, Raymond A.
    1969   *Second Order Consequences.* Cambridge, Mass.: MIT Press.
Bauer, Raymond A. (ed.)
    1966   *Social Indicators.* Cambridge, Mass.: MIT Press.
Bean, J. M. W.
    1968   *The Decline of English Feudalism 1215–1540.* Manchester, England:
            Manchester University Press.
Beckwith, Burnham P.
    1967   *The Next 500 Years.* New York: Exposition Press.
Bell, Daniel.
    1965   "Twelve modes of prediction." Pp. 96–127 in Julius Gould (ed.),
            Penguin Survey of the Social Sciences. Baltimore, Md.: Penguin.
    1967   "The year 2000—the trajectory of an idea." *Daedalus* 96 (Summer):
            639–651.
    1968   *Toward the Year 2000.* Boston: Houghton Mifflin.
    1970   "Commission on the year 2000." *Futures* 2 (September): 263–269.
Blanchi, Herri.
    1970   "Methodology." *Futures* 2 (June): 170–171.
Boguslaw, Robert.
    1965   *The New Utopians: A Study of Systems Design and Social Change.*
            Englewood Cliffs, N.J.: Prentice-Hall.
Bowerman, C. E.
    1964   "Prediction studies." Pp. 215–246 in H. T. Christensen (ed.), *Hand-
            book of Marriage and the Family.* Chicago: Rand McNally.
Bright, James (ed.).
    1968   *Technological Forecasting for Industry and Government.* Englewood
            Cliffs, N.J.: Prentice-Hall.
Churchman, C. West.
    1968a   *Challenge to Reason.* New York: McGraw-Hill.
    1968b   *The Systems Approach.* New York: Delacorte.
Clark, Kenneth B., and Jeannette Hopkins.
    1970   *A Relevant War Against Poverty: A Study of Community Programs
            and Observable Social Change.* New York: Harper & Row.

Coleman, James S.
    1966   *The Game of Democracy.* Washington, D.C.: National 4-H Club
           Federation.
de Jouvenel, Bertand.
    1967   *The Art of Conjecture.* New York: Basic Books.
Deutsch, Karl W., John Platt, and Dieter Senghaas.
    1971   "Conditions favoring major advances in social sciences." *Science* 171
           (February 5): 450–459.
——————.
    1969   *Directory of American Scholars,* 5th ed. Tempe, Ariz.: Cattell.
Dorfman, Robert (ed.).
    1965   *Measuring Benefits of Government Investments.* Washington, D.C.:
           The Brookings Institution.
Dory, John P., and Robert J. Lord.
    1970   "Does TF really work?" *Harvard Business Review* 48 (November–
           December): 16–28, plus other pages.
Dror, Yehezkel.
    1969   *A General Systems Approach to Uses of Behavioral Sciences for
           Better Policymaking.* Santa Monica: RAND Corporation, Paper P-
           4091 (May).
    1970   "A policy sciences view of futures studies." *Technological Forecasting
           and Social Change* 2 (1): 3–16.
Duke, Richard D.
    1966   M.E.T.R.O. Project Technical Report #5: *Report on Phase 1.* Lan-
           sing, Mich.: Tri-Country Regional Planning Commission (January).
Duncan, O. D.
    1969a "Social forecasting—the state of the art." *The Public Interest* 17
           (Fall): 88–118.
    1969b *Toward Social Reporting: The Next Steps.* New York: Russell Sage.
Eldridge, H. Wentworth.
    1970   "Education for Futurism in the United States: an ongoing survey and
           critical analysis." *Technological Forecasting and Social Change* 2(2):
           133–148.
Etzioni, Amitai.
    1961   *Complex Organizations: A Sociological Reader.* New York: Holt.
    1967   "Toward a Macrosociology." Pp. 12–33 in R. William Millman and
           Michael P. Hottenstein (eds.), *Promising Research Directions: Papers
           and Proceedings of the 27th Annual Meeting of the American Acad-
           emy of Management.* Washington, D.C.: The American Academy of
           Management.
    1968   *The Active Society.* New York: Free Press.
Etzioni, Amitai, and Carolyn O. Atkinson.
    1969   *Sociological Implications of Alternative Income Transfer Systems.*
           Washington, D.C.: Bureau of Social Science Research.
Feldt, Allan G.
    1965   *The Community Land Use Game.* Ithaca, N.Y.: Cornell University,
           Division of Urban Studies, Center for Housing and Environmental
           Studies, Miscellaneous Papers #3. (mimeo)

Fellmeth, Robert.
1970   *The Interstate Commerce Omission.* New York: Grossman.
Forrester, Jay W.
1961   *Industrial Dynamics.* Cambridge, Mass.: MIT Press.
1968   *Principles of Systems: Text and Workbook.* Cambridge, Mass.: Wright-Allen.
1969   *Urban Dynamics.* Cambridge, Mass.: MIT Press.
1971a   "Counterintuitive behavior of social systems." *Technology Review* 73 (January): 52–68.
1971b   *World Dynamics.* Cambridge, Mass.: Wright-Allen.
Freeman, Howard E., and Clarence C. Sherwood.
1970   *Social Research and Social Policy.* Englewood Cliffs, N.J.: Prentice-Hall.
Gabor, Dennis.
1963   *Inventing the Future.* New York: Knopf.
Ginzburg, Eli (ed.).
1964   *Technology and Social Change.* New York: Columbia University Press.
Good, Irving J.
1970   "Speculations in hard and soft sciences." *Futures* 2 (June): 176–179.
Gordon, Kermit (ed.).
1968   *Agenda for the Nation.* Washington, D.C.: The Brookings Institution.
Gordon, Theodore J.
1965   *The Future.* New York: St. Martin.
Griffith, Belver C., and A. J. Miller.
1970   "Networks of informal communication among scientifically productive scientists." Pp. 125–140 in Carnot E. Nelson and Donald K. Pollock (eds.), *Communication Among Scientists and Engineers.* Lexington, Mass.: Heath-Lexington.
Gross, Bertram M.
1965   "Planning: let's not leave it to the economists." *Challenge* 14 (September–October): 30–33.
1966   *The State of the Nations: Social Systems Accounting.* London: Tavistock.
1967   "The city of man: a social systems accounting." Pp. 136–156 in William R. Ewald, Jr. (ed.), *Environment for Man: The Next Fifty Years.* Bloomington: Indiana University Press.
1969   "Urban mapping for 1976 and 2000." *Urban Affairs Quarterly* 5 (December): 121–142.
Hare, Van Court.
1967   *Systems Analysis: A Diagnostic Approach.* New York: Harcourt Brace Jovanovich.
Helmer, Olaf.
1966   *Social Technology.* New York: Basic Books.
1967a   "New attitudes toward future." *The Futurist* 1 (February): 8.
1967b   *Systematic Use of Expert Opinions.* Santa Monica, Calif.: RAND Corporation, Paper P-3721 (November).

Hemmens, George C. (ed.).
  1968 *Urban Development Models*. Washington, D.C.: Highway Research
        Board: Special Report no. 97.
Hoggatt, A. C., and E. Balderston.
  1963 *Symposium on Simulation Models: Methodology and Applications
        to the Behavioral Sciences*. Cincinnati: Southwestern.
Horowitz, Irving L.
  1967 *The Rise and Fall of Project Camelot: Studies in the Relationship
        between Social Science and Practical Politics*. Cambridge, Mass.:
        MIT Press.
Jantsch, Erich.
  1967a *Technological Forecasting in Perspective*. Paris: Organization for
        Economic Cooperation and Development.
  1967b "Forecasting the future." *Science Journal* 3 (October): 40–45.
Jantsch, Erich (ed.).
  1968 *OECD Working Symposium on Long Range Planning*. Bellogio, Italy:
        Organization for Economic Cooperation and Development.
Kahn, Alfred J.
  1969 *Studies in Social Policy and Planning*. New York: Russell Sage.
Kahn, Herman, and I. Mann.
  1957 *Techniques of Systems Analysis*. Santa Monica, Calif.: RAND Corpo-
        ration, Paper RM-1829-1.
Kahn, Herman, and Anthony J. Wiener.
  1967 *The Year 2000: A Framework for Speculation on the Next Thirty-
        three Years*. New York: Macmillan.
Lazarsfeld, P. F., William H. Sewell, and H. Wilensky (eds.).
  1967 *The Uses of Sociology*. New York: Basic Books.
Lewinsohn, Richard.
  1961 *Science, Prophecy and Prediction*. New York: Harper & Row.
Low, A. M.
  1950 *What's the World Coming To?* Philadelphia: Lippincott.
Luttwak, Edward.
  1968 *Coup d'État*. Greenwich, Conn.: Fawcett.
Lydon, Fremont J., and G. Ernest (eds.).
  1967 *Planning Programming Budgeting: A Systems Approach to Manage-
        ment*. Chicago: Markham.
McHale, John.
  1969 *The Future of the Future*. New York: Braziller.
Meier, Richard L., and Richard D. Duke.
  1966 "Gaming simulation for urban planning." Washington, D.C.: *Ameri-
        can Institute of Planners Journal* (January): reprint #31.
Moore, Wilbert E.
  1963 *Social Change*. Englewood Cliffs, N.J.: Prentice-Hall.
  1966 "The utility of utopians." *American Sociological Review* 31 (Decem-
        ber): 765–772.
Moynihan, Daniel P.
  1968 "The Negro family: a case for national action." In Lee Rainwater

and William Yancey, *The Moynihan Report and the Politics of Controversy*. Cambridge, Mass.: MIT Press.

1969 *Maximum Feasible Misunderstanding*. New York: Free Press.

Nagelberg, Mark, and Dennis Little.

1970 *Selected Urban Simulations and Games*. Middletown, Conn.: Institute for the Future (March).

Ogburn, W. F., J. L. Adams, and S. C. Gilfillan.

1946 *The Social Effects of Aviation*. Boston: Houghton Mifflin.

Ohlin, L. E., and O. D. Duncan.

1949 "The efficiency of prediction in criminology." *American Journal of Sociology* 55 (March): 441–451.

Olson, Mancur, Jr.

1969 "The purpose and plan of a social report." *The Public Interest* 15 (Spring): 85–97.

Pool, Ithiel de Sola, Robert P. Abelson, and Samuel L. Popkin.

1964 *Candidates, Issues and Strategies: A Computer Simulation of the 1960 and 1964 Presidential Elections*. Cambridge, Mass.: MIT Press.

Rainwater, Lee, and William Yancey.

1968 *The Moynihan Report and the Politics of Controversy*. Cambridge, Mass.: MIT Press.

Russett, Bruce M., Hayward R. Alker, Karl W. Deutsch, and Harold D. Lasswell.

1964 *World Handbook of Political and Social Indicators*. New Haven, Conn.: Yale University Press.

Schuessler, Karl.

1971 "Continuities in social prediction." Pp. 302–329 in Herbert Costner (ed.), *Sociological Methodology*. San Francisco: Jossey-Bass.

Sheldon, Eleanor, and Wilbert E. Moore (eds.).

1968 *Indicators of Social Change: Concepts and Measurements*. New York: Russell Sage.

Shostak, Arthur B.

1966 *Sociology in Action*. Homewood, Ill.: Dorsey.

Skolnick, Jerome.

1969 *The Politics of Protest*. New York: Ballantine.

Smith, Bruce L. R.

1966 *The Rand Corporation: Case Study of a Non-Profit Advisory Corporation*. Cambridge, Mass.: Harvard University Press.

Springer, Michael.

1970 "Social Indicators, Reports and Accounts: Toward the Management of Society." *Annals* 388 (March) 1–13.

Taeuber, Karl E.

1970 *Review of Toward a Social Report*. Santa Monica, Calif.: RAND Corporation, Paper P-4356 (April).

Taylor, John L. (ed.).

1969 *Social Science Instructional Simulation Systems: A Selected Bibliography*. Sussex: Sussex University, Suriss Project Papers #4.

————.

various   *Technological Forecasting and Social Change*. New York: American
years   Elsevier.

U.S. Department of Health, Education, and Welfare.
1969   *Toward a Social Report*. Washington, D.C.: Government Printing
       Office (January).

U.S. House of Representatives, Research and Technical Programs Subcommittee
of the Committee on Government Operations, Staff Study.
1967   *The Use of Social Research in Federal Domestic Programs*. 4 vols.
       Washington, D.C.: Government Printing Office (April).

U.S. House of Representatives, Subcommittee on Science, Research, and Development of the Committee on Science and Astronautics.
1969   *A Technology Assessment of the Vietnam Defoliant Matter*. Wash-
       ington, D.C.: Government Printing Office.
1970   *Hearings: Technology Assessment*. Washington, D.C.: Government
       Printing Office.

U.S. National Resources Committee.
1937   *Technological Trends and National Policy*. Washington, D.C.: Gov-
       ernment Printing Office.

U.S. President's Research Committee on Social Trends.
1934   *Recent Social Trends in the United States*. New York: McGraw-Hill.

U.S. Senate, Subcommittee on Government Research of the Committee on
Government Operations.
1967   *Hearings on S836, A Bill to Provide for the Establishment of the Na-
       tional Foundation for the Social Sciences*. 3 vols. Washington, D.C.:
       Government Printing Office (February and June).

Werner, Roland, and Joan T. Werner.
1969   *Bibliography of Simulations: Social Systems and Education*. La Jolla,
       Calif.: Western Behavioral Sciences Institute.

Winthrop, Henry.
1968   "The sociologist and the study of the future." *American Sociologist*
       3 (2): 136–145.

Wold, H. O.
1967   "Forecasting and scientific method." Pp. 1–65 in *Forecasting on a
       Scientific Basis*. Lisbon: Gulbenkian Foundation.

Wright, Quincy, William M. Evan, and Morton Deutsch (eds.).
1962   *Preventing World War III: Some Proposals*. New York: Simon &
       Schuster.

Young, Michael (ed.).
1968   *Forecasting and the Social Sciences*. London: Heinemann.

CHAPTER 8
ETHNOMETHODOLOGY
The Specialty That
Came in from the Cold

**Social and intellectual properties
of ethnomethodology**

Intellectual leaders	A. V. Cicourel
	H. Garfinkel
	H. Sacks
Social organization leaders	A. V. Cicourel
	H. Garfinkel
Research–training centers	University of California, Los Angeles
	University of California, Santa Barbara
Paradigm content	The study of commonplace rationality, ordinary language, and commonplace events
Success	Garfinkel, "Some Rules of Correct Decision Making that Jurors Respect" (1967 reprint)
Program statements	Garfinkel, "Conditions of Successful ..." (1956)
	Cicourel, **Method and Measurement** (1964)
Example of secondary work	Douglas, **Understanding Everyday Life** (1970)
Examples of critical work	Hill and Crittenden, **Purdue Symposium on Ethnomethodology** (1968)
	Denzin, "Symbolic Interactionism and Ethnomethodology: A Proposed Synthesis" (1969)
	Wilson, "Normative and Interpretive Paradigms" (1970)
Text	None

he term "ethnomethodology" was coined by Harold Garfinkel to reflect his belief that the proper subject for social science is the way in which ordinary people establish rational behavior patterns. Ordinary people use various methods to determine what is happening in society; this methodology is "ethno" in that, like "ethnobotany," it is derived from folk knowledge rather than from professional scientific procedures (Hill and Crittenden, 1968: 8–9). Hence ethnomethodology is the study of the methods used by members of a group for understanding communication, making decisions, being rational, accounting for action, and so on.

Ethnomethodologists plus a few other sociologists are concerned with the sociological analysis of everyday life. Ethnomethodologists are emphasized in this chapter, however, since they have had the most profound impact on this area. Furthermore, ethnomethodology exemplifies an "encapsulated" group in sociology.[1] Related work by other sociologists is discussed as it explicates the growth and development of ethnomethodology. With reference to the model presented in Chapter 2, ethnomethodology is just moving into specialty status. The cluster had a very specific location in southern California (at the University of California campuses at Santa Barbara and Los Angeles) between 1966 and 1971. However, the processes that pull a cluster apart and cause it to spread out had begun operating by late 1970 and were hastened by Aaron V. Cicourel's departure from Santa Barbara, first to London (1970–1971) and then to the University of California at San Diego. Table 8.1 sets forth highlights of the group's social and intellectual activities. Each point on the table is taken up during discussion of the stage in which it occurred.

TABLE 8.1 Social and intellectual highlights in the development of ethnomethodology

Stage	Social	Intellectual
Normal: to 1957	First seminar at UCLA; Schutz teaches at New School	Garfinkel, "Conditions . . ." (1956)
Network: 1957–1966	Second UCLA seminar; Berkeley group begun	Attack on standard American sociology; Cicourel, **Method and Measurement** (1964)
Cluster: 1966–1971	Santa Barbara group forms	Garfinkel, **Studies in Ethnomethodology** (1967)
Specialty: 1971–	Cicourel moves to San Diego	Research studies appear

NORMAL STAGE:
TO 1957

SOCIAL

Ethnomethodology began with the work of Harold Garfinkel, originally one of Parsons' students at Harvard. Between 1950 and 1952 he was at Princeton, working and finishing his dissertation. While still a student, Garfinkel had visited and studied with Alfred Schutz at the New School of Social Research. The ultimate result of his study with both Schutz and Parsons was ethnomethodology.

After receiving his doctorate from Harvard in 1952 (ASA, 1959), Garfinkel took a job at Ohio State. He left Ohio State in March 1954, even though his next job (in UCLA's Department of Sociology) was not to begin until September. At the time, Fred Strodtbeck (see Chapter 5) was directing a research project on juries at the University of Chicago Law School. He hired Garfinkel (a contemporary at Harvard) for the time between March and September to work with Saul Mendovitz, of the law school, analyzing some tape recordings of jury deliberations.

Garfinkel went to UCLA in September but continued to follow up on the jury study, especially on the question of how the jurors "knew what they were doing in doing the work of jurors" (Hill and Crittenden, 1968: 5–6), particularly since they were in no way trained as jurors. This concern with the procedures and methods of rationality among the jurors came to typify empirical research in ethnomethodology. Garfinkel was impressed with the jurors' abilities to sort evidence and to make decisions in a "common-sense" way that was not problematical until one asked how they knew certain things. Indeed, what did they actually know? Some time later, he summarized his conclusions in "Some Rules of Correct Decision Making that Jurors Respect" (Garfinkel, 1967: 104–115).

At UCLA Garfinkel came to know Dell Hymes, then in anthropology and developing his basic approach to anthropological linguistics (Cicourel, 1972). Garfinkel also received a National Institute of Mental Health (NIMH) career investigator grant, which allowed him the time and resources to do research (Cicourel, 1972). Whether because of prior impetus, the psychiatric aspect of standard American sociology which he had acquired at Harvard, or some later development of which I am not aware, Garfinkel began working with colleagues in UCLA's medical school, several of whom (e.g., Sheldon Messinger—see Chapter 4—and Craig MacAndrew) have since been important to Garfinkel's word (Churchill, 1972).

Garfinkel influenced very few graduate students at UCLA in ways that are reflected in the literature. His relationships have tended to be quite informal, particularly after he received the NIMH grant. Nevertheless, in the spring of 1955, he and Cicourel, a Master's degree candidate at UCLA, organized an informal seminar. (A 1956–1957 seminar was also held, but under the guidance of Garfinkel and Edward Rose; Egon Bittner was a participant; Churchill, 1972.) Cicourel received his Master's degree from UCLA in 1955 and left to do graduate work at Cornell.

Table 8.2, the basic data table for this chapter, lists the names of several persons—Peter L. Berger, Thomas Luckmann, Edward Tiryakian, and Helmut Wagner—who completed their degrees during the period 1955–1957. All were strongly influenced by phenomenomology, either directly (for those trained at the New School for Social Research) or indirectly (see below). All have been productive sociologists with respect to papers and books, but they have had few students. Although these individuals do not consider themselves ethnomethodologists, they have nevertheless been sympathetic to that school of thought.

The lack of students is understandable. Wagner has been at small colleges. Berger and Luckmann have spent much time at the New School, which has never had a *group* of students, even though it has had many good students. Tiryakian spent six years at Princeton, which has a very small graduate program, and four years at Harvard; not until 1966 did he move and become chairman of Duke University's Department of Sociology. Of the early person listed in Table 8.2, then, only Garfinkel had the opportunity to influence many students during the 1950s and early 1960s. His first real student group developed when Cicourel returned from Cornell in 1957, after completing his doctorate.

INTELLECTUAL

As is true of all contemporary theory groups in sociology, the intellectual content of ethnomethodology comes from a variety of sources. One of the most important of these, social phenomenology, is of European (largely German) origin and is not shared with the other theory groups. Phenomenology was introduced to American sociology mainly through the teaching of Alfred Schutz, a social philosopher (i.e., both a social scientist and a philosopher) at the New School for Social Research in New York. A banker who had left Germany in 1939 to avoid the Nazis, Schutz took a daytime position in a New York bank to support himself. Starting in 1943, though, he began to teach an evening course in social philosophy at the New School.

Schutz was a follower of Husserl, who suggested (*Ideas*, Vol 1, 1913) that each person has a "natural attitude" of everyday life which he takes toward the world. This attitude suspends doubt and supports a theory of intersubjectivity. Husserl devoted only a few pages to this notion, but Schutz spent a lifetime extending the idea, studying the features that characterize the natural attitude of everyday life's work (Gurwitsch, 1970).[2] His work considers the following major topics:[3]

1. The dimensions of the social world:
   a. Social reality within the reach of direct experience;
   b. The world of contemporaries as a structure of typifications;
   c. The world of predecessors and the problems of history.
2. The problem of rationality in the social world.
3. The meaning structure of the social world, including the various interpretations of the world taken for granted.

Schutz' work combined the purely philosophical interests of Husserl and other German phenomenological philosophers with those of social thinkers. Particularly important was Weber, who, through his use of the concept of *verstehen*, or understanding, provided an approach that was congenial to the social philosopher interested in phenomenology. Schutz was critical of Weber for not going far enough, but his approach was dependent on Weber (Schutz, 1967).

Schutz' conceptions do not necessarily lead only to ethnomethodology. His work also heavily influenced Berger, Tiryakian, Luckmann, and Maurice Natanson. Although all these individuals share some ideas with ethnomethodology, they are perceived by both themselves and ethnomethodologists as being different. Other thinkers close to Schutz' position are Arlene Daniels, Allen Blumensteil, Donald Ball, Jack Petras, and Jack D. Douglas. Still other similar thinkers such as S. M. Lyman and Robert Scott take less from Schutz' approach than they do from symbolic interactionism as interpreted by Erving Goffman. We can say, then, that Schutz' ideas were perhaps necessary to the development of ethnomethodology, but they were not sufficient to create it.

In addition to Schutz, the combination of writers considered important by ethnomethodologists includes both strict phenomenologists (e.g., Aron Gurwitsch, Martin Heidegger, Edmond Husserl, and Maurice Merleau-Ponty) as well as linguistic philosophers (e.g., John Austin, Ludwig Wittgenstein). The two types of philosophy were seen as inimical by their practitioners, but this circumstance is unimportant to their selection by ethnomethodologists as their forebears. Within the two categories, of course, each of these philosophers differs from the others to some degree. The linguistic philosophers have been accepted in most American philosophy departments, but this is not true of the phenomenologists.

This selection demonstrates the more general principle that the

TABLE 8.2   Important ethnomethodologists: degree
(date and place) and selected job locations

| Name | Ph.D. | | 1955 |
	Date	Place	
Adato, Al	ni	UCLA	*
Berger, Peter L.	1954	NEWS	NEWS
Bittner, Egon	1961	UCLA	*
Bloombaum, Milton	1961	UCLA	*
Blum, Alan	1964	CHIC	*
Boese, Robert J.	1971	UCSB	*
Churchill, Lindsey	1961	HARV	*
Cicourel, Aaron V.	1957	CORN	UCLA
Crowle, Anthony	1971	UCSB	*
Douglas, Jack D.	1965	PRIN	*
Duster, Troy	1962	NWU	*
Elliott, Henry	1970	UCSB	*
Garfinkel, Harold	1952	HARV	UCLA
Gurwitsch, Aron	ni	ni	ni
Hajjar, Ted	ni	UCSB	*
Ima, Kenji	ni	NWU	*
Jennings, Kenneth	1971	UCSB	*
Kitsuse, John	1958	UCLA	*
Leiter, Kenneth	1971	UCSB	*
Luckmann, Thomas	1956	NEWS	NEWS
MacAndrew, Craig	ni	CHIC	*
MacKay, Robert	1971	UCSB	*
McHugh, Peter	1961	NWU	*
Mead, Earl	ni	ni	*
Mehan, Hugh	1971	UCSB	*
Mintz, Warren	ni	NYU	*
Natanson, Maurice	ni	NEWS	ni
Platt, Gerald	1964	UCLA	*
Pollner, Melvin	1970	UCSB	*
Riquelme, Antonio	1970	UCSB	*
Rose, Edward	1942	STAN	COLO
Roth, David	1971	UCSB	*
Sacks, Harvey	1966	BERK	*
Schenbein, (ni)	ni	UCI	*
Schegloff, Emanuel A.	1967	BERK	*
Schutz, Alfred	1923	VIEN°	NEWS
Schwartz, Howard	1971	UCLA	*
Shumsky, Marshall	1971	UCSB	*
Smith, Joan	1971	NYU	*
Speier, Matthew	1969	BERK	*
Sudnow, David	1967	BERK	*
Thalheimer, Fred	1962	UCLA	*
Tiryakian, Edward	1956	HARV	HARV
Turner, Roy	ni	BERK	ni

Sources: ASA (various years, a, b); Churchill (1972); Cicourel (1972); Douglas (1970);
Dreitzel (1971); Mehan (1971b; 1972); Natanson (1970).

Job held during academic year ending in				
1960	1964	1967	1970	1972
*	*	ni	ni	UCSB
HART	HART	NEWS	NEWS	RUTG
UCLA	UCR	LPNI	BRAN	BRAN
UCLA	USC	HAWI	HAWI	HAWI
*	HARV	COL	NYU	NYU
*	*	UCSB	UCSB	UBC
HARV	UCLA	RUSS	RUSS	CUNY
NWU	UCR	UCSB	UCSB	UCSD
*	*	UCSB	UCSB	OXFO
PRIN	UCLA	UCLA	UCSD	UCSD
NWU	ni	BERK	BERK	BERK
*	*	UCSB	UCSB	UA
UCLA	UCLA	UCLA	UCLA	UCLA
ni	ni	ni	NEWS	ni
*	*	UCSB	UCSB	SFVC
*	*	NWU	UCSB	IIT
*	*	UCSB	UCSB	UCSD
NWU	NWU	NWU	NWU	NWU
*	*	*	UCSB	RICE
NEWS	NEWS	GOET	GOET	GOET
NPI	NPI	NPI	NPI	UCI
*	*	UCSB	UCSB	YORK
NWU	COL	COL	NYU	NYU
ni	ni	ni	ni	SFVC
*	*	*	UCSB	INDU
*	ni	ni	HOFS	HOFS
ni	ni	ni	UCSC	ni
UCLA	UCLA	HARV	MASS	MASS
*	BERK	UCSB	UCLA	UCLA
*	*	*	UCSB	PURI
COLO	COLO	COLO	COLO	COLO
*	BERK	UCSB	UCSB	TEX
BERK	UCLA	UCI	UCI	UCI
*	ni	ni	UCI	GRON
BERK	BERK	COL	COL	COL
d				
*	*	*	UCLA	HARV
*	*	UCSB	UCSB	SFVC
*	*	COL	NYU	DART
*	ni	UCSB	UBC	UBC
BERK	BERK	STON	UCI	UCI
UCLA	ni	ni	SFST	SFST
PRIN	HARV	DUKE	DUKE	DUKE
ni	BERK	ni	UBC	UBC

TABLE 8.2   (continued)

Name	Ph.D. Date	Ph.D. Place	1955
Wagner, Helmut	1955	NEWS	NEWS
Washington, Jules	ni	HARV	*
Weinberg, Martin S.	1965	NWU	*
Wieder, D. Lawrence	1969	UCLA	*
Wood, Houston	ni	UCSB	*
Zimmerman, Don H.	1966	UCLA	*

Key:

BERK	University of California, Berkeley	HARV	Harvard University
BRAN	Brandeis University	HAWI	University of Hawaii
BUCK	Bucknell University	HOBA	Hobart and Smith College, Geneva, N.Y.
CHIC	University of Chicago	HOFS	Hofstra College
COL	Columbia University	IIT	Illinois Institute of Technology
COLO	University of Colorado	INDU	Indiana University
CORN	Cornell University	LPNI	Langley Porter Neuropsychiatric Institute, Los Angeles
CUNY	City University of New York		
d	Deceased	MASS	University of Massachusetts
DART	Dartmouth College	NEWS	New School for Social Research
GOET	Goethe University, Frankfort	ni	No information
GRON	Gronigen University, Gronigen, Holland	NPI	Neuropsychiatric Institute, San Francisco
HART	Hartford Theological Seminary	NWU	Northwestern University

recognized intellectual forefathers of a group are usually a "mixed bag," rather than a group of thinkers who are obviously and necessarily related in any way. In terms of influences and sources, the individual intellectual biographies of group members probably differ in significant ways, but those differences can be submerged in a "creation myth" on which all can agree. As with all collections of forefathers, this one can be rationalized. Some of the work of Austin and Wittgenstein dealt with ordinary language use, as opposed to the language formulations of ideas. Their concern was to discover the logic of everyday language rather than to force language into an ideal rational system. In the perception of ethnomethodologists, this concern for everyday language, and almost nothing else in the two thought systems, joined the linguistic philosophies with phenomenology (see foregoing discussion of Husserl) as well as with two other intellectual systems that have informed ethnomethodology—linguistics and cognitive anthropology.

Linguists, particularly generative linguists (including Noam Chomsky), are primarily concerned with the knowledge and logic necessary to construct sentences. The cognitive anthropologists (e.g., Harold Conklin, Charles Frake, Ward Goodenough, John Gumperz, and Dell Hymes) are interested in the social knowledge necessary for personal interaction within a given segment of a society. These last two groups

Job held in academic year ending in				
1960	1964	1967	1970	1972
BUCK	BUCK	HOBA	HOBA	ni
*	*	*	HARV	HARV
*	UCLA	UCSB	UCSB	UCSB
*	NWU	INDU	INDU	INDU
*	*	*	UCSB	UCSB
*	UCLA	UCSB	UCSB	UCSB

NYU	New York University	UBC	University of British Columbia
OXFO	Oxford University	UCI	University of California, Irvine
PRIN	Princeton University	UCLA	University of California,
PURI	University of Puerto Rico		Los Angeles
RICE	Rice Institute	UCR	University of California, Riverside
RUSS	Russell Sage Foundation	UCSB	University of California,
RUTG	Rutgers		Santa Barbara
SFST	San Francisco State College	UCSC	University of California,
SFVC	San Fernando Valley State		Santa Cruz
	College	UCSD	University of California,
STAN	Stanford University		San Diego
STON	State University of New York,	USC	University of Southern California
	Stony Brook	VIEN	University of Vienna
		YORK	York University, Toronto
TEX	University of Texas	*	Not in system
UA	University of Alberta	°	Doctor of Laws

are more than important sources of ideas for ethnomethodology; they talk with and learn from the ethnomethodologists. However, it should be emphasized that although all these schools of thought belong to the common heritage claimed by ethnomethodology, members of these groups are seldom aware of the other groups; their commonality exists only in the perceptions of ethnomethodologists.

The first program statement for ethnomethodology appeared in 1956. Rather than producing comprehensive, long-range statements (see discussion of Parsons' and Merton's statements, pp. 58–59), ethnomethodology has adopted the technique of limited program statements, generally by Garfinkel, which sketch out restricted goals by setting an example. For example, in "Conditions of Successful Degradation Ceremonies" (1956: 422), Garfinkel points out that a public denunciation transforms the essence of a person ". . . by substituting another socially validated motivational scheme for that previously used to name and order the preferences of the denounced." He then notes that "essences" are not a scientific concept but a construction of daily life and proceeds to show *how* this construction is used in daily life. This analysis of "socially validated motivational schemes" capable of transforming the essence of individuals subsequently became a central concern of ethnomethodology. Later program-type statements have been clearer in the sense of setting out more rules for activity (e.g., Cicourel's *Method and Measurement*, 1964); but the basic style of limited program statements continued.

NETWORK STAGE:
1957–1966

SOCIAL

The beginning of the network stage was marked by Cicourel's return to UCLA for a postdoctoral year. Once again he and Garfinkel organized a seminar. That 1957–1958 seminar included Egon Bittner, Milton Bloombaum, Troy Duster, Peter McHugh, Kenneth Polk, Gerald Platt, and Fred Thalheimer (Cicourel, 1972). Of this group, Bittner and McHugh have since become important ethnomethodologists. The importance of that seminar was its ability to attract and hold students who themselves later became teaching ethnomethodologists.

As we saw with structural functionalism, student groups do not occur regularly, but once a budding theory group has had *any* students who have subsequently moved into the field, the potential for acquiring many more students is much greater. Even with a first group of students maturing, however, ethnomethodology developed slowly. This was partly because Garfinkel and Cicourel were not in prime locations for students: Chicago, Harvard, and Columbia dominated the 1950s and early 1960s; the expansion of graduate education had not yet occurred. Garfinkel continued at UCLA. Cicourel and Bittner spent 1960 to 1965 at the University of California, Riverside, a poor environment for the developing specialty because it lacked a graduate program, and Cicourel was at the University of Buenos Aires during 1963–1964.

By the end of the network period, both Garfinkel and Cicourel were fairly well known. In 1964 Cicourel had published his first major work, *Method and Measurement in Sociology* (1964), which subsequently functioned as a program statement. (He and John Kitsuse had previously written *Educational Decision Makers*, 1963.) Garfinkel had published several pieces. Their reputations were also aided by the undergraduate and graduate students who were discussing their work. An important example of this activity was the organization, by Harvey Sacks, of a group of Berkeley graduate students to discuss the work of Garfinkel and Cicourel (Sudnow, 1971: preface; Cicourel, 1972).

By 1964 several students had received degrees and jobs. An active, communicating network existed, and the group had a few outside supporters (e.g., John Kitsuse). Ethnomethodologists' work had been successful but not startlingly so. Garfinkel, established at UCLA, was known but largely ignored by the rest of sociology, which still saw ethnomethodology not as a movement but as a personal quirk of Garfinkel's and, to a lesser extent, of Cicourel's.

In 1965–1966, though, during Cicourel's stay at Berkeley, the same large group of students that had been organized earlier by Sacks surfaced again. This group of students included Gail Jefferson, Michael Moerman, Emanuel A. Schegloff, Matthew Speier, David Sudnow, and Roy Turner. Their focus was on Garfinkel's work (Sudnow, 1971: v). Interview material suggests that several members of this group (e.g., Sudnow, Schegloff) commuted occasionally between Berkeley and Los Angeles for seminars with Garfinkel. Cicourel operated primarily as a "cover" for these students within the Berkeley department so that they could use their study of ethnomethodology toward degrees at Berkeley. For example, he chaired Sacks' dissertation committee, which also included a linguist and an anthropologist as well as Herbert Blumer. Cicourel's own intellectual development in linguistics at Berkeley is discussed later.

It was clear by this time that Garfinkel and Cicourel together provided the group's intellectual and social organizational leadership. Berkeley and UCLA had each trained a few students. The research center was UCLA, although Cicourel was working elsewhere on *Juvenile Justice* (1968) and other projects. Within the UCLA context, Garfinkel has been quite effective as both advisor and colleague. Lindsey Churchill's experience of coming to UCLA fresh from Harvard and finding Garfinkel to be the most intellectually influential colleague is apparently not atypical (Churchill, 1972). Equally important, Garfinkel has also been able to obtain money for research. In addition to the NIMH grant, he was supported for at least three years by the Air Force Office of Scientific Research for research with Churchill and Sacks on "Decision Making in Common-Sense Situations of Choice"; he continued with Sacks after Churchill left UCLA in 1966 (see Zimmerman, 1970a: 221n; Zimmerman and Pollner, 1970: 80n; Churchill, 1972). Garfinkel and Sacks' work on the suicide prevention project was another major effort of the network stage.

Cicourel emerged as an intellectual leader with the publication of *Method and Measurement* (1964). His social organizational talents became visible through his department chairmanships (first at Riverside and later at San Diego), his encouragement of students to complete their degrees (e.g., the Berkeley group of students), and his creation of the Santa Barbara group, at the end of the network stage and the beginning of the cluster stage.

The relationship between Cicourel and Garfinkel has been complex. Both are strong-willed, intelligent persons who have experienced friction and misunderstanding in their relationship. Some of their differences have arisen over the way in which ethnomethodology should be done (e.g., contrast Garfinkel, 1967, with Cicourel, 1968); others have derived from practical activities, such as when and where material is to be published. These difficulties, however, should not detract from the realization that the two have provided their most successful training when working together.

Socially, the network stage brought together Cicourel, the group organized by Sacks, and the group at UCLA headed by Garfinkel; furthermore a new center was already forming at the University of California, Santa Barbara, with Cicourel as the central person. Zimmerman went from UCLA to Santa Barbara in 1965; Sudnow went there from Berkeley at the same time. Kenneth Jennings had also been at Berkeley but transferred to Santa Barbara at Cicourel's suggestion (Cicourel, 1972).

INTELLECTUAL

During the network stage, ethnomethodology's intellectual roots became more public because of the appearance of a sequence of the *Collected Papers* of Alfred Schutz, edited by Maurice Natanson and others (the last volume appeared in 1966). Berger and Luckmann (1967), in a continuation of the Schutz tradition, indicated what ethnomethodology might have become under other circumstances.[4] Their book concentrates on what Schutz had to say and modifies his approach, rather than using it as a springboard to new research. By contrast, it is the research aspect of ethnomethodology that has made it different, exciting, and important to its adherents.

The research aspect was obvious to those inside the group, since unpublished results were widely circulated within it. Most of the research completed by 1966 had not yet been published, however, and thus it was not known to the rest of the profession.

The network period of ethnomethodological work was dominated by Harold Garfinkel's concern with everyday rationality. This concern began with the jury work described earlier and proceeded with discussions of the rationality of mental patients and the problems of the suicide prevention center at UCLA. Garfinkel's collected articles were being widely circulated. His intellectual concerns continued to develop along the same lines, his teaching and seminar work constituting his major contribution. During the network stage, he was seen by traditional sociology as the primary ethnomethodologist.

The fundamental difference between ethnomethodology and structural functionalism was over the latter's assumption of a stable system of symbols and meanings shared by members of a society. Hence the typical survey does not consider respondents' interpretive problems in answering questions. These problems have long been considered either (1) not researchable or (2) not important, since the regularity of responses and the ways in which those regularities correlate with regularities in status or behavior are seen as more significant than the interpretation of those meanings being invested in the questions by respondents. With the impetus from a program statement in Cicourel (1964), those involved began to ask whether meanings are shared. Furthermore, ethnomethodologists questioned how actors know what is expected of them and what roles of the many that are possible are being evoked by different situations. The regularity of human behavior is sufficiently great that some systematic process clearly exists; ethnomethodology's question is: How does it proceed?

Ethnomethodology's answer requires studying the accounting and describing procedures for each member of a social order. Social order, then, is precarious, having no existence at all apart from those accounting and describing procedures. The focus is not on activity but rather on the process by which members manage to *produce and sustain a sense of social structure.* The attempt to understand these accounting procedures by members of a social order constituted ethnomethodology's radical break from standard American sociology.[5]

Both the basic position and some of its variations continued development during this period. Garfinkel's concerns had been clear: (1) the cognitive orientation of work and (2) the way in which man makes meaning in situations (i.e., unknowingly does methodology). At Berkeley, yet another interest of the ethnomethodologists was being developed. Cicourel, working with John Gumperz, an anthropological linguist, and Susan Ervin-Tripp, a linguist (Mehan, 1972), learned linguistics, which subsequently became a major theme in the ethnomethodological mixture (through a combination of linguistics training by Cicourel and his students at Santa Barbara and a continuation of prior interests by Harvey Sacks). Cicourel and his students were studying the acquisition and use of language and interpretive abilities. Sacks' work has concentrated particularly on language acts and the analysis of statements. The social effects of Sacks' work became important during the cluster period. During the network stage, the three positions developed separately. While the three differed, though, they were still more similar to one another than any was to any other line of research current in sociology.

With ethnomethodology, then, as with the other traditions discussed in this book, the essence of the tradition is contained in the group's work and nowhere else. A summary of the basic position is: By virtue of man's group memberships, the skills, knowledge, and abilities (a general "world view") of his culture accrue to him. Ethnomethodologists circumscribe for study (1) the acquisition of socially distributed cultural knowledge, (2) its occasioned invocation and use in interaction encounters, and (3) the processes by which other members of society judge specific social behaviors as acceptable displays. Ethnomethodology's theoretical orientation centers around the acquisition and use of language, normative rule interpretation, and the structure of common-sense experience and rationality.[6]

In its (1) insistence on a central dogma (the primacy of everyday life knowledge to *all* social knowledge in all science), (2) strong rejection response from the parent discipline, and (3) early circulation of major material only within the group, ethnomethodology resembles the early branch of molecular biology known as phage work (see Mullins, 1972). A further similarity has been ethnomethodologists' frequent response to the world—"If you haven't been trained in it, you really don't understand it." A final similarity is that group members have had numerous factional battles over the purity of various interpretations.

At the end of the network stage, ethnomethodology had both intellectual and social organization leaders, a central dogma, program statements, and some successful work. The total network in 1964 (see Table 8.2) can be estimated at around 25 members, of whom 11 were located in southern California; five more were at Berkeley. Of those 16, eight were students, but several of those (e.g., Douglas, Sacks, Zimmerman) were nearly finished with their degree work. Clearly, another large group of students could push this group into the cluster stage.

CLUSTER STAGE:
1966–1971

SOCIAL

The cluster stage of ethnomethodological development occurred largely at Santa Barbara and UCLA, although a few adherents were at other southern California locations. Seventeen persons—including at least eleven students—were active in the cluster as of 1967 (see Table 8.2). During this period most of the students were at Santa Barbara, as well as a cluster of faculty: Cicourel; two of Garfinkel's students, Don H. Zimmerman and D. Lawrence Wieder; and (for only one year) David Sudnow. Also during this period, a Northwestern Ph.D., Kenji Ima, came to Santa Barbara on a (Social Science Research Council) postdoctoral grant to study ethnomethodology and sociolinguistics (Cicourel, 1972).

The development of curriculum at Santa Barbara was quite important.

Cicourel taught graduate students, especially in seminars. Zimmerman conducted an ongoing seminar in ethnomethodology in which the manuscript of Garfinkel's *Studies in Ethnomethodology* (published in 1967) was read. Wieder taught ethnomethodology to both undergraduates and beginning graduate students. The program thus became: Wieder, introduction; Zimmerman, textual exegesis; and Cicourel, research methods and ethnoresearch (Mehan, 1972).

Acting as the social organization leader for the group, Cicourel brought several students with him from Berkeley (e.g., Jennings, Pollner, and Roth). He was particularly effective in getting students to conceive of and develop their natural situations as research opportunities. Boese (1971) was raised by deaf parents; he was encouraged to do an ethnography of deaf sign language. Shumsky (1971) was an encounter group leader in Los Angeles, and he studied that group's process. Cicourel also started research projects on education and on fertility in Argentina, both involving students. Some students at Santa Barbara commuted to UCLA for Garfinkel's seminars, and Cicourel and an occasional student visited Sacks at Irvine (Mehan, 1972). Twelve new ethnomethodologists graduated in 1970 and 1971, mostly from Santa Barbara. Several more were still working, in 1971, to finish degrees. A few cluster-period students originated with Garfinkel: Zimmerman (Ph.D., 1966), Wieder (Ph.D., 1969), and Howard Schwartz (Ph.D., 1971).

During this same period Sacks moved from UCLA to the University of California, Irvine, taking several students with him. David Sudnow, after one-year visits at Santa Barbara and then at the (State University of New York's) Stony Brook campus, came to Irvine in 1968. In 1970 Craig MacAndrew moved to Irvine. Clearly an Irvine group was beginning to build. Sacks' work was more important at this point than his group-building efforts, however, because it attracted numerous supporters for ethnomethodology. For example, his work was picked up by cognitive anthropologists. Michael Moerman, an anthropologist at UCLA, was particularly interested in Sacks' work. Sacks and Schegloff (who was strongly influenced by Sacks when both were graduate students at Berkeley) have developed good reputations within both anthropology and linguistics. Indeed, Sacks' ethnomethodology is better known outside sociology than within it.[7] Sacks' impact outside sociology has been assisted by the group of graduate students (Schegloff, Sudnow, and Turner) whom he organized into a seminar at Berkeley, and his importance in gaining wider support for ethnomethodology is clear.

Some sociologists have also become supporters of ethnomethodology. Besides John Kitsuse, mentioned earlier, other supporters are Alan Blum, Thomas Wilson, and Jack D. Douglas. Blum was probably recruited by Peter McHugh at Columbia (they are trusted assessors for each other; see below). McHugh had also recruited one of the Berkeley group, Emanuel Schegloff, to Columbia. Blum's interest had always been in the philosophical and sociological bases for theorizing, and he has continued his work in this area. Wilson came to Santa Barbara in 1967 as the cluster group was gathering there. In 1970 he published an important critical paper, "Normative and Interpretative Paradigms in Sociology." As he has become more ethnomethodological in orientation, his importance to the group has increased. His primary function in the group has been as an analyst and interpreter (to outsiders) of the ethnomethodological position.

Wilson, Cicourel, and Churchill have been particularly important to ethnomethodology because all have considerable quantitative skills (e.g., Cicourel has been involved in computer simulation of natural languages). They serve as living refutations to the rather widespread notion that ethnomethodologists are just sociologists who could not pass methods courses. As ethnomethodological theory comes to grips with the necessity of interpreting and displaying the order discovered in the data of everyday life, these quantitative skills are likely to become quite crucial.

The coauthorship network on this group reflects the social groupings (e.g., Cicourel and his students; Garfinkel, Churchill, Sacks, and Schegloff) already noted. This network (see Figure 8.1) includes 22 of the 50 persons listed in Table 8.2. The largest subgroup, Cicourel and his students, includes nine persons; the next largest (Garfinkel et al.), four. Five smaller groups have three each, and four, two persons each. The amount of coauthorship is small, but the group has just emerged from the cluster stage, and its members are quite young (the median Ph.D. degree date in Table 8.2 is 1966). We would expect both more publication and more coauthorships as the group moves further into the specialty stage.

It was during the cluster period that reaction to ethnomethodology really surfaced. Until then, ethnomethodology could simply be ignored because there was relatively little published work and few students. In 1967, however, Garfinkel let his ASA membership lapse, and there was some question about whether he should be permitted to reinstate it (Hill and Crittenden, 1968: 20). The response to ethnomethodology, when it came, was strongest among the quantitative methodologists in standard American sociology. They had been the targets of the ethnomethodologists' attacks, and they counterattacked. The review of Garfinkel's *Studies in Ethnomethodology* (1967) by James S. Coleman (1968) in the *American Sociological Review* was a counterattack to the proddings of the ethnomethodologists. It is important to note that by 1968 the slow movement of ethnomethodology away from structural

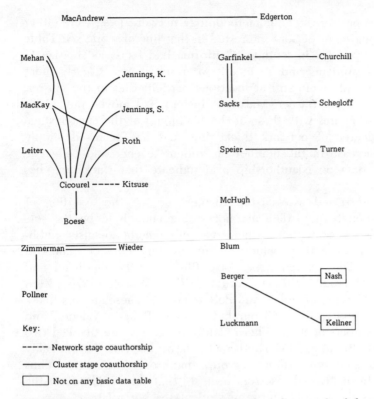

FIGURE 8.1   Coauthorship networks for ethnomethodology, 1963–1972. (**Sources:** Douglas [1970]; Dreitzel [1971]; Mehan [1971b].)

functionalism had produced a situation in which each side could ask the other unanswerable questions. For example, ethnomethodologists consider that Coleman ignored the real issues in his review. *The Purdue Symposium on Ethnomethodology* (1968) shows the effects of several years of discussions, which started with the 1965 ASA meeting, between ethnomethodologists and traditional sociologists.

It is quite significant that the coauthorship network just cited contains no links to persons who appear also in coauthorship networks for other groups. This feature of this group emphasizes the degree to which ethnomethodology has been isolated by sociology in general. In view of this isolation, it is not surprising that, during the cluster stage, there was a series of difficulties between standard American sociologists at Santa Barbara and the ethnomethodologists. These difficulties were over students, money, positions, and program, and the result was the continuation of ethnomethodology at Santa Barbara.

In 1970 Cicourel and Garfinkel were still active leaders, and at least

48 people were part of the ethnomethodology network (i.e., were either ethnomethodologists or persons interested in that line of work; see Table 8.2). The actual cluster in southern California had increased in size to at least 25 (15 students and 10 faculty or researchers). Clearly more than half the people were still at locations participating in the cluster, but a few (e.g., Egon Bittner, Matthew Speier) had moved out. Comparison of these figures with those at the beginning of the cluster stage indicate the degree of network thickening that has occurred simply through the increase in the number of student–teacher and colleague relations. The data on coauthorship also indicate that thickening has occurred.

The data on trusted assessorship further support the assertion of thickening, although these data are not strong enough to be the sole support for such a contention. Among the ethnomethodologists' publications, I found seven that include an introductory note of thanks to critical readers. These seven papers are Blum (1970), Garfinkel and Sacks (1970), McHugh (1970a), Turner (1970), Wilson (1970), Zimmerman (1970a), and Zimmerman and Pollner (1970). These authors thank 27 persons; five individuals (Cicourel, Garfinkel, Pollner, Wieder, and Wilson), all members of the southern California group, are thanked two or more times. Blum and McHugh, who have been at best weakly linked with the southern California group, thank only each other. Thus the limited data on trusted assessors indicate that those links form the same pattern as the coauthorship and student–teacher relations.

INTELLECTUAL

The cluster stage was productive both of students and of the first major publications of ethnomethodological research: Sudnow's *Passing On: The Social Organization of Dying* (1967), Garfinkel's *Studies in Ethnomethodology* (1967), Cicourel's *The Social Organization of Juvenile Justice* (1968), McHugh's *Defining the Situation* (1968), and MacAndrew and Edgerton's *Drunken Comportment* (1969). Cicourel (1968) and MacAndrew and Edgerton (1969) in particular typify what ethnomethodologists would call "ethnomethodological work." Both books report single pieces of research in which meanings are explored in depth from many angles. Another piece of such work (on the Santa Barbara public school system) presently underway has already produced some Ph.D. dissertations (e.g., Mehan, 1971a) and is due for later publication (Cicourel et al., forthcoming). That piece, beyond the simple reporting of research results, is expected to be an important application of theory. Much of the debate over the value and status of ethnomethodology (i.e., is it really sociology?) can be understood when it is realized that ethnomethodologists have seen each others' forthcoming papers, but the rest of sociology has not. Research during this period was largely guided by program statements on the approach of ethnomethodology as made in Garfinkel's *Studies in Ethnomethodology* (1967), Zimmerman and Pollner (1970), and Wilson (1970). *The Purdue Symposium* (Hill and Crittenden, 1968) provided yet another position statement.

During this stage, ethnomethodology's arguments with standard American sociology, begun during the mid-1960s, became ritualized on both sides. The ethnomethodologists continued to object to the hidden quality of social science explanation which assumed that people do not know the reasons for their actions. For example, Zimmerman and Pollner (1970:80) argued that:

> In contrast to the perennial argument that sociology belabors the obvious, we propose that sociology has yet to treat the obvious as a phenomenon. We argue that the world of everyday life, while furnishing sociology with its favored topics of inquiry, is seldom a topic in its own right.

Ethnomethodologists assume that practical reasons exist and that those reasons are necessary and sufficient for activity. Strangely, Émile Durkheim has taken on the character of representing the standard American sociology position, not because he is a standard American sociologist but because (particularly in *Suicide*, 1951, a work much used in methods courses) he clearly separates what people *do* from what they *say* they are doing.

By 1970 Jack Douglas had become the anthologist of ethnomethodology. He has included ethnomethodological materials in many of his books; one collection, *Understanding Everyday Life* (1970), is explicitly about ethnomethodology. His own research in deviance is not ethnomethodological, although his approach shares some common perspectives.

As of 1971, ethnomethodology had not produced a positive public contribution to sociology. It has had critically strong negative effects in its analysis of structural functionalism (see Cicourel's *Method and Measurement in Sociology*, 1964, and Garfinkel, 1963, which concentrates on game models). Furthermore, the papers on rule following by Garfinkel (1962) and others were basically attacks on formal organization theory. Publication of the Santa Barbara studies, Cicourel's Argentine fertility research, and Sacks' linguistic research (see this chapter's bibliography) may well prove to be important positive contributions.

By mentioning the ethnomethodologists' successful publications, I do not intend to imply that ethnomethodologists have found it easy to publish. They have not. The traditional journals in American sociology have published very little of their work (particularly by contrast with their willingness to publish the work of new causal theorists; see

Chapter 9). In response, ethnomethodologists developed the habit of mimeographing their papers and distributing them privately, usually through the sociology department office at Santa Barbara (Mehan, 1972). The few "outlanders" received them by mail. Needless to say, this "publication" practice produced some feeling of mystery about the ethnomethodologists. By 1971, however, the outlanders outnumbered those in southern California, and the centrality of the Santa Barbara campus has been reduced as its membership has declined. This decline has resulted in the need to develop a journal or other general distribution form. Secondary materials (readers and published conference proceedings) have been helpful, but it may be that a monograph series would be preferable, since full ethnomethodological presentations are apt to be very long.

An important function of secondary material has been to provide histories, interpretation, and discussion of work within the tradition. Interpretations of ethnomethodological work (e.g., this chapter) by persons who are in other traditions or no tradition at all are being made. This process provides an entry to ethnomethodology for those who were not part of the original theory-building group.

SPECIALTY STAGE: 1971–

SOCIAL

The end of the cluster stage was signaled by the end of encapsulation. Too many students were graduated in 1970 and 1971 to be reabsorbed into jobs related to the cluster. Whereas the majority of ethnomethodologists were still in southern California in 1970 (most at UCLA and UCSB), by 1972 only 15 of 46 (see Table 8.2) were still there, and by 1971 two locations (University of British Columbia and York University) had managed to hire at least three ethnomethodologists each, thus acquiring the potential to become new research and training centers. As ethnomethodologically trained professionals moved to more and more campuses, the discipline of sociology could no longer deal with ethnomethodology as a localized aberration produced, like smog, by a combination of sun and hydrocarbons. The group by then was large and stable enough to ensure that it would continue to grow, as long as training centers and research questions continued to exist.

As of 1971, seven locations had three or more ethnomethodologists (see Table 8.2). Five are in southern California, four of these being part of the University of California system (Irvine, Los Angeles, Santa Barbara, and San Diego); the fifth is San Fernando Valley State College.

The two others were just noted: University of British Columbia and York University. York, with Blum, McHugh, and MacKay, may exemplify a situation in which numbers alone aren't enough: Differences in approach among these three may make coherent training difficult if not impossible.

Ethnomethodology now has two strings in its bow. Either the various centers may achieve separate productive status *or* a southern California ethnomethodological consortium may develop among the four universities in the area (plus UC Riverside), to produce a concentration of people and a coherent program having the potential to produce many students.

It is also possible that ethnomethodology may develop in Europe. The independent tradition of European phenomenology has been making some contacts with ethnomethodology (see Dreitzel, 1971, which contains readings from both sources). Second, ethnomethodology has been imported through the visits of Cicourel and Turner to Goldsmith's College, London, and the hiring of Anthony Crowle at Oxford as a permanent lecturer.

Ethnomethodology certainly has had the marks of a successful specialty: intellectual leadership from Garfinkel, Cicourel, and Sacks; organizational leadership from Garfinkel and Cicourel; training and research centers; intellectual successes; and substantial secondary work. A text has still not been written, but critical work, both positive and negative, has appeared in some quantity.

Traditional sociology's hostility to ethnomethodology will hinder its spread to each new center. The number of centers is still small. The issue now is whether ethnomethodology will remain within sociology or become a new and separate discipline, with its own meetings, places of publication, and degrees, to replace the informal communication channels it still frequently uses. In either case, the group is now too large and too widely dispersed to return to cluster status.

INTELLECTUAL

In the specialty stage, a group's intellectual production should begin to show some differentiation. Groups in this stage are so large and so widely spread that the immediate mechanisms of conversations and seminars cannot hold exeryone to a dogmatic line. The impact of the real differences among members' individual intellectual biographies, as well as differences in skills and interests, should cause parts of the group to drift away. In these respects the ethnomethodologists are fitting the model well. For example, an East Coast–West Coast split is appearing. This split was inherent in the original structure (see Table 8.2), since Blum and McHugh were not connected strongly with Garfinkel, Sacks, and Cicourel. They had some common interests and some common contacts—Schegloff was at Columbia for a time when Blum and McHugh were in New York—but they also had differences.

The content of the East–West split seems to be the claim of Blum and McHugh to be antipositivists, engaged in "pure" analysis. McHugh's *Defining the Situation* (1968) is the most research-oriented piece from the East Coast group, but it contains more talk about analysis than actual research data and analysis. The kinds of research that Cicourel and Sacks have done are very different from McHugh's work.

Within the West Coast group, there are also potential splits. Conversational analysis (Sacks, Sudnow, Schegloff) and the language acquisition and rule-using analysis (Cicourel and students) have long constituted distinct analytic styles. Furthermore, Cicourel has added computer simulation and applied research interests to the ethnomethodological mixture. In 1972 all ethnomethodologists were a little unhappy over the term "ethnomethodology." Even Garfinkel had suggested earlier (Hill and Crittenden, 1968: 5) that the term had outlived its usefulness as a distinctive term. Cicourel has begun calling his work "cognitive sociology" (Cicourel, 1972). Sacks and Garfinkel have not followed suit, however. The terminological dispute may well mask a deeper difference on tactics of analysis within ethnomethodology.

The difficulty with the term "ethnomethodology" introduces an important aspect of each of the groups examined in Part Three of this book. Each has aspects of being a "fad" as well as a serious research emphasis. The fad aspects are perhaps clearest with ethnomethodology and structuralism, but all the groups have them. The term "fad" here indicates the adoption of a term and the parading of a brief, surface knowledge of a theory, by a series of largely passive carriers who are not doing serious work in the area. The lack of organization within sociological literature makes it difficult for an outsider to a group to determine whether a person is representative of a position. Thus many standard American sociologists have responded to the whole of ethnomethodology solely on the basis of the enthusiastic but intellectually feeble efforts of someone who had designated himself an ethnomethodologist but had not done real work in the area.

IN CONCLUSION

Of the locations that have harbored ethnomethodologists, only Santa Barbara has been highly productive of students. The other centers are either too new, not graduate centers, or inexplicably unproductive. The southern California campuses have been negotiating to establish a "floating graduate center" including courses at all five places, but this proposal has not become reality. If it does, it might resolve the problem of student production. Group members are beginning to publish. A third group of ethnomethodologically trained students have taken jobs in Europe and in East Coast centers, as well as in the more customary West Coast centers. Thus connections have been made from the West to the East Coast group and to a group of European phenomenologists.

The spread of centers, increasing publication, and increasing connections are all positive signs for further group development. In the transition from cluster to specialty, with the number of centers doing this style of work increasing, the group has begun to take on the trappings of a discipline. Clearly much of the future depends on ethnomethodology's relationship with sociology; a continuation of hostilities will obviously push the ethnomethodologists out on their own. The potential for complete separation exists. The ethnomethodologists have been meeting regularly among themselves during the summer (as did phage workers: see Mullins, 1972); if relations with sociology become more strained, these meetings could become those of a new discipline. However, the question of ethnomethodology's near-term (i.e., ten-year) survival has been answered affirmatively by the number of persons who have thus far been trained in this approach.

The transition to specialty status has not been easy. If Santa Barbara survives the loss of Cicourel, and San Diego, the University of British Columbia, and York begin producing students, the transition will be complete. If they do not, ethnomethodology may not survive beyond 1983. Two important factors presently favor the survival of ethnomethodology: (1) Its contacts with anthropologists (particularly anthropological linguists), other linguists, cognitive psychologists, and computer scientists are very important, since they provide for the entry of nonsociological ideas and methodology to act as a springboard for further development. (2) Strong contacts have been made between American ethnomethodologists and European phenomenological social scientists. The contacts with other disciplines and with European social scientists may provide a source of legitimacy that will prevent the simple absorption of ethnomethodologists into a new version of standard American sociology. There is no longer a cluster, and one cannot again develop. If the transition to specialty or discipline is not completed, ethnomethodology will gradually disappear, and its insights will be parceled out to new groups of sociologists.[8]

NOTES

1. The ethnomethodologists have encountered an intense and hostile reaction from many sociologists, who have attempted to place firm boundaries around the specialty, to keep it "encapsulated" like an infection. In this sense,

ethnomethodologists are similar to the phage workers in biology, who received a similar reaction from nonphage biologists.

2. Schutz' work, available in the three volumes of his *Collected Papers* (1962, 1964, 1966), is summarized in Helmut Wagner, *Schutz on Phenomenology and Social Relations* (1970).

3. See the subject titles of sections in Schutz' *Collected Papers*, Vol. 2 (1964).

4. Berger and Luckmann's book is discussed here rather than in the next stage, where it belongs by date, because it represents a pure extension of Schutz' work finally published in English by 1966.

5. I should note that not all of sociology was unhappy with Garfinkel. As I noted in Chapter 6, Erving Goffman early quoted from both Sacks and Garfinkel, and Albert K. Cohen (1959, 1965) used some materials from Garfinkel's paper on trust. The paper was given originally at an ASA meeting chaired by Cohen; later it was published (Garfinkel, 1963).

6. This position was stated by Hugh Mehan (1972).

7. Cicourel had also maintained ties with linguists, taking courses in linguistics at Santa Barbara from an MIT linguist who had been trained by Noam Chomsky (Cicourel, 1972).

8. A revised version of this material appeared as "The Development of Specialties in Social Science: The Case of Ethnomethodology," *Science Studies* 3 (July). Used here by permission.

BIBLIOGRAPHY

American Sociological Association.
  various   *Directory of Members 1959*; also for years 1963, 1967, 1970.
  years a   New York and Washington, D.C.: American Sociological Association.
  various   *Guide to Graduate Departments of Sociology 1965*; also for
  years b   years 1969, 1971. Washington, D.C.: American Sociological Association.
Austin, John L.
  1962   *Philosophical Papers*. Oxford: Clarendon Press.
Bar-Hillel, Yehoshva.
  1954   "Indexical expressions." *Mind* 63 (July): 359–379.
Berger, Peter L., and Thomas Luckmann.
  1967   *The Social Construction of Reality*. Garden City, N.Y.: Anchor.
Bittner, Egon.
  1965   "The concept of organization." *Social Research* 32 (Autumn): 239–258.
  1967a   "The police on skid row." *American Sociological Review* 32 (October): 699–715.
  1967b   "Police discretion in emergency apprehension of mentally ill persons." *Social Problems* 14 (Winter): 278–292.
Blum, Alan.
  1970   "Theorizing." Pp. 301–319 in Jack D. Douglas (ed.), *Understanding Everyday Life: Toward a Reconstruction of Sociological Knowledge*. Chicago: Aldine.

Blum, Alan, and Peter McHugh.
1971 "The social ascription of motives." *American Sociological Review* 36 (February): 98–109.
Boese, Robert J.
1971 "Natural Sign Language and the Acquisition of Social Structure." Santa Barbara: Unpublished Ph.D. Dissertation, University of California, Santa Barbara.
Chomsky, Noam.
1968 *Language and Mind.* New York: Harcourt Brace Jovanovich.
Churchill, Lindsey.
1966 "On everyday quantification practices." Paper presented at the Annual Meeting of the American Sociological Association, Chicago (August).
1971 "Some limitations of current quantitative methods in sociology." Paper presented at American Sociological Association Meetings, Denver, Colo. (August).
1972 Personal communication (April).
forth-   "Interrogation procedures."
  coming
Cicourel, Aaron V.
1964 *Method and Measurement in Sociology.* New York: Free Press.
1967 "Fertility, family planning, and the social organization of family life." *Journal of Social Issues* 23 (October): 57–81.
1968 *The Social Organization of Juvenile Justice.* New York: Wiley.
1970a "The acquisition of social structure: toward a developmental sociology of language and meaning." Pp. 136–168 in Jack D. Douglas (ed.), *Understanding Everyday Life: Toward a Reconstruction of Sociological Knowledge.* Chicago: Aldine.
1970b "Basic and normative rules in the negotiation of status and role." Pp. 4–45 in Hans P. Dreitzel (ed.), *Recent Sociology No. 2: Patterns of Communicative Behavior.* New York: Macmillan.
1970c "Generative semantics and the structure of social interaction." Pp. 173–202 in *International Days of Sociolinguistics.* Rome: Luigi Sturzo Institute.
1970d "Language as a variable in social research." *Sociological Focus* 3 (Winter): 43–52.
1972 Personal communication (May).
forth-   "The attribution of responsibility."
  coming a
forth-   "Ethnomethodology." To appear in Thomas Sebeok et al.
  coming b (eds.), *Current Trends in Linguistics.* The Hague: Mouton.
forth-   *Interviews as Situated Accounts: Comparative Methodological*
  coming c *Issues in a Study of Argentina Fertility.* Wiley-Interscience.
Cicourel, Aaron V., and Robert J. Boese.
1969 "Natural sign language and the acquisition of social structure." Paper presented at American Sociological Association Meeting, San Francisco (August).

Cicourel, Aaron V., Kenneth Jennings, Sybillyn Jennings, Kenneth Leiter, Robert MacKay, Hugh Mehan, and David Roth.
forth-   *Language Socialization in Testing and Classroom Settings*. New
coming   York: Seminar.
Cicourel, Aaron V., and John Kitsuse.
1963   *Educational Decision Makers*. Indianapolis: Bobbs-Merrill.
Cohen, Albert K.
1959   "The study of social disorganization and deviant behavior." Pp.
461–484 in Robert K. Merton, Leonard Broom, and Leonard S. Cottrell, Jr. (eds.), *Sociology Today; Problems and Prospects*. New York: Basic Books.
1965   "The sociology of the deviant act: anomic theory and beyond."
American Sociological Review 30 (February): 5–14.
Coleman, James S.
1968   "Review Symposium." *American Sociological Review* 33 (February):
126–130.
Denzin, Norman.
1969   "Symbolic interactionism and ethnomethodology: a proposed synthesis." *American Sociological Review* 34 (December): 922–934.
Douglas, Jack D.
1970   *Understanding Everyday Life: Toward the Reconstruction of Sociological Knowledge*. Chicago: Aldine.
Dreitzel, Hans P. (ed.).
1971   *Recent Sociology No. 2: Patterns of Communicative Behavior*. London: Macmillan Co.
Durkheim, Émile.
1951   *Suicide: A Study in Sociology*. Translated by John A. Spaulding and George Simpson. New York: Free Press.
Garfinkel, Harold.
1956   "Conditions of successful degradation ceremonies." *American Journal of Sociology* 61 (March): 420–424.
1959   "Aspects of the problem of common sense knowledge of social structures." *Transactions of the Fourth World Congress of Sociology*, IV. Milan: Stressa.
1960   "The rational properties of scientific and common sense activities." *Behavioral Science* 5 (January): 72–83.
1962   "Common sense knowledge of social structure: the documentary method of interpretation." Pp. 689–712 in Jordan M. Scher (ed.), *Theories of the Mind*. New York: Free Press.
1963   "A conception of and experiments with 'trust' as a condition of concerted stable actions." Pp. 187–238 in O. J. Harvey (ed.), *Motivation and Social Interaction*. New York: Ronald.
1967   *Studies in Ethnomethodology*. Englewood Cliffs, N.J.: Prentice-Hall.
Garfinkel, Harold, and Harvey Sacks.
1971   "On formal structures of practical actions." Pp. 338–366 in John C. McKinney and Edward Tiryakian (eds.), *Theoretical Sociology*. New York: Appleton.

Gouldner, Alvin W.
   1970   *The Coming Crisis in Western Sociology.* (Particularly "Ethnomethodology as a happening," pp. 290–295.) New York: Basic Books.
Gurwitsch, Aron.
   1964   *The Field of Consciousness.* Pittsburgh: Duquesne University Press.
   1966   *Studies in Phenomenology and Psychology.* Evanston, Ill.: Northwestern University Press.
   1970   "Problems of the life world." Pp. 35–61 in Maurice Natanson (ed.), *Phenomenology and Social Reality: Essays in Memory of Alfred Schutz.* The Hague: Nijhoff.
Heidegger, Martin.
   1962   *Being and Time.* Translated by John Macquarrie and Edward Robinson. New York: Harper & Row.
Hill, Richard J., and Kathleen Stones Crittenden.
   1968   *Proceedings of the Purdue Symposium on Ethnomethodology.* Lafayette, Ind.: Institute for the Study of Social Change, Purdue University, Monograph # 1.
Husserl, Edmond.
   1967   *Ideas: General Introduction to Pure Phenomenology.* Translated by R. Boyce Gibson. London: Allen & Unwin.
Jennings, Kenneth.
   1971a "The Acquisition of Language and Developmental Social Competence." Santa Barbara: Unpublished Ph.D. Dissertation, University of California, Santa Barbara.
   1971b "The social organization of psycholinguistics research." Paper presented at American Sociological Association meetings, Denver, Colorado (August).
Kjolseth, Rolf.
   1969   "We the Gods." Davis, Calif.: Department of Sociology, University of California, Davis. (mimeo)
Leiter, Kenneth.
   1971   "Telling It Like It Is: The Structure of Teachers' Accounts." Santa Barbara: Unpublished Ph.D. Dissertation, University of California, Santa Barbara.
MacAndrew, Craig, and Robert Edgerton.
   1969   *Drunken Comportment: A Social Explanation.* Chicago: Aldine.
MacKay, Robert.
   1971   "Ethnography of the Classroom and Language Learning." Santa Barbara: Unpublished Ph.D. Dissertation, University of California, Santa Barbara.
MacKay, Robert, Hugh Mehan, and David Roth.
   1971   "Communicative competence and school performance." Paper presented at American Sociological Association Meetings, Denver, Colorado (August).
Mannheim, Karl.
   1952   *Essays on the Sociology of Knowledge.* London: Routledge & Kegan Paul.

McHugh, Peter.
   1968   *Defining the Situation: The Organization of Meaning in Social Inter-*
          action. Indianapolis: Bobbs-Merrill.
   1970a "On the failure of positivism." Pp. 320–335 in Jack D. Douglas (ed.),
          Understanding Everyday Life: Toward the Reconstruction of Socio-
          logical Knowledge. Chicago: Aldine.
   1970b "A common sense conception of deviance." Pp. 61–88 in Jack D.
          Douglas (ed.), *Deviance and Respectability.* New York: Basic Books.
Mehan, Hugh.
   1971a "Accomplishing Understanding in Educational Settings." Santa Bar-
          bara: Unpublished Ph.D. dissertation, University of California, Santa
          Barbara.
   1971b "A Bibliography in Ethnomethodology." Bloomington, Ind.: Indiana
          University Department of Sociology. (mimeo)
   1972   Personal communication.
Merleau-Ponty, Maurice.
   1962   *Phenomenology of Perception.* Translated by Colin Smith. New York:
          Humanities.
   1964   *Sense and Nonsense.* Translated by Hubert L. Dreyfus and Patricia
          A. Dreyfus. Evanston, Ill.: Northwestern University Press.
Moerman, Michael.
   1968   *Analysis of Lue Conversation.* Berkeley: University of California,
          Berkeley, Language-Behavior Research Lab, Working Paper #12.
   1969   "A little knowledge." Pp. 449–469 in Stephen Tylor (ed.), *Cogni-*
          tive Anthropology. New York: Holt.
Mullins, Nicholas C.
   1972   "The development of a scientific specialty: the Phage Group and the
          origins of molecular biology." *Minerva* 10 (January): 51–82.
Natanson, Maurice (ed.).
   1970   *Phenomenology and Social Reality: Essays in Memory of Alfred*
          Schutz. The Hague: Nijhoff.
Palmer, E. R.
   1968   *Hermeneutics.* Evanston, Ill.: Northwestern University Press.
Rose, Edward.
   1967   *A Looking Glass Conversation.* Boulder, Colo.: University of Colorado
          Institute of Behavioral Sciences, Report 12.
   forth-   "Small languages."
   coming
Roth, David.
   1971   "Children's Linguistic Performance as a Factor in School Perform-
          ance." Santa Barbara: Unpublished Ph.D. Dissertation, University of
          California, Santa Barbara.
Sacks, Harvey.
   1963   "Sociological description." *Berkeley Journal of Sociology* 8 (1): 1–17.
   1966   "The Search for Help: No One to Turn To." Berkeley: Unpublished
          Ph.D. Dissertation, University of California, Berkeley.
   forth-   "The baby cried; the mommy picked it up."
   coming a

forth-   *Social Aspects of Language: The Organization of Sequencing*
coming b   *in Conversation.* Englewood Cliffs, N.J.: Prentice-Hall.

Schegloff, Emanuel A.

1967 "The First Five Seconds." Berkeley: Unpublished Ph.D. Dissertation, University of California, Berkeley.

1968 "Sequencing in conversational openings." *American Anthropologist* 70 (6): 1075–1095.

1971 "Notes on a conversational practice: formulating place." Pp. 75–124 in David Sudnow (ed.), *Studies in Interaction.* New York: Free Press.

Schegloff, Emanuel A., and Harvey Sacks.

1969 "Opening up closings." Paper presented at American Sociological Association Meetings, San Francisco (August).

Schutz, Alfred.

1962 *Collected Papers.* Vol. I: *The Problem of Social Reality.* The Hague: Nijhoff.

1964 *Collected Papers.* Vol. II: *Studies in Social Theory.* The Hague: Nijhoff.

1966 *Collected Papers.* Vol. III: *Studies in Phenomenological Philosophy.* The Hague: Nijhoff.

1967 *The Phenomenology of the Social World.* Translated by George Walsh and Frederick Lehnert. Evanston, Ill.: Northwestern University Press.

1970 *Reflections on the Problem of Relevance.* Translated by Richard M. Zaner. New Haven, Conn.: Yale University Press.

Shumsky, Marshall.

1971 "Encounter Groups: A Forensic Science." Santa Barbara: Unpublished Ph.D. Dissertation, University of California, Santa Barbara.

Sudnow, David.

1965 "Normal crimes: sociological features of the penal code in a public defender office." *Social Problems* 12 (Winter): 255–276.

1967 *Passing On: The Social Organization of Dying.* Englewood Cliffs, N.J.: Prentice-Hall.

1971 *Studies in Social Interaction.* New York: Free Press.

Swanson, Guy E., Anthony F. C. Wallace, and James S. Coleman.

1968 "Review Symposium of Harold Garfinkel's *Studies in Ethnomethodology.*" *American Sociological Review* 33 (February): 122–130.

Turner, Roy.

1969 "Some features of the construction of conversations." Paper presented at American Sociological Association Meetings, San Francisco (August).

1970 "Words, utterances, and activities." Pp. 169–187 in Jack D. Douglas (ed.), *Understanding Everyday Life: Toward a Reconstruction of Sociological Knowledge.* Chicago: Aldine.

Wagner, Helmut.

1970 *Schutz on Phenomenology and Social Relations.* Chicago: University of Chicago Press.

Weber, Max.
1947   *The Theory of Social and Economic Organization.* Translated by A. M. Henderson and Talcott Parsons. Edited by Talcott Parsons. New York: Oxford University Press.

Wieder, D. Lawrence.
1969   "The Convict Code." Los Angeles: Unpublished Ph.D. Dissertation, University of California at Los Angeles.

Wieder, D. Lawrence, and Don H. Zimmerman.
1971   "The problem of the competent recognition of social action and the phenomenon of accounting." Paper presented at American Sociological Association Meetings, Denver, Colo. (August).

Wilson, Thomas.
1970   "Normative and interpretive paradigms in sociology." Pp. 57–79 in Jack D. Douglas (ed.), *Understanding Everyday Life: Toward the Reconstruction of Sociological Knowledge.* Chicago: Aldine.

Wittgenstein, Ludwig.
1953   *Philosophical Investigations.* Oxford: Blackwood and Mont.

Zimmerman, Don H.
1966   "Paper Work and People Work." Los Angeles: Unpublished Ph.D. Dissertation, University of California, Los Angeles.
1970a   "The practicalities of rule use." Pp. 221–238 in Jack D. Douglas (ed.), *Understanding Everyday Life: Toward the Reconstruction of Sociological Knowledge.* Chicago: Aldine.
1970b   "Record keeping and the intake process in a public welfare agency." Pp. 319–354 in Stanton Wheeler (ed.), *On Record: Files and Dossiers in American Life.* New York: Basic Books.

Zimmerman, Don H., and Melvin Pollner.
1970   "The everyday world as a phenomenon." Pp. 80–103 in Jack D. Douglas (ed.), *Understanding Everyday Life: Toward the Reconstruction of Sociological Knowledge.* Chicago: Aldine.

Zimmerman, Don H., and D. Lawrence Wieder.
1970   "Ethnomethodology and the problem of order: comment on Denzin." Pp. 285–298 in Jack D. Douglas (ed.), *Understanding Everyday Life: Toward the Reconstruction of Sociological Knowledge.* Chicago: Aldine.

CHAPTER 9
NEW CAUSAL THEORY
The New Model Army

**Social and intellectual properties
of the new causal theorists**

Intellectual leaders	H. M. Blalock, Jr.
	O. D. Duncan
Training centers	University of Chicago
	University of Michigan
	University of Wisconsin
Research centers	University of Chicago
	University of Michigan
	University of North Carolina
	University of Wisconsin
Social organizational leaders	Numerous (cluster and specialty stages)
Program statement	Blalock, **Causal Analysis in Non-Experimental Research** (1964)
Success	Blau and Duncan, **The American Occupational Structure** (1967)
Paradigm content	Theoretical statements can be constructed by empirical analysis.
Example of secondary work	Borgatta and Bohrnstedt (eds.), **Sociological Methodology** (1969; also 1970)
Example of critical work	None
Texts	Dubin, **Theory Building** (1969)
	Blalock, **Theory Construction** (1969b)
	Abell, **Model Building in Sociology** (1971)
	Davis, **Elementary Survey Analysis** (1971)
	Mullins, **The Art of Theory** (1971)

he new causal theorists have wrought (1) a complete change in the acceptable intellectual discourse surrounding the substantive, sociological areas of social stratification, social mobility, and (to some extent) intergroup relations and (2) a revision of the role divisions characteristic of standard American sociology. The techniques they use (path analysis from genetics, structural equation models from econometrics, and error estimation from psychometrics) had to await the advent of large sample sizes (e.g., more than 1500 persons), fairly accurate measurement, and full use of the underlying statistical correlation and regression procedures. These causal techniques have had a powerful effect on social theory because they require the clear statement of both assumptions and variable interrelationships.

The revision in sociology's role divisions is a social indication of the degree to which traditional sociology, particularly standard American sociology, has been superseded by contemporary theory. Structural–functionalist theorists were expected to use the results of others' research to build theory, providing, in turn, theoretical ideas for others to test. The methodologists furnished techniques; those interested in substantive problems used the more general statements of the theorists and the specific methods of the methodologist to study particular areas, usually defined by an institution (e.g., religion) or a process (e.g., socialization). This pattern was established by Robert K. Merton and Talcott Parsons; neither man was methodologically sophisticated, but both were able to find methodologically sophisticated colleagues (e.g., Paul Lazarsfeld and Samuel Stouffer, respectively) and students with whom to work. Since sociological questions have never been so neatly packaged, this role division was artificial at best. Indeed, the major difference between past theories as a category and contemporary ones is that older theories are organized by subject matter, whereas the newer ones focus on *ways* to do theory, regardless of the subject area involved. A person who did both theory and methodology was considered an exceptional sociologist, and there were very few exceptional sociologists. The new causal theorists, by contrast, routinely use the methodologist's tools in addition to doing theory in a substantive area (their major successes thus far have been in stratification and mobility research because of the availability of good data in those areas). However, as the methods pioneered by this group increasingly become a part of standard sociological techniques, and as theory *construction*, in addition to theory *testing*, becomes a standard part of graduate training, the uniqueness of the new causal theory position will probably dissolve into redefined areas of theory and methodology.

This group provides a particularly interesting case study of group formation. The whole history emphasizes that (1) a group may form on the basis of a series of small changes that, taken singly, may not seem to be especially important; (2) the division between group members and others may not be seen in terms of different training and background (as

TABLE 9.1   Social and intellectual highlights in the
development of new causal theory

Stage	Social	Intellectual
Normal: to 1962	Blau and Duncan begin collaboration on occupation research.	Beginning of large-scale analysis
Network: 1962–1966	Chicago—training center Michigan—research center, few students	Program statement: Blalock (1964) Path models
Cluster: 1966–1970	Michigan expands; decline of Chicago; rise of Wisconsin	Blau and Duncan (1967), **Sociological Methodology**; economic models
Specialty: 1970–	Polycentric development	Psychological input

is true of the ethnomethodologists) but, rather, in terms of professional quality and ability; (3) the response to the group's work by the rest of the profession, particularly as evidenced in the successful recruiting of senior high producers to the original group, can construct an "elite" specialty (Griffith and Mullins, 1972). By contrast, the rejection of a specialty by the rest of the profession can create a revolutionary specialty, such as ethnomethodology. Table 9.1 summarizes the major social and intellectual events in the development of new causal theory.

NORMAL STAGE: TO 1962

SOCIAL

The intellectual leaders in the development of new causal theory were H. M. Blalock, Jr., and O. D. Duncan.[1] Duncan has made major contributions to theory, methodology, and substantive research (see Blau and Duncan, 1967). Blalock's most significant work has been in methodology (see Blalock, 1964), but he has also been responsible for both substantive and theoretical advances (see Blalock, 1967a). The impact of Duncan and Blalock on the area was partly the result of their high status—and, hence, visibility—rather than clear intellectual priority or direction. The development of new causal theory has been actively supported by numerous established professionals and by students, although by no means all the students were trained directly by members of the group. (This picture of broad-based development contrasts sharply with the much smaller and more teacher–student-oriented development of ethnomethodology.) Many sociologists could not become involved in new causal theory's development because only those with above-average statistical skills could use its techniques. However, among those possessing the requisite skills in the early 1960s were (listed in order of year in which each Ph.D. degree was granted): William H. Sewell, Karl Schuessler, O. D. Duncan, Edgar F. Borgatta, Donald Pelz, Blalock, Archibald O. Haller, James S. Coleman, James A. Davis, B. Duncan, Edward McDill, Elton Jackson, Robert Leik, Doris Entwisle, Herbert L. Costner, Joe L. Spaeth, and Robert W. Hodge. Some of these people developed techniques (e.g., Duncan) and others concentrated on application of the techniques (e.g., Sewell). All were demographers, methodologists, or survey technologists who possessed considerable quantitative skill. These skills were valued by standard American sociology, and many of the sociologists named already held high prestige within the discipline. At least one reason for their interest in new causal theory has been well expressed by Dubin (1969: vii):

> I was educated in the social sciences at the University of Chicago in an atmosphere permeated by constant clashes between self-conscious empiricists and rather defensive theorists. The empiricists were clearly on the attack, and their parade caught me up in the vanguard. But I was not a wholehearted marcher under the banner because of a nagging need to find purposes for my own research in the products of the archenemy, the theorists.

Similar origins, similar itches, and similar conclusions, differing only with respect to the particular intellectual biography of each person involved, apparently affected Duncan and Blalock and—once the issue was joined —their students and others.

The collaboration between Blau and Duncan which led to *The American Occupational Structure* (1967) began during the normal stage. Blau, a Merton student, had started the research in 1955, at the height of structural functionalism, when he was teaching at the University of Chicago. He had begun the work in discussion with several persons, particularly Nelson Foote and Clyde W. Hart, both associated with the National Opinion Research Center (NORC). From the description in the preface of the book, it is clear that the theory–method role division was quite well accepted when Duncan became formally associated with the project in 1960[2] (although the two had often discussed the project and its problems before this date). Duncan left Chicago in 1961 for the University of Michigan and has remained there since. Blau and Duncan continued their work, however, each receiving support for his research through his own institution. Duncan's status as a demographer helped make the

(Census) Current Population Survey (CPS) available as a vehicle for research into the American stratification system as expressed in inheritance and achievement of status in education, occupation, and income in the United States (see Blau and Duncan, 1967). The study, involving 20,700 respondents, was considerably larger than any done before and was the first of several quite large surveys.

The large survey became possible during this period because technological improvements had become available, as well as more money for social research. The technological improvements were largely computer-based. Computers became available to the general university user in the early 1960s. Previous analysis had been dependent on extensive personnel to sort through cards using counter-sorters. These devices were relatively inflexible, prone to error, and dependent on human labor to keep them going. (Those who remember the heroic days of data analysis on the counter-sorter and tabulator know that the experience was long and difficult!) The advent of magnetic tape to store both data and programs to manipulate those data in the machine made much more intensive data analysis possible (although still not easy) and thus removed the previously existing practical limitations on sample size.

The influx of money initially derived from the National Institutes of Health's (NIH) interest and, somewhat later, the Kennedy administration's commitment to social change through government programs. Other funds came through the gradual acceptance of the social sciences by the National Science Foundation (NSF) and other funding agencies. These monies helped directly and indirectly. For example, part of the Blau and Duncan study (1967: Preface) was directly funded by the NSF; in addition, equipment and training were provided for persons who later did other projects. By 1962 Blau and Duncan's study was well underway and several people were working on the project. They began doing path analysis, the first of several causal techniques that give the group its name. The technique produced interesting results, which caused its use to spread among a group of sociological methodologists and statisticians, as well as a few others who were doing research during the late normal and early network stages. This broadening exemplifies the effectiveness of informal communication (by comparision with formal, e.g., published, channels) as a way of disseminating information: In 1962 the potential success that later caused the group to solidify was still an insider's success; nothing had been published.

INTELLECTUAL

New causal theory developed from the methodological and philosophical underpinnings of standard American sociology. Ten years ago, its practitioners would have been considered methodologists; they would not have qualified for inclusion in a book on social theory. Most of those who became interested in this approach were methodologists or were very sophisticated (by the criteria of standard American sociology) in methodology. It was not the pure methodologists who pioneered this work, however (although they certainly were capable of it), but rather those few methodologists who also did their own substantive research.

We have already noted standard American sociology's strong division between theory and methods. The accepted philosophical basis for theory in standard American sociology was stated in Hans L. Zetterberg's *Theory and Verification in Sociology*, first published in 1953. This very successful little book became the basis for many graduate courses and exams on theory. Zetterberg began with the notion that sociology included hundreds of small-scale studies presumbaly done by persons with substantive interests and aided by methodologists. Each study could contribute one or two or perhaps three propositions (empirically verified statements) to a general theory. Without ever explaining the mechanism clearly, Zetterberg asserted that it was possible to generate a set of *axioms* from which interested researchers could deduce all the propositions of interest in a given area. The fundamental idea of axiomatization was that, by strict propositional logic, one could derive all the empirical statements of a science from a set of axioms. These axiomatized theories would, in turn, make possible other deductions. By testing the consequences of a set of axioms, one could gradually build a tested, axiomatized deductive theory.

This positivist style of theory as supported by Nagel (1961), Hempel (1959), and others has become less central in the general philosophy of science as the philosophical implications of Kuhn (1962), the work of Popper (1959) and his disciples (e.g., see some of the chapters contributed to Lakatos and Musgrave, eds., 1970), and the school of linguistic philosophers (Hanson, 1958; Toulmin, 1961; Black, 1962a, 1962b) have come to be considered valid orientations to science. The difference is between normative philosophies (positivism), which state how theories *should* be done, and descriptive philosophies, which describe how they *are* done. The status of positivism in the general philosophy of science aside, however, the simple fact is that almost no theories of this type were ever tried in sociology.

George Homans was moving in the direction of Zetterberg's approach when he tried to develop a set of axioms within his *Human Group* (1950). He also continued, on a different basis, to discuss axiomatic (or at least propositional) theory in *Social Behavior: Its Elementary Forms* (1961) and later in his Presidential Address to the ASA, "Bringing Men Back In" (1964). Unfortunately, Homans' substantive writing on this topic does not contain any formal manipulations of the theory.

The other type of activity sparked by the same approach was the propositional inventory. There have been several, the most interesting being Williams' (1947) summary of intergroup relations (an empirical forerunner of Zetterberg, 1953) and Berelson and Steiner's (1964) collection of propositions, *Human Behavior*. The Williams collection, done for the SSRC, is an unusual example of these collections because the author explicitly tried to axiomatize, or at least to provide a structure for, the propositions he reported. This collection has aged; some of its statements are now known to be inaccurate. However, it still stands as an indication of what could have been done, had the philosophical program been carried out. The Berelson and Steiner collection, by contrast, is a caricature of the propositional inventory. The order in which the hundreds of propositions are collected is vague, and there has been little attempt at systematization. This collection has proved largely useless.

This approach to combining theory and methods, then, never achieved its promise. The occasional attempts to follow it were generally well received, but even those seem to have ceased. There are several possible explanations for this cessation. First, there were no really interesting results. With very few exceptions, the inventories (like Berelson and Steiner) tended to be unsystematic literature reviews, rather than enlightened contributions to knowledge. Second, the training in symbolic logic required as a foundation for doing serious theory manipulation in logical terms was not then, nor has it been (as of 1972), generally included in sociological training. A third problem, that of testability, is discussed later. Zetterberg's was not the only approach to theory formalization made during the 1940–1960 period (indeed, Chapter 10 deals with another attempt to formalize theory). His just happened to be the most popular, since it best fitted structural functionalism.

With respect to methodology, approaches to statistical manipulation have developed gradually, each based on a standard method. Two of the more interesting were a package of table manipulation techniques, championed by Columbia sociologists (particularly Lazarsfeld) and used principally in public opinion and voting studies (e.g., Lipset, Trow, and Coleman's *Union Democracy*, 1956; Campbell et al., *Voting*, 1960); and a set of correlation- and regression-based techniques, made popular by sociologists at Chicago, which were used chiefly in population, mobility, and stratification studies.[3] Both kinds of techniques were included in the general methods taught to most sociologists during the 1950s and 1960s. Every sociologist was presumed to need some familiarity with these techniques, if only through a course in statistics, which was often forgotten once the requirement for the Ph.D. degree had been passed. The accepting response of sociology to the development of new causal theory was probably conditioned in part by this presumed familiarity.

It is important to note that all the basic techniques used by the new causal theorists had already been introduced to sociology at least once. In an early article in the *American Sociological Review*, Rose (1949) had rejected partial correlation as a useful tool for sociological theory building, on the ground that statements about correlation were not statements of causation. Herbert A. Simon (1954; later incorporated into *Models of Man*, 1957) had discussed partial correlation techniques and had referred to the econometric literature. Psychometric techniques were actually used in testing, particularly by sociologists at the Educational Testing Service in Princeton, N.J. Some of the most sophisticated sociologists used these techniques purely as methods. That these ideas had not been developed for their theory-building potential constitutes additional support for the hypothesis that a good idea without a group will not develop.

New causal theory began with development of the algebra of correlation and regression techniques arising from the reimportation of these techniques and conceptualizations from the fields of economics, genetics, psychology, and statistics. As a consequence of the use for which it had been developed, the technique involved in each case of importation had the ability to deal with three or more variables in a system of variables whose interrelations were simultaneously testable. This type of testing went well beyond the simple, "one proposition at a time" type of testing that had led to Zetterberg's style of theory construction, and it called for new methods of formalizing theories.

In 1962, then, there were: (1) social scientists skilled enough to use causal techniques if such were developed, (2) a study large enough and well-enough staffed to put such new techniques to good use, (3) a body of techniques available in other disciplines which had been introduced to sociology at least once before, and (4) some people beginning to work together on path analysis. The last development marked the end of the normal stage.

NETWORK STAGE:
1962–1966

SOCIAL

The social side of new causal theory is best discussed with reference to Table 9.2, which lists new causal theorists as defined by authors of work in major sociological journals and several books that have collected new causal theory material (see Appendix for complete details on selection). Other social scientists were added to this basic list if they had produced well-known work clearly characteristic of new causal theory but published elsewhere. Table 9.2 is probably overinclusive in retaining persons (1) whose major contribution to new causal theory development was standard survey skills or (2) whose substantive interests were in stratification and mobility, although their interests and skills were not those of the core new causal theorists. With this probable inflation of the numbers in mind, we can now examine the social structure of this group.

Table 9.2 shows that in 1963 future new causal theorists were quite scattered. University of North Carolina, Wisconsin, Columbia, Chicago, Indiana, Michigan, Johns Hopkins, University of Washington, Vanderbilt, Penn State, and others all had one or two. Only Chicago, with three faculty and five students, exhibited any concentration. We can assume some informal communication among persons at different locations who shared a prior training or colleague tie (e.g., Duncan was trained by Ogburn and Hauser; Duncan trained Hodge). Persons like Edward McDill and Richard A. Rehberg (trained and employed at Vanderbilt and Penn State, respectively) are unlikely to have been part of a communicating network. Thus the communicating network, although it had a potential size of at least 32 persons, was probably much smaller. Some sort of formal tie to the University of Chicago seems to be the key factor—as of 1963, 13 of the 32 potential members listed in Table 9.2 either were at Chicago (e.g., Crain, Davis, Hodge) or have Chicago degrees (e.g., Cutright, Dubin, the Duncans).

In Chicago, as Dubin has noted (1969: vii), the elements of the itch and the ability to scratch it were all present. Hodge, although officially a student (his Ph.D. date is 1967), was a faculty member and part of NORC from about 1963. NORC, directed by Peter Rossi and with James A. Davis, Robert L. Crain, and Robert A. Gordon, among others on its staff, was a center of activity (e.g., see Crain and Rosenthal, 1962). In 1963 Chicago's group was fairly large for a network stage group and was supported by two factors: (1) its long-standing concern with the theory–method relationship, mentioned by Dubin, and (2) the existence of NORC. Michigan began only with the Duncans and two students. Wisconsin had three faculty and two students.

The end of the network stage was marked by the beginning of the "second generation's" heavy involvement in teaching and research. When persons recruited as students have matured almost to the point of being professionals, they in turn acquire students and become important colleagues in the network of association. Fifteen students (see Table 9.2) received their Ph.D. degrees during this four-year period (1962–1966).

Table 9.3 summarizes the locations of new causal theorists in 1966, just at the close of the network stage. The network had a potential size of at least 58 members. At that time Chicago had increased its numbers to six faculty and six students, and Michigan had three each. By 1966 also, Wisconsin had five faculty and two students. No social organization leader had yet emerged.

TABLE 9.2 Important new causal theorists: degree (date and place) and selected job locations

Name	Ph.D. Date	Ph.D. Place	1963	1966
Adams, Bert	1965	UNC	UNC	WISC
Althauser, Robert P.	1967	UNC	*	UNC
Armer, J. Michael	1964	WISC	WISC	ORE
Bailey, Kenneth D.	1968	TEX	*	TEX
Bayer, Alan E.	1965	FSU	*	res
Blalock, Jr., H. M.	1954	UNC	UNC	UNC
Blau, Peter M.	1952	COL	CHIC	CHIC
Blum, Zahava	ni	CHIC	*	*
Bohrnstedt, George W.	1966	WISC	*	WISC
Bonacich, Phillip	1968	HARV	*	HARV
Borgatta, Edgar F.	1952	NYU	WISC	WISC
Boudon, Raymond (French)	F	*	*	*
Boyle, Richard P.	ni	IOWA	ni	IOWA
Carlos, Serge	ni	CHIC	*	*
Carter, Lewis	1966	TEX	*	TEX
Carter, T. Michael	ni	WISC	*	ni
Cleary T. Anne	ni	WISC	*	ni
Coleman, James S.	1955	COL	JHU	JHU
Costner, Herbert L.	1960	INDU	WASH	WASH
Crain, Robert L.	1963	CHIC	CHIC	CHIC
Curtis, Richard F.	1959	MICH	ARIZ	ARIZ
Cutright, Phillips	1960	CHIC	SOCA	VAND
Davis, James A.	1955	HARV	res	CHIC
Dubin, Robert	1947	CHIC	ORE	ORE
Dumont, Richard C.	1968	MASS	*	*
Duncan, Beverly	1957	CHIC	MICH	MICH
Duncan, O. D.	1949	CHIC	MICH	MICH
Elder, Jr., Glen H.	1961	UNC	BERK	BERK
Entwisle, Doris	1960	JHU	JHU	JHU
Featherman, David	1969	MICH	*	*
Fennessey, James	ni	JHU	*	*
Glockel, Galen	ni	ni	*	*
Goldberger, Arthur (economist)	*	*	*	*
Gordon, Robert A.	1963	CHIC	CHIC	CHIC
Gove, Walter R.	1968	WASH	*	WASH
Haller, Archibald O.	1954	WISC	WISC	WISC
Halter, Albert	ni	ni	ni	ni
Hannan, Michael	ni	ni	ni	ni
Hauser, Robert M.	1968	MICH	*	*
Heberlein, Thomas	ni	WISC	*	*
Heise, David	1964	CHIC	CHIC	WISC

Sources: American Journal of Sociology (various years); **American Sociological Review** (various years a, b, c); Blalock and Blalock (1968); Borgatta and Bohrnstedt (1969, 1970); Costner (1971).

Job held during academic year ending in				
1967	1968	1969	1970	1971
WISC	WISC	WISC	WISC	WISC
UNC	PRIN	PRIN	PRIN	PRIN
ORE	ni	NWU	INDU	INDU
TEX	TEX	UCLA	UCLA	UCLA
res	res	res	res	res
UNC	UNC	UNC	UNC	UNC
CHIC	CHIC	CHIC	CHIC	COL
CHIC	CHIC	ni	JHU	JHU
WISC	WISC	WISC	MINN	MINN
UCLA	UCLA	UCLA	UCLA	UCLA
WISC	WISC	WISC	WISC	RUSS
*	*	*	*	*
HARV	UCLA	UCLA	UCLA	UCLA
*	*	CHIC	CHIC	CHIC
UNC	UNC	UNC	UNC	UCR
ni	ni	WISC	WISC	WISC
ni	ni	WISC	WISC	WISC
JHU	JHU	JHU	JHU	JHU
WASH	WASH	WASH	WASH	WASH
CHIC	JHU	JHU	JHU	JHU
ARIZ	ARIZ	ARIZ	ARIZ	ARIZ
VAND	WSTL	JUC	JUC	JUC
CHIC	DART	DART	DART	DART
ORE	ORE	ORE	UCI	UCI
MASS	MASS	MAIN	MAIN	MAIN
MICH	MICH	MICH	MICH	MICH
MICH	MICH	MICH	MICH	MICH
BERK	BERK	UNC	UNC	UNC
JHU	JHU	JHU	JHU	JHU
*	MICH	MICH	PRIN	WISC
*	JHU	JHU	CHIC	CHIC
ni	ni	CHIC	ni	ni
*	WISC	WISC	WISC	WISC
CHIC	JHU	JHU	JHU	JHU
WASH	WASH	VAND	VAND	VAND
WISC	WISC	WISC	WISC	WISC
ni	ORST	ni	ni	ni
ni	ni	ni	STAN	ni
BROW	BROW	BROW	WISC	WISC
*	*	*	WISC	WISC
WISC	WISC	WISC	WISC	QUEE

TABLE 9.2 (continued)

Name	Ph.D. Date	Ph.D. Place	1963	1966
Herrick, Clinton	ni	JHU	JHU	JHU
Hodge, Robert W.	1967	CHIC	CHIC	CHIC
Jackson, Elton F.	1960	MICH	YALE	INDU
Jöreskog, Karl (Swedish)	*	*	*	*
Klatzky, Sheila R.	1970	CHIC	*	*
Klein, Robert E.	ni	MICH	*	*
Krippendorff, Klauss	ni	ni	ni	ni
Land, Kenneth	1969	TEX	*	TEX
Lane, Angela	1972	CHIC	*	CHIC
Leik, Robert K.	1960	WISC	WASH	WASH
Lew, Robert	ni	ni	ni	ni
Linn, Robert L.	ni	ni	ni	ni
Lyons, Morgan	1971	WISC	*	*
Marzuki, Ariffinbirr	ni	ni	ni	ni
Mason, Robert	ni	ni	ni	ni
Mason, William	1970	CHIC	CHIC	CHIC
McDill, Edward	1959	VAND	VAND	JHU
Miller, Alden	ni	ni	ni	ni
Oppenheim, Karen	1969	CHIC	*	*
Palmore, James A.	1966	CHIC	*	CHIC
Pelz, Donald	1952	MICH	MICH	MICH
Portes, Alejandro	1970	WISC	*	*
Rehberg, Richard A.	1965	PNST	PNST	ORE
Rosenthal, Donald B.	ni	ni	ni	ni
Rossi, Peter	1951	COL	CHIC	CHIC
Rubin, Zick	1969	MICH	*	*
Schafer, Walter E.	1965	MICH	MICH	ORE
Schild, E. (Israeli)	F	*	*	*
Schnaiberg, Allan	1968	MICH	*	MICH
Schuessler, Karl	1947	INDU	INDU	INDU
Scott, Robert	1961	STAN	ni	RUSS
Seiler, Lauren	ni	ILL	*	*
Sewell, William H.	1939	MINN	WISC	WISC
Shah, Vimal	1966	WISC	WISC	WISC
Siegel, Paul M.	1970	CHIC	*	CHIC
Spaeth, Joe L.	1961	CHIC	CHIC	CHIC
Stinchcombe, Arthur	1960	BERK	ni	JHU
Sullivan, John L.	ni	ni	ni	ni
Summers, Gene	1962	TENN	ILL	ILL
Sweet, James	1968	MICH	*	MICH
Treiman, Donald	1968	CHIC	*	CHIC
Upshaw, Harry (psychologist)	*	*	*	*
Van Valey, Thomas L.	ni	UNC	ni	ni
Walster, G. William	ni	WISC	ni	ni
Warren, Bruce	ni	MICH	*	MICH

Job held during academic year ending in				
1967	1968	1969	1970	1971
JHU	JHU	JHU	STON	STON
CHIC	CHIC	CHIC	MICH	MICH
INDU	INDU	INDU	INDU	INDU
*	*	*	ETS	ETS
*	CHIC	CHIC	MICH	WISC
*	MICH	MICH	MICH	ni
ni	ni	ni	PENN	ni
TEX	TEX	RUSS	RUSS	RUSS
CHIC	CHIC	CHIC	CHIC	INDU
WASH	WASH	WASH	WASH	WASH
ni	MICH	ni	MASS	ni
ni	ni	ni	ETS	ETS
*	*	WISC	WISC	FSU
ni	ni	ni	MICH	ni
ni	ORST	ORST	ORST	ni
CHIC	CHIC	CHIC	CHIC	DUKE
JHU	JHU	JHU	JHU	JHU
ni	ni	ni	BOSU	ni
CHIC	CHIC	CHIC	WISC	WISC
MICH	MICH	MICH	MICH	HAWI
MICH	MICH	MICH	MICH	MICH
*	WISC	WISC	WISC	ILL
ORE	ni	ni	BING	ni
CHIC	ni	ni	ni	ni
CHIC	JHU	JHU	JHU	JHU
MICH	MICH	MICH	HARV	HARV
ORE	ORE	ORE	ORE	ORE
JHU	*	*	*	*
MICH	MICH	NWU	NWU	NWU
INDU	INDU	INDU	INDU	INDU
RUSS	RUSS	ni	PRIN	PRIN
*	*	ILL	ILL	ni
WISC	WISC	WISC	WISC	WISC
WISC	WISC	WISC	WISC	WISC
CHIC	MICH	MICH	MICH	MICH
CHIC	CHIC	CHIC	CHIC	CHIC
JHU	ni	BERK	BERK	BERK
ni	ni	ni	IOST	ni
ILL	ILL	ILL	ILL	WISC
MICH	MICH	WISC	WISC	WISC
CHIC	WISC	WISC	WISC	COL
*	*	*	*	*
ni	ni	ni	UNC	CSU
ni	ni	ni	WISC	WISC
MICH	MICH	MICH	MICH	ni

TABLE 9.2 (continued)

| Name | Ph.D. | | 1963 | 1966 |
	Date	Place		
Wells, Caryll	ni	ni	ni	ni
Werts, Charles E.	ni	ni	ni	ni
Wiley, David E. (psychologist)	*	*	*	*
Wiley, James A.	ni	VAND	*	*
Wilson, Thomas	1965	COL	COL	DART
Wilson, William J.	1965	WAST	WAST	MASS
Woelfol, Joseph	ni	ni	ni	ni

Key:

ARIZ	University of Arizona, Tempe	HARV	Harvard University, Cambridge
BERK	University of California, Berkeley	HAWI	University of Hawaii
BING	State University of New York, Binghamton	ILCH	University of Illinois, Chicago Circle
BOSU	Boston University	ILL	University of Illinois
BROW	Brown University, Providence, R.I.	INDU	Indiana University, Bloomington
CARL	Carleton University, Ottawa	IOST	Iowa State University, Iowa City
CHIC	University of Chicago	IOWA	University of Iowa
COL	Columbia University	JHU	Johns Hopkins University
CSU	Colorado State University, Fort Collins	JUC	Joint Urban Center, Cambridge, Mass.
DART	Dartmouth College	MAIN	University of Maine
DUKE	Duke University	MASS	University of Massachusetts, Amherst
ETS	Educational Testing Service, Princeton, N.J.	MICH	University of Michigan, Ann Arbor
FSU	Florida State University, Tallahassee	MINN	University of Minnesota, Minneapolis

INTELLECTUAL

The network stage produced two intellectual developments of interest. One was the beginning of a series of massive surveys on the relation among education, father's occupation, and achievement (in terms of education, occupation, or income).[4] Several of the earlier ones were done from material incorporated into the CPS. Surveys of the scale and precision of the CPS studies (analyzed by Blau and Duncan) were not just extensions of the much smaller studies done earlier. The increase in size *and* care in design permitted increased sophistication in the data manipulation. These surveys, then, were proposed because previously impossible analyses could now be done with the data. For example, the huge sample size (e.g., Blau and Duncan's sample of 20,700) made tests of statistical significance almost unnecessary. Any statistical differences were almost automatically significant. Furthermore, because models could be developed and tested against data, the models themselves could be more

Job held during academic year ending in				
1967	1968	1969	1970	1971
ni	ni	UNC	CARL	CARL
ni	ni	ni	ETS	ETS
*	*	*	CHIC	*
VAND	VAND	WSTL	ILCH	ILCH
DART	UCSB	UCSB	UCSB	UCSB
MASS	MASS	MASS	MASS	MASS
ni	WISC	ni	ni	ILL

ni	No information	UCI	University of California, Irvine
NWU	Northwestern University	UCLA	University of California,
NYU	New York University		Los Angeles
ORE	University of Oregon, Eugene	UCR	University of California,
ORST	Oregon State University, Corvallis		Riverside
PNST	Pennsylvania State University	UCSB	University of California,
PRIN	Princeton University		Santa Barbara
QUEE	Queens College, Brooklyn	UNC	University of North Carolina
res	Research	VAND	Vanderbilt University
RUSS	Russell Sage Foundation	WASH	University of Washington, Seattle
SOCA	Social Security Administration	WAST	Washington State University,
STAN	Stanford University		Pullman
STON	State University of New York,	WISC	University of Wisconsin, Madison
	Stony Brook	WSTL	Washington University, St. Louis
TEX	University of Texas, Austin	YALE	Yale University
		*	Not in system

complicated than an unconnected series of one-proposition statements logically held together, and an entire model could be tested at once.

Many of the problems that normally occupy a researcher's attention did not concern Blau and Duncan. In particular, they did not have to administer a survey organization; the Census did that for them. Duncan already knew Census procedures; only the specific procedures for the CPS surveys had to be learned. The absence of such necessities freed them for work on analytic techniques.

In addition to Blau and Duncan's work, the 1964 NORC study was underway (Hodge and Treiman, 1965). Duncan, Hodge, and Blalock, among others, were researching the properties of this new type of theory that they were proposing. Chicago personnel were aided by the NORC operation with its large and expert field staff and highly trained survey technicians. Those who did research with NORC were in the position of being able to think about their work rather than having to worry about details. In addition, because NORC did research in many areas, Chicago's

TABLE 9.3 Summary of locations for degrees and positions for 93 new causal theorists

Location	Number of Ph.D.'s	1963	1966	1967	1968	1969	1970	1971
University of North Carolina	5	2	2	3	2	3	4	2
University of Wisconsin	11	5	7	7	10	15	17	15
University of Texas	3	0	3	2	2	0	0	0
University of Chicago	18	8	12	14	8	9	7	3
University of Michigan	11	4	6	8	12	9	9	5
Johns Hopkins University	3	3	5	6	8	8	7	7
Others	22	16	21	23	25	26	42	41
Subtotal	(73)	(38)	(57)	(63)	(68)	(70)	(86)	(73)
No information	13	16	15	16	17	17	4	17
Not in system; no degree, foreign, or other area	5	39	22	14	9	6	3	3
Total	93	93	93	93	93	93	93	93

Source: Table 9.2.

steady flow of bright students could almost always find an interesting topic, and each individual could thus pursue a different substantive concern. Thus Chicago research has not been marked (as has Wisconsin's) by a single kind of output (e.g., analysis of educational data).

The article by Duncan and Hodge (1963) demonstrated one research interest. Its topic is education and occupational mobility, and its purpose is to show the independent effect of education on the social status of persons. This theme is reechoed in the later work of the Wisconsin group. Hodge and Siegel (1964) on rating occupations presents another major interest. The rating of occupations in order to use occupational status as a variable in measuring achievement is an old concern at NORC. The North–Hatt scale and other work summarized in Reiss (1961) were earlier efforts along this same line. Such later work of Chicago students as Lane (1968), Klatzky (1970), and Carlos (1970) represents a continuation of this Chicago tradition of survey analysis with theoretical concerns.

The second development was the debate over whether axiomatic theory produced propositions that were themselves empirically testable. In 1962 theory formalization had essentially meant the kind proposed by Zetterberg: a series of empirically established propositions connected by logical manipulations. During the normal stage, objections to the deductive pattern had developed. These objections culminated in a series of publications during the network period; in them Duncan (1963), Costner and Leik (1964), and Blalock (1964, 1966) all pointed to problems in, and raised explicit objections to, deductive theory. Much later, Bailey (1970) discussed the status of such theories, pointing out especially that the empirical status of deductions from the theory had been much criticized. In addition to rejecting the Zetterberg model, the new causal theorists took the first steps toward establishment of an alternative through Duncan's "Axioms or Correlations" (1963), an explicit criticism of axiomatic theory, and Blalock's *Causal Inferences* (1964).

It is an interesting commentary on the "insider" quality of new causal theory that, at the same time, Zetterberg chose to reissue his book (1963, 2nd ed.) and George Homans' Presidential Address to the ASA (Homans, 1964), although questioning some aspects, continued to champion deductive theory. It is important that Homans' disagreement was *not* with the new causal theorists but with Parsons' slightly different approach to theory. The former were not a significant factor to the old-line theorists, who still saw them as methodologists. Homans' specific disagreement was with Parsons' classificatory theory; the argument was over the appropriate strategy for applying the logic of classes that Parsons was distinguishing. Parsons, Zetterberg, and Homans agreed on the general model of theory; the "methodology" of the new causal theorists was a side issue, at best.

Blalock's *Causal Inferences* (1964) proved to be new causal theory's first program statement. Costner and Leik (1964) had proposed the necessity of a positive alternative, and Blalock specifically proposed the partial-correlation techniques of Simon. Duncan, who had seen Blalock's work before it was published and while he was analyzing the CPS data, felt that Simon's approach was not quite appropriate for his data. In searching for alternatives, he discovered the path analysis techniques of Sewell Wright and then the path regression techniques of John Tukey. The assumptions of these techniques could be met by the CPS data. The eventual result of all these efforts was synthetic theory, supported by an asymmetrical causal model (*synthetic* indicating that it summarizes the data as a whole rather than in separate parts). Synthetic theory, by contrast with analytic-deductive theory, is more easily translated into a statistical model. With the publication of *Causal Inferences*, Blalock emerged as an intellectual leader for new causal theory. Duncan also functioned as an intellectual leader, although this status did not become clear to nongroup members until 1967, when Blau and Duncan's *American Occupational Structure* appeared.

It should be noted that, while Blalock was at North Carolina, it functioned as a research center. It was never a training center, as we can see by studying Tables 9.2 and 9.3.

To the outside observer, the network stage was a time of rejection and waiting. To the inside observer, however, it was clear that a new development was occurring, organized around synthetic theory. In addition to the social properties noted earlier, new causal theory had an intellectual leader, research centers, and small training centers. Indeed, the Chicago training center appeared to need only a heavy influx of students to push it into the cluster stage.

THE CLUSTER STAGE: 1966–1970

SOCIAL

The cluster stage was marked by the development at Chicago, Michigan, and Wisconsin of new causal theory clusters (although Chicago's disintegrated before the end of that stage). Each school had a central figure and a group of other professionals. Both Wisconsin and Johns Hopkins had hired large groups of Chicago people who brought the new causal theory approach with them. However, their effect on training and research was not felt for a few years, since graduate students take at least three years to complete their degree work, and usually longer.

In 1967 Chicago (with Hodge at the center) had increased in size from 12 to 14 people. In 1968, however, the number dropped to eight and by 1971 was down to three. Thus the promise of a strong cluster at Chicago, which had seemed evident in 1966, was not fulfilled.

Instead, strong clusters developed at Michigan, which never had less than nine people between 1968 and 1970, and Wisconsin, which ranged in size from seven (1967) and ten (1968) to 17 (1970) (see Table 9.3.) North Carolina continued as a research center.

During this stage an important link developed between Arthur Goldberger, an econometrician at Wisconsin, and Duncan at Michigan. It started when Goldberger suggested some changes in Duncan's (1966) paper (Blalock, 1971: 136n), and the two have corresponded since then (Duncan, 1972). Goldberger has now made some direct contributions to the sociological literature (e.g., R. M. Hauser and Goldberger, 1971).

The group at Johns Hopkins grew from just two highly qualified methodologists—Coleman, who had never been integral to this group, and Doris Entwisle—to include Arthur Stinchcombe, a Berkeley Ph.D., plus Peter Rossi, Robert L. Crain, Robert A. Gordon, and James Fennessey, a graduate student from Chicago. The techniques of new causal theory were imported wholesale, although the output from this particular group has not been exceptional. Hopkins obviously had sufficient faculty, but the graduate program failed to attract a student group larger than two (see Table 9.3). Hence a cluster never developed. The data, then, show three new causal theory clusters, each at its strongest in a different year.

The presence in Table 9.2 of names of sociologists like Kenneth Land, who was not taught by a group member but developed his understandings from the literature, demonstrates the accessibility of this work to others in sociology with similar skills. Thus we have an explanation for the large number of new causal theorists, throughout the 1960s, at locations that were not training–research centers. This situation contrasts strongly with that of ethnomethodology, which recruited a few older scientists, but the young persons—by Ph.D. date—were trained only by the group. Table 9.3 makes the same point; more people who later took up new causal theory work were trained during the normal stage than in either the network or the cluster stages. In short, colleagues influenced other colleagues more than teachers influenced students to take up new causal theory techniques.

Members of the new causal theory group are joined by coauthorship and trusted assessor linkages reflecting both the total group's growth and the various subgroupings over time. Figure 9.1 is the coauthorship network for new causal theory. A total of 49 people are included, 37 of them from Table 9.2 (40 percent of the table). The largest group is 14; it includes the older University of Chicago group (Cutright, Duncan, Hodge, Rossi, Treiman), together with the older University of Wisconsin group (Armer, Haller, Sewell, and Shah). This group created all the normal and network stage ties that appear on the figure.

The second largest group (which includes ten persons) is the "new" University of Wisconsin group (Borgatta, Bohrnstedt, T. M. Carter, Cleary, Heise, Lyons, Walster); Robert I. Linn is the bridge to a group at the Educational Testing Service (Jöreskog, Linn, and Werts). Other small groups of two, three, four, and five are scattered on the page.

An important feature of this network is that the three largest groups include members who also appear in Table 3.3, Figure 3.3, or both. New causal theory's connection to standard American sociology, then (particularly by contrast with ethnomethodology's totally isolated network), is quite clear.

A second feature is that, relative to other coherent groups in sociology, the new causal theorists are prone to coauthorship; 36 percent (24/67) of the articles analyzed are coauthored, and six of these by three persons. The group has been in the specialty stage for a very short time, and as group members continue to move to new locations, forming new colleague relations, the number of coauthorships should increase.

Although some subgroups are fairly large, the scattered appearance of the network understates the total connectedness among subgroups.

First, all but one group is interconnected to all the others, if only through coauthorship links with standard American sociologists (even though some of the connections are distant in time and through another intellectual country). Second, many of these persons use each other as trusted assessors. As in Chapter 8, we can use information on footnotes that thank various groups for reading earlier versions of papers. In Borgatta and Bohrnstedt (1969, 1970), Blalock (1971), and Costner (1971), these footnotes are frequently seen.

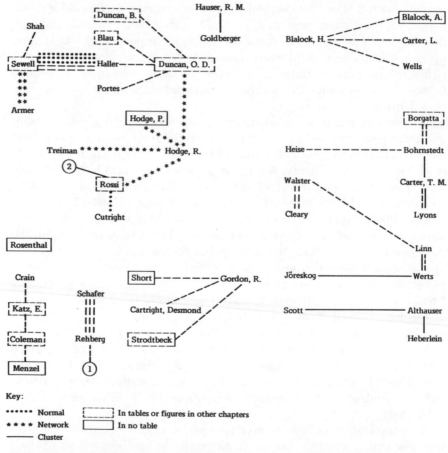

FIGURE 9.1 Coauthorship networks for new causal theory, 1962–1971. (**Sources: American Journal of Sociology** [various years]; **American Sociological Review** [various years a, b, c]; Blalock and Blalock [1968]; Borgatta and Bohrnstedt [1969, 1970]; Blalock [1971]; Costner [1971].)

Looking at the acknowledgments (see Figure 9.2) we find one large network of 33 persons and a very small network of four. The large network is highly connected, since some persons receive many expressions of appreciation. Goldberger receives five; Duncan four; Blalock and Bohrnstedt receive three each. Each of the large receivers thanks at least one other large receiver; these links provide the basic structure for the network.

If we consider the trusted assessor network in conjunction with the coauthorship network, we find that assessor links connect the two largest coauthor groups, the two four-person groups, and two other smaller

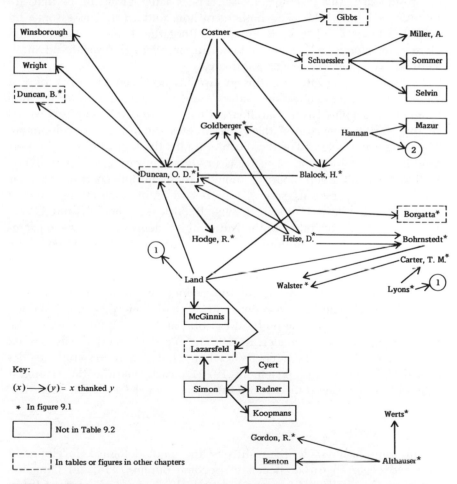

FIGURE 9.2 Trusted assessor network for new causal theory.
(**Sources:** Borgatta and Bohrnstedt [1969, 1970]; Blalock [1971]; Costner [1971].)

groups. Still unconnected directly is a group of five, which is connected through standard American sociology, and a completely unconnected group of three. The group of five includes two long-term colleagues (1967 to the present) Coleman and Crain, who are also linked by colleagueship to Gordon and Rossi, who are included in another subgroup in the figure.[5]

The coauthorship links alone include 37 people from Table 9.2. The trusted assessor links plus the coauthor links combine to include four more persons who are in Table 9.2: Costner, Land, Miller, and Schuessler. There are 13 people in Figure 9.2 who are not in Table 9.2. Five are either not sociologists (i.e., are economists and psychologists) or are older standard American sociologists. The smaller group of 14 that are in Figures 9.1 *and* 9.2 (i.e., both coauthors and trusted assessors) includes Althauser, Blalock, Bohrnstedt, Borgatta, Duncan, Goldberger, Heise, and Hodge, who have all been important to the social and intellectual development of new causal theory.

The social organization of this group has not been the work of just one or two social organization leaders, partly because the group has had three clusters (plus North Carolina acting as a research center as well). In this respect, new causal theory resembles small group development. The geographical spread of these centers, plus the high status of the persons located at the centers, made a single organization leader unlikely. Unlike the small group theorists, though, these clusters coordinated their activities. Many persons served together on ASA committees. Several served together (e.g., Duncan, Davis, Blalock; see Smelser and Davis, 1969) on a study committee of the National Academy of Sciences to examine social science. In addition, a committee of the NIH on methodology in sociology, including Duncan, Blalock, Borgatta, Davis, Schuessler, and Bohrnstedt (for some of the time), met from 1965 to at least 1969. Such opportunities made it possible for the people involved to keep up with research developments at locations other than their own and enabled coordination of research opportunities, jobs, and so on. (For more on the NIH committee, see Schuessler, 1966.) The end of this period was marked by Chicago's decline as a center (when Hodge and his students departed). Wisconsin (17 people in 1970) clearly became the strongest location for new causal theory in terms of personnel (see Table 9.3).

INTELLECTUAL

During the cluster stage, the results of the methodological development that had occurred earlier began to become public. Blau and Duncan's *American Occupational Structure* and Blalock's *Toward a Theory of Intergroup Relations* were both published in 1967. The former constituted a second program statement for new causal theory, even though it had already had substantial effects on research through informal communication. Both books have curious anachronisms (e.g., Blau's chapters in the book he coauthored with Duncan, and the propositional inventory aspect of Blalock's book), but both also point to a new style of discourse in these areas. Other technical materials (Duncan, 1966; Blalock and Blalock, eds., 1968) were also published during this period.

The growing acceptance of this style can be seen in the dedication of one-fourth of Borgatta and Bohrnstedt's (eds.) *Sociological Methodology* (1969) to discussions of path analysis, and the curiously titled research note by Werts, "Path Analysis: Testimonial of a Proselyte" (1968). Another important element in the growing acceptance was Arthur Stinchcombe's remarkable *Constructing Social Theory* (1968), which attempted to introduce into theory analysis techniques that would make path analysis or partial-correlation analysis the natural way to test theory. Stinchcombe, probably influenced by frequent contacts with Coleman and Duncan, took many of the standard theories and inquired about the sorts of relations among the variables proposed by each theory. He depicted the answers in diagrams that are very much like path diagrams. His discussion of such diagrams is based on Huggins and Entwisle (1968), a general discussion of relations within empirical, linear systems.

Intellectually, the new causal theory group had moved from an initial concern with the spurious correlation phenomenon and three-variable problems to the structure of theories as represented by path models imported from genetics. Subsequently, interest shifted to the set of structural equations which, if properly set up, represent the path model, and then to more general sets of linear equations (e.g., those which have characterized economics). Attention next focused on measurement error, first as represented in path models including error and then as a general problem, using the techniques of psychometrics to illuminate the subject. Another major concern was for the analysis of panel and other over-time analyses (e.g., Heise, 1970). During the late cluster stage, psychometric inputs became important. Together and in combination with other sociologists, Werts, Linn and, particularly, Karl Jöreskog—all working at the Educational Testing Service—made major contributions to sociological understanding of the problems of measurement error (Cleary, Linn, and Walster, 1970; Werts, Linn, and Jöreskog, 1971). In each case, the contention of Deutsch, Platt, and Senghaas (1971; see Chapter 6) that sociology is not an innovative discipline has been supported. The basic technology has been imported and then adapted for use.

More specifically during the cluster stage, the two intellectual leaders, Blalock and Duncan, took different approaches to causal modeling. Blalock (1971: 73-74) is quite clear on the difference between the two approaches to causal modeling. He sees these as differences in (1) the kinds of measures utilized to build causal models (those following him —and through him, Simon and the econometric literature—tended to use unstandardized measures) and (2) the explicit attention paid to error terms. Fundamentally, the two model types are the same, although they appear to be quite different (see Blalock, 1971: 74).

Blalock (ed., 1971), although published in the specialty stage, is a book of readings collected from earlier publication. Many of the authors included have ties to North Carolina. For example, Michael Hannan, John L. Sullivan, and Thomas Van Valey have ties to North Carolina (see references to earlier North Carolina publications by these authors, Blalock, ed., 1971: 330, 508). The book gives considerable attention to econometric simultaneous equation models. As Blalock says (1971: vii) in his introduction:

> The most systematic discussions of this general approach have appeared in the econometrics literature, where several general texts are available. Many of these discussions are too technical for most sociologists, political scientists, and others who lack strong backgrounds in mathematics, however. In editing this volume I have attempted to integrate a few of the less technical papers written by econometricians such as Koopmans, Wold, Strotz, and Fisher with discussions of causal approaches in the biological sciences and with relatively more exploratory treatments by sociologists and other social scientists.

If Blalock (1971) is a North Carolina–econometrics book, Borgatta and Bohrnstedt (1969, 1970) are Wisconsin–path-model books. The Wisconsin center has had two different intellectual involvements, which are visible as different parts of Figures 9.1 and 9.2. The first development centered on the early analysis of Sewell's education data on Wisconsin high school graduates in 1957 (see Sewell and Armer, 1966). The second stage began with Sewell and Shah (1968a, 1968b) and Sewell, Haller, and Portes (1969). A reexamination of the Sewell and Amer results using the new techniques appeared in Duncan, Haller, and Portes (1968). Wisconsin's interest in education and its fundamental place in the stratification system was underlined by Robert M. Hauser's move to Wisconsin. His concerns with education are shown in Hauser (1969, 1970).

Michigan's development centered on Duncan. As I noted, he originally became interested (Duncan, 1972) in various causal models after reading Blalock (1964) in draft form. Michigan's intellectual development during the cluster stage grew largely out of earlier efforts. Duncan's (1968a) paper on the inheritance of poverty continues Blau and Duncan's effort to assess the relative effects of parental influence (including, in this case, race) and the relative achievement of persons with respect to social status. The fundamental problem is that both factors have effects on social status as well as other effects not yet measured The solution of this problem does not lend itself to easy verbal formulations, and the need for careful investigation, particularly given the governmental policy implications of wrong (or right) analyses, is truly awesome. For example, consider the matter of school integration and the basis on which integration should be achieved; analyses such as Duncan (1968a) have tremendous potential implications for such policies.

A Johns Hopkins center never developed. The people there had methodological concerns (e.g., Coleman's *Introduction to Mathematical Sociology*, 1964; Fennessey, 1968; and Gordon, 1968), theoretical concerns (e.g., Stinchcombe, 1968), and deep explorations of the general linear model (Huggins and Entwisle, 1968). Yet in the presence of all this work in the late 1960s, when large education research projects were underway, as well (see Coleman and Campbell, 1966; McDill, Rigsby, and Meyers, 1969), there was no coming together. My guess is that the relatively small size of the entire operation made a development along the lines of Michigan or Wisconsin unlikely.

The mass of publication during the cluster stage provided a continuing string of intellectual successes which, in retrospect, makes the group's activities seem inevitable and smooth. Acceptance of that work by those who were statistically oriented was very quick, although some modifications occurred. During this period the work of Robert M. Hauser (a student of Duncan's) and Arthur Goldberger (1970) drew heavily on econometrics and treated unobserved variables. Also during this stage—perhaps inevitably, given the group's acceptance—some work based on new causal theory concepts was published which was *not* very good. Without pointing to any specific work, Duncan (in Borgatta and Bohrnstedt, eds., 1970: 38–39) addressed this problem:

> In a good deal of recent sociological discussion, published and unpublished, one senses an implicit assumption that the objective of a piece of research is best served by a partitioning of the "explained variance" or by the calculation of a partial correlation. I wish to argue, to the contrary, that achieving an algebraically consistent partitioning or system of partialing is secondary in importance to setting up an appropriate representation (or "model") of the structure of the problem. Much confusion arises because of the protean character of regression and correlation statistics, which permits their algebraic manipulation into a large number of essentially equivalent, but apparently distinct, forms. Preoccupation with this algebra is not likely to generate anything new, for many capable statisticians have had a go at the subject during the twentieth century. Even worse, it is likely to distract one from the more urgent task of making sure that the regression setup itself is suited to the inferences and interpretations to be attempted. The viewpoint of this paper is that of the analyst seeking a rationally defensible and substantively interesting interpretation of a set of data. His objectives are distinct from those of the technician seeking an optimal prediction instrument. . . .

The foregoing statement clearly indicates the difference between new causal *theoretical* work and regression-prediction maximizing alone.

The clusters at Michigan and Wisconsin were still active at the end of the cluster stage in 1970. The group had social and intellectual leadership, research and training centers, program statements, successes, and secondary work.

SPECIALTY STAGE: 1970–

SOCIAL

By 1971 the concentration at cluster centers had lessened. Wisconsin was still large (15 persons), but Chicago, Johns Hopkins, Michigan, and the University of North Carolina had declined in size (see Table 9.3). Table 9.2 reveals a wider spread than ever of new causal theorists over locations.

Wisconsin, although strong in 1971, may well be dissolving as a cluster location. In 1971 Borgatta, Bohrnstedt, Oppenheim, Treiman, and some of the students had left. Only Robert M. Hauser was added to the staff. Furthermore, the editorship of *Sociological Methodology*, which had been at Wisconsin in 1969 and 1970, had moved to the University of Washington (under Herbert L. Costner).

The specialty stage shows that many of the expected events have occurred. New causal theory's ideas have become part of most graduate student training, particularly at major universities, as people trained in new causal theory have been added to their faculties. The style of research has spread from its original areas (stratification, occupational mobility, etc.) to new areas (e.g., ecology; see Kasarda, 1972). Furthermore, the group's success as a specialty (in this case, taking over a large portion of the parent discipline) also signaled its end as a coherent group. As Table 9.3 shows, people had begun to disperse quite widely. In 1970, for the first time, the "other schools" employed more new causal theorists than the top six combined.

The group has not completely taken over the discipline, although some of its members are very highly regarded within sociology. Competition for major positions among forecasters, new causal theorists, ethnomethodologists, structuralists, and radicals, as well as more traditional sociologists, makes complete and immediate control by new causal theorists unlikely. Given the group's size, wide geographical spread, prestige within the discipline, and continued leadership, we would expect a flood of research, publications, and coauthorships similar to that produced by standard American sociology between 1951 and 1958.

INTELLECTUAL

The specialty stage of new causal theory has already been marked by the publication of numerous papers, as the work that had supported graduate students for years has reached the public (see Costner, ed., 1971). In addition, new book series and journals (e.g., *Sociological Methodology, Social Science Research*) have been created to carry the written material, the research has enjoyed broad acceptance, and there is competition for the graduates of the major new causal theory training programs. The group's intellectual concerns still include technical problems and ideas that will continue to provide material for research. Indeed, the founders are still doing new causal theory research, and the shift in the editorship of *Sociological Methodology* to Costner retains that series as a major published source of secondary work in new causal theory.

Also during this stage the dialogue with other sciences using statistical techniques has continued. Psychometrics and other levels of econometric thinking have been aided by work such as Goldberger's (1970). Now that there is more and broader graduate training that includes causal techniques, more sociologists are becoming capable of dealing with the most sophisticated analytical techniques. The methodological work is growing in difficulty and technicality as it centers increasingly on model specification, errors of measures, and nontractable models (e.g., unobserved variables) and less on substantively important questions.

The textbooks necessary for large-scale training of students in new causal theory began being published in 1969. Blalock (1969b), Dubin (1969), and Davis (1971) were written by long-term group members. Abell (1971) and Mullins (1971) were written by outsiders. Dubin (1969) and Blalock (1969b) were written simultaneously at North Carolina. Dubin's book was read by Blalock and his graduate class in theory building at the University of North Carolina (Dubin, 1969: vii) at the same time as Blalock's own more methods-oriented book was being used. Davis (1971) and Mullins (1971) were also written together for a pair of experimental sociology courses at Dartmouth College. They were the methods and the theory textbooks, respectively, for underclassmen. These two books, together with Abell (1971), will enable the training of undergraduates as well as graduates in new causal theory. The end result should be a revamping of sociological training as complete as was standard American sociology's (see Chapter 3). The fact that two of these texts were produced by nonmembers of the group testifies further to the spread of new causal theory and its acceptance by the profession at large.

A recent development (see Goodman, 1972) suggests that ordinal and nominal data are tractable to causal modeling. No research using the Goodman techniques has yet been published, but their introduction has been greeted with considerable interest by those who do data analysis in the new causal theory style. A success in this effort would be very important to future theory development.

IN CONCLUSION

The area is at once a success and a failure. Its success was its revision of theoretical discourse in sociology and the changes it has wrought in profesional roles and graduate training. The basic ideas of causal analysis have spread widely. Its failure is that its synthesizing effect on professional roles seems to be weakening as divisions occur between those who are continuing to do causal analysis for substantive research purposes (e.g., Duncan and Hodge) and those who seem to be more interested in the development of models for their own sake (e.g., Land). This division has reintroduced the theorist–methodologist split, although the theorist now has new skills in his repertoire.

The new causal theorists are like the structuralists (see Chapter 10) in that their theories are mathematical formulations. However, where the new causal theorists have tried to develop an algebra of variables useful for interpreting properties, structuralists have been interested in the algebra of relations. The two groups tend to admire one another's work and there is some drift back and forth between them; nevertheless, essential intellectual and social differences exist.

The new causal theorists have been like the ethnomethodologists in rejecting standard American sociology's division between theory and method and insisting that theory be rebuilt. Also like the ethnomethodologists, they have been rebuilding from a methodological base, although the methods involved are totally different. Both groups reached the specialty stage at about the same time. Their similarity in form, however, only sharpens their contrast in history and content. The ethnomethodologists totally rejected the methods of standard American sociology, whereas the new causal theorists chose to build theory on the most sophisticated of those methods (i.e., correlation and regression techniques).

The budding relationship between new causal theory and forecasting was discussed in Chapter 7.

As we noted earlier, an elite specialty is one that is accepted, although not necessarily joined, by the rest of the discipline. New causal theory's elite status is reflected in the acceptance of its researchers' papers in major journals and its students in jobs at major institutions, as well as its major proponents' receipt of traditional professional honors and positions (e.g., the editorship of *Sociological Methodology*, an official publication of the ASA). By contrast with ethnomethodology, there was little antipathy to new causal theory, even though the requirement of some mathematical (or at least statistical) sophistication was sufficient to keep much of the discipline from participating in the group's initial development. However, ethnomethodology's critique of sociology was more fundamental, denying the basic acceptability of much prior and then-current research. New causal theorists, rather, rejected the work as not good enough. In addition, their research developed at three of the recognized, great centers of graduate training. Given these basic differences between the two specialties, the differing reactions of the parent discipline are understandable.

As an elite specialty, new causal theory has redefined the people at the top of sociology with the qualification that some circulation (reshuffling) of elites has occurred. Moreover, the characterization of those at the top of the profession now differs somewhat (with respect to skills, interests, focuses, etc.) from the picture of those who were at the top earlier. New causal theory's leaders, instead of being considered structural–functionalist theorists, have been seen as methodologists doing theory in a new way. My expectation is that new causal theory's relatively few differences with standard American sociology will gradually be resolved and that the two will synthesize; the result will be a more useful sociology because new causal theory will have added the synthetic approach to the theorist's ideas and skills.

NOTES

1. Both were trained by University of Chicago sociologists—Duncan by Ogburn and Philip M. Hauser at Chicago, Blalock by L. S. Cottrell, Jr., at North Carolina. Blalock's substantive work has been in the area of intergroup relations (e.g., *Toward a Theory of Minority Group Relations*, 1967a). He taught at the University of North Carolina until 1971, when he moved to the University of Washington. Duncan was at the University of Chicago until he moved to the University of Michigan, in 1962. His work at Chicago was primarily in demography and ecology. He has maintained strong ties to Chicago, and several of his students, notably Robert Hodge, were at Chicago during the 1960s.
2. Duncan has spent much of his professional life in demography, a subspecialty of sociology in which the professional roles have not been quite so sharply divided. Demographers have long been expected to be conversant both with the mathematical methods of demography and with its theory (although there is some debate about how much theory actually exists in demography), whereas a (general) sociologist may be a perfectly acceptable sociologist with no mathematical skills at all.
3. Other statistically trained social scientists working at that time included the Minnesota group of psychometrically sophisticated sociologists (Chapin, Guttman, and Sewell). The point is simply that table analysis and regression techniques became recognized as alternative methods championed by

different groups. Goodman's work (1972), which is naturally theoretical in the same way as path analysis is well on the way to supplanting both techniques in many social analysis applications.

4. Among the comprehensive surveys done during the 1960s on stratification, occupational mobility, and education were Blau and Duncan's on "Occupational Changes in a Generation," given in March 1962, to about 30,000 respondents; Hodge's NORC survey, given in October 1964, to roughly 934 respondents; J. A. Davis and Spaeth's NORC–Education survey; Sewell's work on high school graduates (in Wisconsin in 1957) with about 2060 respondents; and Coleman and Campbell's Office of Education study of educational differences by race with 900,000 respondents.

5. The coauthorship networks are symmetrical—two coauthors have obviously chosen each other. The assessor networks differ from the coauthorship networks in that the choices are asymmetric—if A chooses B, B does not necessarily choose A; A may see himself as close to B if A chose B, but B may not see himself as close to A. If C also chose B, A and C share a choice of reviewers. This choice probably indicates something more substantial about the work done by A and B than a shared preference for pistachio ice cream might, but not very much more. For details on how to think about the asymmetries of networks, see Harary, Norman, and Cartwright (1965).

BIBLIOGRAPHY

Abell, Peter.
   1971   *Model Building in Sociology.* New York: Schenckman.
Althauser, Robert P., and Donald Rubin.
   1970   "Computer sampling." *American Journal of Sociology* 76 (September): 325–346.
American Journal of Sociology.
   various   *Cumulative Index to the American Journal of Sociology 1895–*
   years   *1965;* also for years 1966–1970. Chicago: American Journal of Sociology.
American Sociological Association.
   various   *Directory of Members 1959;* also for years 1963, 1967, 1970.
   years a   New York and Washington, D.C.: American Sociological Association.
   various   *Guide to Graduate Departments of Sociology 1965;* also for
   years b   years 1969, 1971. Washington, D.C.: American Sociological Association.
   various   *Index to the American Sociological Review.* Vols. 1–25 (1936–
   years c   1960), 26–30 (1961–1965), and 31–35 (1966–1970). New York and Washington, D.C.: American Sociological Association.
Bailey, Kenneth D.
   1970   "Evaluating axiomatic theories." Pp. 48–71 in Edgar F. Borgatta and George W. Bohrnstedt (eds.), *Sociological Methodology 1970.* San Francisco: Jossey-Bass.

Bayer, Alan E.
  1969   "Marriage plans and educational aspirations." *American Journal of Sociology* 75 (September): 239–244.
Berelson, Bernard, and Gary A. Steiner.
  1964   *Human Behavior: An Inventory of Scientific Findings.* New York: Harcourt Brace Jovanovich.
Black, Max.
  1962a   *The Importance of Language.* Englewood Cliffs, N.J.: Prentice-Hall.
  1962b   *Models and Metaphors: Studies in Language and Philosophy.* Ithaca, N.Y.: Cornell University Press.
Blalock, H. M., Jr.
  1962   "Four-variable causal models and partial correlations." *American Journal of Sociology* 68 (September): 182–194.
  1963   "Making causal inferences for unmeasured variables from correlations among indicators." *American Journal of Sociology* 69 (July): 53–62.
  1964   *Causal Inferences in Nonexperimental Research.* Chapel Hill, N.C.: University of North Carolina Press.
  1966   "The identification problem and theory building: the case of status inconsistency." *American Sociological Review* 31 (February): 52–61.
  1967a   *Toward a Theory of Minority-Group Relations.* New York: Wiley.
  1967b   "Status inconsistency, social mobility, status integration and structural effects." *American Sociological Review* 32 (October): 790–801.
  1969a   "Multiple indicators and the causal approach to measurement error." *American Journal of Sociology* 75 (September): 264–272.
  1969b   *Theory Construction: From Verbal to Mathematical Formulation.* Englewood Cliffs, N.J.: Prentice-Hall.
  1970   "Estimating measurement error using multiple indicators and several points in time." *American Sociological Review* 35 (February): 101–111.
Blalock, H. M., Jr. (ed.).
  1971   *Causal Models in the Social Sciences.* Chicago: Aldine-Atherton.
Blalock, H. M., Jr., and Ann Blalock (eds.).
  1968   *Methodology in Social Research.* New York: McGraw-Hill.
Blalock, H. M., Jr., Caryll S. Wells, and Lewis Carter.
  1970   "Statistical estimation in the presence of random measurement." Pp. 75–103 in Edgar F. Borgatta and George W. Bohrnstedt (eds.), *Sociological Methodology 1970.* San Francisco: Jossey-Bass.
Blau, Peter M., and O. D. Duncan.
  1965   "Some preliminary findings on social stratification in the United States." *Acta Sociologia* 9 (FASC. 1-2): 4–24.
  1967   *The American Occupational Structure.* New York: Wiley.
Bohrnstedt, George W.
  1969   "A quick method for determining the reliability and validity of multiple-item scales." *American Sociological Review* 34 (August): 542–548.
Borgatta, Edgar F., and George W. Bohrnstedt (eds.).
  1969   *Sociological Methodology 1969.* San Francisco: Jossey-Bass.
  1970   *Sociological Methodology 1970.* San Francisco: Jossey-Bass.

Boudon, Raymond.
   1965   "A method of linear causal analysis." *American Sociological Review* 30 (June): 365–374.
   1968   "A new look at correlation analysis." Pp. 199–235 in H. M. Blalock, Jr., and Ann Blalock (eds.), *Methodology in Social Research.* New York: McGraw-Hill.
Boyle, Richard P.
   1966   "Causal theory and statistical measures of effect: a convergence." *American Sociological Review* 31 (December): 843–851.
   1970   "Path analysis and ordinal data." *American Journal of Sociology* 75 (January): 461–480.
Campbell, Angus, Philip E. Converse, Warren E. Miller, and Donald E. Stokes.
   1960   *The American Voter.* New York: Wiley.
Carlos, Serge.
   1970   "Religious participation and the urban–suburban continuum." *American Journal of Sociology* 75 (March): 742–759.
Cleary, T. Anne, Robert L. Linn, and G. William Walster.
   1970   "Effect of reliability and validity on power of statistical tests." Pp. 130–138 in Edgar F. Borgatta and George W. Bohrnstedt (eds.), *Sociological Methodology 1970.* San Francisco: Jossey-Bass.
Coleman, James S.
   1964   *Introduction to Mathematical Sociology.* New York: Free Press.
Coleman, James S., and Ernest Q. Campbell et al.
   1966   *Equality of Educational Opportunity.* Washington, D.C.: Government Printing Office.
Costner, Herbert L.
   1969   "Theory deduction and rules of correspondence." *American Journal of Sociology* 75 (September): 245–263.
Costner, Herbert L. (ed.).
   1971   *Sociological Methodology 1971.* San Francisco: Jossey-Bass.
Costner, Herbert L., and Robert K. Leik.
   1964   "Deductions from 'axiomatic theory.'" *American Sociological Review* 29 (December): 819–835.
Crain, Robert L., and Donald B. Rosenthal.
   1962   "Community status as a dimension of local decision making." *American Sociological Review* 32 (October): 970–984.
Curtis, Richard F., and Elton F. Jackson.
   1962   "Multiple indicators in survey research." *American Journal of Sociology* 68 (September): 195–204.
Cutright, Phillips.
   1967   "Inequality: a cross-national analysis." *American Sociological Review* 32 (August): 562–578.
Davis, James A.
   1971   *Elementary Survey Analysis.* Englewood Cliffs, N.J.: Prentice-Hall.
Davis, James A., Joe L. Spaeth, and Carolyn Huson.
   1961   "A technique for analyzing the effects of group composition." *American Sociological Review* 26 (April): 215–225.

Deutsch, Karl W., John Platt, and Dieter Senghaas.
  1971   "Conditions favoring major advances in social science." *Science* 171
            (February 15): 450–459.
Dubin, Robert.
  1969   *Theory Building.* New York: Free Press.
Dumont, Richard G., and William J. Wilson.
  1967   "Aspects of concept formation, explanation and theory construction
            in sociology." *American Sociological Review* 32 (September): 985–
            995.
Duncan, O. D.
  1963   "Axioms or correlations?" *American Sociological Review* 28 (June):
            452.
  1966   "Path analysis: sociological examples." *American Journal of Sociology*
            72 (July): 1–16.
  1968a   "Inheritance of poverty or inheritance of race?" Pp. 85–110 in Daniel
            P. Moynihan (ed.), *On Understanding Poverty.* New York: Basic
            Books.
  1968b   "Ability and achievement." *Eugenics Quarterly* 15: 1–11.
  1970   "Partials, partitions and paths." Pp. 38–47 in Edgar F. Borgatta and
            George W. Bohrnstedt (eds.), *Sociological Methodology 1970.* San
            Francisco: Jossey-Bass.
  1972   Personal communication (June).
Duncan, O. D., Archibald O. Haller, and Alejandro Portes.
  1968   "Peer influences on aspirations: a reinterpretation." *American Journal
            of Sociology* 74 (September): 119–137.
Duncan, O. D., and Robert W. Hodge.
  1963   "Education and occupational mobility: a regression analysis." *American Journal of Sociology* 68 (May): 629–644.
Elder, Glen H., Jr.
  1969   "Appearance and education in marriage mobility." *American Sociological Review* 34 (August): 519–533.
Fennessey, James.
  1968   "The general linear model: a new perspective on some familiar topics."
            American Journal of Sociology 74 (July): 1–27.
Goldberger, Arthur.
  1970   "On Boudon's method of linear causal analysis." *American Sociological Review* 35 (February): 97–101.
Goodman, Leo.
  1972   "A model for the analysis of surveys." *American Journal of Sociology*
            77 (May): 1035–1086.
Gordon, Robert A.
  1968   "Issues in multiple regression." *American Journal of Sociology*
            73 (March): 592–616.
Griffith, Belver C., and Nicholas C. Mullins.
  1972   "Coherent groups in scientific change: 'Invisible Colleges' may be
            consistent throughout science." *Science* 177 (4053, September 15):
            959–964.

Hanson, Norwood.
  1958   *Patterns of Discovery: An Inquiry into the Conceptual Foundations of Science.* Cambridge: Cambridge University Press.
Harary, Frank, Robert Z. Norman, and Dorwin Cartwright.
  1965   *Structural Models.* New York: Wiley.
Hauser, Robert M.
  1969   "Schools and the stratification process." *American Journal of Sociology* 74 (May): 587–611.
  1970   "Context and consex: a cautionary tale." *American Journal of Sociology* 75 (January): 645–664.
Hauser, Robert M., and Arthur Goldberger.
  1971   "The treatment of unobservable variables in path analyses." Pp. 81–117 in Herbert L. Costner (ed.), *Sociological Methodology 1971.* San Francisco: Jossey-Bass.
Heise, David.
  1967   "Cultural patterning of sexual socialization." *American Sociological Review* 32 (October): 726–739.
  1969   "Separating reliability and stability in test–retest correlation." *American Sociological Review* 34 (February): 93–101.
  1970   "Causal inferences from panel data." Pp. 3–27 in Edgar F. Borgatta and George W. Bohrnstedt (eds.), *Sociological Methodology 1970.* San Francisco: Jossey-Bass.
Hempel, C. G.
  1959   "The logic of functional analysis." Pp. 271–307 in Llewellyn Gross (ed.), *Symposium on Sociological Theory.* Evanston, Ill.: Row, Peterson.
Hodge, Robert W., and Paul M. Siegel.
  1964   "Methods and procedures for rating occupations." Chicago: Unpublished NORC manuscript, January.
Hodge, Robert W., and Don Treiman.
  1965   "Class identification in the United States." *American Sociological Review* 73 (March): 535–547.
  1966   "Occupational mobility and attitudes toward Negroes." *American Sociological Review* 31 (February): 93–101.
  1968   "Social participation and social status." *American Sociological Review* 33 (October): 722–740.
Homans, George C.
  1950   *The Human Group.* New York: Harcourt Brace Jovanovich.
  1961   *Social Behavior: Its Elementary Forms.* New York: Harcourt Brace Jovanovich.
  1964   "Bringing men back in." *American Sociological Review* 29 (December): 809–818.
Huggins, W. H., and Doris R. Entwisle.
  1968   *Introductory Systems and Design.* Waltham, Mass.: Ginn-Blaisdell.
Kasarda, John D.
  1972   "The impact of suburban population growth on central city service functions." *American Journal of Sociology* 77 (May): 1111–1124.

Klatzky, Sheila R.
  1970 "Organizational inequality: the case of the public employment agencies." *American Journal of Sociology* 76 (November): 474–491.
Kuhn, Thomas S.
  1962 *The Structure of Scientific Revolutions*. Chicago: University of Chicago Press (2nd ed., 1970).
Lakatos, Imre, and Alan Musgrave (eds.).
  1970 *Criticism and the Growth of Knowledge*. Cambridge: Cambridge University Press.
Lane, Angela.
  1968 "Occupational mobility in six cities." *American Sociological Review* 33 (October): 740–749.
Leik, Robert K., and Walter R. Gove.
  1969 "The conception and measurement of asymmetric monotonic relationships in sociology." *American Journal of Sociology* 74 (May): 696–709.
Lipset, Seymour M., Martin A. Trow, and James S. Coleman.
  1956 *Union Democracy*. New York: Free Press.
Maris, Ronald.
  1970 "The logical adequacy of Homans' social theory." *American Sociological Review* 35 (December): 1069–1081.
McDill, Edward, Leo Rigsby, and Edmund D. Meyers, Jr.
  1969 "Educational climates of high schools: their effects and sources." *American Journal of Sociology* 74 (May): 567–586.
Moynihan, Daniel P.
  1969 *On Understanding Poverty*. New York: Basic Books.
Mullins, Nicholas C.
  1971 *The Art of Theory: Construction and Use*. New York: Harper & Row.
Nagel, Ernest.
  1961 *The Structure of Science: Problems in the Logic of Scientific Explanation*. New York: Harcourt Brace Jovanovich.
Palmore, James A., Robert E. Klein, and Ariffinbirr Marzuki.
  1970 "Class and family in a modernizing society." *American Journal of Sociology* 76 (November): 375–398.
Pelz, Donald, and Robert A. Law.
  1970 "Heise's causal model approach." Pp. 28–37 in Edgar F. Borgatta and George W. Bohrnstedt (eds.), *Sociological Methodology 1970*. San Francisco: Jossey-Bass.
Popper, Karl.
  1959 *The Logic of Scientific Discovery*. New York: Basic Books.
Rehberg, Richard A., Walter E. Schafer, and Judie Sinclair.
  1970 "Toward a temporal sequence of adolescent achievement variables." *American Sociological Review* 35 (February): 34–48.
Reiss, Albert J., with O. D. Duncan, Paul K. Hatt, and Cecil C. North.
  1961 *Occupations and Social Status*. New York: Free Press.
Rose, Arnold M.
  1949 "A weakness of partial correlation in sociological analysis." *American Sociological Review* 14 (December): 536–539.

Rubin, Zick.
  1968 "Do American women marry up?" *American Sociological Review* 33 (October): 750–760.
Schnaiberg, Allan.
  1970 "Measuring modernism: theoretical and empirical explorations." *American Journal of Sociology* 76 (November): 399–424.
Schuessler, Karl.
  1966 "Communication to the Editor." *American Sociologist* 1 (February): 82.
Sewell, William H., and J. Michael Armer.
  1966 "On neighborhood context and college plans." *American Sociological Review* 31 (April): 156–168.
Sewell, William H., Archibald O. Haller, and Alejandro Portes.
  1969 "The educational and early occupational attainment process." *American Sociological Review* 34 (February): 82–92.
Sewell, William H., and Vimal Shah.
  1968a "Social class, parental encouragement and educational aspirations." *American Journal of Sociology* 73 (March): 559–672.
  1968b "Parents' education and children's educational aspirations and achievements." *American Sociological Review* 33 (April): 191–209.
Simon, Herbert A.
  1954 "Spurious correlation: a causal interpretation." *Journal of the American Statistical Association* 49 (September): 467–479.
  1957 *Models of Man.* New York: Wiley.
Smelser, Neil J., and James A. Davis.
  1969 *Sociology.* Englewood Cliffs, N.J.: Prentice-Hall.
———.
       Social Science Research: A Quarterly Journal of Social Science Methodology and Quantitative Research. New York: Seminar.
Spaeth, Joe L.
  1968 "Occupation prestige expectations among male college graduates." *American Journal of Sociology* 73 (March): 548–558.
  1970 "Occupational attainment among male graduate students." *American Journal of Sociology* 75 (January): 632–644.
Stinchcombe, Arthur.
  1968 *Constructing Social Theories.* New York: Harcourt Brace Jovanovich.
Toulmin, Stephen.
  1961 *Foresight and Understanding: An Enquiry into the Aims of Science.* Bloomington: Indiana University Press.
Turk, Arthur.
  1966 "Conflict and criminality." *American Sociological Review* 31 (June): 338–352.
Werts, Charles E.
  1968 "Path analysis: testimonial of a proselyte." *American Journal of Sociology* 73 (January): 509–512.
Werts, Charles E., Robert L. Linn, and Karl Jöreskog.
  1971 "Estimating the parameters of path models involving unmeasured variables." Pp. 400–409 in H. M. Blalock, Jr. (ed.), *Causal Models in the Social Sciences.* Chicago: Aldine-Atherton.

Wiley, David E., and James A. Wiley.
    1970   "The estimation of measurement error in panel data." *American Sociological Review* 35 (February): 112–117.

Williams, Robin M., Jr.
    1947   *The Reduction of Intergroup Tensions: A Survey of Research on Problems of Ethnic, Racial, and Religious Group Relations.* Prepared under the direction of the Committee on Techniques for Reducing Group Hostility. New York: Social Science Research Council, Bulletin 57.

Woelfol, Joseph, and Archibald O. Haller.
    1971   "Significant others, the self-reflexive act and the attitude formation process." *American Sociological Review* 36 (February): 74–87.

Wold, Herman, and Lars Juréen.
    1953   *Demand Analysis: A Study in Econometrics.* New York: Wiley.

Zetterberg, Hans L.
    1965   *On Theory and Verification in Sociology.* Totowa, N.J.: Bedminster Press. (3rd ed.; first issued in 1953.)

CHAPTER 10
THE STRUCTURALISTS
Tracking Something

**Social and intellectual properties
of structuralism**

Intellectual leader	H. C. White
Training center	Harvard
Research center	Harvard
Social organization leader	None
Program statement	White, "The Use of Mathematics in Sociology" (1963b)
Success	White, **Chains of Opportunity** (1970a)
Paradigm content	The relations of persons and positions are fundamental to social process
Secondary work	None
Critical work	None
Textbook	None

Hallo," said Piglet. "*What are you doing?*"
"*Hunting*," said Pooh.
"*Hunting what?*"
"*Tracking something*," said Winnie-the-Pooh, *very mysteriously.*
"*Tracking what?*" said Piglet, *coming closer.*
"*That's just what I ask myself. I ask myself, 'What?'* "
"*What do you think you'll answer?*"
"*I shall have to wait until I catch up with it*," said Winnie-the-Pooh.

(Milne, 1954: 36)

This chapter, like the previous one, describes a group concerned with formal theory in sociology. Structuralism is as socially undeveloped as the forecasters; however, unlike the forecasters, it has developed naturally and was not called together for a specific purpose. Although very slow to develop and a relatively late arrival on the contemporary sociological scene, this group focuses on work that has a long history within general social science (particularly in anthropology and linguistics; see Piaget's *Structuralism*, 1970). The group had moved into the network stage by 1970. The group is included, in part, because the research from which this book has been drawn is heavily influenced by structuralism. Furthermore, the slow development of structuralism, like the failure of small group work, indicates that promising ideas by themselves will not develop in the absence of support from specific social factors, because without support, the theoretical potential of those ideas is not exploited. Finally, structuralism's development contrasts with that of small group work (from which it borrows some intellectual elements): Those studying small groups ended as an atheoretic group, whereas structuralism has become a relatively developed theory, lacking a solid group.

Despite their mathematical sophistication, the new causal theory group and structuralists differ in the type of theory each does (see pp. 258 ff.) and have only a few people in common (e.g., Phillip Bonacich and J. A. Davis). Since relatively few sociologists have any mathematical skills whatsoever, the two groups have something in common simply in possessing those skills. However, the differences in style of work have lead to the lack of understanding and occasional lack of mutual appreciation, which are characteristic of fundamentally different theory groups in spite of the respect for one another's skills. To attempt collection of the two groups into a more general category, such as mathematical sociology, would be both difficult and not very useful; nevertheless, we should allow for the possibility that, in the future, the structuralists might combine with another group.

Like all the newer groups discussed in this book, the structuralists have both interdisciplinary and international aspects. However, since this breadth has been more important to structuralism than to the groups discussed earlier, this chapter gives more explicit attention to those aspects.[1] Table 10.1 summarizes highlights of this group's development to date.

TABLE 10.1   Social and intellectual highlights in the development of structuralism

Stage	Social	Intellectual
Normal: to 1970	White trains future structuralists at Harvard; Social Relations 10 course.	White, **Anatomy of Kinship** (1963a); "The Use of Mathematics in Sociology" (1963b)
Network: 1970–	Seminars and conferences begun; research grants.	White, **Chains of Opportunity** (1970a); increased publication by White's students

NORMAL STAGE: TO 1970

SOCIAL

Structuralism had an early start in the 1950s in the flurry of work growing out of the mathematicization of small group work and the efforts of the Social Science Research Council's (SSRC's) Mathematics and Social Science Committee. Then a gap occurred from the late 1950s to the late 1960s, when very little work in formal theory was done (McFarland, 1970). This gap is curious because high excitement had greeted the early articles (many were reprinted and discussed), but it gives further support to the hypothesis that promising ideas in a field will not develop without serious follow-through in terms of student training and group development.[2] The data on persons working in the field further support this suggestion. Herbert A. Simon, one of the important thinkers, spread his talents across a number of fields, including sociology, but trained no sociologists. Neither did any of the other early workers (e.g., Dorwin Cartwright, a psychologist; Frank Harary, a mathematician).

One major exception to the publication gap was Harrison C. White's *Anatomy of Kinship* (1963a). White's concern in that book was stated first by Lévi-Strauss (1949; translated as 1969a), then given mathematical form by Weil (1949), extended by Bush (1953), and subsequently restated by Kemeney, Snell, and Thompson (1957) in their *Introduction to Finite Mathematics*: Are some kinds of kinship structures amenable to description in terms of formal relations such that the phenomenon of kinship is necessarily implied by the relations among groups? Anthropology largely ignored White's book, and the reviewer in the *American Anthropologist* (Kennard, 1964) remarked that he might be the only one in the United States with sufficient mathematics to review the book. White, however, continued his work, writing numerous papers between 1963 and 1970, as well as *Canvasses and Careers* (1965), another structurally oriented book, which he coauthored with his wife Cynthia. A holder of two Ph.D. degrees (1955, MIT, theoretical physics; 1960, Princeton, sociology), he has been at Harvard since 1963; before that he was at the University of Chicago (1961–1963). At Chicago, Morris F. Friedell was one of White's few students; at Harvard he has had several.

Another early structuralist was James A. Davis, a long-standing friend and former colleague (at Chicago, 1961–1963; see Table 10.2) of White's. Davis, a widely respected survey researcher who is now Director of NORC, has also done research on structuralist problems, particularly with Samuel Leinhardt (see Davis and Leinhardt, 1973). Davis (1963) was a second exception to the publication gap; however, since much of Davis' structuralist work was done while he was at Dartmouth College, which has no graduate program in sociology, he has trained no advanced students in structuralism.

McFarland (1970) noted that the mathematical *statisticians* of standard American sociology (particularly Lazarsfeld at Columbia and Goodman at Chicago) have had a disproportionate effect on the discipline (see Chapter 9). However, the impact of *mathematicians* interested in social science problems (by contrast with mathematical statisticians) has been very muted because three of their small number—John Kemeny, J. Laurie Snell, and Robert Norman—teach at Dartmouth. This is not the most advantageous location because, again, Dartmouth has no graduate training in the social sciences, and because its small social science faculty (with the exception of a few sociologists) has not utilized the mathematical expertise available.

Kemeny, Snell, and Thompson (1957) first influenced the field by working with Joe Berger, then a sociologist at Dartmouth College. After Berger left Dartmouth (1962), he went to Stanford, where he has since trained a few students with his orientation, although largely in small group work (an indication of the link between structuralism and small group theory). Berger and Snell (1962) and Berger, Zelditch, and Anderson (1966) provide good examples of Berger's thinking.

Table 10.2 lists the American sociologists actively working as structuralists. The group is clearly small and quite young (the median Ph.D.

TABLE 10.2   Important structuralists: degree (date and place) and selected job locations

Name	Ph.D.		Job held during academic year ending in				
	Date	Place	1960	1965	1967	1970	1972
Adams, Bert N.	1965	UNC	*	UNC	WISC	WISC	WISC
Berkowitz, Harriet	cand	HARV	*	*	*	HARV	SASK
Berkowitz, Steven	cand	BRAN	*	*	BRAN	BRAN	SASK
Bernard, Paul	cand	HARV	*	*	*	HARV	HARV
Bonacich, Phillip	1968	HARV	*	HARV	UCLA	UCLA	UCLA
Boorman, Scott	cand	HARV	ni	ni	ni	HARV	HARV
Boyd, J. P.	ni	ni	ni	ni	ni	ni	UCI
Boyle, Richard	ni	ni	*	IOWA	HARV	UCLA	UCLA
Chase, Ivan	1971	HARV	*	*	HARV	HARV	DART
Crain, Robert	1963	CHIC	CHIC	CHIC	JHU	JHU	JHU
Davis, James A.	1956	HARV	CHIC	CHIC	DART	DART	CHIC
Friedell, Morris F.	1965	CHIC	CHIC	CHIC	MICH	UCSB	UCSB
Granovetter, Mark	1970	HARV	*	*	HARV	HARV	JHU
Howard, Leslie	cand	HARV	*	HARV	MICH	TORO	TORO
Kadushin, Charles	1960	COL	COL	COL	COL	COL	COL
Katz, Fred E.	1961	UNC	UNC	MISO	BUFF	BUFF	BUFF
Lee, Nancy Howell	1968	HARV	*	HARV	HARV	PRIN	PRIN
Leinhardt, Samuel	1968	CHIC	*	*	CHIC	CARN	CARN
Levine, Joel H.	1968	HARV	*	HARV	HARV	MICH	DART
Lorrain, Francois	1972	HARV	*	*	HARV	HARV	MICH
Matras, Judah	1962	CHIC	ni	ni	HEBR	WISC	WISC
Mullins, Nicholas C.	1967	HARV	*	HARV	VAND	DART	INDU
Schwartz, Michael	1970	HARV	*	HARV	HARV	UCLA	STON
Useem, Michael	1971	HARV	*	*	HARV	HARV	HARV
Wellman, Barry	1971	HARV	*	HARV	HARV	TORO	TORO
White, Harrison C.	1960	PRIN	CHIC	HARV	HARV	HARV	HARV

Sources: AJS (various years) ASR (various years a, b, c); my knowledge of the group as an insider; White, 1972.

Key:

BRAN	Brandeis University	ni	No information
BUFF	State University of New York, Buffalo	PRIN	Princeton University
cand	Doctoral candidate	SASK	University of Saskatchewan
CARN	Carnegie Institute of Technology	STON	State University of New York, Stony Brook
CHIC	University of Chicago		
COL	Columbia University	TORO	University of Toronto
DART	Dartmouth College	UCI	University of California, Irvine
HARV	Harvard University	UCLA	University of California, Los Angeles
HEBR	Hebrew University		
INDU	Indiana University	UCSB	University of California, Santa Barbara
IOWA	University of Iowa	UNC	University of North Carolina
JHU	Johns Hopkins University	VAND	Vanderbilt University
MICH	University of Michigan	WISC	University of Wisconsin
MISO	University of Missouri	*	Not in system

date for those with degrees is 1967). The core of the original group is composed of White, Phillip Bonacich, Ivan Chase, Mark Granovetter, Nancy Howell Lee, Joel H. Levine, Nicholas C. Mullins, Michael Schwartz, and Barry Wellman. Their interest in structuralism dates from 1965 and 1966, when all were White's teaching assistants for Harvard's introductory course, Social Relations 10. That course has to be one of the few introductory courses ever taught which, at completion, had almost as many graduate as undergraduate students attending lectures faithfully.

The relative lack of theoretical development when a cluster of persons is lacking, as well as another link between structuralism and small group theory, can be observed in the data of Table 10.2 for the University of North Carolina. Four years apart, far enough so that they did not overlap in time, Fred E. Katz and Bert N. Adams completed Ph.D. degrees at UNC. Both were interested in networks (Katz in occupational networks, Adams in kinship networks), and UNC has long had several small group theorists (see Chapter 5) whose work has been close to the interests of structuralists. Thus far, however, neither has carried the structuralist aspects of research very far.

At Columbia University, Charles Kadushin (1966, 1968) has also done research on the same sort of phenomena that interest structuralists. Both his conceptualizations (in terms of social circles) and his methodology (utilizing Lazarsfeld's latent structure analysis to develop group structure) are quite distant from the concern with social networks and their analysis customarily found among structuralists trained by White. When a group is in the early network stage, however, it is very difficult to predict what work will eventually become part of the final mixture.

In addition to Kadushin, Katz, and Adams, who have had some contact with other structuralists in Table 10.2, other scholars more isolated from the Harvard group have also done structuralist-style work. Anatol Rapoport is a classic example. He has influenced the intellectual development of structuralism because many people have read his books, but his location at the University of Michigan at the Center for Conflict Resolution, which is *outside* the Department of Sociology, has virtually deprived him of sociology graduate students. James S. Coleman at Johns Hopkins is another important figure; however, he has not trained people along the lines of his work with Elihu Katz and Herbert Menzel (1966); on his own, however, Coleman (1958, 1964) has produced several excellent works that are structural in intent.

The continuation of the network stage may see the persons just mentioned brought into the group. Table 10.3 lists supporters of structuralism who were not group members as of 1970. They are all poten-

TABLE 10.3 Supporters of structuralism as of 1970[a]

Supporters	Mathematicians
Peter Abell (English)	T. Atkin (Essex, England)
Joseph Berger	Frank Harary
Elizabeth Bott (English)	Paul Holland (statistician)
Dorwin Cartwright	John G. Kemeny
James S. Coleman	Robert Z. Norman
Thomas Farraro	J. Laurie Snell
J. Mitchell (English)	G. L. Thompson
Anatol Rapoport	
Herbert A. Simon	

[a] Social scientists whose work is related in intent although the individuals themselves are not group members.

tial group members, however, assuming that the structuralists continue to make theoretical progress and begin inviting these supporters to their gatherings.

INTELLECTUAL

Structuralist theory draws on linguistics, formal mathematical theory in the social sciences, and anthropological structural studies. The fundamental structuralist perspective is that social structures show at least two levels of structural regularity: a surface, obvious level known to the structure's participants (e.g., a table of organization known to those listed in it) and a nonobvious "deep" level produced in certain fundamental behaviors and limited by the nature of those behaviors (e.g., the networks formed in an organization by those who talk to one another regularly—these communication systems are limited in size by the requirement of regular conversation). Structuralists argue that surface-level structure has been examined in some detail by sociologists and that, although some useful findings have been made, surface-level study thus far has produced only hypotheses, having little ability to predict regularities in a whole social system.

The fundamental metaphor for the structuralists is formal grammar, in particular the analysis of that grammar by Noam Chomsky. For any theoretical system in sociology, the fundamental question is: What aspects of the given social system need explanation? Structural functionalists tried to explain various aspects of social systems in terms of the motives (usually shared values) and perceptions of persons sharing certain attributes. The structuralist studies patterns of fundamental behaviors (e.g., regular conversation between two persons; the giving of food by one person to another). Behavior within a network of relations and behaviors is a component of structure and joins with other behaviors to form the deep structure in a social system. For example, scientists talk with and train other scientists; "talking" and "training" are fundamental behaviors. One of this book's purposes, as a piece of structural research, is to describe the structures (patterns) formed by these fundamental behaviors.

Fundamental behaviors parallel morphemes in linguistics; similarly, the status and role construction tasks in structuralism parallel the sentence construction task in linguistics. The ways in which status roles articulate into structural systems of roles parallel syntax. Structuralists interpret the relationship(s) of unit behaviors to one another as providing an explanation for behavior within specific social systems. Chomsky has been particularly important for his conception of the "deep structure" of language and analysis through rules by which all the grammatical sentences in a given language—and only these—can be generated.[3]

The contribution of formal mathematics to structuralism is older than structural linguistics. In 1874 Francis Galton presented a formal mathematical theory to explain the observed circulation of elites. Another classic in this area is Simon's article (1952) which uses propositions originally stated by Homans in *The Human Group* (1950). Homans' verbal formulations were based on early research in the small groups tradition and on anthropological data. Simon subsequently demonstrated that the propositions were minimally consistent. Simon's initial attempt was later extended by Coleman (1964). Systematic theory that includes a small group element has since been a frequent combination for structuralists. Examples are Harary, Norman, and Cartwright (1965); Simon and Guetzkow (1955a, 1955b); and Cartwright and Harary's mathematical reformulation of Heider's balance theory (1956). The effort to reformulate known sociological or social psychological theories (e.g., Homans, 1950; Heider, 1946) into normal mathematical theory has sputtered sporadically.

At one time or another, all structuralists have considered the problems of analysis within social networks. James A. Davis, joined by Samuel Leinhardt and Paul Holland in later developments, has followed out the theoretical mathematics and empirical fit of balance theory to social networks. Most of these networks are person-to-person, small group, classroom-choice situations (again we see how structuralism has picked up an old problem from small group research). Some, however, are small social systems such as towns or neighborhoods. Davis (1963) initially based his generalization on Heider's balance theory and has slowly, through a series of papers, generalized it into a wider and wider set of situations (Davis, 1967, 1968). By and large, however, the effort to reformulate known sociological or social psychological theories mathematically has been minimal.

This effort was sporadic in spite of the programs of the SSRC's Mathematics and Social Science Committee, which has been one of the SSRC's more successful committees in its ability to attract both money and the interest of the profession. Several programs have been established to train social scientists in mathematics, but they have had little success, particularly in retraining professionals (see White, 1963b). An alternative approach—the attempt to attract mathematically inclined graduate students to the study of social science—has been more productive, but even this strategy has not been overly successful.

Anthropology's contribution to structuralism has come from two types of studies. The first are exemplified by the explicitly structural studies of Lévi-Strauss (1963, 1966, 1967, 1969a, 1969b, and 1970) and Edmund Leach (1965) and those of other anthropologists who have collected data on small-scale societies which lend themselves to similar structural consideration, particularly on kinship patterns; see Frederick G. G. Rose's (1960) data on Groote Eylandt (see also Firth, 1966, 1967; Fortes, 1949; and Malinowski, 1922). Lévi-Strauss, both stimulating and puzzling, has been the key figure for the structuralists. Anthropological structuralism has been a specialty under considerable attack within anthropology. (Part of this attack has centered on Lévi-Strauss's study of myth, his area of interest since roughly 1955.) The French anthropologist's early work on kinship (see *The Elementary Forms of Kinship*, 1969a translation) and several of the essays in *Structural Anthropology* (1967), however, has been of more concern to American structuralists.

A second anthropological development has been comprised of the English studies of urban social networks, particularly those of Bott (2nd ed., 1971), Mayer (1960), and Mitchell (1969). This work appears to have its base in Meyer Fortes' work and to be an independent, English development in anthropology; its products have been much admired, if not emulated, in the United States (see Barnes, 1971, for a critical appraisal of the area).

Fundamentally, structuralism is a cross-disciplinary, international movement. It has attracted more attention in Europe than in the United States. The distinctive aspect of structuralism is its practitioners' belief that all manifestations of social activity in any society constitute languages in a formal sense (see Lane, *Structuralism*, 1970: 13–14). Structuralism is a cognitive perspective, concerned with social system logic. Lévi-Strauss talks of systems playing themselves out through people. Structuralists see human behavior as ordered by a small number of simple systems that can be described in terms of boundaries, self-regulation, and transformation rules (Piaget, 1970). *Boundaries* define a set. *Self-regulation* implies control of a set's activities by itself rather than by either historical or external systems; and *transformation* is the property of moving from one state to another in a regular, lawful manner.

Structuralists thus give logical and analytic priority to a whole over its parts, emphasizing the complex web of relationships (e.g., a social network) that link and unite those elements. The complex web may be quite extended and weak (e.g., the communication network among friends); yet stronger relations (e.g., marriage choice) can be constructed from it.

The structuralists' conception of formal theory is different from that of the new causal theory group, whose fundamental theoretical operation is to use the intricate algebra of correlation and regression statistics to support theoretical statements. The structuralists tend to use the finite algebras of groups, sets, networks, and lattices. The data and problems that each group member uses are different, and it is not important to determine whether this is by simple choice, or because different methods and conceptualizations require different data, or vice versa. As we know, new causal theorists tend to use the results of massive sample surveys, done on a random sample of a population, which report a series of attributes for each individual surveyed. The manipulation of variables is intended to show how the values of the variables for each individual are causally related. For example, a person who has blackness as one attribute will, on the average, have less education as another attribute. The *way* in which those two facts fit into a causal theory—which may include availability of education, motivation, character of the educational experience, and so on—is the new causalist's issue.

Structuralists are more likely to use unobtrusive data (e.g., records) or, if a survey, a survey of persons connected by a relation of interest. For example, White's *Chains of Opportunity* (1970a) analyzed occupational mobility using job records of three Protestant denominations in America over the last century. Manipulating the reports of relations among the persons in the data is intended to reveal how the relations fall into certain simple patterns and how those simple patterns then order other phenomena. Mullins (1968), based on survey data, uses a simple network of relations to order data on the basis of similarity of orientations to scientific work.

For some structuralists (e.g., Lévi-Strauss), structuralism is profoundly noncausal. Instead of cause-and-effect relations, the structuralist conception emphasizes laws of transformation by which one structure is transformed into another. Causality emphasizes the effect of prior variables on later variables, whereas structuralism stresses the transformations of relational structures into other structures. Causality is embedded in the concept of necessary and sufficient conditions for change. The assumption is that, if proper analysis is done, these conditions will become clear. New causal theory is concerned with the necessary and sufficient conditions for *any* change. Structuralists, by contrast, are more interested in *what* forms will appear if change in deep structure occurs, not *whether* change will occur. Deep structure results from the operation of a small set of transformations which produce a limited number of patterns (structures) within a system. The effect of this deep structure is to provide a basic orderliness to relations and behavior.

Structuralists differ among themselves about the types of relations that may be used in rules of transformation. Partly because they lack mathematical sophistication, anthropological structuralists have tended to emphasize short-range binary relations, whereas sociologists have used graph theory (e.g., Flament, 1963; Ore, 1963). White has used group theory (White, 1963a) and semigroup theory (Lorrain and White, 1971). Although the forms of analysis are formally equivalent, their focus—e.g., local orders (binary relations) or long-range orders (graph or group theory)—differs.

Perhaps the most important intellectual event during the normal stage was White's (1963b) publication of "The Uses of Mathematics in Sociology." This piece, published three years prior to Duncan's "Path Analysis . . ." (1966), clearly reveals structuralism's difference from new causal theory. The paper has served as structuralism's program statement; as such, it came very early in the history of the group's development.

At the end of the normal stage, the structuralists had an intellectual leader, a program statement, and a research–training center. There were 25 people in the group—12 of them still students—and several supporters. Numerous people had been working—separately, for the most part—on various pieces of structural research; some of these (e.g., Lee, 1969) had been published. Some of White's former students had kept in touch with him and with one another, but few social mechanisms such as current colleague ties and conferences existed to ensure regular contact among people other than those at Harvard.

NETWORK STAGE:
1970–

SOCIAL

Socially, the beginning of the network stage was marked by deliberate attempts to begin regular gatherings of structuralists. Late in 1970 Levine at Dartmouth began organizing a seminar series which was held at Harvard throughout the spring and summer of 1971. Many structuralists at Harvard and Dartmouth attended these seminars, but others came also (e.g., Steven Berkowitz, Brandeis; Paul Holland, a Harvard statistician). At each session a different participant discussed his current research and received comments and criticism from the others.

A second gathering was the Camden (Maine) conference, held in June 1972 and organized by White, at which 19 persons, led by White and Davis, gathered for a week to discuss both current research and the group's future.[4] The seminar served to solidify communication links and encourage more frequent communication among group members between gatherings. The result has been a developing network among structuralists. The Camden meeting should encourage further network formation through increased communication.

This stage has seen some of the previously independent researchers make contact; for example, Fred Katz, whose work developed quite independently from that of White and his students, has recently talked with White (White, 1972), who noted the similarities in their work. Mullins and Katz met in 1971. As I noted in Chapter 2, this gradual coming together of independent researchers is a characteristic of the network stage.

Attrition from the group, due to inactivity or shifts into other kinds of work (e.g., Bonacich into new causal theory) is quite likely. Not all of White's Social Relations 10 assistants attended the Camden conference. The group must recruit more members and train many more students if structuralism is to move into the cluster stage. At present, as Table 10.2 shows, the linkages are primarily created by present or former student–student and student–teacher ties and less by colleague ties. These relations have been strengthened by the seminar and the conference. If the group grows, we would expect to see more colleague ties developing, as well as a numerical increase in students.

The network that exists is small; it includes White, his students, and a very few others (see Tables 10.2 and 10.3); some of the others are not sociologists, and some are not Americans. The American group of sociologists is thus very small. The network clearly exists, however, and a few of White's students (e.g., Mullins, Schwartz, Wellman) are now beginning to train students of their own. Furthermore, a recent research grant has enabled White to cluster several of his students at Harvard; the possibility thus exists for future, cluster-style student production at Harvard, heretofore a bastion of structural functionalism.[5] Table 10.2 shows that group members are beginning to form possible research centers (more than one person) away from Harvard. Such colleague formations are crucial if the group is to continue development.

INTELLECTUAL

A success, although not necessarily a publicly validated one, is necessary if a group is to be inspired to continue doing research along nontraditional lines. White's (1970a) *Chains of Opportunity* provided that kind of success. The public recognition gained through this book's receipt of the Sorokin award in 1971 may also serve to attract established sociologists. Continued publication of structural research and theory *not* written by White (e.g., Davis, 1970; Levine, 1972; Mullins, 1972a, 1972b) has also been important in demonstrating that this work is not simply one individual's style.

The Camden meeting may prove to have been crucial through its consideration of a narrowed research focus (in order to produce comparability of research results). The possibility now exists that structural research in the future will focus on social elites, particularly in the economic area. It is important at this stage to remember that the structuralists have not had time to develop a fully differentiated theory. Beyond the metaphors of "deep structure" and "network," the style of research and theory is still relatively unformed. Structuralism is clearly different from either structural functionalism or new causal theory, but what it will eventually be is not yet clear. If the group continues its growth, the differences between structuralism and other varieties of sociology will certainly grow and become generally noticed.

I noted earlier the surface similarity between structuralism and new causal theory. The combination of the two into "mathematical sociology" (largely by the ignorant) has made the structuralist perspective difficult to maintain at centers other than Harvard which have employed structuralists. Conversely, the lack of a new causal theory leader at Harvard has had a beneficial effect on White's recruiting efforts.

Mathematically oriented sociologists have long enjoyed the option of becoming primarily structural or primarily statistical (new causal theory); however, they have not recognized these options as opposites. As I noted earlier, Peter Abell (the English sociologist), Richard Boyle of UCLA, J. A. Davis of Chicago and NORC, and Coleman of Johns Hopkins have switched back and forth between the causal-oriented statistical analysis of survey data based on the answers of individual respondents and the noncausal, usually nonstatistical analysis of relational structures, frequently of small groups. My own work has also moved between causally oriented theory development (*The Art of Theory*, 1971, describes my teaching approach) and sociology of science research, in which I use a structural, transformational model (1968, 1972a, 1972b). If structuralism continues to grow and differentiate, such moving back and forth will no longer be a casual event.

Although this group is small and young, the model's first prerequisites have been met: Structuralism has an intellectual leader, a program statement, a research–training center, and a success. There are also others who may be brought into the group. White, continuing to attract and train students, is now working on a concept totally different from vacancy chains; this research may lead to another success.

The recruitment pool for structural studies among current professional sociologists is not very large. It could be increased somewhat by the reeducation of already mathematically inclined sociologists into this style of work; however, its development will probably occur largely through graduate student training. In any case, a wider recruiting effort is necessary if the group is not to collapse quickly. Of structuralists active in 1972, 15 were at institutions with graduate training programs (see Table 10.2). The future of structuralism probably lies with them: Will a social organizational leader emerge? Another success? More students? Secondary and critical work?

IN CONCLUSION

Analysis of the structuralists provides interesting data for our under-standing of the interaction between social groups and sociological theory. Although the basic ideas have been around for some time, the structuralists are still a young group. Ideas thus can and do develop outside a group context. Isolated persons and pairs can work on problems for various periods of time. Parts of the problems now collecting under the title of structuralism have been considered before through small group work (Davis', 1963, work on networks), anthropo-logical kinship studies (White, 1963a), and organization study (Friedell, 1967).

Nevertheless, these ideas were not seen as connected until a group began to put them together. They were not central to a theory until a group began to develop that theory. The parts of a theory (one idea in a skein of ideas) can be developed by a set of unconnected persons, but the data so far suggest that a detailed, fairly general theory cannot develop without a coherent group. Independent theorists simply are not able to grind their ideas against those of others on a daily or monthly basis—shaping, trimming, and fitting their ideas, and moti-vating one another to the hard work of theory. Most of the questions about a theory and about the social world cannot be asked by single investigators; one person alone cannot be sufficiently self-aware and self-critical. The group at present is linked largely by student–teacher relations; continued growth will require an increase in colleague and coauthorship[6] relations and, hence, a thickening in the group's communication structure.

The development of structuralism has not been the result of a consciously philosophical movement; structuralists have been more interested in doing research than in exploring metaphysics. In 15 to 20 years when someone writes a history of structuralism, or perhaps, later, a festschrift to Harrison C. White, people will say that there was a continuing thread running back to 1874, when Galton and Watson invented a type of mathematics called branching theory because they wanted to explain the circulation of elites. This concern is now once again a sociological problem. Someone will study citations or some other such feature and trace structuralism back to 1874; yet it's very clear that, until four or five years ago—perhaps even not until now— there were just random pieces sitting out in the midst of the desert (forest?) of sociological knowledge.

NOTES

1. European structural thinking has provided not only theoretical foundations but active colleagues who are developing a European school of thought parallel to the American development. European structuralists have been more concerned about philosophical and metaphysical speculations than have the Americans, but their empirical concerns are very similar to ours.
2. McFarland (1970) believes that reward theory explains this failure. He argues that people will choose to do work for which they will be rewarded. Since Homans had already received eponymic credit for the propositions that others later mathematized, the latter stopped working on them. The lack of students, however, provides a much simpler explanation.
3. Chomsky's first book (*Syntactic Structures*) appeared in 1957; it was followed by *Aspects of the Theory of Syntax* (1965) and *Cartesian Linguistics* (1966). His development of a group at MIT and his training of many students have enabled a substantial modification of the basis for linguistic study. These persons working on transformational grammar, although not yet studied, appear to exemplify a coherent group in linguistics. The actual input of linguistic ideas into structuralism probably began with Zellig S. Harris, an earlier structural linguist.
4. Participants in the Camden conference were Harriet and Steven Berkowitz, Paul Bernard, Daniel Bertaux (a French sociologist), Scott Boorman, James A. Davis, O. D. Duncan and Beverly Duncan (not group members but interested in structuralism), Gregory Heil (a computer specialist), Leslie Howard, Tsuneo Ishikawa (a Harvard economist), Warren Lavey (then a Harvard undergraduate working with White), Nancy Howell Lee, Joel H. Levine, Paul Levitt, François Lorrain, Nicholas C. Mullins, Michael Schwartz, Barry Wellman, and White, himself.
5. Dartmouth's group can be considered to be part of the Harvard group. All thus far have had Harvard doctorates, and members of the group travel

back and forth frequently for seminars or just conversation. During the spring of 1972, Levine worked part-time with White at Harvard and part-time at Dartmouth. Dartmouth's fine interactive computer and the presence of J. A. Davis (through 1971) made Dartmouth an attractive location for structural researchers.

6. No coauthorship network has been done for this group. It is still in the early network stage, and thus we would not expect to find many coauthorships (this chapter's bibliography supports that expectation). If the group develops a cluster, we would expect some coauthorship at that time, as well as considerable during the specialty stage if one occurs.

BIBLIOGRAPHY

American Journal of Sociology.
　　various　　*Cumulative Index to the American Journal of Sociology 1966*;
　　years　　　also for year 1971. Chicago: American Journal of Sociology.
American Sociological Association.
　　various　　*Directory of Members 1959*; also for years 1963, 1967, 1970.
　　years a　　New York and Washington, D.C.: American Sociological Association.
　　various　　*Guide to Graduate Departments of Sociology 1965*; also for
　　years b　　years 1969, 1971. Washington, D.C.: American Sociological Association.
　　various　　*Index to the American Sociological Review*, Vols. 1–25 (1936–
　　years c　　1960) and Vols. 26–30 (1961–1965). New York and Washington, D.C.: American Sociological Association.
Barnes, J. A.
　　1971　　*Three Styles in the Study of Kinship*. Berkeley, Calif.: University of California Press.
Berger, Joseph, and J. Laurie Snell.
　　1962　　*Types of Formalization in Small-Group Research*. Boston: Houghton Mifflin.
Berger, Joseph, Morris Zeldich, and Bo Anderson (eds.).
　　1966　　*Sociological Theories in Progress*. Boston: Houghton Mifflin.
Bott, Elizabeth.
　　1957　　*Family and Social Network: Roles, Norms, and External Relationships in Ordinary Urban Families*. London: Tavistock.
　　1971　　*Family and Social Network*. 2nd ed. (includes "Reconsiderations"). New York: Free Press.
Bush, Robert R.
　　1963　　"An algebraic treatment of rules of marriage and descent." Pp. 159–172 in Harrison C. White, *An Anatomy of Kinship*. Englewood Cliffs, N.J.: Prentice-Hall (originally published in 1953).
Cartwright, Dorwin, and Frank Harary.
　　1956　　"Structural balance: a generalization of Heider's theory." *Psychological Review* 63 (September): 277–293.

Chomsky, Noam.
  1957   *Syntactic Structures*. New York: Humanities Press.
  1965   *Aspects of the Theory of Syntax*. Cambridge, Mass.: MIT Press.
  1966   *Cartesian Linguistics: A Chapter in the History of Rationalist Thought*. New York: Harper & Row.
Coleman, James S.
  1958   "Relational analysis: the study of social organizations with survey methods." *Human Organization* 17 (Winter): 28–36.
  1964   *Introduction to Mathematical Sociology*. New York: Free Press.
Coleman, James S., Elihu Katz, and Herbert Menzel.
  1966   *Medical Innovation: A Diffusion Study*. Indianapolis: Bobbs-Merrill.
Davis, James A.
  1963   "Structural balance, mechanical solidarity and interpersonal relations." *American Journal of Sociology* 68 (January): 444–462.
  1967   "Clustering and structural balance in graphs." *Human Relations* 20 (May): 181–187.
  1968   "Statistical analysis of pair relationships." *Sociometry* 31 (March): 102–119.
  1970   "Clustering and hierarchy in interpersonal relations: testing two graph theoretical models on 742 sociometrices." *American Sociological Review* 35 (October): 843–851.
Davis, James A., and Samuel Leinhardt.
  1972   "The structure of positive interpersonal relations in small groups." Pp. 218–251 in Joseph Berger, Morris Zelditch, and Bo Anderson (eds.), *Sociological Theories in Progress*, Vol. II. Boston: Houghton Mifflin.
Duncan, O. D.
  1966   "Path analysis: sociological examples." *American Journal of Sociology* 72 (July): 1–16.
Firth, Raymond.
  1966   *We, the Tikopia: A Sociological Study of Kinship in Primitive Polynesia*. Boston: Beacon.
  1967   *Elements of Social Organization*. 3rd ed. Boston: Beacon.
Flament, Claude.
  1963   *Applications of Graph Theory to Group Structure*. Englewood Cliffs, N.J.: Prentice-Hall.
Fortes, Meyer.
  1949   *The Web of Kinship Among the Talensi*. London: Oxford University Press.
Friedell, Morris F.
  1967   "Organizations as semilattices." *American Sociological Review* 32 (February): 46–54.
Galton, Sir Francis, and H. W. Watson.
  1874   "On the probability of extinction of families." *Journal of the Anthropological Institute* 6: 138–144.
Harary, Frank, Robert Z. Norman, and Dorwin Cartwright.
  1965   *Structural Models*. New York: Wiley.

Harris, Zellig S.
  1961   *Structural Linguistics.* Chicago: University of Chicago Press. (First printed in 1951.)
Heider, Fritz.
  1946   "Attitudes and Cognitive Organization." *Journal of Psychology* 21 (2): 107–112.
Holland, Paul, and Samuel Leinhardt.
  1970   "A method for detecting structure in sociometric data." *American Journal of Sociology* 76 (November): 492–513.
Homans, George C.
  1950   *The Human Group.* New York: Harcourt Brace Jovanovich.
Kadushin, Charles.
  1966   "The friends and supporters of psychotherapy: on social circles in urban life." *American Sociological Review* 31 (October): 786–802.
  1968   "Power, influence and social circles: a new methodology for studying opinion makers." *American Sociological Review* 33 (August): 685–699.
Katz, Fred E.
  1966   "Social participation and social structure." *Social Forces* 45 (December): 199–210.
Katz, Fred E. (ed.).
  1971   *Contemporary Sociological Theory.* New York: Random House.
Katz, Fred E., and Harry W. Martin.
  1962   "Career choice processes." *Social Forces* 42 (December): 149–154.
Kemeny, John G., J. Laurie Snell, and Gerald L. Thompson.
  1957   *Introduction to Finite Mathematics.* Englewood Cliffs, N.J.: Prentice-Hall.
Kennard, Edward A.
  1964   Review of Harrison C. White's *An Anatomy of Kinship: Mathematical Models for Structures of Cumulated Roles. American Anthropologist* 66 (December): 1403–1404.
Lane, Michael (ed.).
  1970   *Structuralism: A Reader.* London: Cape.
Leach, Edmund.
  1965   *Political Systems of Highland Burma: A Study of Kachin Social Structure.* Boston: Beacon.
Leach, Edmund, and S. N. Muberjee (eds.).
  1970   *Elites in South Asia.* Cambridge: Cambridge University Press.
Lee, Nancy Howell.
  1969   *The Search for an Abortionist.* Chicago: University of Chicago Press.
Lévi-Strauss, Claude.
  1963   *Totemism.* Translated by Rodney Needham. Boston: Beacon.
  1966   *The Savage Mind.* Translated by George Weidenfeld. Chicago: University of Chicago Press.
  1967   *Structural Anthropology.* Translated by Claire Jacobson and Brook G. Schoepf. Garden City, N.Y.: Doubleday.

1969a *The Elementary Forms of Kinship*. Translated by James H. Bell, John R. von Sturmer, and Rodney Needham. (First published in French in 1949.) Boston: Beacon.

1969b *The Raw and the Cooked: Introduction to a Science of Mythology*, Vol. I. Translated by John Weightman and Doreen Weightman. New York: Harper & Row.

Levine, Joel H.
1972 "The sphere of influence." *American Sociological Review* 37 (February): 14–27.

Lorrain, François, and Harrison C. White.
1971 "Structural equivalence of individuals in social networks." *Journal of Mathematical Sociology* 1 (January): 49–80.

McFarland, David.
1970 "The Future of Mathematical Sociology." Chicago: University of Chicago Center for Mathematical Studies in Business and Economics. Report # 7036.

Malinowski, Bronislaw.
1922 *Argonauts of the Western Pacific: An Account of Native Enterprise and Adventure in the Archipelagoes of Melanesian New Guinea*. London: Routledge & Kegan Paul.

Mayer, Adrian C.
1960 *Caste and Kinship in Central India: A Village and Its Region*. Berkeley: University of California Press.

Milgram, Stanley.
1967 "The small world problem." *Psychology Today* 22 (May): 61–67.

Milne, A. A.
1954 Winnie-the-Pooh. New York: Dutton.

Mitchell, James Clyde (ed.).
1969 *Social Networks in Urban Situations: Analyses of Personal Relationships in Central African Towns*. Manchester, England: Manchester University Press.

Mullins, Nicholas C.
1968 "The distribution of social and cultural properties in informal communication networks among biological scientists." *American Sociological Review* 33 (October): 786–797.

1971 *The Art of Theory: Construction and Use*. New York: Harper & Row.

1972a "The development of a scientific specialty: the Phage Group and the origins of molecular biology." *Minerva* 10 (January): 51–82.

1972b "The structure of an elite: the advisory committees of the Public Health Service." *Science Studies* 2 (January): 1–29.

Nadel, Siegfried F.
1957 *The Theory of Social Structure*. New York: Free Press.

Ore, Oystein.
1963 *Graphs and Their Uses*. New York: Random House.

Piaget, Jean.
1970 *Structuralism*. Translated by Chaninah Muschler. New York: Basic Books.

Rapoport, Anatol.
  1963 "Mathematical models of social interaction." Pp. 493–580 in R. Duncan Luce, Robert Bush, and Eugene Galanter (eds.), *Handbook of Mathematical Psychology*, Vol. 2. New York: Wiley.

Rose, Frederick G. G.
  1960 *Classification of Kin, Age Structure, and Marriage Amongst the Groote Eylandt Aborigines: A Study in Method and Theory of Australian Kinship*. Berlin: Akademie-Verlag.

Simon, Herbert A.
  1952. "A formal theory of interaction in social groups." *American Sociological Review* 17 (April): 202–212.

Simon, Herbert A. (ed.).
  1957 *Models of Man*. New York: Wiley.

Simon, Herbert A., and Harold Guetzkow.
  1955a "A model of short- and long-run mechanisms involved in pressures toward uniformity in groups." Pp. 115–130 in Herbert Simon (ed.), *Models of Man*. New York: Wiley.
  1955b "Mechanisms involved in group pressures on deviate members." *British Journal of Statistical Psychology* 8 (Part 2): 93–102.

Travers, Jeff, and Stanley Milgram.
  1969 "An experimental study of the small world problem." *Sociometry* 32 (December): 425–443.

Weil, André.
  1963 "On the algebraic study of certain types of marriage laws (Murngin's system)." Translated by Cynthia White. Pp. 151–157 in Harrison C. White, *An Anatomy of Kinship*. Englewood Cliffs, N.J.: Prentice-Hall. (First published in 1949 in French.)

White, Harrison C.
  1963a *An Anatomy of Kinship: Mathematical Models for Structures of Cumulated Roles*. Englewood Cliffs, N.J.: Prentice-Hall.
  1963b "The Uses of Mathematics in Sociology." Pp. 77–94 in James C. Charlesworth (ed.), *Mathematics and the Social Sciences*. Philadelphia: The American Academy of Political and Social Science.
  1970a *Chains of Opportunity: System Models of Mobility in Organizations*. Cambridge, Mass.: Harvard University Press.
  1970b "Simon out of Homans by Coleman." *American Journal of Sociology* 75 (March): 852–862.
  1971 "Search parameters for the small world problem." *Social Forces* 49 (December): 259–264.
  1972 Personal communication (July).

White, Harrison C., and Cynthia White.
  1965 *Canvasses and Careers: Institutional Change in the French Painting World*. New York: Wiley.

CHAPTER 11
RADICAL-CRITICAL THEORY
Here There Be Tygers

Thus far each group discussed in this book has shown explicit social and intellectual properties, manifested in specific stages, of the kind described in Chapter 2. This chapter examines two traditions that have some cohesion both internally and between themselves, but this cohesion differs from that of earlier groups. Since the radicals and criticals have developed partly outside the largely academic processes presumed in Chapter 2, they have thus devised other institutional arrangements to deal with the same underlying problems. For example, recruitment (of either colleagues or students) and publication have occurred at least partly outside normal academic channels. In looking through collections of work by both radical and critical sociologists (e.g., Deutsch and Howard, 1970; Fischer, 1971), I have been struck by how few of the articles were originally published in traditional sociological journals (zero of 16 in Fischer; five out of 46 in Deutsch and Howard, although 16 of Deutsch and Howard's had been published elsewhere in nonsociological books and magazines). Most were originally published in nonprofessional (i.e., not refereed) magazines or radical newspapers.

Radical-critical sociology has some of the marks of a successful specialty. However, as far as I can discover, it has not progressed through the four stages described in Chapter 2. The necessary linkages and network patterns have not formed. In brief, the radicals have had a structure that has very little academic basis; rather they have clustered and declustered around specific events. In order to obtain the concentrated attention and criticism necessary for theoretical clarity, they have frequently held day- and night-long discussions of strategy and tactics around particular events (e.g., protests). The participants in these discussions have included both experienced and inexperienced individuals, and professional and nonprofessional social scientists. Whatever formal ties have been made through these gatherings have been continually broken by the constant reshuffling of political alignments and participants. The critical sociologists are not a theoretical offshoot from standard American sociology; they have developed from the importation of a European specialty group, the Frankfort School (of Frankfurt am Main), and its subsequent impact on American social scientists and philosophers. The incorporation of both groups into academic sociology seems possible since several graduate departments have recently begun employing two or more radicals or criticals.

Whereas the other groups studied in this book began their development within the more or less sheltered boundaries of academic sociology, the radical-criticals have been especially open to nonacademic influences—even more than the forecasters. The involvement of many radical-criticals in activities that expose them to legal action plus the changing relation of the people, organizations, and ideas loosely labeled the Movement (see p. 278 ff.) to the rest of the society make day-to-day accounting for their activities very difficult; as a result, a specific group is almost impossible to define and trace. Indeed, in some respects only a person who is part of this movement can sense the making and breaking of cohesion, and his awareness applies only to his particular area of involvement. The radical and critical traditions are discussed in this book both because they have had a pronounced effect on contemporary sociological theory and because they diverge substantially from the model. Later in this chapter, I consider the inconclusiveness of linkages as shown by the data.

A detailed history of both radical and critical sociology would require tracing (1) the growth and spread of Marxian theory from the middle nineteenth century and (2) social developments within the United States in the 1950s and early 1960s. Some comments on the intellectual foundation of radical-critical sociology precede my discussion of the social properties of this school of thought.

INTELLECTUAL CONCERNS

Discussion of the history of Marxian theory here is limited to the most recent and pertinent developments[1] from the perspective of their impact on the sociological profession and on sociological theory. In beginning this brief summary, I feel like Raymond Aron (1971: 131) when he remarked: "When we deal with a great thinker, a great personality, and especially a controversial personality, it is of course possible to imagine several interpretations of this man's work and thought. I am not convinced that I would give exactly the same interpretation next year. . . ."

For more than a century, the theories, life, and meanings of Karl

Marx have been the subjects of detailed study. His work has been a landmark of Western thought, and those who have written about it have been plagued by the problems that Aron notes. Hundreds of scholars have produced hundreds of different and shifting interpretations of what Marx said and what he meant. Indeed, the European tradition of literary criticism and the use of Marxist texts as quasi-sacred documents has had the effect of building subtlety upon subtlety and fine point upon fine point.

The fine distinctions have had some meaning to the European public because adherence to one or another interpretation has had immediate and deadly political consequences in revolution and counterrevolution: Revolutionaries in Europe have generally been Marxist, fascist, or anarchist, and all these views have been affected by Marxian thought. Furthermore, Soviet Marxism's existence has forced every Marxist scholar, at some point, to clarify his position with respect to the USSR (and now China), in addition to many European political movements now dead. He must understand these movements because much of the argument in his field is in terms of "Bernsteinism" or "Trotskyism" or other such references to persons and times of the European past rather than to present events. This typology of events is important because, for many, it serves as an historical lesson on what may happen again.

The intellectual content of critical Marxism has been a synthesis of idealistic (formal) and substantive (empirical) statements about the way in which society operates. On the idealistic side, the concept of history moving irresistibly to a final synthesis in the communistic society is fundamental. On the substantive side, primacy is given to economic matters and organization over other interests (including political arrangements) in a society. Thus the parliamentary democracy in a capitalistic society is seen as a mechanism only for protecting the interests of the middle class. The necessity to integrate economic theory, political insight, and philosophical subtlety makes critical analysis difficult but interesting.

For sociology, an important concept derived from Marxist theory has been that intellectual content, both ideology and theory, is at least partly determined by the social position of the persons expounding that content. The sociology of knowledge, which proceeds from this premise, is now more important to the discipline than it has been since the subsiding of the brief flurry of interest during the 1930s (from German, Marxist-trained scholars such as Karl Mannheim and Werner Stark). Occasional brilliant pieces, such as Sorokin's *Social and Cultural Dynamics* (1941), have not been used to develop the sociology of knowledge until recently. However, the rise of radical and critical thought has raised these issues again, and many articles and books, including this one, have been written in response to this new questioning of the foundations of social thought.

The sociology of knowledge, though, has been virtually the only sociological specialty to benefit from Marxian thought. Possibly, Bottomore (1972: 3) asserts, this is because "programmatic" rather than empirical studies have been typical of Marxist sociology (by contrast with Marxist history). He argues that the difference may be that sociology and history constitute two different world views and that

> this rivalry had produced controversies which are largely methodological and philosophical in character, especially on the Marxist side, where a preoccupation with the inner structure of Marxist thought, and criticism of "bourgeois" thought, tend to assume preeminence over any study of the external world.

American social science largely ignored the direct study of Marx during the 1940s and 1950s (incidentally, the reasons for this neglect call for serious historical study). This disuse has contributed to making American sociology quite different from European sociology. Gradually, though, the importation of European sociology, initially in the heads of refugees and subsequently in translations and some originals, has supplied the basis for the radical and critical movements. This importation has introduced numerous complexities. One complication in particular has been the discovery and rediscovery of new Marxist texts. For example, much of the English language discussion of Marx in the first half of the 1960s was predicated on reading the 1956 translation of the "early" manuscripts (i.e., primarily the economic and philosophical manuscripts of 1844, but referring to anything before 1847), which contain much of the philosophical and humanist side of Marx's thought (see Bottomore, 1964a). Just recently, the *Grundrisse* (Marx, 1971), a massive work (mostly incomplete and existing only in notes) of which *Capital* was only a section, has been translated. This manuscript has provided a totally new framework for Marx's economic concepts. European scholars, in particular Lukács (1971) and Fromm (1964), saw all these manuscripts when they were first published in German in 1932. Since that time they have worked out interpretations that incorporate Marx's humanism with his economics and philosophy. Americans and other English-speaking scholars have had translations only since the mid-1950s and thus have just begun to incorporate these ideas into their work. Interpretation and analysis of the *Grundrisse* should occupy English-speaking critical scholars for quite some time (Mandel, 1971: 174). Obviously, then, American critical scholars have been handicapped by the general inability of their students (and occasionally themselves) to read other languages with any subtlety. This limitation on critical scholarship is being reduced as the newly awakened interest in critical sociologists makes translations a profitable activity for English and American publishing houses. However, the language barrier is still a considerable hurdle for the professional who wants to become a contributor to critical studies.

Critical sociologists have been primarily concerned with historical and theoretical work and only secondarily interested in *praxis*, the working out of the theoretical in practical action. The three main sources of the American critical tradition reflect this priority. One source has been the activities of the American Socialist party; these activities hit a high point during the 1920 election and have continued to inspire critical intellectuals such as Irving Howe, Michael Harrington, and Bayard Rustin. However, the other two sources clearly favor the theoretical. One is the German scholars who emigrated before World War II, and their American students. Among the Germans are Max Horkheimer, Erich Fromm, and Herbert Marcuse; among the students, black activist Angela Davis and critical scholar Trent Schroyer. Less clearly identifiable than the other two sources are previously established scholars who have gradually moved to a radical perspective, often from a discipline other than sociology, (e.g., Noam Chomsky, 1969; Anatol Rapoport, 1969; and Paul Goodman, 1962).

Horkheimer and Marcuse were part of the Frankfort School, originally established in Germany. Horkheimer was the guiding spirit for the development of the School. In 1920 he became the occupant of a university chair following a successful and prolific professor, Carl Grunberg, at Frankfort, and he thus acquired control of both a journal and an operating research institute. When Hitler came to power, the institute emigrated first to Paris and then to the United States, where it became part of Columbia University. Horkheimer himself became involved in research on anti-Semitism. Franz Neumann and Otto Kircheimer joined Columbia's government department. Theodor W. Adorno (of Adorno et al., 1950) was another member of the Frankfort group (see Shils, 1970: 785 ff. for details on the data in this paragraph).

Ralf Dahrendorf was a (German) student of Horkheimer's whose discussion of societal organization (*Class and Class Conflict in Industrial Society*) was published in English in 1959. This work directly challenged structural–functionalist theory, which had never considered Marxism, from a European, Marxist perspective. The critique had no effect on structural–functional theory, in part because American students lacked the training in Marxist thought to digest and utilize the criticism. Dahrendorf spent 1956–1957 at the London School of Economics, where he took part in the "Tuesday Economy Seminar" with David Lockwood and others. The following year, he visited the Stanford Center for Advanced Study, where he discussed his views with American scholars (Dahrendorf, 1959: Preface). Because there was no routine way in which Marxists could enter American sociology, Dahrendorf remains an historical figure within critical sociology, even though he is quite alive and well today in Germany. Socially, though, the generally accepting response to the study of Dahrendorf's ideas helped to pave the way for the serious study of Marx by sociologists.

The intellectual history of radical thought within sociology began with C. Wright Mills, an early nonconformist (to standard American sociology) who nevertheless fashioned a distinguished academic career for himself at Columbia. A graduate of the University of Wisconsin who had studied with Han H. Gerth (a German refugee), among others, Mills retained his ties with German thought through his Columbia–Frankfort colleagues; his scholarly work throughout the 1940s and 1950s (particularly *The Power Elite*, 1956) was more than conventionally controversial.

He was not a simple figure. Over a period of time, he moved from a complex but basically symbolic interactionist perspective into a radical perspective. This radical perspective was basically a moralistic approach, which contained as much midwest Populism as Marxist analysis. As one of the founding fathers of American radical sociology, Mills' importance lies in one book (*The Power Elite*, 1956), two pamphlets ("The Causes of World War III," 1959a, and "Listen Yankee," on Cuba, 1960a), an article ("Letter to the New Left," 1960b), and a reader (*The Marxists*, 1962), all produced during the late 1950s and early 1960s. These works had firm foundations in classical sociological theory. While at Columbia, Mills became interested in using data to test theoretical concepts; indeed *The Power Elite* shows the author's interest in this aspect of standard American sociology. However, the book's impact in promoting discussion of the American system was far more valuable than its rather unreliable and overinterpreted data. Mills' roots may have been American, but the German socialist influence is unmistakable.

Despite Mills' early theoretical importance for radical sociology, his somewhat Marxist orientation (exactly how Marxist he was is a point of debate; see I. M. Zeitlin, 1971), and his consciousness of Marxism through his ties to Gerth (and, to some extent, Howard P. Becker, an historically oriented scholar at Wisconsin), the radicals have roots that are not explicitly Marxist. Both the civil rights and the antiwar movements had their origins in Christian ethics (e.g., the Christian ministers Martin Luther King, Jr., and A. J. Muste were early leaders of the civil rights and peace movements, respectively). The pacifism and humanism of Gandhi was also important for these movements. Veblen's non-Marxian radicalism (e.g., *Theory of the Leisure Class,* 1899) also presented a possible alternative structure for radical theory. Nevertheless, Mills' theory and the "humanism" of Erich Fromm (a member of the Frankfort School and a Marxist) have been the most influential factors in providing an intellectual basis for the radicals' activity. Fromm's *Escape from Freedom* (1941) and other psychoanalytic work, plus his (1966) championing of the view of Marx as a humanistic scholar, have been quite important to the radicals.

The ties between radical social movements and the more critical intellectual movement, both complex and ever-changing, are easy to document in specifics but hard to perceive in overall perspective. In general, the notable differences in style and content among the more social movements can be attributed to their centrality (or marginality) to intellectual movements. Speaking of the pre-World War I German socialist movement, Coser (1972) argues that the intellectually central group was postulating revolution while the peripheral groups (e.g., Rosa Luxemburg's group) were being revolutionary. Likewise in the United States, the largely critical group, trained in socialist orientations, is more discursive, whereas the socially peripheral radical group has been more revolutionary.

There are intellectual ties among the critical analyses of Birnbaum, Habermas, and Schroyer (see Table 11.2), Habermas being the central figure. Among other European critical scholars, he is thanked in Birnbaum's introduction for having read and commented on the manuscript of the *Crisis of Industrial Society* (Birnbaum, 1969: ix). Schroyer (1971: 297) sees his work in part as an extended interpretation of "the pioneering work of Jürgen Habermas."

The radical activists have connections to other radical activists through membership in the same activist groups. For example, Tom Hayden, Carl Oglesby, and Todd Gitlin—radicals with varying degrees of prominence—are all present or past members of Students for a Democratic Society (SDS), although they differ on radical strategy and tactics. The National Conference for New Politics (Newfield, 1967: 152) is an example of a collection of several radical groups, including SDS. Group memberships are constantly shifting, and this fluidity encourages social linkages.

There are also recent ties between the radicals and criticals. For example, Herbert Marcuse is part of the critical tradition, yet he is, and has long been, revered by radicals. However, documentation of some radicals' reanalysis of their basis in Marxian theory (Weinstein and Eakins, 1970) and of the criticals' greater concern for *praxis* (e.g., their concern for injustice, war, and racism, Fischer, 1971: ix) should not obscure the fact that these two groups were not totally independent before.

These connections are very difficult to assess. We know that some members of an organization may be quite isolated from others; others (e.g., in a teacher–student relationship) can be quite close. There are clearly a few strong relationships within the Movement, as some members will testify (see, e.g., Newfield, 1967; Jacobs, 1970). The intellectual ties noted previously are probably more influential than the social ties, which at present are rarely permanent. Beyond these observations, I lack a means of assessing these relations accurately; the radical (and to some extent, critical) sociologists lack a means for regularly producing strong, intellectually significant relations. One rather weak measure of this deficiency is that there are only 13 coauthored items out of 107 (12 percent) in this chapter's bibliography, a fairly low coauthorship rate. However, three of these pieces are by collectives (the editors of *Ramparts* and *Liberation*); these three may thus indicate a closer collaboration than the usual coauthorship.[2]

The major difference now between European Marxist sociology and its American critical counterpart plus the sociology of the radicals is the addition of a strong pragmatic bias to the radical perspective. This pragmatism comes in part from the work of Mills (who studied the pragmatic philosophers from a sociology of knowledge perspective for his doctoral thesis; see Mills, 1964, reprint) and in part from the need to have effective programs for social change. From the radical perspective, such programs are needed; and if they happen to be "right" by some theoretical criterion, that circumstance has been seen as nice (although not necessary). The strain to synthesize the theoretical and the pragmatic is now being felt.

A program-type statement by Richard Flacks (1972) suggested a series of projects that radical sociologists need to investigate. Like the ethnomethodologists up to 1971, the radicals have been more critical of sociology than productive of positive work of their own (Bottomore, 1972: 5). Indeed, work that is critical of other sociology (e.g., Mills, 1959b; Birnbaum, 1969: 11–44; Williams, 1969: 3–11) has been the bread and butter of radical sociology. The list of critical work could be extended indefinitely. These critics, however, have used much of the same material, many of the same arguments, and many adumbrations of Mills and now Gouldner (1970). The result has been a plethora of repetition. Nevertheless, some positive contributions, including Mill's *Power Elite* (1956), Domhoff's *Who Rules America?* (1967), and the articles in Maurice Zeitlin's *American Society Inc.* (1970) constitute important beginnings for positive radical analysis. This work could eventually prove to be the stream of small intellectual successes, which are a necessary element to building a group within the academic community. More such work, along the same lines suggested by Flacks, would be quite important.

SOCIAL ASPECTS

The social aspects of the radical and critical groups are more separate than their intellectual heritage. I am therefore discussing the social aspects with respect to each group separately.

THE RADICALS

The 1960s brought new elements crucial to the growth of radical sociology. One was the appearance of the Movement. In addition, several socialist groups (ranging from the Communist party to Progressive Labor to the old Students for a Democratic Society) became important, although not as central as the Movement. Flacks (1971a: 231) points out the sources of the Movement. Students from the 1950s and 1960s going into service occupations (particularly education, but all the new professions) had gradually become a new intelligentsia. Flacks remarks:

> By 1960, the development of the American Intelligentsia as a class had come to this: Demographically, it had grown over several decades from small pockets of isolated independent intellectuals to a substantial stratum of the population, including many in new white-collar vocations. Culturally, it had begun to develop a family structure and value system that was at odds with the traditional capitalist, Protestant Ethic, middle-class culture. Politically, it had passed through a period of optimistic reformism toward increasing disillusionment.

A significant difference between this group and those discussed in preceding chapters is that recruits for radical sociology came largely through the Movement. For many, their new radical political positions had little or no immediate impact on their more strictly sociological education. Some, however, saw that their formal education did not fit with their work in the Movement and withdrew from school. Still others consciously decided to complete their degrees so that they could work within the system, either to change or to subvert it. Students in sociology could only constitute a small part (a few hundred) of the total number of radicalized graduate students. However, because radical activity was concentrated at centers such as Berkeley, Harvard, Michigan, Columbia, and Wisconsin, which were major centers for graduate training in general, an important part of sociology's graduate student population was involved.

Interacting with the Movement were civil rights and peace movements, community development movements and demonstrations, political groups and political rallies, building takeovers, and communes. Of particular importance was the "permanent floating seminar" organized at "trouble spots" or "scenes of constructive activity" (depending on your viewpoint) for the purpose of discussing tactics and proposals for action. Some of the places that had permanent floating seminars during the 1960s are listed in Table 11.1. These seminars were at least as open to the discussion of ideas as seminars in more formal educational settings. When a major event was to take place, branch seminars readied people prior to action. The lessons learned in them were reinforced by the testing of ideas in action, followed by more discussion and reinterpretation at hundreds of other such "seminars," some held "on the scene," others not.

The level of understanding of Marxist or critical ideas varied from complete ignorance to high sophistication; philosophical points might be made, but they had to have some relation to reality (i.e., the action at hand). The kind of theory involved was neither complete nor consistent; however, the moral position (opposition to the system and insistence on the practical utility of theory in action) provided a very different basis for learning that theory than did the more traditional

TABLE 11.1 Examples of locations of "permanent floating seminars"

Date		Event
1962		In Students for a Democratic Society, around Port Huron, Mich., and fight with League for Industrial Democracy
1963–1968		Education Research Action projects in Newark, N.J.
1964		At Berkeley during Free Speech Movement; Freedom Summer in Mississippi
1965		Student Non-Violent Coordinating Committee, Nashville, Tenn., conference
1966	August	SDS National Convention, Clear Lake, Iowa
1967	June	Ann Arbor, Mich., SDS National Convention: "new working class" concept
1968	May	Paris–Nanterre Student Uprising
	August	Chicago Democratic National Convention: "student power concept"
	April-May	Around campuses, Columbia, Harvard: building takeovers
1969	June	Chicago: SDS National Convention: "Weatherman" concept
1970	May	Many campuses (e.g., Jackson State and Kent State) at the time of the Cambodian crisis

Sources: Newfield (1967); Jacobs (1970).

learning situations. Only a few of these seminars were directly educational in intent. They had in common an interest in analysis of the present general situation in tension with an antianalytic, anarchist viewpoint, highly moralistic in content and action-oriented in perspective.

Besides the seminar, other, more permanent, institutional forms developed. The New University Conference and the various caucuses within each of the major social science disciplines helped hold the radical group together. There were also explicitly Movement groups (e.g., SDS, Progressive Labor party) which served as rallying points for radicals in and out of the academic world.

Table 11.2 lists some of the major figures in radical and critical sociology.[3] These persons have had varying amounts of sociological training. Members of the group do not share a common graduate training, but they do have the common experience (and concomitant relations) developed from having been at the same places at the same time (e.g., SDS conventions; Chicago in 1968). Indeed, every new action (particularly on campuses) between 1964 and 1970 acted as a recruiting device for radical sociology.

For radical sociology, the 1970s thus far have been a period of retrenchment. By 1971 the Movement had considerably reduced its political activity. The coalition of academics and revolutionaries of various sorts had been split by a shift from mass action, in which the academics were welcome allies, to covert action, in which academics have become unnecessary baggage. The 1971 situation has thus left those who were once radical academics without the sustained high activity levels necessary to maintain their impression of being "on the firing line." The range of possible social involvements since 1971 (from the Weathermen to New University Caucuses) has been extensive, but these involvements seem to have lacked the focus and the feeling of historical necessity that characterized pre-1971 involvement. Perhaps as a consequence, the post-1971 situation thus far has been more prone to theoretical and historical analysis by those involved, as they seek guidance for the future. Rapidly changing events, however, may well enable frequent shifts between mass and covert action, and between action and analysis. I expect that the factionalism of these groups will continue to confuse the scene as some groups go one way and some, others.

Three (roughly) radical training centers have recently materialized: one at Santa Barbara around Richard Flacks; one at Washington University, St. Louis (with David Colfax and Henry Etzkowitz); and a third at Rutgers (with Irving L. Horowitz, Martin Oppenheimer, and John Leggett). All three centers are still quite small; but they are starting to train students and are working hard on theoretical issues. Radical sociologists as they function within sociology can best be understood by contrast with the social forecasters. The forecasters have been building on a politically liberal philosophy. They argue that society has power

TABLE 11.2 Data on some prominent radical–critical sociologists

Name	(1)	(2)	(3)	(4)	(5)	(6)
Anderson, Charles	A	R	—	—	UMEA	1971
Birnbaum, Norman	A	C	—	1969	AMHE	1970
Blackburn, Robin	E	C	SSC	1969	OXFO	1970
Cammett, John M. (historian)	A	C	SSC	1967	NYU	1970
Colfax, David	A	R	—	—	WSTL	1970
Dixon, Marlene	A	C	SSC	—	MCGI	1970
Eakins, David W.	A	C	—	1970	—	—
Etzkowitz, Henry	A	R	—	—	WSTL	1970
Fischer, George (historian)	A	C	SSC	1971	CUNY	1970
Flacks, Richard	A	R	—	1972	UCSB	1970
Gitlin, Todd	A	R	—	—	BERK	1970
Habermass, Jürgen	E	C	F	1970	FRAN	1970
Hamilton, Richard	A	C	—	1972	MCGI	1970
Hayden, Tom	A	R	—	1970	—	—
Hobsbawm, Eric J.	E	C	F	1968	FRAN	1970
LeFebvre, Henri	E	C	—	1969	PARI	1970
Leggett, John	A	R	—	—	RUTG	1970
Löwenthal, Leo	E	C	F	—	BERK	1970
Lynd, Staughton	A	R	—	1969	—	—
Marcuse, Herbert (philosophy)	E	C	F	1968	UCSD	1970
Menashe, Louis	A	C	SSC	—	BPLT	1970
Miller, Samuel M.	A	—	—	1970	NYU	1970
Moore, Barrington	A	C	—	1966	HARV	1970
Nicolaus, Martin	A	R	—	1970	SIFA	1968
O'Connor, James	A	C	—	1970	SJST	1970
Oglesby, Carl	A	R	—	1969	—	—
Oppenheimer, Martin	A	R	—	—	RUTG	1970
Parris, Robert Moses	A	R	—	—	—	—
Schaflander, Gerald	A	R	—	—	BOSU	1970
Schroyer, Trent	A	C	—	1971	NEWS	1970
Touraine, Alain	E	C	—	—	—	—
Wiley, Norbert	A	C	—	—	ILL	1970
Williams, John S.	A	R	—	—	NEWS	1970
Zeitlin, Irving M.	A	C	—	1967	WSTL	1970
Zeitlin, Maurice	A	R	—	1970	WISC	1970
Zinn, Howard (historian)	A	R	—	—	—	—

Sources: Birnbaum (1969: ix), Dreitzel (1969), ASA (1970), Fischer (ed.) (1971: vi–xiv), **Sociologist Insurgent** (1971).

Key:
Col. 1. E = European; A = American.
Col. 2. C = critical; R = radical.
Col. 3. F = Frankfort School; SSC = Socialist Scholars' Conference.
Col. 4. Date of an important item in this chapter's bibliography.
Col. 5. Locations:

AMHE	Amherst College
BERK	University of California, Berkeley
BOSU	Boston University
BPLT	Polytechnic Institute of Brooklyn
CUNY	City University of New York
FRAN	Frankfort, Germany
HARV	Harvard University
ILL	University of Illinois
MCGI	McGill University
NEWS	New School for Social Research
NYU	New York University
OXFO	Oxford University
PARI	University of Paris
RUTG	Rutgers
SIFA	Simon Frasier University
SJST	San Jose State University
WISC	University of Wisconsin
WSTL	Washington University, St. Louis
UCSB	University of California, Santa Barbara
UCSD	University of California, San Diego
UMEA	Umea University, Sweden

Col. 6. Date for Col. 5 location.

centralized in its government. The bureaucratic portions of the government (the executive department staffs) are experts who have the possibility, by their superior knowledge and position, to direct society toward the greater good. Forecasters, therefore, support an administrative, bureaucratic response to social problems. Government bureaucracies have needed information both to propose programs and to control those which have been approved, and the forecasters have attempted to provide that information.

By contrast, the radical-critical approach to achieving a better society has been through the organization of persons with needs. With organization, the adherents to this group expect to be able to demand what is needed by working within the system (through elections), by engaging in revolutionary activities, or by some combination of the two. Radicals believe that if organizations remain responsive to the groups that founded them, then in a direct political confrontation, they can win and control some portion of social goods.

The opposition of these two perspectives was clearly pointed out in the confrontation at the 1968 ASA meetings, for within its little teapot, this confrontation reflected the larger tempest simultaneously occurring in Chicago around the Democratic National Convention. The Secretary of the U.S. Department of Health, Education, and Welfare, Wilbur Cohen, was a featured speaker at the ASA meetings; he was chosen partly because of his involvement with the social indicators effort. As the epitome of the liberal bureaucrat, he was protested and picketed. Finally several counteraddresses (e.g., Nicolaus, 1970) to his address were given.

The confrontation between forecasters and radicals was seen with particular clarity in the Moynihan Report (Rainwater and Yancey, 1968) and Project Camelot (I. Horowitz, 1967) episodes. The same sort of philosophy produced both the report (discussed in Chapter 7) and the project. The latter, an attempt to assess which of a series of Latin American countries was more likely to have revolutions, was a research effort by American academics. Although it probably would not have resulted in any accurate predictions, it was seen by Latin Americans as an affront to them and their nationalism. As Nicolaus (1970) points out, not until the rich are studied and the resulting information is spread throughout poor communities will there be less opposition to the idea of studies.

In both Project Camelot and the Moynihan Report, relatively powerless communities were investigated by social scientists to aid those in power in making decisions that would affect the lives of the people studied. The radicals' objection to this approach is simple: If power were more evenly distributed, there would be no need for studies, since those who knew an area would be making the decisions that affected it (see Birnbaum, 1969: 81–83). Yet sociologists have an interest in studies that goes beyond that of a study's sponsor: They want to advance general understandings of how society operates. Unfortunately, the money needed to do research can usually be obtained only through agency sponsorship, which is clearly a mixed blessing. Good sociology, even good radical sociology, can be done on agency sponsorship; but the tendency would certainly be to pander to what the agency wanted.

H. S. Becker and Horowitz (1972: 62) assign two other probable causes to the opposition between the forecasters and the radical-criticals: (1) the conservative influence of conventional technical procedures and (2) common-sense standards for the credibility of explanations. The conservative influence of standard methods results from the limit on kinds of causes that can be examined with pencil-and-paper questionnaires, tests, and experiments. The common-sense notions of what constitutes an acceptable cause for either radical or conservative sociology also limit sociology. Interestingly, Becker and Horowitz argue that radical sociology is likely to be better sociology, if only because it must take both the official and the opposition (i.e., radical) common-sense notions into account.

THE CRITICALS

The critical sociologists have always worked more within the academic tradition than have the radicals. Again, in contrast to the radicals, the criticals are primarily theoretical and historical, rather than being action-oriented. They have a relatively unified theory, notwithstanding the existence of intergroup disagreements on specific points and, thus far, the failure of Marxism to achieve the status of a major intellectual movement in America. In Europe, with the exception of Nazi Germany, critical sociology has been more generally accepted. The persons (e.g., Adorno, Gerth, Horkheimer) who came to the United States from Germany varied in socialist affiliation from mildly social democratic to communist.

Table 11.2 lists both Europeans and Americans. Most of the Americans, however, were trained by Europeans or have spent time studying at European universities. The American criticals are important to contemporary social theory largely for their analysis of radical actions in the 1960s. Without the radicals, the criticals probably would have continued as a parallel development, peripheral to sociology and generally ignored by it. The radicals' actions opened up departments to their concerns and have thereby made critical sociology more acceptable.

The critical theorists have developed their own extradisciplinary institutions in socialist groups and journals. One of the most important institutions was the Socialist Scholars' Conference (SSC; 1964–1970). Table 11.2 lists some of those who were organizers and major figures for the SSC (as well as for some journals). The SSC first met in 1965 and ceased to exist in 1970, having reached a high point of activity and membership in 1967 (Fischer 1971: vii–x). Its most likely successor, the Telos Conferences, is more philosophical in orientation, like the journal of the same name. Other groups of critical social theorists have also developed around journals. *Telos, The Monthly Review* (with Paul Sweezy and the late Paul Baran), and others have groups of editors who act as colleagues for one another. Table 11.3 lists important journals and some persons associated with some of them.

The simple passage of time has added senior sociologists to both groups as earlier Ph.D. recipients have matured. The New School for Social Research in New York City has had a long tradition of critical socialist studies and presently has Trent Schroyer on its faculty. Marcuse is on the University of California, San Diego faculty. Critical scholars have also been trained in history and philosophy departments, such as those at Rutgers and Brandeis. Critical studies thus have the same interdisciplinary aspect as other contemporary theory groups in sociology.

Because critical sociologists have been more academically oriented than their radical colleagues, they have been more likely to finish their academic training. This tendency suggests the possibility of a sharp increase, during the 1970s, in the number of trained critical sociologists.[4]

TABLE 11.3 Journals that serve as bases for critical groups

Monthly Review—Sweezy; Magdoff
Ramparts—mostly radical; David Horowitz
New Left Review—critical journal
Telos—mostly critical; philosophical perspective; Paul Piccone (ed.); Paul Breines
Radical America—Breines; Dale Domich;[a] SDS publication ·
Socialist Revolution—O'Connor (ed.); Stanley Aronowitz
Politics and Society—ni[b]
Berkeley Journal of Sociology—ni
New York Review of Books—Christopher Lasch (contributor)
Studies on the Left—John Cowley (ed.)
Zeitschrift für Sozial Forschung (ed. by Horkheimer in 1930s)
Dissent—Irving Howe (ed.)
Root and Branch—Stanley Aronowitz
Anarchos—Murray Bookchin

Sources: Deutsch and Howard (1970); Jacobs (1970); Fischer (1971).
[a] First name shown if person is not listed in Table 11.2.
[b] ni = No information.

IN CONCLUSION

The radicals initially recruited and trained new members through action situations. The Movement, the campus actions that attracted new members, and the permanent floating seminars around radical actions have constituted a social situation in which both new and old members mixed together informally. The actions themselves have constituted practical tests of radical theory. However, as the actions have decreased in number and the opportunities for permanent floating radical seminars have declined, the need to provide more regular training has increased, and the division that existed during the 1960s between the radicals and the critical intellectuals is being healed.

For the group to become institutionalized within the profession, the drift toward establishing active centers of radical and critical theory must continue. The group might then develop a few clusters for the training of new radical and critical sociologists. Regardless of whether formal institutionalization occurs, however, we can confidently predict the continued existence of nontraditional, nonacademic, institutional forms of radical and critical thought (in social groups, journals, caucuses, etc.). In turn, their presence on the scene guarantees that, unlike the forecasters, both the group and the impact of its concepts will continue, whether radical-critical thought becomes part of mainstream sociology or whether it remains separate.

The radical-criticals have already made some permanent contribution to the content of sociology through their influence on forecasting (discussed in Chapter 7), ethnomethodology, and structuralism. The humanistic perspective of Marxism (e.g., Schaff, 1970), which bases much of its interpretive weight on Marx's 1844 manuscripts (see Bottomore, 1964a, 1964b), has become quite prominent in recent Marxist scholarship. It has been suggested (Dreitzel, 1969: ix–x) that the combination of ethnomethodology's phenomenological concerns with the humanistic Marxist perspective is quite likely. Indeed, Habermas (1970a) appears to be attempting such a synthesis, and Schroyer (1971) cites Habermas heavily, as well as Schutz, Garfinkel, and Cicourel (see Schroyer, 1971: 312).

There have also been some attempts in Europe to combine structuralism and radical-critical thought. The writings of Lévi-Strauss have been taken as the starting point for a philosophical movement in which the empirical aspects of social science seem to be buried in discussion of the differences between economic and mental organization in determining social structure. This attempt to combine Lévi-Strauss with radicalism has been made by Althusser (1969), an important French Marxist intellectual.[5]

Marxist interpretation and utilization of new causal theory is quite possible; to the best of my knowledge, however, only Stinchcombe (1968: 93–98) has begun such a combination.

In short, each of the schools considered in Chapters 1 to 10 can be or is being actively combined with Marxist interpretations. This cross-fertilization makes it hard for us to predict the immediate future of sociology in general and radical-critical thought in particular. Chapter 12 examines future possibilities in more detail.

The basic questions now for this group are whether the radicals will spend the necessary time in academic research and whether the criticals will respect the revolutionary experience of the radicals. If both answers are affirmative, the two subgroups will probably continue to grow together.

NOTES

1. A good history of Marxian developments from 1870 to 1940 can be found in Lichtheim (1970). Marxism's impact on sociology is assessed in I. M. Zeitlin (1968). A history of the radical movement in the early 1960s can be found in Jack Newfield (1967). Some history of the development of socialist and communist thought through the Russian Revolution is given in Edmund Wilson (1953).
2. The existence of other nonacademic collective efforts such as the Liberation News Service and the (Detroit) Radical Education Project suggests that formal attribution of authorship or coauthorship is not to be the style among some radicals. Likewise, the radical-criticals tend not to use footnotes of acknowledgment. This situation presents obvious problems for my data collection procedures and represents another way in which this group departs from the academic pattern of the other groups.
3. Table 11.2 was particularly difficult to construct. The requirement of professional status used in prior chapters to help define who should be included and who excluded provides misleading data on the radicals. I have chosen a "strict constructionist" approach to the data, including in Table 11.2 only those who were sociologists by training (e.g., Flacks) or whose work has become very important to sociologists (e.g., Marcuse). As a result I have omitted some persons mentioned in this chapter who have made little impact on sociology but a major impact on society. Because these persons seem, at first glance, to be glaring omissions from the table, I feel that their absence demands an explanation.
4. On the other hand, since the precise analysis prized by critical theorists is very time-consuming, recent students have sometimes required as long as ten years to finish their degrees. Brandeis, long a critical center when Herbert Marcuse and Kurt Wolff were there, did not grant a single Ph.D. in sociology during the first seven years of its existence.
5. French critical sociology differs from the German that has been the central influence on American radical-critical sociology. The French Marxist sociology has been both more intellectual and perhaps more integrated into

French sociology. French Marxism emanates largely from Henri LeFebvre, a distinguished Marxist sociology professor, plus Marxist students and some faculty, chiefly on the sociology faculty at Nanterre. The French intellectual atmosphere is heavily Marxist.

BIBLIOGRAPHY

Adorno, Theodor W., Else Frenkel-Brunswik, Daniel J. Levinson, and R. Nevitt Sanford.
1950   *The Authoritarian Personality.* New York: Harper & Row.
———.
1969   *Alternative Press Index*, Vol. 1 (July–December). Northfield, Minn.: Carleton College, Radical Research Center.
Ali, Tarig (ed.).
1969   *The New Revolutionaries: A Handbook of the International Radical Left.* New York: Morrow.
Althusser, Louis.
1969   *For Marx.* Translated by B. Brewster. London: Allen Lane.
Althusser, Louis, and Etienne Balibar.
1970   *Reading "Capital."* Translated by B. Brewster. London: NLB Press.
American Sociological Association.
1970   *Directory of Members, 1970.* Washington, D.C.: American Sociological Association.
Aron, Raymond.
1971   "Conclusion." Pp. 131–132 in Otto Stammer (ed.), *Max Weber and Sociology Today.* Translated by Kathleen Morris. New York: Harper Torch Books.
Aronowitz, Stanley.
1971   "Does the United States have a new working class?" Pp. 188–216 in George Fischer (ed.), *The Revival of American Socialism: Selected Papers of the Socialist Scholars' Conference.* New York: Oxford University Press.
Avineri, Shlomo.
1968   *The Social and Political Thought of Karl Marx.* London: Cambridge University Press.
Aya, Roderick, and Norman Miller (eds.).
1971   *The New American Revolution.* New York: Free Press.
Baran, Paul, and Paul Sweezy.
1969   *Monopoly Capital: An Essay on the American Economic and Social Order.* New York: Monthly Review Press.
Becker, Howard S., and Irving L. Horowitz.
1972   "Radical politics and sociological research: observations on methodology and ideology." *American Journal of Sociology* 78 (July): 48–66.
Birnbaum, Norman.
1969   *The Crisis of Industrial Society.* New York: Oxford University Press.
1971   "Late capitalism in the United States." Pp. 133–153 in George Fischer (ed.), *The Revival of American Socialism: Selected Papers*

of the Socialist Scholars' Conference. New York: Oxford University Press.

Blackburn, Robin, and Alexander Cockburn (eds.).
1969   *Student Power: Problems, Diagnosis, Action.* Baltimore, Md.: Penguin.

Boorstein, Edward.
1968   *The Economic Transformation of Cuba, A First-Hand Account.* New York: Monthly Review Press.

Bottomore, T. B.
1964a "Preface." Pp. v–vii in Karl Marx, *Selected Writings in Sociology and Social Philosophy.* Edited and translated by T. B. Bottomore. New York: McGraw-Hill.
1964b "Introduction." Pp. v–xi in Karl Marx, *Early Writings.* Edited and translated by T. B. Bottomore. New York: McGraw-Hill.
1968   *Critics of Society: Radical Thought in North America.* New York: Pantheon.
1972   "Introduction." *American Journal of Sociology* 78 (July): 1–8.

Breines, Paul.
1970   *Critical Interruptions: New Left Perspectives on Herbert Marcuse.* New York: Herder & Herder.

Cammett, John M.
1967   *Antonio Gramsci and the Origins of Italian Communism.* Stanford, Calif.: Stanford University Press.

Chomsky, Noam.
1969   *American Power and the New Mandarins.* New York: Pantheon.

Coser, Lewis A.
1972   "Marxist thought in the first quarter of the 20th century." *American Journal of Sociology* 78 (July): 173–201.

Dahrendorf, Ralf.
1959   *Class and Class Conflict in Industrial Society.* Stanford, Calif.: Stanford University Press.

Deutsch, Steven E., and John Howard.
1970   *Where It's At: Radical Perspectives in Sociology.* New York: Harper & Row.

Dibble, Vernon K.
1972   "Political judgments and the perception of social relationships: an analysis of some applied social research in late 19th century Germany." *American Journal of Sociology* 78 (July): 155–172.

Domhoff, G. William.
1967   *Who Rules America?* Englewood Cliffs, N.J.: Prentice-Hall.

Dreitzel, Hans Peter (ed.).
1969   *Recent Sociology* No. 1. London: Macmillan.

Fischer, George (ed.).
1971   *The Revival of American Socialism: Selected Papers of the Socialist Scholars' Conference.* New York: Oxford University Press.

Flacks, Richard.
1971a "Revolt of the young intelligencia: revolutionary class-consciousness

in a post-scarcity America." Pp. 223–259 in Roderick Aya and Norman Miller (eds.), *The New American Revolution*. New York: Free Press.

1971b *Youth and Social Structure*. Chicago: Markham.

1972 "Toward a socialist sociology." *Insurgent Sociologist* 2 (Spring): 18–27.

Friedenberg, Edgar Z.

1965 *Coming of Age in America: Growth and Acquiescence*. New York: Random House.

Fromm, Erich.

1941 *Escape from Freedom*. New York: Holt.

1964 "Introduction." Pp. xiii–xviii in Karl Marx, *Selected Writings in Sociology and Social Philosophy*. Edited and translated by T. B. Bottomore. New York: McGraw-Hill.

Fromm, Erich (ed.).

1961 *Marx's Concept of Man*. New York: Ungar.

1966 *Socialistic Humanism: An International Symposium*. Garden City, N.Y.: Doubleday.

Goodman, Mitchell.

1970 *The Movement Toward a New America*. New York: Knopf.

Goodman, Paul.

1962 *The Community of Scholars*. New York: Random House.

Gouldner, Alvin W.

1970 *The Coming Crisis of Western Sociology*. New York: Basic Books.

Gramsci, Antonio.

1971 *Selections from the Prison Notebooks*. Edited and translated by Quintin Hoare and Goeffrey Nowell Smith. New York: International Publishers.

Habermas, Jürgen.

1970a "Toward a theory of communicative competence." Pp. 114–148 in Hans Peter Dreitzel, *Recent Sociology* No. 2. New York: Macmillan.

1970b *Toward a Rational Society; Student Protest, Science, and Politics*. Translated by Jeremy J. Shapiro. Boston: Beacon.

Hamilton, Richard F.

1971 "Class and race in the United States." Pp. 81–106 in George Fischer (ed.), *The Revival of American Socialism: Selected Papers of the Socialist Scholars' Conference*. New York: Oxford University Press.

1972 *Class and Class Politics in the United States*. New York: Wiley.

Hayden, Tom.

1970 *Trial*. New York: Holt.

Hobsbawm, Eric J.

1968 *Industry and Empire*. New York: Pantheon.

Horowitz, David.

1969 *Empire and Revolution: A Radical Interpretation of Contemporary History*. New York: Random House.

Horowitz, Irving L.

1967 *The Rise and Fall of Project Camelot*. Cambridge, Mass.: MIT Press.

Howe, Irving.
    1970   *Beyond the New Left.* New York: McCall.
Israel, Joachim.
    1971   *Alienation: From Marx to Modern Sociology; A Macrosociological Analysis.* Boston: Allyn & Bacon.
Jacobs, Harold (ed.).
    1970   *Weatherman.* Berkeley, Calif.: Ramparts Press.
Jay, Martin.
    1970   "How utopian is Marcuse?" Pp. 244–256 in George Fischer (ed.), *The Revival of American Socialism: Selected Papers of the Socialist Scholars' Conference.* New York: Oxford University Press.
King, Martin Luther, Jr.
    1963   *Strength to Love.* New York: Harper & Row.
Knowles, Louis L., and Kenneth Prewitt (eds.)
    1969   *Institutional Racism in America.* Englewood Cliffs, N.J.: Prentice-Hall.
Kolko, Gabriel.
    1969   *The Roots of American Foreign Policy; An Analysis of Power and Purpose.* Boston: Beacon.
Korsch, Karl.
    1938   *Karl Marx.* New York: Russell & Russell. (Reissued, 1963.)
    1970   *Marxism and Philosophy.* Translated by Fred Halliday. New York: Monthly Review Press.
Lasch, Christopher.
    1970   *The Agony of the American Left.* New York: Knopf, 1969.
    1971   "From culture to politics." Pp. 217–226 in George Fischer (ed.), *The Revival of American Socialism: Selected Papers of the Socialist Scholars' Conference.* New York: Oxford University Press.
LeFebvre, Henri.
    1969   *The Explosion: Marxism and the French Upheaval.* Translated by Alfred Ehrenfeld. New York: Monthly Review Press.
Leites, Nathan, and Charles Wolf, Jr.
    1970   *Rebellion and Authority.* Chicago: Markham.
Liberation, Editors of,
    1969   "The Movement: 10 years from now." *Liberation* 14 (August–September): entire issue.
Lichtheim, George.
    1970   *A Short History of Socialism.* New York: Praeger.
Lipset, Seymour M., and Everett C. Ladd, Jr.
    1972   "The politics of American sociologists." *American Journal of Sociology* 78 (July): 67–104.
Lothstein, Arthur.
    1970   *"All We are Saying . . ." The Philosophy of the New Left.* New York: Putnam.
Lukács, Georg.
    1971   *History and Class Consciousness Studies in Marxist Dialectics.* Translated by Rodney Livingstone. Cambridge, Mass.: MIT Press.
Lutz, William, and Harry Brent.
    1971   *On Revolution.* Cambridge, Mass.: Winthrop Publishers.

Lynd, Staughton.
    1969   *The New Left*. Boston: Porter Sargent.
Magdoff, Harry.
    1969   *The Age of Imperialism: The Economics of U.S. Foreign Policy*. New York: Monthly Review Press.
Malcolm X. (Little, Malcolm)
    1965   *Malcolm X Speaks*. New York: Merit Publishers.
Mandel, Ernest.
    1968   *Marxist Economic Theory*. 2 vols. Translated by Brian Pearce. New York: Monthly Review Press.
    1971   "Workers and permanent revolution." Pp. 169–187 in George Fischer (ed.), *The Revival of American Socialism: Selected Papers of the Socialist Scholars' Conference*. New York: Oxford University Press.
Marcuse, Herbert.
    1962   *Eros and Civilization; A Philosophical Enquiry into Freud*. New York: Vintage.
    1968a *Negations: Essays in Critical Theory*. Translated by Jeremy J. Shapiro. Boston: Beacon.
    1968b *One-Dimensional Man: Studies in the Ideology of Advanced Industrial Society*. Boston: Beacon.
    1969   *An Essay on Liberation*. Boston: Beacon.
Marx, Karl.
    1946   *Capital*. London: Allen & Unwin (reprint).
    1964a *Selected Writings in Sociology and Social Philosophy*. Edited and translated by T. B. Bottomore. New York: McGraw-Hill. (First published in 1956.)
    1964b *Early Writings*. Edited and translated by T. B. Bottomore. New York: McGraw-Hill.
    1971   *The Grundisse*. Edited and translated by David McLellen. London: Macmillan.
Merton, Robert K.
    1972   "Insiders and outsiders: a chapter in the sociology of knowledge." *American Journal of Sociology* 78 (July): 9–47.
Miliband, Ralph, and John Saville (eds.).
    1967   *The Socialist Register 1967*. London: Merlin.
Miller, Samuel M., and Pamela A. Roby.
    1970   *The Future of Inequality*. New York: Basic Books.
Mills, C. Wright.
    1956   *The Power Elite*. New York: Oxford University Press.
    1959a *The Causes of World War III*. London: Serber & Warburg.
    1959b *The Sociological Imagination*. New York: Oxford University Press.
    1960a *Listen Yankee: The Revolution in Cuba*. New York: Ballantine.
    1960b "Letter to the New Left." *New Left Review* 1 (5) 18–23.
    1964   *Sociology and Pragmatism: The Higher Learning in America*. New York: Paine-Whitman.
Mills, C. Wright (ed.).
    1962   *The Marxists*. New York: Dell.

Moore, Barrington.
  1966   *Social Origins of Dictatorship and Democracy: Lord and Peasant in the Making of the Modern World.* Boston: Beacon.
Muste, A. J.
  1940   *Non-violence in an Aggressive World.* New York: Harper & Row.
Newfield, Jack.
  1967   *A Prophetic Minority.* New York: Signet.
Nicolaus, Martin.
  1970   "Text of a speech delivered at the ASA convention, August 26, 1968." Pp. 274–278 in Larry T. Reynolds and Janice M. Reynolds (eds.), *The Sociology of Sociology.* New York: McKay.
O'Brien, James.
  1968   *A History of the New Left, 1960–68.* A pamphlet of the New England Press based on three articles printed in 1968 in *Radical America.*
O'Connor, James.
  1970   *Origins of Socialism in Cuba.* Ithaca, N.Y.: Cornell University Press.
Oglesby, Carl (ed.).
  1969   *The New Left Reader.* New York: Grove.
Oglesby, Carl, and Richard Shaull.
  1967   *Containment and Change.* New York: Macmillan.
Rainwater, Lee, and William Yancey (eds.).
  1968   *The Moynihan Report and the Politics of Controversy.* Cambridge, Mass.: MIT Press.
Ramparts, Editors of,
  1970   *Divided We Stand.* San Francisco: Canfield.
  1971   *Two, Three, Many Vietnams.* San Francisco: Canfield.
Rapoport, Anatol.
  1969   "Have the intellectuals a class interest?" Pp. 215–238 in Hans P. Dreitzel (ed.), *Recent Sociology* No. 1. London: Macmillan.
Schaff, Adam.
  1970   *Marxism and the Human Individual* (Introduction by E. Fromm). New York: McGraw-Hill.
Schroyer, Trent.
  1971   "The critical theory of late capitalism." Pp. 297–321 in George Fischer (ed.), *The Revival of American Socialism: Selected Papers of the Socialist Scholars' Conference.* New York: Oxford University Press.
Shils, Edward A.
  1970   "Tradition, ecology and institution in the history of sociology." *Daedalus: The Making of Modern Science: Biographical Studies* 99 (Fall): 760–825.
The Sociologist Insurgent.
  1971   "Apologia." *The Sociologist Insurgent* 1 (April): 1, 7.
Sorokin, Pitirim A.
  1941   *Social and Cultural Dynamics.* New York: American Book.
Stammer, Otto (ed.).
  1971   *Max Weber and Sociology Today.* Translated by Kathleen Morris. New York: Harper & Row.

Stein, Maurice R., and Arthur Vidich (eds.).
  1963 *Sociology on Trial.* Englewood Cliffs, N.J.: Prentice-Hall.
Stinchcombe, Arthur.
  1968 *Constructing Social Theories.* New York: Harcourt Brace Jovanovich.
Teodori, Massimo (ed.).
  1969 *The New Left: A Documentary History.* Indianapolis: Bobbs-Merrill.
Veblen, Thorstein.
  1899 *Theory of the Leisure Class.* London: Macmillan.
Weinstein, James, and David W. Eakins (eds.).
  1970 *For a New America: Essays in History and Politics from Studies on
        the Left 1959–1967.* New York: Random House.
Wellmer, Albrecht.
  1971 *Critical Theory of Society.* Translated by John Cumming. New York:
        Herder & Herder.
Wilcox, Laird M.
  1969 *Guide to the American Left.* Kansas City, Mo.: U.S. Directory Serial.
Williams, William A.
  1969 *Roots of the Modern American Empire: A Study of the Growth and
        Shaping of a Social Consciousness in a Marketplace Society.* New
        York: Random House.
Wilson, Edmund.
  1953 *To the Finland Station.* Garden City, N.Y.: Doubleday.
Zeitlin, Irving M.
  1967 *Marxism: A Re-examination.* New York: Van Nostrand.
  1968 *Ideology and the Development of Sociological Theory.* Englewood
        Cliffs, N.J.: Prentice-Hall.
  1971 "The Plain Marxism of C. Wright Mills." Pp. 227–243 in George
        Fischer (ed.), *The Revival of American Socialism: Selected Papers
        of the Socialist Scholars' Conference.* New York: Oxford University
        Press.
Zeitlin, Maurice (ed.).
  1970 *American Society Inc.* Chicago: Markham.

CHAPTER 12
CONCLUSIONS
The Dusty Crystal Ball

Ⓘn this chapter I compare the data in Chapters 7 to 11 with Chapter 2's model and evaluate the results. Then I compare that model with those proposed by others to explain group development in sociology. Finally, I place my bets on the shape of sociological theory in the future.

EVALUATION OF THE MODEL

The specifics of the model do not fit the data as closely as we might wish. I have already noted that the model does not explain the development of radical–critical sociology. The model's assumption of an academic base simply does not hold for this group. Comments in this section, therefore, refer largely to the groups discussed in Chapters 7 to 10. The data are summarized in Table 12.1.

GENERAL OBSERVATIONS

By contrast with the three groups (standard American sociology, symbolic interactionism, and small group theory) discussed in Chapter 6, the forecasters, ethnomethodologists, structuralists, and new causal theorists show somewhat less sloppiness in transition from stage to stage. The forcasters' shift into network status was marked by the establishment of government commissions and the publication of critical work (Moore, 1966; for this and all references to group work used as examples, see the appropriate chapter bibliographies). The ethnomethodologists' attainment of cluster status was clearly indicated by an increase in students in 1966–1967. Similarly, their shift into cluster status was signaled by a marked change in location (from southern California to elsewhere) for many group members. New causal theory's move into specialty status was

TABLE 12.1 Outline of model, including data from Chapters 7 to 10

Feature	Stage			
	Normal	Network	Cluster	Specialty
Theory group[a]				
SF	to 1965	1966–	—[b]	—
ETH	to 1957	1957–1966	1966–1971	1971–
NCT	to 1962	1962–1966	1966–1970	1970–
STR	to 1970	1970–	—	—
Intellectual leader				
SF	None	None yet	—	—
ETH	Garfinkel	Garfinkel, Cicourel, Sacks	Garfinkel, Cicourel, Sacks	Garfinkel, Cicourel, Sacks
NCT	Blalock	Blalock, Duncan	Blalock, Duncan	Blalock, Duncan
STR	White	White	—	—
Social organization leader				
SF	—	None yet	—	—
ETH	—	Cicourel, Garfinkel	Cicourel	Cicourel
NCT	—	Many	Many	Many
STR	—	None yet	—	—
Training–research center				
SF	—	Hudson Institute, Institute for the Future, Russell Sage Foundation	—	—
ETH	—	Berkeley, UCLA	UCLA, UCSB	Many
NCT	—	Chicago, Michigan, UNC	Chicago, Michigan, Wisconsin	Wisconsin; many others
STR	—	Harvard	—	—
Success				
SF	None	Two potentials	—	—
ETH	Garfinkel (1956)[c]	Cicourel (1964)	Garfinkel (1967)	Many

TABLE 12.1 (continued)

Feature	Stage			
	Normal	Network	Cluster	Specialty
NCT	None	Blalock (1964)	Blau and Duncan (1967)	Many
STR	None	White (1970)	—	—
Program statement				
SF	—	U.S. Department of Health, Education, and Welfare (1969)	—	—
ETH	Garfinkel (1956)	Cicourel (1964)	Garfinkel (1967)	None
NCT	—	Blalock (1964)	Blau and Duncan (1967)	None
STR	White (1963b)	None	—	—
Secondary work				
SF	—	Bell (1968), Rainwater and Yancey (1968)	—	—
ETH	—	—	Douglas (1970)	Sudnow (1971)
NCT	—	—	Borgatta and Bohrnstedt (1970)	Costner (1971)
STR	—	—	—	—
Critical work by group				
SF	None	Moore (1966)	—	—
ETH	None	Cicourel (1964)	Wilson (1970)	None
NCT	None	Duncan (1966)	None	None
STR	None	None yet	—	—
Critical of group				
SF	—	Horowitz (1967); Rainwater and Yancey (1968)	—	—

TABLE 12.1   (continued)

Feature	Stage			
	Normal	Network	Cluster	Specialty
ETH	—	—	Hill and Crittenden (1968); Denzin (1970)	None yet
NCT	—	—	—	—
STR	—	—	—	—
Textbook				
SF	—	—	—	—
ETH	—	—	—	None yet
NCT	—	—	Blalock (1969b); Dubin (1969)	Abell (1971); Davis (1971); Mullins (1971)
STR	—	—	—	—
Group size[d]				
SF	9	Around 37	—	—
ETH	Around 7	Around 25	25 in cluster	Many
NCT	Numerous	Around 58	28 at Chicago, Michigan, Wisconsin .	Many
STR	25	Around 25	—	—

[a] SF = Social forecasters, ETH = ethnomethodologists, NCT = new causal theory, STR = Structuralists.
[b] — = Not applicable.
[c] For full references, see appropriate chapters.
[d] Counting:

Normal: SF: People discussed on pp. 157–159.
ETH: People listed in Table 8.2 as active in 1955.
NCT: Not counted individually.
STR: People listed in Table 10.2 as active in 1970.

Network: SF: People listed in Table 7.2 as active in 1971.
ETH: People listed in Table 8.2 as active in 1964.
NCT: People listed in Table 9.2 as active in 1966.
STR: People listed in Table 10.2 as active in 1970.

Cluster: SF: Not applicable.
ETH: People listed in Table 8.2 as active at cluster locations in 1970.
NCT: People listed in Table 9.2 as active at cluster locations in 1970.
STR: Not applicable.

Specialty: SF: Not applicable.
ETH: People listed in Table 8.2 as active in 1971.
NCT: People listed in Table 9.2 as active in 1971.
STR: Not applicable.

characterized by comparable shifts to out-of-cluster locations. When the structuralists reached network status, both social events (the deliberate structuring of meetings) and intellectual ones (White, 1970; publications by other structuralists) occurred.

The majority of these signals are social, however. The two most highly developed groups, the ethnomethodologists and the new causal theorists, show the same lack of transitional precision with regard to intellectual characteristics as did the earlier groups, and for the same general reason (i.e., the lack of organization in the literature). Ethnomethodology has been further hampered by the habitual unwillingness of sociological journals to publish work by ethnomethodologists.

Network Thickening With respect to network thickening, the model seems to be adequately supported. The forecasters and the structuralists are groups that are just beginning to form their initial links. In the forecasters' case, we concentrated on those people who have participated, on request, in several projects related to social forecasting. Obviously some social scientists have an honest interest in the area (many responded to the government's call for assistance); but an undeniably strong factor in the group's beginnings has been governmental interest and funding. The government's desire for immediate results and the group's need for students may well be at cross purposes. The forecasters are similar to the small group researchers in their split origins and publication patterns. Both groups have published in diverse locations, and both have found it necessary to produce bibliographies early in their development.

In the structuralists' case I included those people who were trained by Harrison C. White or who had a specific relationship either with White or with persons trained by him. The structuralists are just beginning to become visible in sociology. Their position is somewhat like that of the ethnomethodologists in 1964: Those who have noticed them see them not as a group but rather as individuals having very specific idiosyncrasies. If the forecasters and the structuralists ultimately succeed, it will probably become evident that, in discussion, I omitted some names of people who will then be considered to be members of these groups.

Both network growth and thickening can be more clearly observed for the ethnomethodologists and the new causal theorists as formal ties replace, or are added to, previous informal ties. Coauthorship and trusted assessor information on these two groups reinforce the assertions of thickening that can be made on the basis of data included in Tables 8.2 and 9.2. For the ethnomethodologists, the network thickening can be very clearly seen. Since the group is small and more isolated, links are much easier to trace completely. Second, I was very fortunate in having the help of several members of this group, who told me the group's history and indicated where to look for public information on group members that I might not otherwise have found. The new causal theorists and the ethnomethodologists constitute the core of contemporary theory. Both groups have moved into the specialty stage and have begun to spread out.

Elite vs. Revolutionary Groups Furthermore, they represent the two different types of the model, the revolutionary and the elite. The difference between a clearly revolutionary (ethnomethodology) and a clearly elite group (new causal theory; the three groups studied in Part Two) is striking in almost every particular. The fundamental difference lies in ethnomethodology's total rejection of standard American sociology's methodology (especially survey research), whereas the new causal theorists sought to build on earlier methods by improving them and using them in a radically different way—to build theory. We might hypothesize that if conflict or exchange theory were suddenly to start attracting groups of students who refrained from totally rejecting standard American sociology, they might also produce elite rather than revolutionary groups.

The new causal theorists are the largest and most successful of the new groups. They are the first sociology group to demonstrate that the rapid shift of professionals to a new research area need not result solely because the work of one person has continued to interest his former students. Of course many of Duncan's students are new causal theorists (as many of Parsons' are structural functionalists). However, the new causal theory group includes others (e.g., Schuessler and Land) who follow the core group's work, although they were not brought into the group through having been, originally, either students or colleagues of one of the leaders. The inclusion of such "outsiders" suggests that the statistical analysis of data was well enough understood throughout the discipline to permit the spread of new ideas simply on the basis of an understanding of regression techniques, without the added commonality of training. As a result, new causal theory differs somewhat from the model in having many more early members and relatively fewer teacher–student relations.

As an elite group, new causal theory's leadership was drawn from among the best standard American sociologists. It developed at highly regarded graduate schools—by the mid-1960s, thanks to earlier expansion, Michigan and Wisconsin had joined Chicago and Harvard as schools having respected graduate programs in sociology. New causal theory attracted many adherents early (at least 58 by the end of the network stage). It has had many successes, and its members have had easy access to publication. As of 1972, this group had not been the target of serious public opposition; instead, persons trained in this perspective have been eagerly hired by many institutions, and the group's leaders continue to be very well thought of in the profession at large.

Several characteristics of the new causal theorist group—multiple clusters, relatively few student–teacher relations, multiple organization leaders, lack of criticism, and accumulation of multiple texts (the first two of which were written by group members)—reinforce our need to recognize that the development pattern proposed in Chapter 2 must be modified somewhat for elite specialties developing within disciplines that have a large number of graduate centers. My suspicion is that, had the expansion of graduate centers (see Chapter 6) occurred before 1946, we might well have seen multiple clusters for standard American sociology and symbolic interactionism. In this regard it should be noted that, over the total cluster–specialty period combined, Columbia outproduced Harvard in number of students graduated, even though the New York location never had very large student groups at any one time. Whether elite specialties following the new causal theory pattern have developed in other disciplines remains to be seen.

Although it also benefited from the expanded number of graduate centers, ethnomethodology, by contrast, is clearly a revolutionary specialty. Since the mid-1960s, traditional sociologists, particularly methodologists, have become alternately outraged and disdainful simply at the mention of ethnomethodology. The group's leadership was trained at respected schools (Cicourel at Cornell; Garfinkel at Harvard; Sacks at Berkeley in the 1960s), but its leaders were long ignored, and its development occurred most strongly at the Santa Barbara campus of the University of California, which has never been accepted as a prestige school. Lacking a consistent training center, the group has always been much smaller than the new causal theory group both in number of persons and in number of strong locations. Ethnomethodology's narrower base suggests that a lack of common training may necessitate the teacher–student basis of revolutionary groups. However, as ethnomethodology expands and adds more linguistic skills, this characteristic may change. Few sociologists have yet learned or seen any need for the linguistic skills that already constitute much of the basis of ethnomethodology. Only those who have already absorbed ethnomethodological ideas understand this requirement; thus, unlike new causal theory, ethnomethodology has had no large body of untapped skill from which to draw personnel. Only time will tell whether, in the specialty stage, the ethnomethodologists will catch up numerically with the new causal theorists.

When Models Fail   Data on the radical-criticals do not fit the model at all. One of their intellectual and social sources is European. Furthermore, since they have recruited and published through both academic and non-academic sources, they have not been bound by the constraints that tend to limit early growth and thus to define an intellectual group. Radical-criticals have been very successful as a group that has concentrated on a limited set of topics (e.g., a controlling elite and its class interests; the composition of the working class; imperialism and imperialistic war).

Thus far, however, they have done only limited kinds of research and, unlike the other contemporary groups, they have not concentrated fundamentally on a new way to do theory.

"Piling on" Groups function as a mechanism for focusing the attention of several trained persons on a set of problems. This "piling on," as we might call it, is a characteristic of science. The radical-critical group reminds us that piling on can occur through other mechanisms—in this case, the floating seminar, combined with temporary mobilizations in response to crisis situations. Other possible mechanisms are conceivable (e.g., the national laboratory pattern used in physics). The piling-on mechanism of science is not as effective in sociology as it is elsewhere in science for at least three reasons: (1) the literature is disorganized and slow, (2) the profession is small with few active training centers, and (3) only recently have there been enough students to make possible the existence of multiple, concurrent "piles."

Regardless of the specific area involved, the piling-on mechanism leaves us with the problem of determining who is really in a group. In this regard we must remember that the perceptions of members are neither singular nor determining of membership—not singular in that every person in a group has not been polled on group membership; not determining because, for groups in which such polling has been done, it is clear that very different "membership" lists result from: (1) differing perceptions of events, (2) tricks of memory and recall, and (3) position-controlled differences in interpretation. Furthermore, as any historian can testify, the problem of ascertaining with accuracy who was where and when, and what each party at a gathering said, is very difficult.

The Data and Their Effects Each data chapter in this book is based on a reconstruction of reality from public, documentary data on the members and events of the group being considered. The connections that exist between group members are as careful as can be created. There is room for argument in only two directions: (1) that the relations described were not the most significant ones and that, in fact, other relationships were more important to theory development; or (2) that the impacts of the relations described differed from those proposed for it. It is *not* important that we know the history of the developments. Whitehead (cited in Merton, 1968a: 1) once remarked that a science that hesitates to forget its forefathers is lost; Derek Price expressed the same concept in a less elegant phrase—"packing down" science (Price, 1965). One need not recapitulate the history of physics to understand the second law of thermodynamics. This history is interesting and strongly felt by those involved, but it is not essential to an understanding of thermodynamics. Likewise, the notion of "revolution" permits us to move ahead without a feeling of loss for not having probed a development's history; in short, the process of group formation has become an important way of "forgetting history."

This assertion is not likely to be popular. Every professor has the feeling that he was trained in the "right way" and that his students should learn in much the same way. For example, there are many professors now who believe that the hand manipulation of statistical computations has some magic property. They seem to believe that the particular setup of statistical problems for hand calculation permits one to understand such calculations. Others believe that a person can learn just as much about, say, correlation coefficients, from a computer process and, having learned what he needs to know, spend his time studying questions of interpretation and trying multiple approaches, rather than doing lengthy calculations.

The process of forgetting works as follows. A new group surfaces. Its research is of interest to me. I study that research. Only if I am close to the group do I learn the background, and even then I will not learn it all. From the viewpoint of the group, my knowledge is shallow. From my perspective, however, I understand both the group's research and, more important, how it relates to my specific interests. Our knowledge is thus of two distinctly different kinds.

This contrast between knowledge per se and knowledge as a group member forces us to consider the effects of environment. Not long ago a prominent sociologist and I were discussing his time as a graduate student at a major university. The remark was made that similar training turned out different people. He noted that his school had seemed to be full of symbolic interactionists, although if a census had been taken there, it would have been clear that symbolic interactionists hardly constituted a majority of the faculty. Given roughly the same training he had, he went on, a classmate of his later became a well-known symbolic interactionist, but my informant did not. The gist of his reminiscence was that his friend had "caught the faith" and he hadn't. This same effect was noted earlier with respect to Robert Bellah and Harold Garfinkel—both trained by Talcott Parsons (see Table 3.2): Bellah became a structural functionalist, whereas Garfinkel started ethnomethodology.

Group boundaries are not clear. To argue that any individual either is (or is not) a new causalist (or a structuralist or an ethnomethodologist) and nothing else is non-sense. Each person has many ties to others. We can speak of a coherent group, however, if many of those ties thicken into cluster that virtually cuts off its members from others in the parent discipline, such that the members become a separate collectivity, generating new members through training to maintain itself. Ethnomethodology behaved in precisely that fashion for a while; it is still doing so to a degree, although there are good indications (see Chapter 8) that the group is now spreading too widely to maintain itself as a closed group. New causal theory behaved similarly, but in several locations. Therefore, assertions of group membership for ethnomethodologists and new causal theorists can be made with some assurance. To date, structuralists have not behaved this way. The present criterion for identifying a person as a structuralist is assertion of (1) informal connections through social ties that do not necessarily bind and (2) a similarity in research style. (Clearly similarities in research style must be postulated in a somewhat fuzzy manner.) The same twin statements must also be made for the social forecasters.

Ethnomethodologists and new causalists do work that shows distinct similarity to that of other persons in their respective groups, as well as clear social ties. In that sense we say that these sociologists constitute distinct social categories (e.g., new causal theorists, ethnomethodologists). Individually, though, I should repeat that many group members have other interests. Duncan, as we know, has also done forecasting and follows structuralist work with some interest. He himself sees his work from its beginning as a continuity (Duncan, 1972). When we move to this level, however, we are talking about individual behavior rather than *patterns of social behavior* (and it is these patterns that are the proper concern of sociology). There is thus no necessary contradiction between Duncan's perception of continuity and my perception of two distinct social groups to which he has made substantial contributions.

STAGE-SPECIFIC VARIATIONS

Normal The normal stage shows three deviations from the model (see Table 12.1). Both the ethnomethodologists and the structuralists produced program statements during the normal stage. The ethnomethodologists' statement was quite late (Garfinkel, 1956), but that of the structuralists (White, 1963b) appeared very early in the normal stage. The ethnomethodologists' program statement is understandable when we note that that group has been guided not by one but by several such statements, each appearing during a different stage. The structuralists' early program statement has no readily visible explanation.

Network The exceptions during the network stage are all produced by the forecasters. Although lacking an intellectual leader, a training center, and recognized successes, the group has a program statement. Secondary and critical work has also been published. I examined the reasons for these anomalies in Chapter 7. The reasons are adequate and quite specific to the group's unusual status as both important to government and highly visible through its activity in nonacademic channels.

Cluster The only variations are those noted for new causal theory with respect to its elite status.

Specialty The only deviation from the model during the specialty stage is that the intellectual leaders have continued to work within the specialties they founded. For sociology, then, the evidence is overwhelmingly against the leaders' leaving their fields for greener pastures once their chosen specialty has been established.

At this point we can conclude that social support for intellectual developments is absolutely necessary if these developments are to prosper. That support can come from extraordinary external circumstances (as it does with the radicals) or, in the present academic situation, it can come from the social and intellectual characteristics listed in Table 12.1. Since nonacademic support is the exception rather than the rule, the presence of the model's properties and the operation of its processes seem to be necessary if a group is to produce significant change in its parent discipline's acceptable intellectual discourse. Transition points in the stages may not always be clear, but the overall progression is quite recognizable. Finally, specific manifestations for elite specialties will differ from those for the revolutionary case from which the model was initially developed.

Except for ethnomethodology, the contemporary theory groups show some of the same sharing of personnel (e.g., Duncan and J. A. Davis) as did the early groups. Ethnomethodology and structuralism have been found to be quite similar conceptually by some structuralists (White and Mullins). Lindsey Churchill has continued his interest in problems of data analysis and new causal theory (see his review of Hannan's book in *Contemporary Sociology*, 1972). The forecasters, except for their link to new causal theory, seem to be less integrated intellectually into whatever will eventually prove to be sociology's new mainstream. The radicals have recruited persons from various backgrounds, but I have found no recent examples of persons who are as well accepted in two or more groups as are Duncan and Homans, for example. (The late C. Wright Mills had connections both to symbolic interactionism and radical-critical thought.)

In this book I have established that:

1. If we examine data on people who are doing similar work, social connections usually appear. (A possible exception is represented by Kenneth Land and his new causal theory work.)
2. The social connections will include some people who were trained prior to a theory's developments, either by one person or by a small group of persons, and their later students. After the first group of persons (elite groups excepted), there will be very few or no additions other than students.

3. At first the work of a forming group will be much the same as that of researchers in the parent discipline, but differences will grow slowly over time. To the insider, the change will appear as a process of gradual evolution. To the outsider, and that is most of us most of the time, the new development will land squawking on our desks with a name tag on its neck. We will exclaim "revolutionary development!" without knowing any of the history of its development (nor, as I have noted, is it important that we do).
4. The details of the model vary from that of the physical and biological sciences, largely because of sociology's disorganized publication system.
5. Institutional forms are not fixed. The ethnomethodologists used a moving, single program at several graduate training centers in southern California. The new causal theorists had three cluster locations, plus an additional research center.
6. The social processes of science must be manipulated by someone to produce the conditions necessary for group growth. This necessity is contrary to the presumed norms of science (Merton, 1968b, 1968c), but it is necessary for scientific development.
7. There is an orderly sequence of events, although the order requires institutional arrangements to maintain it. Given different institutional arrangements (e.g., a different university system), other combinations of events might happen. The spacing and the length of events are also dependent on a group's competition situation and the degree to which that group can be mobilized to concentrate on an activity. If each new entrant must be specially trained, a group will grow slowly; if basic training is evenly scattered across the discipline, a group will grow quickly, given the necessary social and intellectual properties.

When we compare the five contemporary groups with those discussed in Part Two, one important difference becomes very clear: Early sociology conceived and organized its theory and its methodology separately; later that theory was tried in specific content areas (e.g., sociology of religion, sociology of knowledge). Furthermore (as noted in Chapter 4), standard American sociology and symbolic interactionism concentrated on different content areas. Contemporary theory, by contrast, has organized itself mainly around *how* theory is to be done; thus far, the theory itself has not been separable from methodology and content. Ethnomethodology has been used in fertility studies (Cicourel, 1967) that would have been considered demography if done by a standard American sociologist, in studies of schools (Cicourel et al., forthcoming) that formerly would have been classed as "sociology of education," in jury studies (Garfinkel, 1967) that once would have been called sociology of law, as well as in studies of small groups (Shumsky, 1971), formerly small group research. As a result, some have objected that new causal theory is not theory because it has been applied widely to studies of education (Sewell's Wisconsin studies), mobility and stratification (Blau and Duncan,

1967), and aspiration, (Rehberg et al., 1970), and because it seems to be quite applicable to a range of other problems when the data are available.

A review of earlier chapters will convince the reader that forecasting and structuralism have applied their theories to numerous specific, substantive problems. They also have concentrated on ways to *do* theory. These areas are less developed, but substantive diversity is the rule. For example, a key forecasting book edited by Sheldon and Moore (1968) has chapters on mobility, science, the family, and so on. Structuralist theory has been used for mobility studies (White, 1970a) and deviance research (Lee, 1969) as well as for sociology of knowledge studies (e.g., this book).

Inevitably, this reorganization has caused some sociologists to wonder if there is anything called "theory" any more, while others are deciding that "theory" is more important than "methods." Stehr and Larson (1972), counting the areas of specialization listed in the 1959 and 1970 ASA directories, found that among sociologists, theory had moved from fifth rank in 1959 to third rank in 1970. Methods and statistics retained their place as the second largest specialty, and social psychology was ranked number one.

When perceived from the Olympian heights of the sociologist of knowledge, sociological theory has a great deal of continuity. Ideas have developed over time, and although some research (e.g., Sorokin's, 1928, 1941; and Mannheim's, 1946, 1952) has long awaited development, that development seems eminent. The skein of ideas has not been broken in the recent past. But as I noted earlier, the effect of forgetting is to concentrate a group on work to be done in the present and future. Certainly that effect allows for the possibility of repeating earlier work; but even that repetition can be useful, since the purpose for which it is done often differs entirely from the original aim. Most important, the perceived continuity is not incompatible with the perceived, specific histories of these groups.

OTHER MODELS FOR SCIENTIFIC DEVELOPMENT

The major alternative conceptualizations of intellectual development in sociology problems are:

1. Shils' (1970) institutionalization view.
2. Gouldner's intellectual history (1965; 1970; when tradition and conceptualization begin to move away from one another, a crisis occurs).

3. Friedrichs' (1970) analysis of sociology in terms of a modification of Kuhn's (1962) conception of paradigm.

Each of these conceptualizations contains some truth. The problem is to sort out what the authors have said, what they have implied, and how both statements and implications apply to the findings reported in this book.

In terms of time and persons, Robert K. Merton's career symbolizes the past 35 years of most sociology. As Nelson (1972) notes, Merton published both "Science, Technology and Society in Seventeenth Century England" and "Social Structure and Anomie" in 1938. In Nelson's (1972: 231) poetic language:

> The suggestion of the present review is that the road Merton was to take [following "Social Structure"] was to become the high road of American sociology and the one he was to visit only occasionally was to undergo very great neglect. . . . The "road less traveled by" was the road which led toward the comparative historical sociology of sociocultural process in the spirit of Max Weber, Alfred Weber, Mauss, Durkheim. . . .

The questions that each of these four theories (Shils', Gouldner's, Friedrichs' and mine) must answer are: Why were specific choices made, not just by individuals but by most of the professionals? Is a shift occurring now? What is the shape of the future? The first three theories are examined in this section; mine was examined earlier and is considered again in the final section of this chapter.

SHILS

Shils' emphasis is on the central importance of institutionalization, a contention that is well supported by his short but excellent case studies of the difference between Mannheim and Horkheimer and on the failure of sociology to institutionalize in France and England, as well as his "insider's" discussion of the University of Chicago. He remarks (1970: 777):

> Institutionalization is not a guarantee of truthfulness; it only renders more probable the consolidation, elaboration and diffusion of a set of ideas. It is not the sole determinant of the acceptance or diffusion of ideas. Intellectual persuasiveness, appropriateness to "interesting" problems, correspondence with certain prior dispositions and patterns of thought of the potential recipient are also very significant. Institutionalization serves however to make ideas more available to potential recipients, it renders possible concentration of effort on them, it fosters interaction about them, and it aids their communication.

The centrality of institutions, a social factor, makes it necessary for Shils to seek and find a dialectic diversity in the intellectual traditions.

Sociology is both coherent as a set of traditional problems and very diverse, incorporating as substantive traditions both (1) traditions regarding procedure (Shils, 1970: 806) and (2) external intellectual traditions, such as Freudian psychology, comparative religious studies, economic analysis, animal and plant ecology, cybernetics and others (Shils, 1970: 804–805). Shils summarizes the complexity of tradition roughly as follows: The exogenous influences have affected the substantive areas but not the vague and ambiguous analytical framework of sociology, which has experienced relatively little differentiation (paraphrase of Shils, 1970: 810).

Shils' undeveloped theory of how social groupings interact with institutionalization fails to consider how the impact of students affects science and why the Chicago school's disorganization did not push Sorokin, MacIver, or Becker into prominence instead of or in addition to Parsons. This weakness at the subinstitutional level also makes Shils' summary of traditions strangely dated for a document published in this decade. For as we have insisted in the last five chapters, it is precisely the analytic framework that has undergone the most profound changes during the past few years.

GOULDNER

The best early research on the subject of social theory development may be Alvin W. Gouldner's *Enter Plato* (1965). In that book the author clearly grasped a major element in group development: the necessity for at least two persons to share a viewpoint and, hence, to support a development. What he fails to note, however, is that even two persons cannot necessarily protect themselves against the failure rate for new developments in science. In pointing out the necessity for support, then, his concern is for the binary student–teacher relation rather than for the exchange of ideas among three or more persons.

Gouldner's failure is the mirror image of Shils'. Gouldner understands that basic changes have occurred. Furthermore, he sees clearly that events external to the institutional framework of sociology have had a substantial effect, although he is ambiguous about how this effect operates. He also understands the social psychological structure of persons that drives theorists to seek students to support their new ideas, yet he lacks an appreciation of the discipline's institutional structure.

Part of the reason for Gouldner's failure to see that phenomenon may be that his subjects, Socrates and Plato, lacked the institutional framework which creates the temptation of multiple, and therefore relatively diffuse, short-lived relationships focused on intellectual problems. Modern science presents an enormous quantity of research problems, and the competent researcher is free to work on anything that interests him. Such a situation can spread commitment so thin that no concentrated research ever gets done.

Gouldner also failed to realize that students must be strongly encouraged into research interests and jobs, and not necessarily on grounds of merit. Groups manipulate situations to provide positions, support, and preference for friends. The history of the Phage Group, particularly as told by James D. Watson in *The Double Helix* (1968), is very instructive on this subject.

In 1970 Gouldner published *The Coming Crisis of Western Sociology*. In this work he departs from the insights that made *Enter Plato* such an excellent book. Instead, he seems to have decided that society is the major force in changing sociology. He depicts sociology as both shaped and driven by society, possessing little of its own motivation or structure. In doing so, the author weakens his earlier argument and creates a caricature. In Gouldner's initial statements and in the counterattack by Lipset and Ladd (1972), it appears that both parties want to prove that the political inclinations of persons and the social control of institutions (in particular, of journals and of society) can explain the intellectual development of the discipline. The argument between them revolves around whether structural functionalists controlled the journals and the ASA (Gouldner's assertion) or whether these were controlled by a theoretically pluralistic group (according to Lipset and Ladd). The case rests unproved in that Lipset and Ladd, even though naming names, do not show how the persons listed differ from structural functionalists, and Gouldner offers no data on which a decision might be reached. Even if a decision could be made, the effects of that "control" on the content of the discipline would still need to be demonstrated.

FRIEDRICHS

The coincident publication in 1970 of Friedrichs' *A Sociology of Sociology* with Gouldner's *The Coming Crisis* and Shils' essay typifies the sort of data discussed by Friedrichs. His approach is almost totally intellectual, and he gives little attention to the social aspects of intellectual growth. To him, the issues are what people said and how those statements fit into a total intellectual tradition. Friedrichs (following Kuhn, 1962) argues that sociology has had a paradigm—namely, structural functionalism—and that that paradigm is now in an intellectual crisis. He then examines other parts of sociology as possible sources of a new paradigm.

Friedrichs' importance is as a collector of themes from which a new paradigm of social analysis might be built. He includes very little social dynamic in his theory, depending largely on the intellectual. His intellectual analysis is interesting, but it does not provide (as Kuhn does not) an explanation for how new theory can be built.

THE SHAPE OF
THE FUTURE

The test of any theory, naturally, is how well it predicts future events, given explicit assumptions, certain facts about the past, and statements about the way those facts relate. Hence writing Part Two was a relatively unrisky venture: All the groups studied were part of the past; I was not required to make predictions about the future, only to explain what had happened. In Part Three, however, I examined groups that have not completed the developmental sequence; the model has been used to explain events in the immediate past (the radical-critical group excepted). Now I feel required to put my hypotheses to the iron test and predict, from what I already know, the shape of the future.

The future is always more complicated than we can imagine. The possibilities and the main lines can be estimated if we have a very good theory and if "all other things" are more or less equal. But what will sociology look like in 20 years? First we must respond to the quality of students in the 1970s: They are both more educated and less accepting than even the students of my generation (1963–1966). Second, the non-sociological academic world may not remain as it is. In fact, it is rather unlikely that sociology will remain well insulated, either from other disciplines or from the outside world. There is presently some instability in the whole institutional structure of the social sciences. Anthropology, linguistics, and geography do not seem to me to be either large enough or stable enough to maintain independent existences. The disagreements within sociology are obvious, and political science appears to be similarly afflicted. The failure of the social relations experiment at Harvard and the lack of stable reformulations suggest that the fundamental conditions underlying the splits in various disciplines could force the total reorganization of the social sciences in the near future.

A further consideration is that the number of Ph.D. degrees granted in sociology has changed notably. From 1920 to 1950, 1000 Ph.D.'s were granted in sociology. In 1970 and 1971, 1100 Ph.D.'s were granted (NAS, 1972). Since the absolute numbers are increasing (even if there were no increase in rate), that increase will make money (for educational centers and research support) a major limitation on future theory group development. (If the resource situation eases at all, however, we should expect a number of even newer contemporary groups to appear. In addition, the older groups should then be able to support somewhat greater separateness.) A further implication of growth is that, at present rates, in just ten years we will have more than doubled the present number of sociologists ($10 \times 500 = 5000$). This larger profession should require a substantially increased number of journals and publications.

There are also other likely changes whose effects will be seen. The number of sociologists with some quantitative skills will increase, and capabilities of the very skilled should increase also (although their relative number may not). This probability does not necessarily mean that there will be an increase in the number of mathematical statisticians in sociology; however, there should be an increase in the number of sociologists with mathematical skills. This increase should make statistics and mathematics ordinary "tools of the trade." There will also be more sociologists in nonacademic jobs. We have noted an increase in nonacademic jobs over the past few years, and I see no decline in that trend (see Smelser and Davis, 1968). The increased quantity of the literature and the development of searching devices such as the Science Citation Index (SCI) raise the possibility that the literature may become more current and, hence, more responsive to change. The sociology literature will thus become more like that in the natural sciences.

The sum of these trends suggests a larger, more diversified field, characterized by practitioners able to use a broader range of techniques and more interesting problems. From the viewpoint of sociological theory, the future will be very much more complicated than the past. Given these qualifications to protect myself, let me proceed. I have telegraphed my punches somewhat by doing a bit of evaluation at the conclusion of each preceding chapter. In general, unlike standard American sociology and symbolic interactionism, the groups considered (the radicals excepted) have developed with a simultaneous concern for substantive research, theory, and methods. Although the development of specific methodological concerns within the new causal theorists, for example, is possible, my feeling now is that these groups will continue to be better integrated than were the earlier groups.

With respect to the forecasters, I noted that the group may already have died. Given the group's present lack of intellectual and organizational leadership and training centers plus the recent shift of persons such as Eleanor Sheldon into jobs that effectively move them away from forecasting research, I expect the dissolution of whatever remains of the group. Its problems and technology will probably be incorporated into the work of the new causal theorists. I also expect that the most important person in effecting that incorporation will be O. D. Duncan, who is active and respected by researchers in both areas.

The forecasters in general are scattered; they are held together mainly by their differences from other parts of their various disciplines, both in terms of group origin and with respect to the federal government's need for their projections. If a series of accurate predictive exercises were to be successfully developed and exploited by someone, that success might attract a group relatively quickly. Since the forecasters' basic skills and concerns are held by many other sociologists, a mobilization of this group would probably be in the elite pattern. As long as the forecasters' concerns are kept alive by some group, and as long as they continue to be important to government policies, radical-critical sociology should also continue to be important simply because its practitioners will feel compelled to both active and academic response. Just as the radical-criticals have thus far kept themselves largely separate from mainline sociology, however, I expect them to continue to retain their distance. Almost by definition, if they begin to synthesize with another group, radical-critical sociology will cease to exist, not only as a group but as an intellectual entity.

For the radical-criticals, the major question is whether that group can coalesce in a setting that is principally academic. The closing off of the radicals' primary nonacademic recruitment source in the recent past (due to the relative inaction of the Movement over the past few years) and the maturing of radicals and criticals within the academic system have made them eligible to control resources and to support students in a more traditional academic fashion. Since this "reformed" group would have to build from its present basis in Marxism (including all the various interpretations of Marx) as well as on empirical research, its intellectual output might be a very powerful and interesting combination of its sources. The possibility of a fusion between humanistic Marxism and some parts of ethnomethodology, based on similar phenomenological approaches to society, has been mentioned. Such a fusion would be limited, by strong differences in philosophical focus, but it might be temporarily fruitful.

New causal theory has already become quite strong within sociology, and I expect it to remain strong. Thanks to its improved theory construction techniques and methods for reducing error, effects of bias, and so on, I expect this group eventually to be able to combine its insights with those of the ethnomethodologists in improving survey research. In addition, some new causal theorists have been using not survey approaches but the unobtrusive data that is often preferred by structuralists. Johnson and Cutright (1973) demonstrate the use of largely unobtrusive data within a new causal theory approach. I would expect, eventually, that the interest in unobtrusive data will draw structuralists and some new causal theorists together, for the purpose of trying to combine their approaches. I think it quite likely that the new causal theory group will become the new "traditional" sociologists, as the skills involved in their work (e.g., path analysis) become as routine as the obligatory footnote to Merton and the use of "middle-range theories" were to structural functionalism.

I expect the ethnomethodologists to succeed the symbolic interactionists as the social psychologists of the new sociology. I further expect the ethnomethodologists' next group of research publications to make important theoretical contributions to sociology and that these new concepts will make ethnomethodology highly attractive to many who have thus far ignored it. I also expect, over the next decade or so, to see the ethnomethodologists' insights relative to valid interviewing (see Mehan, 1973) gradually incorporated into survey research. That incorporation will find researchers taking variety in interviewers and interviewing situations into account as an important variable for sociological analysis.

The ethnomethodologists have the potential for developing into an alternative discipline, which would not be "sociology" but perhaps "ethnoscience," in combination with parts of anthropology and linguistics. This possibility will become more likely if ethnomethodologists' future contributions to sociology are rejected simply on the basis of continuing hostility, and without consideration of their merits. This group's introduction of an entirely new set of skills into sociology, as well as the possible reintroduction of those skills (combined with a sociological perspective) into linguistics and anthropology, make ethnomethodology a very strong contender as an alternative to new causal theory.

The structuralists, like the forecasters, have barely begun. They are all future. They may develop independently of the other groups, particularly if they have more immediate successes (or the strongly held feeling of success) in areas on which structural research is beginning to focus. There is also the possibility that this group, or parts of it, will join with others. I have already mentioned the potential for joint interest of both structuralists and new causal theorists in unobtrusive data.

In addition, there is an unquestionable parallel between at least the linguistic ethnomethodologists and the structuralists. Both have judged the work of Chomsky to be important, and both have been constructing theory on the basis of the same linguistic metaphors. The difference thus far is that the ethnomethodologists have been explicitly social psychological, whereas the structuralists have explicitly avoided that aspect. Based on my reading and my conversation with ethnomethodologists, however, it seems to me that there may be great promise in the merging of these two perspectives.

The ultimate theoretical possibility—a basic combination of structuralism with the improved sociology which might result from the combined attack of ethnomethodology and new causal theory on old problems—could produce a very strong new synthesis. Such a synthesis would be based on ways to do theory regardless of the substantive area involved, and it could easily incorporate the work that is presently central to both the forecasters and the radical-criticals.

Finally, if such a synthesis ultimately results, it will last only until research support becomes readily available again and that support begins to underwrite the clustering and research of even newer theory groups.

BIBLIOGRAPHY

Baltzell, E. Digby.
  1972 "Epilogue: to be a Phoenix—reflections on two noisy ages of prose."
        American Journal of Sociology 78 (July): 202–220.
Bottomore, T. B.
  1972 "Introduction." *American Journal of Sociology* 78 (July): 1–8.
Churchill, Lindsey.
  1972 "A review of *Problems of Aggregation and Disaggregration in Socio-
        logical Research.*" *Contemporary Sociology* 1 (July): 321–322.
Duncan, O. D.
  1972 Personal communication (June).
Gouldner, Alvin W.
  1965 *Enter Plato: Classical Greece and the Origins of Social Theory.* New
        York: Basic Books.
  1970 *The Coming Crisis of Western Sociology.* New York: Basic Books.
Friedrichs, Robert W.
  1970 *A Sociology of Sociology.* New York: Free Press.
Johnson, David R., and Phillips Cutright.
  1973 "Problems in the analysis of Latin American illegitimacy." In
        Michael Armer and Allen D. Grimshaw (eds.), *Comparative Social
        Research: Methodological Problems and Strategies.* New York: Wi-
        ley–Interscience.
Kuhn, Thomas S.
  1962 *The Structure of Scientific Revolutions.* Chicago: University of Chi-
        cago Press.
Lipset, Seymour M., and Everett C. Ladd, Jr.
  1972 "The politics of American sociologists." *American Journal of Sociology*
        78 (July): 67–104.
Mannheim, Karl.
  1946 *Ideology and Utopia.* New York: Harcourt Brace Jovanovich.
  1952 *Essays on the Sociology of Knowledge.* Edited by Paul Kecskemeti.
        London: Routledge & Kegan Paul.
Mehan, Hugh.
  1973 "Assessing children's language-using abilities: methodological and
        cross-cultural implications." In Michael Armer and Allen D. Grim-
        shaw (eds.), *Comparative Social Research: Methodological Prob-
        lems and Strategies.* New York: Wiley–Interscience.
Merton, Robert K.
  1938 "Science, technology and society in seventeenth century England."
        Osiris 4 (Part II): 360–632.
  1968a *Social Theory and Social Structure*, rev. ed. New York: Free Press.
  1968b "Science and the social order." Pp. 591–603 in *Social Theory and
        Social Structure*, rev. ed. New York: Free Press.
  1968c "Science and democratic social structure." Pp. 604–615 in *Social
        Theory and Social Structure*, rev. ed. New York: Free Press.
  1968d "Social structure and anomie." Pp. 185–214 in *Social Theory and
        Social Structure*, rev. ed. New York: Free Press.

National Academy of Science.
    1972   *Summary Report 1971: Doctorate Recipients from United States Universities.* Washington, D.C.: National Research Council.
Nelson, Benjamin.
    1972   "Review essay of Robert K. Merton, *Science, Technology and Society in Seventeenth Century England.*" *American Sociological Review* 78 (July): 223–231.
Price, Derek J. de S.
    1965   "Networks of scientific papers." *Science* 149 (3683, July 30): 510–515.
Shils, Edward A.
    1970   "Tradition, ecology and institution in the history of sociology." *Daedalus: The Making of Modern Science: Biographical Studies* 99 (Fall): 760–825.
Smelser, Neil J., and James A. Davis (eds.).
    1969   *Sociology.* Englewood Cliffs, N.J.: Prentice-Hall.
Sorokin, Pitirim A.
    1928   *Contemporary Sociological Theories.* New York: Harper & Row.
    1941   *Social and Cultural Dynamics.* New York: American Book Co.
Stehr, Nico, and Lyle E. Larson.
    1972   "The rise and decline of areas of specialization." *American Sociologist* 7 (August): 3, 5–6.
Watson, James D.
    1968   *The Double Helix.* New York: Atheneum.
Webb, Eugene J., Donald T. Campbell, Richard D. Schwartz, and Lee Sechrest.
    1966   *Unobtrusive Measures: Nonreactive Research in the Social Sciences.* Chicago: Rand McNally.

METHODOLOGICAL APPENDIX

Several methodological questions need to be answered. First, how did I select groups to investigate? Are there other groups, and how would one find a group to work with? Second, what data were collected, and how were they used?

In the beginning (October, 1970) was an itch. Had I realized that it would ultimately take two years and more than 600 typed pages to scratch it thoroughly, I might have borne the discomfort. I had finally finished a paper on the Phage Group (Mullins, 1972) and was beginning to see the outlines of a more general model of group growth and development (Griffith and Mullins, 1972). The itch was: Would the model explain intellectual development in the social sciences? I chose sociology because I am a sociologist; this area has a certain intrinsic interest for me.

The model's central concept is that major developments in an area require not only intellectual content but social support which must be generated in a specific way. The material researched was the American academic context of sociology from the 1930s to the present. Some differences between sociology and physical science groups were found, but these were not sufficient to discredit the model.

ABOUT GROUP SELECTION

I selected groups by a process of inventory. I read recent articles and books, talked to many sociologists, and surveyed the range of articles and books included in the major sociological journals (*American Journal of Sociology, American Sociological Review*, and *Social Forces*) and their book review sections. My basic question in this process was: What different kinds of theory are implicit in these works?

The process of finding a group can be demonstrated with the way in which I discovered the standard American sociologists. I started off with

Wallace (1969), *Sociology Today* (Merton et al., 1959), and *American Sociology* (Parsons, 1968). In each case I took the list of authors of papers. Then I added to that list: (1) those on Parsons' list of students (Table 3.2) who were on the faculties of major institutions (such data can be found in the ASA *Directories* for various years) and (2) those publishing six or more papers in the *ASR* and *AJS* over the period 1935–1965 or having three books reviewed during the same period (information contained in the *AJS* and *ASR Indexes*; see Chapter 3 for full references on standard American sociology). I removed from this provisional list anyone who had one or no publications and anyone who had not been a faculty member at one of the major schools at some time during the 1935–1970 period. The large group remaining probably includes the core persons in the development of standard American sociology. The other two early groups were similarly determined.

The reasons for each group's selection are stated at the beginning of each chapter. In addition to their intrinsic importance as theory groups, careful study of the early groups was necessary to lay a foundation for the study of contemporary groups. In determining contemporary groups, I looked first for differences between standard American sociology and what was being published during the late 1960s and early 1970s. The radicals were easy to find, although the critical group was more hidden in the standard literature. The ethnomethodologists were an unmistakable something by 1971, and the new causal theory group had already produced a coherent literature that was clearly different from previous research, particularly with respect to stratification research.

I was part of the structuralist group and felt that it merited inclusion both for intellectual reasons (its contribution to the literature) and for social reasons (as part of the group I know something about its social structure). The forecasters gradually appeared as I did research on people who were using management techniques (e.g., program budgeting) and/or technological forecasting techniques. I examined conflict theory and exchange theory, but both proved, as of the early 1970s, to be modest variants from standard American sociology. The eight groups finally chosen provided a respectable range of groups in different stages of development as well as involvement in research which, by publication measures at least, accounts for most of the variety in sociological theory. For all chapters except Chapter 3, the sources for group membership selection are listed in the basic data tables.

The general group-finding process is not particularly difficult. If you find a new perspective showing up in a series of papers or books, examine the authors' backgrounds. If they seem totally unconnected, investigate them more deeply, because you may have found a most interesting case. Try a survey of the field that appears to be involved; define that field as broadly as is necessary. Make determinations—by expert judges, content analysis, or your own estimation—of the differences in research style noticeable between that kind of work and other kinds; look also for differences within the work. Once a group of work has been defined and researched, isolate the authors of that work and examine their careers. Look particularly for data on training, early jobs, participation in major research projects, and coauthorships. These are crucial events in determining later work.

If you start systematically through the literature of a discipline as defined by the boundaries of a journal, abstract service, or bibliography, you will find many groups (depending on which criteria you select). For example, the graduates of a particular school may number in the hundreds over a particular decade (see Chapter 6). Theory categorized under the same topic in subject listings may seem to fall into several groups. A secondary source (e.g., McGrath and Altman, 1966) may suggest a major division. Or an informant may give you some clues.

In any case, the group defined by any *one* method alone is rarely the group of interest. For example, had I continued to follow out the network of coauthors in Chapter 3 to its fullest, I would eventually have included almost all the groups in the book, with the exception of the ethnomethodologists and the structuralists. To report that network as a group would have been insane. In the same way, the list of students mentioned by Talcott Parsons, although interesting in its own right, does not include all major standard American sociologists. In short, the use of any single source or technique provides a bounded group; my process requires overlapping and isolating a subset of those bounded groups through triangulation of methods.

This procedure follows from the theory discussed in Chapter 2. Of the major relations identified by that theory (teacher–student relations, colleagueships, trusted assessorship, and communication), only the first two can be observed. The paucity of public data on trusted assessors was demonstrated in Chapters 8 and 9. Since the actual process by which social conditions influence intellectual development is hidden, we can observe only indicators, and these are affected by the way in which a group chooses to work. For example, if a group generally does not use acknowledgment footnotes (see Chapter 11), such material is not available for use as data. Likewise, if coauthorship rarely occurs (e.g., see Chapter 4), we can only describe that rarity, note its possible effects, and go on.

ABOUT DATA COLLECTION

All the groups presented data-gathering problems. Ethnomethodologists, for example, generally do not join the ASA; thus they do not appear in its *Directories*. I therefore gathered degree and job data largely through interviews and descriptions of authors included with many ethnomethodological books and papers. The forecasters' group (Chapter 7) includes many persons who are listed as members of one or another committee but who are not sociologists or, as far as I can see, participants in events or research other than the specific committee from which I chose them.

The kinds of data collected depend on the types of questions you have about groups. I started with these questions:

1. What kind of theory does a particular group do?
   (a) What are its main topics?
   (b) How is analysis done?
   (c) What prior authors are cited in papers, and why?
2. What kinds of social arrangements (roughly) characterize the theory's practitioners?
   (a) Who is a student of whom?
   (b) Who is a colleague of whom?
   (c) Who has done research with whom, and did this work leave traces in coauthorships, acknowledgments, or published memoirs?
3. What is the theory's time span?
   (a) When does it seem to have begun?
   (b) When does the theory group include its maximum number of people?
   (c) During what time span is the most important work done?
   (d) When does the group's membership begin to decline?

True coauthorships, resulting from joint research (not the more causal coeditorships or joint authorship relations in which each author does part of a book), are the best kind of indicator. They represent extended, detailed interaction in which two people sort out assumptions, ideas, and language. Such a relationship has a profound effect on the work eventually published.

This procedure produced a list of persons. My next task was to determine whether it was a group. First I gathered some data sources, at least five or six per group (including interviews, books, article lists, readers, memoirs, citation lists, etc.). Starting with what seemed to be the largest source, I made a list of persons named. Then I checked their career locations. If this check showed a noticeable group of training locations, a coherent group might be involved. I then checked the second source. If a coherent group was involved, the list generally expanded somewhat, but not by as much as 100 percent. Furthermore, each succeeding pass through the procedure produced: (1) a greater and greater overlapping of persons and (2) a distinct focus on a few locations as training and research centers. As sociology matures—that is, as more people enter the area and theory becomes more clearly defined—we can expect to use other sources (e.g., citation indexes or *American Men of Science* listings of specialties) as basic records from which small coherent groups can be discovered and analyzed.

Insofar as information was available, I systematically collected five types of data for all people in each group:

1. Job Information.
   Job information (shown in basic data tables) was taken from the following sources:
   AJS *Cumulative Index to the AJS* (1966, 1971)
   ASA *Directories* (1959, 1963, 1967, 1970). The 1959 *Directory* was particularly useful because it published career summaries for the years prior to 1959.
   ASA *Guide to Graduate Departments* (1965, 1969, 1971).
   ASA *Index to ASR*, vols. 1–25 and 26–30.
   Listings of job locations on papers, in books, and so on.
2. Degree Information.
   Same sources, plus references to dissertations in other papers and in *Dissertation Abstracts*.
3. Authorship and Coauthorship Information.
   Authorship and coauthorship information are from the *AJS Index*, the *ASR Index*, and books used as sources for specific groups. The specific books used are noted where used.
4. Additional data from memoirs, retrospective or summary papers, and occasional comments in the literature.
5. The chapters on the various groups have been read by the persons listed in the acknowledgments section of the preface. They have been very helpful in correcting direct errors of fact and interpretation insofar as possible.

Those are the data sources. The next questions are:

1. How were that data evaluated?
2. Where does intellectual information come from?
3. How does all this information bear on the concepts used?

The lists of persons are as accurate as double-checking can assure. All names have been checked with at least one printed version (although, as those who have seen the name of Gerhard Lenski, author of *The Religious Factor*, embossed on the spine of his books as "Lensky" are aware, appearance in print is not a perfect check). The quality of the data themselves, therefore, is reasonable. I expect an occasional error because no system is perfect, but I am confident that errors have been minimized.

The ASA *Directories* are compiled from questionnaires mailed to the membership list of the ASA. They are not universally returned (66 percent return for 1970; 70 percent for 1967). In addition, the directories have changed formats radically over the period of their existence. The 1959 volume contained retrospective information on those persons who were still members; the 1970 issue was the next most informative. The 1963 *Directory* contains only a mailing address, whereas the 1967 book contains mailing address and degree information.

For those people holding teaching jobs at major institutions, the ASA *Guides to Graduate Departments* provide other information. These guides are compiled from questionnaires mailed to department chairmen (169 departments in 1969, 170 in 1970, 184 in 1971). There are always some departments that do not respond to the questionnaire (19 in 1971, or 10 percent), and errors are common, particularly with respect to persons who have recently relocated. If the ASA *Directory* and the *Guide* to *Graduate Departments* did not agree, I listed "no information" rather than hazard a guess.

A typical example of a data problem is the inclusion of Nathan Keyfitz on Table 4.2: Important Symbolic Interactionists. Keyfitz is included because he fits the criteria for being on the table. However, his major work has been in mathematical demography—a far cry from symbolic interaction. I do not know why he was included in the festschrift for Blumer except that he had long been a colleague of Blumer's. His inclusion is typical of the data problems in that the model suggests that social closesness, especially when significant research is being done (e.g., for a dissertation or for later research projects), will result in similar intellectual orientations. However, social closeness does not always predict intellectual closeness, as the anomalous case of Keyfitz reminds us.

The data, as I have noted, are only indicators of social ties. These data result from interactions that do not always occur in a form that produces a public record. We are, therefore, best advised to use multiple indicators and methods for determining group boundaries, particularly since those boundaries are expected on theoretical gounds to be rather fuzzy. Each new source increases both the number of peripheral persons (by adding persons previously omitted) as well as the determination of the core group (by overlapping with persons previously included). The effect of multiple indicators, then, is to increase assurance that the people who form the central group are, indeed, included, while decreasing the ability to make sharp distinctions between persons in groups.

Another data interpretation problem is the notation "not in the system—*." This notation indicates that the person so marked is (1) not a Master's degree holder and, hence, in most systems, not a candidate for the Ph.D.; (2) foreign; or (3) otherwise not part of sociology's social structure.

Evaluating intellectual information is more complex. I have read widely in the papers and books that are important to the various groups. However, I have summarized vague and ambiguous intellectual positions (which all complex positions are) in very few words, aiming to produce an adequate "feel" for an area rather than complete faithfulness to every detail. My justification for any interpretation stated in this book is my own understanding of the work. I expect that any serious student of the theoretical schools discussed will use the bibliographies as a starting point to develop his own understandings.

Figure A.1 is a cautionary tale. The "small world phenomenon" (Milgram, 1967) asserts that only a few linkages of one sort or another are needed to connect almost everyone in the world to almost everyone else. Most likely it would require only three links to join any reader of this book to its author, and most likely fewer. The fact that Longman taught Rockne who taught Crowley who taught Lombardi is suggestive. This result is related to Zuckerman's discovery (1967) that Nobel Prize winners are generally trained by Nobel Prize winners. What neither result by itself can demonstrate is *what* is being transmitted, or recognized, and if there is any commonality in the research being done (or the football being taught) that makes the connection important.

This question raises a more general question. Are the coauthorship networks, for example, representative only of a short-range phenomenon, the coauthorships themselves? Or do they imply the existence of longer-range, weak-tie phenomena that transform parts of the figures into "neighborhoods" (Rapoport, 1963) in the sense that similar location and similar research as well as coauthorship are represented? For Figure 3.3, for example, location is represented in a Columbia, a Harvard, a Princeton neighborhood; research, by a criminology and a statistics neighborhood. The discerning of neighborhoods must be done carefully, since we can be very easily misled by the accidents of graph construction (see Harary, Norman, and Cartwright, 1965).

To a historian, this research is obviously not history. I have not tried for the depth in detail that even a reasonably competent historian would bring to these data. I am a sociologist, interested in how changes in com-

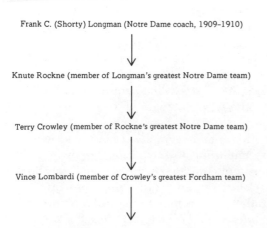

Frank C. (Shorty) Longman (Notre Dame coach, 1909–1910)

↓

Knute Rockne (member of Longman's greatest Notre Dame team)

↓

Terry Crowley (member of Rockne's greatest Notre Dame team)

↓

Vince Lombardi (member of Crowley's greatest Fordham team)

↓

FIGURE A.1   A cautionary tale of linkages. (**Source: Ronald Encyclopedia of Football** [1960].)

munication structures, in particular their bunching together over time, might lead to changes in a discipline's intellectual patterns. From this viewpoint, I am concerned with the core of developments and not with the last detail of the periphery. If I am correct about the developments, the different types of measures should all return the same answers, varying only insofar as the data are unreliable or the core not well defined.

BIBLIOGRAPHY

Baltzell, E. Digby.
   1972   "To be a Phoenix—reflections on two noisy ages of prose." *American Journal of Sociology* 78 (July): 202–220.
Griffith, Belver C., and Nicholas C. Mullins.
   1972   "Coherent groups in scientific change: 'Invisible Colleges' may be consistent throughout science." *Science* 177 (4053, September 15): 959–964.
Harary, Frank, Robert Z. Norman, and Dorwin Cartwright.
   1965   *Structural Models.* New York: Wiley.
McGrath, Joseph E., and Irwin Altman.
   1966   *Small Group Research: A Synthesis and Critique of the Field.* New York: Holt.
Milgram, Stanley.
   1967   "The small world problem." *Psychology Today* 22 (May): 61–67.
Mullins, Nicholas C.
   1972   "The development of a scientific specialty: the Phage Group and the origins of molecular biology." *Minerva* 10 (January): 51–82.
Rapoport, Anatol.
   1963   "Mathematical models of social interaction." Pp. 494–594 in R. Duncan Luce, Robert R. Bush, and Eugene Galanter (eds.), *Handbook of Mathematical Psychology*, Vol. II. New York: Wiley.
————.
   1960   *Ronald Encyclopedia of Football.* New York: Ronald.
Zuckerman, Harriet.
   1967   "The sociology of the Nobel Prizes." *Scientific American* 217 (November): 25–33.

NAME INDEX

SUBJECT INDEX

action theory, 40, 53

American Journal of Sociology, 43, 62, 70, 80, 89, 93, 99, 124, 134, 147, 176, 232, 242, 265

American Sociological Association, 43, 64, 70, 80, 99, 125, 140, 146, 147, 164, 171, 176, 199, 206, 240, 242, 265, 282

American Sociological Review, 62, 124, 134, 232

American Sociological Society. *See* American Sociological Association

Berkeley, University of California, 23, 60, 75, 77, 139, 193

biography, 7, 9–10

boundaries, 258

Bureau of Applied Social Research (BASR), 39, 64

Chicago, University of, 23, 39, 40, 41–46, 60, 75, 76–97, 139, 140, 220

coherent groups, 17, 25–30, 129, 130
  active adherents, 130
  apprenticeship, 19
  cluster stage, 22–24, 25–30, 135–136
  coauthorships, 19, 20, 62–64, 109, 116–117, 134–135, 200, 231–234
  colleagueship, 19, 20, 109
  communication structure, 18–20, 22, 30–31, 109
  group size, 25–30
  informal communication, 134
  institutionalization, 24, 31
  intellectual leader(s), 25–30, 123
  intellectual properties of, 25–30
  literature, 22, 23, 91, 134
  network stage, 21–22, 25–30, 135
  normal stage, 20–21, 25–30, 135
  participation, 78
  passive carriers, 130, 141
  program statement(s), 22, 25–30, 123
  research center, 25–30
  revolutionary, 23–25, 135–136

sizes (group), 136–138
social organizational leader(s), 25–30, 123
social properties of, 25–30
specialty stage, 24–30, 136
success, 21, 25–30, 58, 78, 93, 167
training center, 25–30
trusted assessors, 18, 231–234
collective behavior, 96
Columbia University, 23, 39, 40, 43, 46, 52, 60, 139
concept, 4–5, 7–9, 78, 143–145
conflict theory, 138
critical material, 25–30

elite specialty, 23–25, 135–136, 215, 240
"encapsulated" specialty, 24, 205–206
European social theory, 45, 48–49, 142, 187, 203, 205
  Marxist analysis, 81, 270–277
  phenomenology, 186, 203, 205
exchange theory, 12–13, 138

Frankfort school, 271, 274–275
function. *See* structural functionalism

great society, 141, 143, 155, 159–160

Harvard University, 23, 39, 40, 41, 46, 49, 60, 105, 140
Health, Education and Welfare, U.S. Department of, 155, 161, 164, 170, 182

intellectual history, 7, 10–11
"invisible college." *See* coherent groups
Iowa, University of, 83, 105

Laboratory of Social Relations, 64

Massachusetts Institute of Technology, 105, 108, 167
meaning, 80, 81
methods. *See* techniques